YOUR TOWNS & CITIES IN WO

KENT

AT WAR 1939-45

YOUR TOWNS & CITIES IN WORLD WAR TWO

KENT
AT WAR 1939-45

TANYA WYNN

EDITED BY STEPHEN WYNN

Pen & Sword
MILITARY
AN IMPRINT OF PEN & SWORD BOOKS LTD.
YORKSHIRE · PHILADELPHIA

First published in Great Britain in 2019 by
Pen & Sword Military
An imprint of
Pen & Sword Books Ltd
Yorkshire – Philadelphia

ISBN 978 1 47388 7 404
The right of Tanya Wynn to be identified as Author of this work has been asserted by
her in accordance with the Copyright, Designs and Patents Act 1988.

A CIP catalogue record for this book is available from the British Library.

Printed and bound in England by CPI Group (UK) Ltd, Croydon, CR0 4YY
Typeset by Aura Technology and Software Services, India

Pen & Sword Books Limited incorporates the imprints of Atlas, Archaeology,
Aviation, Discovery, Family History, Fiction, History, Maritime, Military, Military
Classics, Politics, Select, Transport, True Crime, Air World, Frontline Publishing,
Leo Cooper, Remember When, Seaforth Publishing, The Praetorian Press,
Wharncliffe Local History, Wharncliffe Transport, Wharncliffe True Crime and
White Owl.

For a complete list of Pen & Sword titles please contact

PEN & SWORD BOOKS LIMITED
47 Church Street, Barnsley, South Yorkshire, S70 2AS, England
E-mail: enquiries@pen-and-sword.co.uk
Website: www.pen-and-sword.co.uk

Or

PEN AND SWORD BOOKS
1950 Lawrence Rd, Havertown, PA 19083, USA
E-mail: Uspen-and-sword@casematepublishers.com
Website: www.penandswordbooks.com

Contents

Prologue

Kent's war time involvement

King George VI bestowed the award of the George Cross on Malta during the Second World War because of the heroism and devotion shown by the island's people during the great siege they underwent throughout the early months of the war, whilst being bombed almost incessantly by the Luftwaffe.

That being the case, it is amazing that the part Kent played in the war does not appear to have been fully appreciated, because if it had been, it would surely have been deemed worthy of a similar award. It is not overstating the case to suggest that Kent played a pivotal role in the war, an effort that deserves to be fully remembered and commemorated and in this book I will look at as many of the county's achievements as possible.

In the early days of the war as evacuated children from London came flooding into the county, thousands of its young men were leaving to go off to war as part of the British Expeditionary Force (BEF).

In 1939 the old First World War Kitchener Army Camp at Richborough was re-opened to house some 4,000 German Jewish refugees, who had been allowed to leave Nazi Germany.

In May 1940, with British, French and Belgian troops fighting a rearguard action in France, just to survive, the Local Defence Force, which went on to become the Home Guard, was created in towns and cities across the country, including Kent.

The army camp on the Isle of Grain was a prominent location, protecting as it did the mouths of both the River Thames and the River Medway from any potential threat of German amphibious assaults. Its anti-aircraft batteries also added to the numerous defensive positions dotted around the south and south-east coast line of Great Britain.

Nearly all of the 800 vessels which sailed across the English Channel to assist with the Dunkirk evacuations between 26 May and 3 June 1940 as part of Operation Dynamo, left from Sheerness. Collectively their sterling efforts saw some 330,000 troops who had gone to France as part of the British Expeditionary Force, rescued from the beaches at Dunkirk in northern France. If those fighting men had been killed or taken prisoner by the Germans, there is every chance that the war would have been over at that time, with Britain and her Allies being on the losing side, a once proud nation defeated after less than a year of fighting, reduced to being incorporated into part of Germany's burgeoning new world order of the Third Reich.

The Battle of Britain which followed hot on the heels of Dunkirk, and took place between 10 July and 31 October 1940, did so mainly over the skies of Kent. The battle was a determined attempt by Nazi Germany to compel Britain to agree to a negotiated peace settlement and bring a swift end to the war in their favour. With her main enemy out of the way and America still nowhere near entering the fray, Germany would have had a clear run at extending her empire across a forlorn and greatly weakened Europe, with Russia clearly as her new target.

Many of the aircraft and pilots that fought in the Battle of Britain flew out of many of the airfields across Kent such as Biggin Hill, Detling, Eastchurch, Hawkinge, Manston, Lympne, and Rochester. Most of these airfields were actively targeted by the Luftwaffe in the early months of the war.

Although Kent experienced numerous bombing raids on many of her towns and cities throughout the war, Canterbury was the recipient of a particularly hellish air raid on the night of 1 June 1942 which resulted in the loss of many of her historic buildings.

Reculver Bay, in the district of Canterbury, was used to test prototypes of the bouncing bomb, designed by Barnes Wallis, and which were subsequently used in Operation Chastise, the bombing of the Möhne, Sorpe and Edersee dams in the Ruhr valley, on 16 and 17 May 1943.

On D-Day, 6 June 1944, 185,000 troops left Britain's shores and headed for the beaches of Normandy, as part of Operation Overlord. In the build up to D-Day, Operation Fortitude, which was an audacious deception, managed to convince the enemy that the Allied invasion of North West Europe would take place in the Pas de Calais region. The day before the D-Day landings, the false invasion fleet left Dover just after midnight, ensuring that many German divisions remained in the Calais area. June 1944 also saw Kent become a victim of Germany in her military death throws, in the shape of well over 1,000 Flying Bombs or Doodlebugs, which landed across the county. This was followed up by the even more powerful V2 rockets later the same year.

The end of 1944 saw Operation Pluto, a plan to run an oil pipe line across the English Channel in support of the Normandy landings and the invasion of Europe. As Britain and her Allies pushed German forces back towards their own country, a constant supply of fuel was needed for the tanks, other vehicles and aircraft that would assist in that venture.

In the following chapters, I will look at some of these events in more detail.

CHAPTER 1

1939 – The War Begins

Richborough Internment Camp

In the violent November 1938 Pogrom often referred to as *Kristallnacht*, nearly a year before the beginning of the Second World War, the Nazi authorities in Germany came up with a novel way to make money. It involved rounding up some 30,000 Jewish men and holding them against their will, in concentration camps. Their crime in the eyes of the Nazi Party was straightforward and unquestionable: they were Jewish. That was it. The men were given hope with the proviso that if they could acquire an entry visa for a foreign country, then they would be released from their internment and allowed to leave Germany. However, there were two catches. The required visas cost money, for some it was simply a price that they could not afford and secondly the acquiring of these visas had to be done expediently and was not an open-ended offer by the German authorities. For most of those who were released from their incarceration in the concentration camps, at such places as Buchenwald, it was on the understanding that they would finalise their affairs and leave Germany within six months.

Richborough Internment Camp.

Some 5,000 of these men were eventually saved, thanks largely to the efforts of the Council for German Jewry, and then made their way to England having obtained the required transit visas. On their arrival the men, who were joined by others from Austria and Czechoslovakia, as it was then, were provided with accommodation at a dilapidated First World War Army training base, at Richborough, near Sandwich in Kent, known as the Kitchener Camp. The camp was taken over in early 1939 and by February of that year, it had taken in its first refugees.

Originally there had been three Army camps at Richborough during the First World War, Haig, Stonar, and the largest of them all, Kitchener, which was situated west of the Ramsgate Road. Initially what took place there during the First World War was shrouded in an element of secrecy. It was turned into a port area so that the large amount of munitions and equipment needed by the troops on the Western Front had a chance of arriving there. The British authorities had assumed, correctly, that the Germans would have been well aware that the three main ports that Britain had used at the beginning of the war to ferry men, equipment, ammunition and provisions across the English Channel had been Southampton, Dover and Folkestone. Richborough was then built up and used to transport munitions across, in an attempt to reduce the risk of such supply vessels being attacked and sunk by German submarines.

The camp's welfare officer Phineas May, kept a diary from his time spent at the camp as a refugee, which survived. It provides an in-depth insight into what life was like for those who lived there. The men were glad to be out of the danger they had been in back home in Germany, of that there was no doubt, but it was not all plain sailing. It has to be remembered that these men had been forcibly separated from their families, whom they had then had no choice but to leave behind to an uncertain future. They missed them, they worried about them and no doubt some were consumed with guilt because they had not been able to protect their loved ones. Even worse for these men was the not knowing and for many the total lack of any correspondence from them must have been absolutely crushing.

To be accepted at the camp there were two conditions that the men had to meet. Firstly, they had to be between the ages of 18 and 40 years, and secondly, their prospects of being accepted to go and live in another country had to be realistic and not based on a pipe dream.

The camp opened in late January 1939 and its day to day running was down to the Jewish Lads Brigade, at an estimated yearly cost of £80,000, which was a staggering sum of money at the time.

Mr Ernest Joseph, an architect and the man responsible for making arrangements for the camp at Richborough, emphasised that those arriving there wouldn't want to become a burden and liability on either the county of Kent or the country. Each evening saw the refugees learning Spanish and English, and during the day they were given instruction in engineering, agriculture, and trades such as boot making and tailoring. The long-term aim for all of those who found themselves in the camp was to obtain visas for such countries as Canada and America so that they could emigrate, find work and somewhere to live. By April 1939 the number of refugees living at the camp had risen to 500.

In March 1939 two schoolgirls, Freda Pearce and Brenda Friedrich, of Sidcot School in Winscombe, a village in North Somerset, each adopted a German refugee at the Kitchener Camp in Richborough. The girls wrote every week to the two men as well as sending them sixpence a week pocket money. At the time the parents of Brenda Friedrich were both in Germany doing what they could to help Jewish people, who were becoming more and more marginalised in German society by the Nazi regime. Her father was German and her mother was English.

The kindness of the two young girls came about due to Brenda having seen an appeal in her local newspaper. It was a request to help the refugees, if possible by providing them with small amounts of pocket money so that they could purchase a few essential items. The girls were glad of the opportunity to help fellow human beings who through no fault of their own found themselves in an extremely difficult situation.

Freda Pearce sent 4s to be spread out over an eight-week period to the refugee whom she had 'adopted'. The money she sent came out of her own limited pocket-money which she received from her parents.

By the middle of May 1939 the Kitchener Camp had become a self-contained town. It had its own post office, recreation centre, classrooms and a cinema that was only a matter or weeks from completion in May 1939. The camp had its own doctors, a rabbi for religious services, an agricultural expert, and had already started growing its own food. It even had its own newspaper, the *Kitchener Camp Review*, which was written and published by the refugees and gave an insight into their lives in the camp.

Through their camp newspaper the refugees were able to tell their story and express their feelings. Although they were in a foreign land and soon-to-be enemies of their beloved Fatherland, they were content in their new home, in a land of freedom and happiness.

In the first issue of the newspaper, one of the refugees explained what it felt like to him to be 'Under the Union Jack':

Through all the persecution and terrible times we experienced in the last years, we refugees have almost forgotten what it means to honour a flag. The older comrades will surely remember the time, pre-war and during the war (First World War) when we were proud of the colours black, white and red or red, white and red. We elderly fellows were fighting for them and thousands of our co-religionists gave their lives for the flag.

When our home countries came under the dictatorship we learned to hate and despise the flag which was forced on us and so we forgot that in other countries throughout the world the flag is the symbol of might and shelter, that wherever it is flown it is greeted by lifting the hat or standing to attention. And all that is done voluntarily with the heart beating quicker and with pride to be a subject of the country which shows her flag.

Today we were allowed for the first time the hoisting of the Union Jack, the British flag, which you find in every part of the world, which is beloved and respected wherever it flies in the wind. No matter whether in the four corners of the world, or in the midst of the jungle where in a lonely post an English Government official works, or high up in the ice-cold north where a scientific expedition discovers new wonders, it is honoured.

Today we ourselves honour this flag under which we receive shelter, and, whilst standing to attention our thoughts flew back to our own home countries which are no more our homes.

Let us never forget those minutes; let us always think of the moment when we followed the Union Jack climbing up the huge flagpole and flying in brilliant sunshine. Let us do everything that is in our power to build up this camp for those to follow us. Let us work together hard and incessantly to show our gratitude for the generous hospitality we are given here, here in England, the land of freedom, of which the symbol is the Union Jack.

This unknown man's words highlight the level of hatred and persecution that he and his comrades must have experienced in the country of their birth. A nation that had ultimately betrayed them and imprisoned them simply because of their religious beliefs, a nation that had seen fit to strip them of their every belonging, and a nation that would ultimately do even worse, much worse, to those who followed in their footsteps. But to finish from a more positive perspective, the following words are taken from the first edition of the *Kitchener Camp Review*:

When, through happier circumstances, this camp ceases to exist for the use of refugees, it is our modest ambition that this journal will be a record for all time of the life as lived here.

Richborough Camp Plaque.

In June 1939 the Isle of Thanet acquired a new cinema that could cater for 500 people in one sitting, but not one that ordinary members of the public could go to. There was no box office, no usherettes to show customers to their seats, and those who attended the screenings didn't have to pay. The new cinema wasn't to be found in one of the district's busy high streets, instead it was located at the Kitchener Camp and built by the camp's refugees for themselves. Before the refugees moved into Richborough, the First World War mystery port was merely a collection of ugly, drab-looking, derelict stone buildings with leaking roofs and broken windows. It was criss-crossed with rusty disused railway lines and dirt tracks for roads, not the most obvious of places to begin a new life.

The refugees were not a group of workshy individuals who wanted to sit back and have everything done for them, far from it. The construction work for the new cinema, which was designed by two of the camp's men, Mr Kuh and Mr Marmorek, both architects, was carried out by the combined effort of a number of the camp's men and took them only a matter of weeks to complete.

The outside of the new premises was nothing special to look at, and certainly didn't look like a Mecca for entertainment, the only thing that betrayed the building's purpose was the sign above the main doors – 'Kitchener's Cinema'. But inside it was exactly what one would expect the interior of a cinema in the late 1930s to look like. Comfortable seats had been painstakingly screwed to the floor of the building. The previously uninviting grey walls had been painted a pleasant buff colour. A dimming mechanism had been added to the lighting system, making the overall experience no different from that of an ordinary cinema.

The new premises were officially opened on 12 June 1939 by Mrs Marie-Louise de Rothschild, wife of the financier and banker, Lionel de Rothschild, who was accompanied by a distinguished group of individuals including Sir Robert Waley-Cohen, who was the chairman of the committee responsible for refugee camps; Mr Oscar Deutch, the well known film magnate; Lieutenant Colonel W.V.L. Prescott-Westcarr, the Mayor of Sandwich, along with Mr J.A. May, the camp commandant and his brother, Mr P. May, the camp's sports officer.

Before the opening ceremony began all the guests were treated to some renditions from the camp's excellent, eighteen-piece orchestra, which included some of Europe's finest musicians.

All of the cinema equipment had been donated by Mr Oscar Deutsch, who had also kindly agreed to cover the cinema's running costs. Many of the films which had been provided were in English so as to help those in the camp who did not speak English, learn the language faster. One of those who could already speak English fluently was a Mr Eric Saltzmann, also known as and referred to, as Refugee No.1, for obvious reasons. He gave a rousing speech to those present about what the camp had already done for him and how it had made him feel to be one of its inhabitants. He highlighted the difference in the camp in just four months and how it had gone from being an uninviting and unhomely place, because of the state of disrepair it had fallen into, compared what it had become in such a short space of time. He finished by saying that when the time eventually came for him to leave, he would do so with many happy memories and it would be his everlasting endeavour to pass on the spirit of kindness which had given him so much happiness during his stay in the camp.

In July 1939 the organisers of the camp, the Council for German Jewry, had managed to acquire fifty-five acres of land adjacent to the camp, so that it could be used by refugees who wished to train and study in agricultural and gardening work.

With the outbreak of war in September 1939 many of the men who were refugees in the camp enlisted in the British Army and ended up fighting against the same Nazi regime that had persecuted them and forced them to leave Germany.

Mr Kurt Siegal, who was 30 years of age and one of the German Jewish refugees who lived at the Richorough camp, died due to injuries he sustained when he fell from his bicycle on the Crosswell Bridge on 26 August 1939. An inquest in to his death was held on Monday 4 September at the Eastry Institute Mr A.K. Mowll, the Deputy East Kent Coroner, sat with a jury, of which Mr Lawrence Gillman, was the foreman. Dr Ronald E.S. Lewis, who was the resident medical officer, at the Royal Victoria Hospital in Dover, identified the body of the deceased as being that of Kurt Israel Siegal. Prior to leaving his home at 55 Welanerh, Berlin, Germany, he had been a lady's clothier. He was a German Jew, residing at the refugee camp in Richborough.

Mr Siegal was admitted to the Royal Victoria Hospital in Dover on the evening of Saturday, 26 August, at which time he was conscious. Dr Lewis attended the deceased the following morning when he was awake, but he was unable to provide him with an account of what had happened, as he could not speak any English and there wasn't anybody in the hospital who could speak German. He appeared to be suffering with concussion, as he had a bad bruise above his left eye and a small abrasion to the left side of his forehead. He remained under observation for six days until 1 September when he was moved during the evacuation of the hospital. He died at 6am the following morning. The cause of his death was recorded as a cerebral laceration of the brain due to a fracture at the base of the skull. Dr Lewis had a conversation with the deceased's brother and managed to establish that he had been cycling when he crashed into a wall. After the accident Mr Siegal was initially taken to Richborough Camp, but because there were no proper medical facilities there, it was then decided to take him to the town's hospital.

Mr Mowll asked Dr Lewis if he had known Mr Siegal was suffering from a laceration of the brain, would he have allowed him to be moved? Dr Lewis replied that under normal circumstance he would not have been moved, but as the country had just entered into a war with a foreign power, the circumstances were far from normal. Dr Lewis also pointed out that the hospital authorities had no choice in the decision as to whether the patients were to be evacuated or not, but he conceded that the moving of Mr Siegal may have affected his injuries. Dr Lewis further stated that Mr Siegal had become unconscious before he was removed from the hospital. In the circumstances every patient at Dover hospital was moved, each person travelled in a private ambulance with two nurses and a witness travelling with them.

George Henry Sayle of 9 Church Road, Dover, told the inquest that at about 4 pm on 26 August, he was standing on the left hand side of Strond Street, about 25 yards away from the scene of the accident. He explained how he saw two cyclists descending the slope of the concrete foot bridge at the Crosswall. There were warning notices clearly visible on both ends of the bridge, which forbade people from riding bikes down the slopes, but despite this the deceased and another man were seen cycling across the bridge. A short while later he heard a crash and he saw the man that he subsequently knew to be the deceased, Kurt Siegal, lying on the pavement by the foot of the bridge, whilst his bike was lying in the opposite corner. Mr Sayle could see that Siegal appeared to be seriously hurt, and that he believed the man had sustained his injuries by hitting his head against the concrete structure. Mr Sayle then rushed back to his employer to borrow his car so that he could collect Mr Siegal and take him to Dover hospital.

The coroner, Mr Mowll, then read out all of the information and evidence in the case to the deceased's brother, Rudolph Siegal, and then had it translated for him by an interpreter from Richborough camp. Mr Mowll then addressed the jury and said that Mr Siegal, a Jewish refugee, had, by cycling down the slope of the bridge been doing something that he ought not to have been doing. This had led to the crash and Mr Siegal hitting his against the wall, which had subsequently led to his death.

Saturday, 9 December saw a friendly game of football take place at Dumpton Stadium, between Ramsgate Grenville and a team from the Kitchener Camp at Richborough, made up of German and Austrian refugees. After a spirited 90 minutes of football, Ramsgate Grenville ran out winners by a score line of 4 goals to 3.

Grenville supporters were greatly encouraged in the first half by the appearance of Mr C. Hoare, only on the field as a replacement for one of the Grenville players who was late in arriving, and the diminutive brother of Bernard Hoare, their gifted regular right winger. Encouraged by an enthusiastic crowd he sped up and down the wing like a seasoned professional, giving a good account of himself, with his footballing skills aligned with a desire and willingness to work hard when not in possession. Grenville's goals were shared two each by debutant and trialist, Purvis, who played centre forward, and the lively Hoare.

The Kitchener Camp team gave a good account of themselves, with noteworthy performances by Schwarz in goal, Gimpel at centre-half and Rottenberg at centre-forward, who scored the first of the camp's goals. Their other goals coming from Katz and Reitmann. The two teams were:

Ramsgate Grenville
Munday, Martin, Bray, Bray, Sutton, Finch, Hoare, Smith, Purvis, Thompson, Lewis.

Kitchener Camp
Schwarz, Schmerling, Diamnach, Tabate, Gimpel, Foiber, Kassmer, Reitmann, Rottenberg, Uhlfelder, Katz.

Having the names of the two teams was extremely useful, especially those representing the Kitchener Camp as it has provided history with the names of eleven of the men who lived at the camp as refugees during the time of its existence.

On Thursday 28 December the Wingham Petty Sessions were held at Sandwich, Kent. Chairman of the bench was Viscount Hawarden. Before him were Bertha Maria

Mathilda Goldmann, who was summoned for committing a breach of the Aliens Order Act by entering a place of employment at Ash on 6 November 1939. Through an interpreter, she pleaded not guilty. Charged with aiding and abetting the offence by employing the woman, was Colonel Robert Wynne Henderson of Twitham Court in Ash, a charge to which he also pleaded not guilty.

When Goldmann, who at the time was unmarried with the surname Johannsen, entered the country at Dover on 20 July 1939 as a visitor, her passport was endorsed that whilst in the country she could not engage in any kind of work, either paid or unpaid. It had become a common practice where aliens would arrive in the county then work for no pay in exchange for a roof over their head and their meals.

PC Mounsey told the court that he had visited Twitham Court on 6 November and spoken with Colonel Henderson. He admitted that Mrs Goldmann was assisting with the household duties, but as he was not paying her, only providing her keep, he did not consider that constituted employment. Colonel Henderson added that he had taken her in out of pity. It was in fact his wife who had determined to take the woman in after being asked to do so by the Reverend Vischer of Sandwich.

After arriving in England she married a Mr Goldmann, who was a refugee at the Richborough Camp. She could not stay with her husband at the camp but after a period of time her money ran out and she had nowhere to stay, which is why Colonel Henderson and his wife let her stay with them. If she returned to Germany after having married a Jew, she faced a prison sentence of up to eight years. Mrs Goldmann's husband had, since this incident, been accepted as a recruit in the British Army.

Despite all of the mitigation, and Viscount Hawarden adding his personal sympathies, both Mrs Goldmann and Colonel Henderson were found guilty as charged. Mrs Goldmann was fined 5s, whilst the colonel was fined 10s.

Colonel Henderson was born in Calcutta, India, on 20 August 1874, and went on to become an officer in the Indian Army, having first been commissioned as a cavalry captain on 10 October 1894.

At the same Petty Sessions at Wingham two German men who were refugees at the Richborough Camp, found themselves charged with offences which took place on 25 November 1939. Fred Meyer was charged that he had been stopped for riding a bicycle without a front facing light, in Deal Road, Worth, by Special Constable Spinner at 8 pm on the date in question, and twenty minutes later in the same road, the same officer stopped Frederich Lion for riding a bicycle without a rear facing light. Both men pleaded guilty and were each fined 2s 6d.

After the Jewish refugees left in the early years of the war, the Kitchener Camp was initially taken over by elements of the British Army who were engaged in home defence. In 1942 it saw further military use when it became HMS *Robertson* and was used by the Royal Marines. It was also used by the Royal Engineers, who under tight security, helped develop sections of the Mulberry harbour that were used extensively for the D-Day landings on the beaches of Normandy.

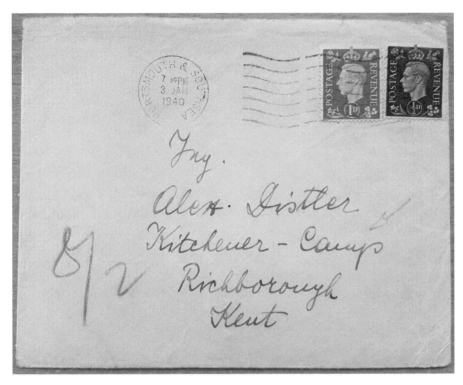

Envelope of letter.

Translation of letters:

Dear Alex,
With this letter I am inviting you to spend a few days with us to relax. You can come to Portsmouth any time for a few days. I don't know how much the trip would cost but we can help with a little bit. We would like to have you here this Saturday if that is possible.

You don't need to write but just come unless you can't come this Saturday then let us know when you can come. We are looking forward to seeing you and hope that you have the opportunity to leave the camp.

By the middle of July, I will be a busy mum. Hope to see you soon and I wish you a good year.

Somebody else is also including regards but is in London today but would also like to see you.

When you are coming, get off the station Portsmouth/Southsea...

Despite the country being at war with Germany, a nation hell bent on conquering the whole of Europe, life on the home front still went on as best it could, although normality now had a totally different meaning to what it had been before the war. It would be five

Lieber Alex,

Hiermit lade ich Dich höflichst ein auf ein paar Tage zu mir auf Erholung zu kommen. Du kannst nach Portsmouth jeder-zeit, nur nicht auf ständig, niemand hat etwas dagegen wenn Du auf paar Tage zu Besuch kommst. Ausserdem wohnen wir in Southsea und nicht im Hafen.

Ich weiß nicht was die Fahrt kostet, aber einen Teil können wir Dir beisteuern wenn nötig.

Wir hätten Dich schon gerne diesen Samstag hier. Wenn das möglich ist, dann schreibe gar nicht sondern fahre, geht es aber nicht diesen Samstag dann teile uns mit

Above and opposite: Letter.

years, eight months and one week, before the war in Europe would eventually come to an end, and a further three months and one week before the war in the Pacific against the Japanese would finally bring the Second World War to a close. So what normal would have looked like throughout Kent, is extremely hard to quantify. The easiest way of showing this would be to look at some of the news items from throughout the year in the Dover area, which looked at preparation and readiness for a possible war, whilst drawing a comparison with where Germany was on the same timeline.

On Tuesday 19 September a meeting took place of the Finance and Consultative Committee of the Kent County Football Association in Dover, under the chairmanship of Mr W.N. Rule. A decision to continue playing competitive football throughout Kent for the duration of the war, but only on a limited basis, was agreed. After the meeting the following statement was issued, which was subject to the agreement of the Football Association:

'Football may be played in Kent during the War as follows:
    In neutral and reception areas friendly and competition matches on Saturdays and public holidays.
    In evacuation areas, both friendly and competition matches, with such restrictions as to the number of spectators as may be subject of instructions. The

conditions named in (a) and (b) may be regarded as applicable to clubs and players who normally are unable to play on Saturdays but participate only in mid-week football. N.B Permission in all cases must first be obtained from the local Police Headquarters, which, it is anticipated, will not be unreasonably withheld.

Under the foregoing decision, and subject to the conditions set out in (a) and (b) (1) Minor Football and Minor Competitions may function on normal lines; (2) Junior Leagues and Competitions may proceed with their arrangements with such modification and variation of their rules as may be necessary for smooth and elastic working.

Owing to transport difficulties and the undesirability of making calls on players for long journeys, it is not considered practicable to run the Kent League on an all-county basis, but the possibility of regional leagues, as an alternative, was considered and will be recommended to the Senior Clubs for adoption. The running of certain out of the County Cup Competitions in a modified form will be considered at a subsequent meeting.'

Now, hopefully all of the above is crystal clear and the question concerning the criteria as to whether it was possible to play football in war time Kent is completely unambiguous!

The coming of the war understandably caused some real concerns amongst the people of Kent, especially in relation to the threat of an invasion. Having county boundaries that stretched from the far reaches of the south coast all the way up to the outskirts of London, left many with a strong feeling of concern. It was obvious to most that there was always going to be a potential for aerial threats, because of the close proximity to the English Channel and the coast line of occupied France.

With war now imminent an announcement was made on 1 September 1939 that arrangements were in hand, as part of the national defence scheme, for a new anti-aircraft battery to be established within the Sevenoaks district of Kent. The battery was to be formed with immediate effect and was to consist of ten officers and 156 men, all of whom had to be between 25 and 50 years of age.

Everyone selected to serve with the newly formed battery became part of the 16th Light Anti-Aircraft Regiment, Royal Artillery, which was a Territorial Army unit. The man responsible for organising recruitment for the new battery was Major V.A. Cazalet MC MP, who was available at the unit's temporary headquarters, at New Beacon, Sevenoaks, each evening between 6 pm and 9 pm from 1 September, to interview perspective candidates looking to sign up. The unit went on to serve during the Second Battle of El Alamein, in North Africa, which took place between 23 October and 4 November 1942.

The rural area of Sevenoaks had been preparing for war from the late summer of 1938, with a number of air raid patrol posts already in place by that time with more in the pipe line. There was certainly an urgency in the desire to be as prepared as possible by members of the local community. Each village had its full complement of trained air raid wardens, and services such as the local fire brigades and the first aid units had been fully tested in a previous black-out drill and an earlier rehearsal, from which valuable lessons had been learnt. The organisers from each of the services were satisfied that they would be fully prepared and able to deal with any such emergency which might take place across the Sevenoaks district.

Captain E.J. Wilson, the organiser of the ARP sections, was of the opinion that such incidents would be of an isolated nature, and that there were sufficient personnel and equipment in the area to cope with them. History and the benefit of hindsight have possibly proved his assessment of the first point of that statement to be incorrect.

If any of the local parishes were affected as the result of an enemy air raid, the civil services in that particular community had the benefit of knowing that they would receive assistance from neighbouring village units, with the same being expected of them in return. This meant that the entire rural area of Sevenoaks was covered with a network of units that were manned by suitably trained men who were capable of dealing with nearly all of the incidents which they might be called upon to deal with.

In the final few days leading up to the outbreak of the war, Captain Wilson stated that everybody in the area should have been provided with their own individual gas masks and asked those, who for some reason or another, hadn't received one, to contact their local air raid wardens. The only known shortfall was a lack of protective helmets for infants along with respirators for children who were between two and four-and-a-half years of age.

The local authorities had determined that there was no need at that time for the digging of any trenches, but that should the need arise for such defences, then the work would be expediently carried out and overseen by the various parish councils, although some potential sites had already been identified.

An important component of protecting local communities from the inherent dangers of enemy air raids, were the sirens which gave early warning of such impending dangers. With this in mind sufficient sirens had been put up in every part of the district, so that advance warnings could be easily given of imminent attacks.

All that remained for residents across the Sevenoaks district was to keep calm and be confident in the knowledge that everything that could possibly be done to help safeguard lives and property had been addressed and put in place.

A letter appeared in the edition of the *Sevenoaks Chronicle and Kentish Advertiser* dated Friday 1 September, concerning precautionary measures which had been taken at the Sevenoaks and Holmesdale Hospital:

Sir,
For your information I give hereunder a few details of the precautionary measures, etc., being taken at this hospital.
(1). Sandbagging is in course of progress. Volunteers to fill and lay sandbags, are still urgently required.
(2). All windows of primary importance are being wired, eg., operating theatre, surgery, x-ray departments, etc.
(3). Every pane of glass is being covered with cellophane on the inside, to prevent injury from splintering should windows be smashed.
(4). Preparations are made for an immediate black out.

(5). Extra supplies of food, drugs, dressings and equipment are in stock.

(6). Only acute medical cases are currently being admitted to the hospital.

(7). Extra beds have been erected, practically doubling the accommodation available.

(8). Arrangements are in hand for the medical, nursing and domestic staffing of the Hospital in the event of an emergency.

The War Ministry originally advised the board to devise a scheme of structural alterations and plans were prepared and tenders obtained for protecting various parts of the building by means of steel scaffolding, etc. Despite this, the ministry subsequently informed us that we were not considered to be a vulnerable area and therefore they deemed such precautions unnecessary.

There are many of your readers who subscribe regularly to the hospital funds: most of them will by this time have already sent in their contributions.

It is impossible for us to carry on with our normal work of serving the district unless funds are available, and I would urge those who have not yet done so to be good enough to forward their subscriptions or donations immediately, in order that the Hospital may carry out its functions with the minimum of inconvenience.

Mr F. Moore

Secretary and House Governor.

Even though the war hadn't yet begun – Britain didn't declare war on Germany until 3 September 1939 – everybody obviously knew that it was about to start, as every possible precaution had been enacted by local authorities in preparation for it.

The prestigious Kent College for Girls was established in 1886 and its home, until the outbreak of the Second World War, had been in the Kent coastal town of Folkestone. That all changed with the beginning of hostilities. Although the school had been looking to move to other premises for some time, Folkestone, in the circumstances was understandably deemed to be too dangerous a location for a girls' educational establishment, so the decision was taken by the Kent Wesleyan Methodist Association, who ran the school, to move it to a safer location further inland.

The headmistress, Miss Walker, the teachers and other staff, along with the sixty girl boarders, moved to Hawkwell Place, in the beautiful surroundings next to Pembury Old Church, in the picturesque village of Pembury, on the outskirts of Tunbridge Wells. One of the big advantages of Hawkwell Place was that it had an air raid shelter in the form of its basement, which had been converted for that very purpose and had the luxuries of lights and running water. It also had exits which led directly in to the sumptuous gardens which came with the property.

The official opening ceremony of the new premises was due to take place on Saturday 30 September, but it was cancelled because of the difficulties of arranging transport for the occasion.

It was sadly ironic that the staff and pupils of The Kent College for girls had moved from their previous address at Folkestone to the comparative peace and tranquillity of Pembury, in part to escape the dangers which war brings with it. But less than a year after the school's official opening in its new premises, death and tragedy literally landed in their own back garden.

On 15 September 1940, with the Battle of Britain at its peak, a young man's life was sadly extinguished, a young man who had no connection with the school in whose grounds he died. But years after his death those at the school would rediscover his story and take him to their hearts, grateful for the sacrifice that he made on their behalf to keep them safe.

The man in question was Sergeant Pilot (742636) Leslie Pidd, who at the time of his death was just 22. He was serving with No.238 Squadron, and he was a member of the Royal Air Force Volunteer Reserve which he had joined before the war. His home was at Dunswell in the East Riding of Yorkshire, and although he lies buried in the churchyard of St Peter's Church in Woodmansey, Yorkshire, a part of him will always remain in Pembury, Kent.

The Hurricane (P 2836) which Leslie was flying was shot down, it is believed by a German Messerschmitt aircraft, before crashing in to an oak tree in the grounds of Kent College, Pembury. It is known that Leslie managed to bale out of his aircraft, but differing reports suggest that he was either strafed by a German aircraft whilst parachuting to the ground or was simply too low when he baled out.

The following was written about the incident at the time: 'The inimitable Miss Barrett, matron at both Folkestone and Pembury, was first on the spot and tended to the fallen pilot, covering the body in a cloth before the stretcher bearers arrived.'

Leslie Pidd.

Leslie Pidd's bullet-ridden Hurricane hit an oak tree in the grounds of the college, managing to miss all of the buildings. Whether that was because of good fortune or the skills of the young pilot, will never be known for certain. But for the rest of the war, luck and good fortune stayed with the school because other than a few broken windows, it did not suffer any structural damage to its buildings.

On 15 September 2010 Kent College Pembury, remembered Leslie Pidd in a memorial service at the college, seventy years to the day that he was killed in action. More than thirty members of the Pidd family attended the service, which included a Hurricane flying over the college.

To mark and celebrate the college's one hundreth birthday, Margaret James, who was the Headmistress of Kent College between 1966 and 1983, wrote a book about its history, entitled *The Kent College Saga*. In chapter eight there was a description of the school taken from an advertisement in *The Times* newspaper dated 13 October 1893, when the property had previously been up for sale. It was described as being 'a well built modern mansion, finely situated in magnificently timbered park and woodland commanding extensive views over the notedly beautiful surrounding country'.

When Kent College were looking to purchase the same property in 1939, a certain amount of additional work had been carried out on the premises. It was described as 'a fine Elizabethan residence. It has a porch and entrance hall, lounge and staircase hall, four reception rooms, billiards room, seventeen bed and dressing rooms, six bathrooms, four attics. It had six capital cellars, one of which has been converted in to an air raid shelter. The outbuildings included garages, stabling, four cottages, and in the beautifully established grounds, there was a hard tennis court, swimming pool, squash court, lake and boathouse, kitchen garden and orchard.'

One afternoon during the war a German aircraft had been heard overhead in the skies above the school, engaged in a 'dog fight' with a British aircraft. This time it was the German aircraft that came off second best, but its pilot managed to bail out and parachute safely to the ground, although on landing his parachute became entangled in the branches of a tree, leaving him dangling in the air before he was arrested by the police.

By Christmas 1939 Britain had been at war with Germany for nearly four months, a time to reflect and put things into perspective on both a local and international level. When it came, the war wasn't a surprise to most people, there had been political rumblings throughout Europe for most of the previous year, many of which had involved Germany, Hitler or the Nazi Party, usually all three together.

On 12 January 1938 Field Marshal Werner von Blomberg, the German Minister for War, married Eva Gruhn. The best man at the wedding was Hermann Göring who was not a well known figure on the international stage at the time.

On 4 February the Nazi Party strengthened their grip on power. Adolf Hitler took military control of the country by abolishing the German War Ministry and replacing it with the High Command of the Armed Forces, or the *Oberkommando der Wehrmacht*. Not stopping there, Hitler dismissed those considered to be unsympathetic to his way of doing things. These included the Foreign Minister, Baron Konstantin, who was replaced by Joachim von Ribbentrop, who was sentenced to death at the Nuremberg trials for waging war and enabling the Holocaust. He was hanged on 16 October 1946. The commander-in-chief of the German Army, General Werner von Fritsch, also fell from favour and was replaced by General Walther von Brauchitsch, after being accused of having committed acts of homosexuality. Seven months later on 22 September 1939, he was dead, shot in the leg during the Siege of Warsaw.

On 12 February 1938 Hitler demanded and received assurances from Kurt von Schuschnigg, the Austrian Chancellor, at a meeting at Berchtesgaden, that the Austrian government would allow greater Nazi influence in their affairs. A refusal would have seen a German invasion of his country, but just a month later, German troops marched into the country and annexed it as part of the German Reich. Then on 28 May Hitler declared his intention to destroy Czechoslovakia by military means and mobilised his troops in readiness. July 1938 saw the construction of the Mauthausen concentration camp in Austria.

On 18 August 1938 General Ludwig Beck, Chief of the German Army General Staff, resigned convinced that Hitler's dispute with Czechoslovakia over the Sudetenland will lead to a war in Europe. Most of the month was taken up with numerous meetings, statements, threats and counter threats by the different nations involved in trying to resolve the situation over the Sudetenland. On 30 September the Munich Agreement, a settlement which allowed Nazi Germany to annex parts of Czechoslovakia, was signed by Germany, France, Britain and Italy, but not Czechoslovakia, who were not invited to the conference. The next day German forces marched into the Sudetenland.

On 18 October Germany expelled 12,000 Polish Jews living in Germany and on 7 November the German politician, Ernest von Rath, was assassinated in Paris by Herschel Grynszpan, a Polish-Jewish refugee. Then on 9 November came *Kristallnacht,* the night of broken glass, with the destruction of Jewish businesses, synagogues, schools and the arrest of thousands of Jewish men; 30,000 are estimated to have been sent to concentration camps.

Despite all of the above happenings and the gradual build up of hostilities, by the time Germany invaded Poland on 1 September 1939, the residents of Dover were enjoying the peace and tranquillity of the town's cricket week while the British authorities were planning for a state of emergency in the case of war.

In November 1938, as part of their future capital expenditure planning, the authorities in Dover had requested £120,000 for the building of deep air raid shelters, so as to be able to offer maximum protection to the town's population. This request was turned down. Instead they were provided with Anderson steel shelters, which were akin to a garden shed with mud added to the sides. As they were above ground, and offered far less protection, they were understandably not very popular.

In January 1939 Dover was informed that they had to receive evacuee children from London and other nominated danger zones, a decision which most towns folk found astonishing, taking into account the town's close proximity to the enemy. Dover Council sent a deputation to the Home Office to challenge this and the decision was changed on 18 March 1939. The deputation was also informed that the town would be receiving steel Anderson shelters, but not every household would automatically be provided with one. To qualify for a free shelter each household had to have a visit from an air raid warden to establish who qualified for one under the £5 per week maximum income limit. For those families who didn't qualify, the price to purchase one was £7. The first batch of Anderson shelters did not arrive until August 1939 and the delivery of them was completed by November.

Anderson shelters were designed in 1938 and named after Sir John Anderson. A simple design, they were intended to be occupied by six people. The shelters consisted of a centre piece of six corrugated steel panels. Further flat, steel, corrugated panels were then bolted on to form the sides and end panels, one of which contained a door. They were 1.4m in width, 2m in length and 1.8m high, which meant that a man of 6ft or taller would not be able to fully stand up in it. Once a shelter had been put together, the base of it was supposed to sit one metre below the surface of the ground and was then to be covered in a thick layer of soil and topped off with turf. In total 3.5 million Anderson shelters were built and distributed, immediately before and during the course of the Second World War. During the cold winter months, especially during the hours of darkness, they were not the most inviting of places. After the war many were used as garden sheds.

On 22 January 1939 Dover Council voted by 19-3 in favour of the latest scheme of the Ministry of Transport which provided for the removal of the remainder of the sea side by Snargate Street, widening it and changing Northampton Street, into quay space. The Ministry of Transport donated the lion's share of the overall cost of the project which came to £42,315.

Although the demolishing of slum areas across the town had been approved by Dover Council earlier in the year, all such schemes came to an abrupt end with the outbreak of war. Plans for the layout of the new Army Barracks at Old Park were made public for the first time in March 1939. The cost of the much-needed project was in the region of £200,000. This came at a time when the Royal Marines Barracks at nearby Deal, which had been constructed shortly after the beginning of the French Revolution in 1789, were being replaced and updated.

Part of Dover's five-year strategic plan from 1939 had included expenditure for the building of additional schools, but not until the latter stages of the plan. The Board of Education wrote a letter on 11 March 1939 to the town planners, threatening the loss of the promised 50 per cent grant towards the total cost of the scheme, if the work wasn't completed before the end of 1940. The big push from central government was centred around ARP plans, certainly for towns such as Dover, although £17,315 was found for a new infant's school at St Radigund's Road, big enough to cater for 300 pupils. It still exists today in the shape of St Radigund's Community Primary School.

At the end of March 1939 the Air Raid Precautions Joint Committee for Dover and Dover Rural District was dissolved after the resignation of Captain Papillon, who had been the ARP co-ordinator since May 1938. In his place Dover pointed the Chief Constable, Mr Marshall Bolt, as the new controller of the local ARP, whilst Mr S.R.H. Loxton, the town clerk, was made the co-ordinating officer. The Dover Rural District Council appointed Mr P.C. Bushell as their ARP clerk and organiser. Less than four months later both councils agreed a local plan that saw the Fire Brigade services for both authorities, provided by Dover. The recruiting and training of all ARP personnel continued throughout the year, highlighting just how seriously the potential threat of air attacks was being taken in the event of the country going to war.

Alderman J.R. Cairns, the Mayor of Dover, laid the foundation stone of the town's new police station on 25 July 1939. Part of the new station included a control room, which during the course of the war was to be used by the town's ARP members. Other such building works in Dover had been postponed as a result of the impending threat of war including building on the St Radigund's Road municipal housing estate, the Buckland Bridge and London Road widening scheme, along with the planned demolition work due to take place in Snargate Street.

Blackout trials took place at different times throughout the year as did siren testing, so that people would be left in no doubt as to what the noise of the air raid siren sounded like, and to monitor just how quickly they would have to move to get to the nearest shelter. On 24 August 1939 the Mayor of Dover, Alderman J.R. Cairns announced that there would be no more siren tests and that the next time the sirens were heard, it would be for real. Residents were made aware of the locations of all air raid shelters in the town over several weeks via the local press.

As soon as Germany invaded Poland on 1 September 1939 a compulsory blackout was ordered between sunset and sunrise, even though it would be two more days before Britain declared war on Germany. The Royal Victoria Hospital moved the same evening to the premises of the Earl and Countess of Guildford at Waldershare Mansion.

At 11.15 am on Sunday 3 September the Prime Minister made a speech that was broadcast via the radio, as Germany had failed to respond to Britain's ultimatum to withdraw her troops from Poland by 11 am on 3 September 1939. Britain was now at war with Germany.

With the outbreak of the war, the Admiralty Harbour at Dover once again became the headquarters of the Dover Patrol, which had been so successful in their efforts to ensure the safety of Allied shipping crossing safely between Britain and the continent, but because of wartime censorship regulations, any reference or any other publicity about the patrol was forbidden. Despite this, and how it passed the censorship of the time is unclear, the BBC broadcast a report that London Press reporters had visited Dover and let the cat out of the bag that the patrol was under the command of Vice Admiral B.H. Ramsy CB MVO. If that wasn't bad enough the report also announced that his headquarters was at Dover Castle.

Once war had been declared, Dover became a closed port which meant that vessels could only enter and leave the harbour with official permission.

When the much-criticised Munich Agreement was signed on 30 September 1938 and Neville Chamberlain muttered those now immortal words, 'I believe it is peace in our time', Kent's Public Assistance Committee obviously believed what he had said without thinking that Chamberlain's comments, no matter how well intended, might not come to fruition. Committee members, supported by the Dover Guardians Committee, became quite indignant earlier in the year because of ARP trenches which had been dug on County Council owned land in Union Road, and asked the town council to have them filled in and the site restored to its previous condition – at best a somewhat short-sighted if not naive approach in the circumstances.

On 4 November 1939 Vice-Admiral Sir Percy Douglas, the Chairman of the Dover Harbour Board, and the Commodore Superintendent of the Dover Naval Dockyard, died suddenly.

The Dover municipal elections weren't due to take place until 9 November 1939, two months after the outbreak of the war, and because of this Alderman J. R. Cairns was re-elected unopposed as Mayor of Dover for the third consecutive year. The latter of the three appointments was due to emergency wartime legislation, that prevented such elections taking place. Stability, particularly of a political nature, was important in wartime Britain. Halfway through the same month, the people of Dover were issued with ration books by the local Food Control Office, in an effort to ensure there was enough food for everybody, and to safeguard against panic buying in the shops of essential items.

Kent was blessed with large coal deposits, which were an absolute necessity, not just for the county but the country as well as the nation headed into a war that nobody knew how long would last. After the First World War, into the 1920s and 1930s, the local coal industry expanded rapidly, providing much needed jobs whilst at the same time bolstering the county's economy, but by the outbreak of the Second World War, there were only four working collieries left: Bettshanger, which is just outside Deal, Chislet, Snowdown and Tilmanstone.

During the summer of 1939, the Coal Commission suggested an amalgamation of Kent's collieries, a proposal that was heavily criticised by the managing director of the Chislet Colliery, Mr Forster Brown. Throughout the course of the year, there had been no major labour disputes at any of the collieries, although had been a three-day stoppage at Snowdon in February, along with minor disagreements at the Tilmanstone and Betteshanger collieries.

On 18 November 1939 a vessel well known to Dover, the SS *Simon Bolivar*, which had first sailed from Dover harbour en route to the West Indies, via Holland, in March 1927, was sunk off the Essex coast after striking a German magnetic mine. Of her crew, 150 perished.

On Sunday, 17 September the Royal Navy aircraft carrier, HMS *Courageous*, on an anti-submarine patrol in the Western Appoaches, an area of the Atlantic Ocean which lies west of the British Isles, with an escort of four destroyers, was attacked by the German submarine, *U-29*, which struck her with two torpedoes on her port side. She sank within 20 minutes and of a ship's complement of 1,202 officers and ratings, 515 were killed, included the commanding officer, Captain William T. Makeig-Jones.

At least two of the crew who survived were from Dover. Signaller Edward Frank Day, who was only 19 years of age, lived with his aunt and uncle, Mr and Mrs Bennett of 183 Clarendon Street, Dover. He had just finished having a bath when a torpedo struck the *Courageous* amidships. All the lights went out immediately and the vessel quickly took a heavy list to her port side. Signaller Day somehow managed to get himself up on deck, and when the order was given to abandon ship he slid down the side of the stricken hulk into the cold water before swimming off to one of the nearby destroyers. Fortunately, he was a strong swimmer, he had been a champion swimmer at his school, St Mary's, in both 1933 and 1934. He ended up in the water for forty-five minutes before he was rescued. He had only been in the Navy for a year at the time of the sinking and the *Courageous* was his first ship. His elder brother Charles, who had previously served on the *Courageous*, was by that time a wireless telegraphist on board HMS *Gloucester*.

Signaller Day was positive that the submarine which had brought about the demise of the *Courageous*, *U-29*, had been sunk in the immediate aftermath, claiming that he had seen the conning tower of the submarine blown 30ft in the air by a depth charge dropped from another vessel. Whatever he saw wasn't the death throws of *U-29* as she was still in front line service until early 1941. After that she was used as a training submarine by the 24th U-Boat Flotilla, before being scuttled on 5 May 1945 in Kupfermuhlen Bay as part of Operation Regenbogen. This was a co-ordinated operation by the German authorities to destroy as many of its submarines as possible so that they didn't fall into Allied hands.

The commander of *U-29* was Korvettenkapitan Georg Lassen, who died on 18 January 2012 in Mallorca, Spain, aged 96. In its time as an operational submarine, *U-29* sank thirteen Allied vessels, but the only military vessel it sunk was the *Courageous*. The other twelve were all merchant ships.

The Commonwealth War Graves Commission website shows that Signalman D/SSX 20742 Edward Frank Day from Dover, who was serving with the Royal Navy, was killed in action on 10 April 1940 whilst serving on board HMS *Hunter*. He was 20 years of age, has no known grave but is commemorated on the Plymouth Naval Memorial. The vessel was sunk by German destroyers during the First Battle of Narvik, killing 107 of her crew, one of whom was Edward Frank Day. A further five later died of their wounds.

A search of the same website showed that a Petty Officer Airman FAA/FX 77376 Charles Aisne Day from Dover, who was serving on board HMS *Courageous* was killed in action on 23 May 1941 aged 26. His name is commemorated on the Lee-on-Solent Memorial in Hampshire.

Sinking of HMS Gloucester.

HMS *Gloucester* was sunk during the Battle of Crete by German Stuka dive bombers on 22 May 1941. Wikipedia records a total of 722 officers and men out of a crew of 807, were lost when it was sunk, yet the Commonwealth War Graves Commission website records the number of dead as being 754. As can be seen there is a discrepancy of one day between when the *Gloucester* was sunk and the date of death shown for Charles Aisne Day. He obviously did not die of his wounds subsequent to the sinking, because if he had, then he would have a grave, but that it is not the case. Maybe it was because a complete list of survivors wasn't known until 23 May 1941.

The other Kent man to have survived the sinking of HMS *Courageous* was Mr G.H. Gerrard, who lived at 10 Beach Street, Dover. He was 27 years of age and an officer's cook, who had been in the Navy for eleven years, having previously served aboard HMS *Malaya* and HMS *Furious*.

Hitler's Invasion of Poland

Adolf Hitler's decision to invade Poland on 1 September 1939, and his then refusal to remove his troops by a given date, ultimately led to Great Britain declaring war on Germany. It was as if Hitler wanted a war, but just needed a way to start it, because up to that moment, nobody had actually stood up to him. Nations throughout Europe had let him do what he wanted, more as a way of trying to prevent a war. Maybe Hitler's decision not to pull his troops out of Poland was born out of a real belief that Britain wouldn't carry out the threat to go to war.

The eventual German invasion of Poland didn't come as a shock, because Hitler had been making rumblings about returning parts of the German speaking territories in Western Poland to German control since soon after the Nazi Party came to power on 30 January 1933. It has to be remembered that under the treaty of Versailles at the end of the First World War, Germany lost lands to Poland, including the city of Danzig. Initially, in an attempt to obtain a veneer of credibility on the international stage, Hitler went as far as signing the German-Polish Non-Aggression Pact of 1934, but with no long term intention of keeping to the agreement. Ironically, Hitler even claimed Poland had attacked Germany to legitimise his subsequent attack.

Relations between Germany and Poland went from bad to worse. In 1937 Germany began to apply political pressure on Poland by making more demands about Danzig whilst at the same time wanting to build a road that would connect East Prussia with Germany, but to achieve this it would have to cut straight through what was known as the Polish corridor. Not surprisingly Poland rejected this proposal fearing that to agree, would mean Germany would have more power and control, which would eventually lead to a loss of independence.

It could be argued that what actually started the Second World War was the military alliance signed by Poland, France and the United Kingdom on 31 March 1939, with each promising to come to the others' assistance in the case of one of them being threatened with war by a belligerent nation. It is almost certain that Poland had Germany in mind when she signed her military alliance with France and the Untied

Kingdom. Less than one month later on 28 April 1939 Germany's aggressive stance towards Poland and the United Kingdom worsened when she withdrew from both the German-Polish Non-Aggression Pact of 1934 and the London Naval Agreement of 1935.

In Lloyd Clark's book *Kursk. The Greatest Battle: Eastern Front 1943*, he records that in May 1939 Hitler wrote the following note to a group of his generals whom he had tasked with planning the invasion of Poland.

With minor exceptions German national unification has been achieved. Further successes cannot be achieved without bloodshed. Poland will always be on the side of our adversaries. Danzig is not the objective. It is a matter of expanding our living space in the east, of making our food supply secure, and solving the problem of the Baltic states. To provide sufficient food you must have sparsely settled areas. There is therefore no question of sparing Poland, and the decision remains to attack Poland at the first opportunity. We cannot expect a repetition of Czechoslovakia. There will be fighting.

The anti-Polish rhetoric didn't end there. On 22 August 1939 Hitler delivered a speech to his commanders at a meeting at the Obersalzberg, the mountainside retreat of the Nazi Party, near to the Bavarian town of Berchtesgaden:

The object of the war is physically to destroy the enemy. That is why I have prepared, for the moment only in the East, my 'Death's Head' formations with orders to kill without pity or mercy all men, women and children of Polish descent or language. Only in this way can we obtain the living space we need.

By now the talking was over as far as Hitler was concerned with the German invasion of Poland due to commence at 4 am on 26 August 1939. The previous day the Polish government signed the Polish–British Common Defense Pact which committed Britain to defending Poland and guaranteeing the preservation of her independence as a sovereign nation. This caused Hitler to postpone his planned invasion, but only for six days. Even then the final scenes of this ridiculous affair still had to be played out to the full by Hitler, apparently feeling the need to convince members of the international community that Germany was being wronged by Poland all they were doing were defending themselves.

This came in the shape of what has become known as the Gleiwitz incident. On the evening of 31 August 1939 an attack took place on the radio station in the German border city of Gleiwitz, purportedly by Polish soldiers, but in fact the attack was carried out by German soldiers dressed in Polish uniforms. The evidence for this comes in an affidavit sworn by SS Sturmbannführer Alfred Naujocks, at the Nuremberg trials in 1945. In it he states that he was ordered by Heinrich Müller, the head of the Gestapo and his boss, Reinhard Heydrich, to carry out the attack on Gleiwitz radio station. As part of the ploy the bodies of Dachau concentration camp internees were left at the scene dressed in Polish Army uniforms. They had been killed by lethal injection and their dead bodies shot through at the scene of the 'raid'. There is today no way of proving or disproving Naujocks' version of the events that took place at Gleiwitz.

The political gamesmanship and manoeuvring had at last come to an end, and Hitler had finally got around to doing what he had been planning for the previous six years. But the strangeness of the situation didn't stop there. After just one month of fighting, on 6 October 1939, Hitler made a peace offering to both Britain and France while making it abundantly clear that the situation with Poland was not up for discussion and that it would be down to Russia and Germany to determine her future. After wrestling with the proposal for six days, Neville Chamberlain rejected it, stating that 'Past experience has shown that no reliance can be placed upon the promises of the present German government.'

Strangely enough throughout August and September 1939, there was hardly a mention of any build up to war, or much about the outbreak of it either, in Kent newspapers. Instead the topics were of a sporting nature, concerning Kent's darts league, football and how it was going to be affected across the county, as well as the county's first class cricket averages. With the war less than a month old there was talk of wage increases in the Kent mining industry, hop pickers on their way to the hop gardens of Kent, the state of the lamb industry and how a man from Borough Green had a heart attack and died whilst driving in Woolwich.

The *Dover Express* had bucked the trend somewhat when an article appeared in their newspaper for Friday 1 September entitled, 'Dover and the Great Preparation'. It spoke of how busy the previous week had been and the amount of work that had been carried out to ensure that the county's defences were prepared for war. This had been mirrored around the country and was in line with a speech the Prime Minister had made on 29 August, the detail of which could not be repeated in the newspaper article, for obvious reasons, although Kent was determined to do what was required of it and in doing so, face its responsibilities.

What could be explained was that Civil Defence measures continued to be made, such as the sand-bagging of important buildings. A notice had been issued by the town clerk and the co-ordinating officer of the Dover ARP committee, which called upon owners and occupiers of industrial and commercial premises to take all practical steps for the protection of their buildings, in the event of the outbreak of war.

On Thursday 31 August the British Government decided that the evacuation of more than 3,000,000 children and others who came into the relevant priority classes, should begin. This included such areas as major cities and coastal areas along the south coast, which included the county of Kent.

On the same day it was also announced that the Royal Navy was to be fully mobilized, which saw plenty of activity in towns such as Chatham, Sheerness, and Dover. Members of the Army Reserve and supplementary reserve, along with members of the Royal Air Force Volunteer Reserve, also received the call to arms.

Police issued the following notice for the residents of Dover in relation to air raid warnings.

'Warnings of impending Air Raids will be given by a fluctuating or warbling signal of varying pitch, or a succession of intermittent blasts sounded by hooters and sirens.

These signals may be supplemented by sharp, loud blasts on Police whistles. The Raiders Passed signal will be a continuous signal at a steady pitch.

If Poison Gas has been used, warning will be given by Hand Rattles. The ringing of Hand Bells will announce that the danger from gas has passed.'

My first thought in relation to a town the size of Dover being the target of a gas attack, is that it would take an awful lot of people equipped with hand rattles, being able to make it onto the streets and then make a loud enough noise to attract the attention of all the other residents, in enough time to warn them about an impending gas attack.

The *Chatham News* for Friday 8 September carried on its front page, in very small print, the news that certain retired Army officers had been employed to purchase large numbers of horses in towns across the county. It also covered news of the location of the ten ARP public shelters that were available in Rochester.

Over the next few months that would change drastically with more and more news items about the war filling more of the pages.

Although this book is about Kent and its people in the Second World War, it includes a narrative from a wider perspective, so that the Kent-related events can be seen in their fullest context. In the early months of the war there were a few battles which took place involving Japanese, Chinese and Russian forces, which were not directly part of the Second World War but of other conflicts. They included the Battle of Changsha (17 September to 6 October 1939) during the Second Sino-Japanese War, which had begun on 7 July 1937; the Battle of Khalkhyn Gol (11 May to 15 September 1939) part of the Soviet – Japanese border disputes; the Battle of Tolvajarvi on 13 December 1939 in which Finnish forces led by Colonel Paavo Talvela defeated forces of the Soviet Union during the Winter War, a conflict fought between those two nations.

Closer to home, the Battle of the Atlantic lasted from 3 September 1939 until 8 May 1945, making it the longest continuous military campaign of the Second World War. It involved the naval blockade of German ports to prevent the Kriegsmarine attacking Allied shipping. Royal Navy ships escorted convoys of merchant shipping, predominantly from ports in North America that were bound for either the United Kingdom or the Soviet Union. Britain relied on a million tons of imported goods per week to survive and continue the war effort.

The term Battle of the Atlantic was coined in February 1941 by Prime Minister Winston Churchill. By the end of the battle Britain and her Allies had lost a total of 36,000 men from the Royal Navy and an equivalent amount from the Merchant Navy. On top of this they lost 3,500 merchant ships, 175 warships and 741 aircraft from the RAF's Coastal Command.

The Battle of River Plate was the first major naval battle of the Second World War on 13 December 1939. The German battleship, *Admiral Graf Spee*, had been active in the Indian Ocean and the South Atlantic since the beginning of the war, and on the day in question it was making its way towards the River Plate when it saw what it thought were three merchant vessels. They were in fact HMS *Achilles* of the Royal New Zealand Navy, along with HMS *Ajax* and HMS *Exeter* of the Royal Navy. Captain Hans Langsdorf directed his vessel directly towards the three ships that were ahead of him. Commodore Henry Harwood on board the *Exeter* who was in charge of the three Allied vessels, split his force to make it more difficult for the German guns.

The initial engagement was between *Graf Spee* and the *Exeter*, and although both ships had taken hits, the latter of the two vessels came off far worse. After an intense battle between the four ships, which also saw *Ajax* struck, the *Graf Spee* made good its escape by laying down smoke and making for the comparative safety of the port of Montevideo, the capital of Uruguay. The Allied and American governments applied political pressure on their Uruguayan counterparts, who in turn directed that the *Graf Spee* had to leave Uruguayan waters within seventy-two hours, whether the needed repairs had been completed or not.

Ajax and *Achilles* had been joined by HMS *Ark Royal* and HMS *Renown*, so Captain Langsdorf knew that his chances of getting out of the harbour and into international waters, were slim. He was running desperately short of ammunition and the *Graf Spee* was still damaged. He contacted the German government and the decision was taken that Langsdorf should scuttle his vessel rather than let it fall in to the hands of the British. To this end, on the evening of 17 December 1939, and with only a skeleton crew on board, Langsdorf steered the *Graf Spee* out of the harbour and abandoned her. She exploded a few minutes later. Unbeknown to the British, the bulk of the German crew had embarked on board the German merchant vessel *Tacoma* which had then made its way to the nearby Argentinian city of Buenos Aires. There they were met by Langsdorf and his skeleton crew.

On the evening of 19/20 December 1939 Captain Langsdorf committed suicide by shooting himself in the head.

Two men from HMS *Achilles* were killed in the incident involving the *Graf Spee*. Telegraphist D/JX 148899 Frank Stennett was only 18 years of age and from Hazel Grove in Manchester and Ordinary Telegraphist D/SSX23288 Neville Jervaise Milburn. Both were killed in action on 13 December and are buried in the Buceo British Cemetery in Montevideo.

Sixty-one of the crew of HMS *Exeter* were also killed whilst engaging the *Graf Spee*. They have no known grave, but their names are commemorated on the Plymouth Naval Memorial. One of the men, Captain Humphrey Ropner Duncan Woods of the Royal Marines (35) was a married man from Walmer in Kent.

Seven of the crew of HMS *Ajax* were also killed. Their names are commemorated on the Chatham Naval Memorial, one of whom, Ordinary Seaman C/JX 151605 William John Farley (18) was from Ramsgate in Kent.

Between the outbreak of the war and 31 December 1939, at least seventy-six men who had Kent connections, and who were serving in either the Army, RAF, Navy, or Merchant Navy, were either killed or died of their wounds, sickness or disease. This number includes six from the Army, five from the Royal Air Force, fifty-three from the Royal Navy and twelve from the Merchant Navy.

The first Kent man to be killed in action during the Second World War was Leading Aircraftman 524808 John Quilter (22), of No.206 Squadron, Royal Air Force, who was killed in action on 5 September 1939, just five days into the war. At that time No.206 Squadron consisted of only twenty-four aircraft, a mixture of Anson and Lockheed Hudsons.

On 5 September 1939, an Avro Anson of No.206 Squadron, with its four-man crew, was on a reconnaissance mission over the English Channel when it came into contact with two German Bv 138 flying boats. This coming together resulted in the RAF Avro being shot down and crashing in the sea. Three of the four crew members, Sergeant Alexander O. Heslop, Aircraftsman 1st Class Geoffrey Sheffield, and Leading Aircraftman John Quilter, were all killed. The bodies of all three men were lost to the sea, but their names are recorded and commemorated on the Runnymede Memorial in Surrey.

Flying Officer Laurence Hugh Edwards, a New Zealander, survived the crash and after the two German aircraft landed next to the wreckage of the downed Anson, they picked up Edwards from the cold waters of the English Channel, taking him prisoner, and in doing so, making him the first Allied officer to be captured by the Germans during the Second World War.

On Monday 9 October two men appeared before the Dover Borough Quarter Sessions for breaking and entering a shop and stealing items of cutlery valued at £1 2s 7d. Overseeing the proceedings was the Recorder, Sir Archibald Bodkin.

About 10.15 pm on the evening of Friday 29 September, three busmen were walking along the High Street in Dover. As they walked past the premises of Frederick Morecroft, they noticed two men standing in the doorway of the shop. They had only walked a few yards further on when they heard the sound of breaking glass. One of the busmen, William Turner, turned around and rushed back to the shop, where the two men were still in the doorway. He grabbed hold of one of the men, whilst the other man ran off. Mr Turner and his colleagues took the man they had detained to Dover police station where they handed him over to one of the constables on duty. He subsequently admitted having broken the window in Mr Morecroft's shop.

The two men in question, Robert Sands and Harry Richard John Record, were both serving soldiers, Gunners in either the 519th or 520th Kent and Sussex (Heavy) Coastal Regiment; the 519th were stationed at Dover whilst the 520th were situated at Dover Citadel. When the police took Sands back to his barracks they found Record who admitted also being involved in the incident.

Inspector Datlen of the Dover police told the court that Sands was a married man with no children. His mother-in-law described him as being lazy and indolent and that his main interests in life appeared to be football matches and picture houses. He had joined the Army in June 1939, even though he had served a three-month prison sentence in 1937 for multiple cases of theft and house-breaking, and for six months in May 1938 for stealing a wireless set and a camera from a house he had broken into.

Record on the other hand was a single man who had served in the Army for three years between 1933 and 1936, when he was then placed on the Army Reserve, and had previously been a man of exemplary character. Captain P.B. Southern, the men's commanding officer was present, and spoke highly of both of them, stating that they both had good Army characters.

The Recorder found both men guilty as charged and bound them over for a period of six months. He thought it in the public interest that Gunners Sands and Record should be disciplined and dealt with by the Army authorities, possibly in the way of further training, rather than spend time in a civilian prison. He advised both men to avoid drinking too much, although he accepted that there were a large number of public houses throughout Dover. They were fortunate that they were serving soldiers and the nation was at war as they would have otherwise undoubtedly received a custodial sentence.

Sir Archibald Bodkin added that the Justices believed that Mr Turner's actions on the night in question, especially with a blackout in progress, were 'first rate', and what would be expected of any 'decent fellow', sentiments echoed by Sir Archibald.

A letter appeared in the *Dover Express* dated Friday 13 October on the subject of Air Raid Precautions at Dover and the need for more volunteers. The letter had been sent to the newspaper by Mr S.R.H. Loxton, the town clerk and co-ordinating officer for Dover.

Dear Sir,

The Corporation would be grateful if you would permit them, through your columns, to express their very sincere thanks for the most valuable work which is being done by all members of the ARP organization. They greatly appreciate the public spirited manner in which voluntary unpaid workers are giving so much of their time to the service of the town, and also the way in which the whole-time paid workers are carrying out their duties, which entail long hours, often in far from congenial circumstances. The Corporation are however, still greatly concerned at the shortage of volunteers for A.R.P. duties, which is the cause of the heavy demands which are now being made on all paid and unpaid A.R.P. personnel. This shortage of personnel could, to some extent, be made up by the employment of more people on a whole-time paid basis, but the Corporation are reluctant to take this course, as it must throw an even heavier expense upon the ratepayers than that which they will in any event have to bear. The only other way in which the required number of A.R.P. personnel can be obtained is, therefore, by more of the people of Dover giving their services in a voluntary capacity.

A considerable number of paid whole-time workers is necessary for all the A.R.P. services, and in the interests of economy this number is being kept as low as practicable, but unless more voluntary workers enrol and undergo such training as may be necessary, the Corporation will have no alternative but to increase substantially the number of paid personnel. The Corporation, therefore most urgently appeal, in the interests of efficiency and economy, to all those who are able to do so, to enrol for voluntary service in one of the branches of the Dover A.R.P. organization.

Volunteers are required for all services, Auxiliary Fire Service, Wardens, Rescue, etc., Parties, Control Room, and most urgently of all for First Aid Posts and Parties and Ambulance work. Please enrol for training now, for the sake of the safety and future prosperity of your town.

The letter highlights just how much work was undertaken on the home front during the Second World War on a voluntary basis by well meaning citizens, who were either too old or simply not physically fit enough to enlist in His Majesty's armed forces.

The Mayor of Dover, Mr J.R. Cairns wrote a letter to the editor of the *Dover Express* on the matter of the Dover Rest and Recreation Room, for the many hundreds of men of His Majesty's forces who were stationed in the town. The letter appeared in the edition dated Friday 3 November.

Dear Sir,

The good welfare of the many men of HM Forces stationed in Dover is, I am sure, a matter which commends itself to the inhabitants of the town generally, and the urgent necessity for the provision of hostels where they can spend a few quiet hours under comfortable conditions for the purpose of recreation or writing home, must be apparent to all, particularly at the present time during the prolonged 'black out' hours and the restriction upon many forms of entertainment. I am therefore pleased to state that in addition to the hostels which have already been established by certain other local organisations, arrangements have been made to open No.4 Gilford Lawn, as the Dover Rest and Recreation Room for men of HM Forces, which premises the Dover Harbour Board have kindly made available at a nominal rental and where a number of beds will be available for the use of men sleeping ashore or away from barracks.

An influential committee, under the able Chairmanship of Lady Douglas, and with the assistance of the Mayoress's Social Committee, has been formed to supervise the arrangements, and Councillor Mrs Langley, of 3 Worthington Street, has kindly consented to act as Honorary Secretary, and Mr E.M. Worsfold, JP., 4 Cambridge Terrace, Dover as Honorary Treasurer.

A number of interested persons have already kindly promised gifts of money and furniture, etc., to assist in equipping the Hostel, and in bringing the matter to the notice of your readers, I confidently appeal for their generous support in this worthy effort. In addition to money, gifts of furniture, blankets and bed linen, writing utensils and paper, books, cards, a dart board and other games are urgently required.

Contributions, however small, may be sent direct to the Honorary Treasurer, Mr E.M. Worsfold, JP., 4 Cambridge Terrace, Dover, or may be paid direct to Barclays Bank, Cannon Street, and will be gratefully acknowledged. Offers of help and gifts or every description should be addressed either to Lady Douglas at the Rest Room, 4, Guildford Lawn, or to the Honorary Secretary, Councillor Mrs Langley, 3 Worthington Street. Arrangements will gladly be made to collect any gifts on receipt of a postcard.

The rest and recreation rooms provided invaluable respite away from their barracks or ships for all military personnel, who were a long way from their homes and families, many not knowing when and if they would ever return to either again. These premises were nothing new to most well established military towns, and for locations which now suddenly found their communities had become large military hubs, they were an invaluable addition.

The No.4 Guildford Lawn Rest and Recreation Room in Dover was officially opened on Monday, 27 November by the Mayor Alderman J.R. Cairns, who was accompanied by the mayoress, and in the presence of a large gathering which included Vice Admiral B.H. Ramsay CB., the commanding officer of Dover Naval base, and Brigadier A.K. Main DSO, commanding officer of the Dover Garrison.

The war affected everybody in many different ways regardless of their social standing – homes, families, businesses and even children's ability to attend school. It was announced in early December 1939 that as of January 1940, Dover College would move for the duration of the war to Poltimore House, about four miles from Exeter. The property had previously been a girl's school for sixteen years but closed in the Christmas term 1939.

The masters and pupils of Dover College were moving to a splendid location and had at their disposal the mansion house, part of the deer park, pleasure grounds and gardens which amounted to 112 acres of land. The governors of the school and the parents of the children had decided that because of the war Dover was too dangerous a location for a public school. Dover College had been evacuated during the First World War and relocated to Leamington in Warwickshire, returning to Dover after the war.

By the end of 1939 the war had been underway for nearly five months, and so much had already changed in Dover, as it had in other towns and villages across Kent and the rest of the country. Nobody had the slightest idea that it would continue for nearly another five years, and that before it was over, hundreds of young men from across Kent would have been killed fighting for their country in the battle to defeat the evil of Nazism, once and for all.

CHAPTER 2

1940 – Britain at Bay

Dunkirk Evacuations

At the start of the war the United Kingdom sent troops in the form of the British Expeditionary Force (BEF), across the English Channel, to help with the defence of France. Ten divisions were under the command of the formidable General John Standish Surtees Prendergast Vereker, 6th Viscount Gort VC GCB CBE DSO and Two Bars MVO MC. He had been mentioned in despatches eight times during the First World War, wounded several times and his award of the Victoria Cross was as a result of his actions at the Battle of the Canal du Nord in September 1918.

The BEF wasn't alone in its efforts to defend France from the German threat. They were working alongside elements of both the Belgian and French Armies, in an effort to hold back the German blitzkrieg, but by 10 May 1940 enemy forces had begun to gain the upper hand as they bulldozed their way into Belgium and Holland. Elements of the BEF had taken up defensive positions on the Belgian side of the River Dyle where they found themselves up against Germany's formidable Army Group B, under the command of Generaloberst Gerd von Rundstedt.

With the men of the BEF holding their own in the middle of the line, they were dependent on the Belgian and French troops to do the same on either flank. Sadly, this was not the case and by 14 May General Vereker had to order a fighting withdrawal to the River Scheldt, which runs through northern France, western Belgium and the south-western part of Holland, because both the French and Belgian armies failed to hold their positions against a fast moving and formidable enemy. What made the situation even more precarious was that the French, under the command of General Gaston Billotte, had astonishingly committed all of their troops to the fight and had not held any back in reserve.

Field Marshal Lord Gort and General John Vereker.

Operation Dynamo – Dunkirk Evacuations

Thankfully for all concerned, General Vereker had grasped the seriousness of the situation, and realized that he was no longer looking at a retreat, but an evacuation, if all the Allied troops were not to be either killed or captured by the Germans. Dunkirk was quickly identified as the nearest and best location for the troops to be extracted from, not only because of the length of its sandy beaches where large numbers of men could assemble, but because the area was surrounded by marshes, which would make it nigh on impossible for the Germans to be able to bring forward any heavy artillery or tanks. The town also had many old, but still usable, fortifications, which would provide a useful defensive platform to try and hold back the enemy long enough to evacuate as many men as possible, before Dunkirk was finally overrun.

Remarkably, the planning for Operation Dynamo had only begun on 20 May 1940 and was overseen by Vice Admiral Bertram Ramsey, at Dover Castle.

When mention is made of the heroic acts that were carried out during the evacuation of Dunkirk, the battle and fighting which preceded these historic events often become lost to history. German forces had captured the French port of Boulogne and surrounded the nearby town of Calais all of this had been achieved by 23 May 1940, as the Germans prepared themselves for the attack on Dunkirk.

General Vereker's appraisal of the potential advantage of the geographical elements surrounding Dunkirk proved to be correct, as on 23 May 1940 von Rundstedt ordered his Panzer units to halt as they approached the outskirts of the town. Part of his reasoning was concern about the marshy ground being unsuitable for his tanks. Von Rundstedt's decision had the total support of Adolf Hitler and was endorsed by him on a visit he made to Army Group A's headquarters on 24 May, whilst later the same day ordering the Luftwaffe to attack the retreating Allied soldiers and cut off their escape. It was a further two days before Hitler decided that the time had come for his Panzer units to continue their advance on Dunkirk, but for some reason, it took many hours before these orders were carried out. This precious time allowed Allied units to dig in, strengthen their defensive positions, and hasten their evacuation plan. This decision alone was without doubt a game changer. If Hitler and von Rundstedt hadn't been so cautious, the evacuation at Dunkirk would not have been anywhere near as successful as it was, which ultimately would have most likely changed the course of the war.

Whilst the British and Allied soldiers were fighting for their lives on the beaches and streets of Dunkirk, preparations in readiness for the flotilla of ships to leave Dover as part of Operation Dynamo, were well under way.

Winston Churchill gave the go ahead for the operation to begin around 7 pm on 26 May. Unbeknown to him at the time, the Luftwaffe had on 25 and 26 May, decided to concentrate their efforts not on Dunkirk, as might have been expected, but on Calais, Lille and Amiens, where groups of Allied soldiers were still holding out. Men of the British Expeditionary Force surrendered at Calais on 26 May. The Belgian Army surrendered on 28 May and, running out of food and ammunition, 35,000 French troops finally surrendered at Lille on 31 May. On each occasion the threat to Dunkirk and those men waiting on the beach to be evacuated, worsened. By 31 May the operation was into its fifth day and 194,620 men, including General Vereker, had been picked up and returned safely to England via Dover. The operation was completed four days later on 4 June by which time a further 143,606 men had safely made it back to Dover.

Operation Dynamo has to go down as one of the most important operations of the entire war, because if it hadn't been the success that it was, Britain and her Allies would have undoubtedly lost the war after just ten months.

The flotilla of some 861 naval as well as 'Little Ships' had been assembled at Sheerness in Kent, before making their way to Dover and then across the English Channel to rescue British and Allied soldiers who had been forced back to the sea by the combined might of the German Army and Luftwaffe. A wide variety of vessels were utilized, some of which were not necessarily intended to be used in open seas. Although many were willingly offered up by their owners free of charge, others were commandeered by the Ministry of Shipping, whilst some were even requisitioned without the knowledge of their owners, such was the urgency for the operation to go ahead as expediently as possible. Although the initial plan was for all of the vessels to have crews made up of men from the Royal Navy, this turned out to be impractical because of the sheer number of boats being used, so some went across the Channel with their owners and civilian crews.

The operation took place over nine days between 27 May and 4 June 1940, and by the time it had been completed, 338,226 British and Allied soldiers had been rescued from the beaches and harbour of Dunkirk and brought safely back to England. It wasn't achieved without pain and sacrifice. Out of the 861 vessels that left Sheerness, 243 of them were sunk, with a further 44 damaged. The RAF lost 145 aircraft during the course of the operation.

Losses of equipment were quite staggering. These included almost 2,500 artillery pieces and 20,000 motor cycles, why so many of them were needed is unclear. There were 65,0000 other vehicles abandoned in and around Dunkirk. Also left behind were 377,000 tons of food and water, 68,000 tons of ammunition and 147,000 tons of fuel. The BEF had taken 445 tanks with them to France; not one of them made it back home. Those that were not destroyed during the fighting were simply left behind, lives rightly deemed to be more important than vehicles.

Between 10 May 1940 and the fall of France on 22 June, the BEF lost a total of 68,000 men who were either killed, wounded, captured or missing. This is not to forget the estimated 40,000 French troops who had been fighting a rearguard action to ensure others, mainly British, would escape, and who finally surrendered on 4 June 1940.

It was never going to be a risk-free operation, Winston Churchill and his military advisors knew that from the outset. If the operation hadn't gone ahead the war would have been lost at that point, which might have resulted in Britain and her Allies having to agree to an unconditional surrender with Germany. A lot of people made sacrifices for the greater good during Operation Dynamo, a sacrifice that would subsequently turn out to be more than worthwhile.

There was a second part to the evacuations at Dunkirk which was codenamed Operation Aerial, whereby a further 192,000 Allied troops, which included 144,000

British military and civilian personnel, were rescued from various French ports. St Nazaire at the mouth of the Loire estuary was one of them where on 17 June 1940 the SS *Lancastria* troopship was attacked by German dive bombers and sank with the loss of 4,000 lives – the greatest single loss of life in British maritime history; fewer than 2,500 survived. Churchill imposed a news blackout on the event, declaring that the newspapers had quite enough of disaster that day; it was never lifted so it was years before the full story became known.

Local Defence Volunteers – Home Guard

There was no coincidence in the timing of the British Government's decision to form a Local Defence Volunteers (LDV) force. The date of the request for volunteers from amongst the civilian population to come forward and do their bit on the Home Front, was 14 May 1940. This was the same day that General John Vereker VC, the man in charge of the BEF, gave the order for his men to begin a fighting withdrawal from their position on the Belgian side of the River Dyle and head back to the River Scheldt, which in no time at all ended up at Dunkirk and the eventual evacuations back to England. At the time of General Vereker's decision to withdraw his men, there was no way of knowing the eventual outcome of his actions but the government had no option but to plan for the worst possible scenario, which ultimately was either the annihilation or capture of hundreds of thousands of men, the entire BEF. If this had happened then the war would have been over with Germany the victors.

In relation to the Local Defence Volunteers, the government placed the following advertisement in national newspapers asking for men to volunteer.

King George VI in Kent, 10 August 1940.

A New Force for Home Service

The War Office announced last night that in order to supplement, from sources as yet untapped, the home defences of the country, it has been decided to create a new force to be known as 'Local Defence Volunteers'.

This force, which will be voluntary and unpaid, will be open to British subjects between 17 and 65 years of age. The period of service will be for the duration of the war. Volunteers accepted will be provided with uniforms and will be armed.

Men of reasonable physical fitness and a knowledge of firearms should give in their names at their local Police stations. The need is great in small towns and villages, and less densely populated areas. The duties of the force can be undertaken in a volunteer's spare time. Members of existing Civil Defence organisations should consult their officers before registering under this scheme.

The force will be under the command of the General Officer Commander-in-Chief, Home Forces.

On 23 August 1940 Winston Churchill changed the name of the volunteers to that of the more commonly known Home Guard. They were a bit of a rag tag group of men, most of them older, veterans of the First World War in some cases, but men who would still be expected to fight in the event of a German invasion. Most of the men who were of age and fit enough, had already enlisted or been called up for service in one of the branches of the military, with the majority of those who were left either being too young, or working in reserved occupations. Despite all this, within just six weeks of the formation of the Local Defence Volunteers, more than one million men had taken up the call and volunteered.

The government had only anticipated that their request would be answered by 150,000 men, so in some respects they were overwhelmed. They certainly were regarding uniforms and equipment, as they simply didn't have enough to go around. Most units in the early days really did have to make do with what they could muster.

Local Defence Volunteers – 1940.

Old shotguns, air rifles, bayonets stuck to a bit of pipe, were all used, anything that they could get their hands on. Eventually the uniforms and weaponry did arrive, albeit the rifles were mostly left overs from the First World War in the form of Lee Enfield .303 rifles. A number of American P14 and P17 rifles were also issued to the Home Guard.

By the end of 1940 there were 1,682,000 volunteers in the Home Guard, but 739,000 of them still didn't have a serviceable weapon.

Kent's Home Guard

Most people's impression of the Home Guard during the Second World War, is based on the TV programme, 'Dad's Army', that aired between 1968 and 1977, and was set in the fictional seaside town of Walmington-on-Sea. None of the programmes were actually filmed in Kent, with nearly all of the episodes coming from locations in Norfolk and Suffolk. Besides the humourous sketches, the programme showed that the men of the Home Guard were just ordinary men, most of whom had day jobs, such as bank managers, butchers, and undertakers.

An interesting point about 'Dad's Army' is that two of the programme's actors, John Laurie who played Private Fraser, the local undertaker, and William Arnold Ridley, who was known by his middle name, and who played Private Godfrey, had served in the Home Guard during the Second World War. Both men had been in the First World War. Arnold Ridley was wounded when he was bayonetted by a German soldier. He also served in the Second World War before being discharged on health grounds and then joined the Home Guard in Caterham where he lived.

Kent ended up with a staggering forty-two battalions of willing men, who wanted to do their bit, but in most cases they were simply too old or not fit enough to enlist in the regular Army. The sections were as follows, and are recorded alphabetically and not in their consecutive battalion number order.

The 1st Kent (Ashford) Battalion of the Home Guard covered the areas between Romney Marsh and Folkestone, with most of the men who served in it, having worked at the Southern Railway Engineering Works. Some of the officers who served with the battalion were:

Lieutenant Colonel L.E. Swann
Major C.A.W. Duffield
Major H. Durling MC
Major D.H. Morton
Major B.S. Bland
Captain W.P. Spens OBE
Captain G.H.D. Metcalfe
Captain W. Hazell DCM
Lieutenant H. Barkworth MC
Lieutenant J.H. Berry, MC
Lieutenant A.G. Le Clercq
Lieutenant H.C. Ratcliffe
Lieutenant J.W. Reynolds

Lieutenant R.J. Martin
Lieutenant P.J. Baxter
Lieutenant C.C. Cameron
Lieutenant A.J. Ray
Lieutenant C.H. Elderkin
Lieutenant F.B. Pinch
Lieutenant F.J. Temblett
Lieutenant R.W. Maughan
Lieutenant A.L. Underwood
Lieutenant S.O. Garnham
Lieutenant H. Wilson
Second Lieutenant G.P. Tappenden
Second Lieutenant F.G. Moon

Second Lieutenant C.H. Bates

Second Lieutenant G. Holland

Second Lieutenant T.H. Jeanes

Second Lieutenant E.J. Burgess

Second Lieutenant F.L. Cloke

Second Lieutenant C.A. Martin

Second Lieutenant J.W. Kennard

Major F.J. Newall (Medical Officer)

The 55th Kent (Beckenham) Battalion, although part of the Kent Home Guard, was also included as part of the London Zone. They came under the command of Lieutenant Colonel, A.F. Hopper OBE TD.

The 51st Kent (Bromley) Battalion was part of the London zone and came under the command of Lieutenant Colonel H.W. O'Brion MC TD. Their HQ was situated in a big house in Oaklands Road and had previously been on the first floor of a building at 48 Widmore Road, next door to Bromley police station.

Private Bernard William Wright was one of those who also served with the battalion between 13 July 1940 and 31 December 1944.

The 3rd Kent (Canterbury) Battalion was under the command of Major A.C. Cussans MC. They covered the Canterbury area, working closely with the Royal Kent Regiment.

The 2nd Kent (Charing) Battalion came under the command of Lieutenant Colonel C.G. Darley DSO and, as a unit, they had dug trenches and dug-outs at Charing Hill. Some of the other officers who served with the battalion, were:

Major Sir John A. Campbell

Major A. Thorp

Major H.C. Hessey

Major L. Chalk

Major W.A.V. Findlater

Captain R.V. Langdon

Captain H.M. Pleydell OBE

Captain J.H. Tinsley

Lieutenant F.V. Scott MM

Lieutenant R.F. Bryant OBE

Lieutenant A.J.P. Scaife DSO TD

Lieutenant Hon. P.J.S. Tufton

Lieutenant C.S. Quin DCM

Lieutenant G.M. Turner

Lieutenant G.S.L. Burroughes

Lieutenant R.H. Neate

Lieutenant C.F.R.N. Weston

Lieutenant J.R. Tafft

Lieutenant E.V. Beard

Lieutenant W.T. Fullagar

Lieutenant A. McL. Wilson

Lieutenant T.K. Barton

Lieutenant C McDowell

Lieutenant S.A. Bates

Lieutenant E.P. Smith

Lieutenant W.J. Sargeaunt

Lieutenant R.F. Goodwin

Lieutenant D.F.R. Howard

Lieutenant I.M. Marsh

Lieutenant H. Romney

Lieutenant R G Martin.

Lieutenant W.E. Vaughan

Second Lieutenant L.F.E. Vamrenen

Second Lieutenant C.T. Miller

Second Lieutenant F.K. Hensley

Captain R.M. Knolles DSO

(Adjutant & Quartermaster)

Major J.C. Hodgson (Medical Officer)

That's a lot of officers for just one battalion; one can only begin to imagine how many men they had.

Chatham had two battalions as part of the Kent Home Guard. One was the 12th Kent (Chatham) Battalion which patrolled the town of Chatham and came under the command of Lieutenant Colonel H. Evans, and the other was the 31ˢᵗ Kent (Dockyard Chatham) Battalion, which just looked after the dockyards and came under the command of Lieutenant Colonel H.B. Forbes.

One of the members of the 31ˢᵗ Battalion was Private 59545 Stanley Lewis Colvill who served between 19 October 1942 and 31 December 1944.

One of the officers of the 54ᵗʰ Kent (Chislehurst) Battalion, was Major Howard Withers Roberts MC. He won his award during the First World War whilst operating a trench mortar in no man's land during the Battle of the Somme for two days whilst under fire of the enemy. He even eclipsed that feat by rescuing wounded soldiers in no man's land, also whilst under fire.

Chislehurst, which was C Company of the 54ᵗʰ Battalion, had a poster printed to assist them with recruitment.

Recruitment drive poster for Chislehurst.

According to the poster, the Chislehurst battalion's HQ was situated at the right-half HQ on the old Conservative Club premises at the corner of Green Lane and Belmont Lane, West Chistlehurst.

The 8th Kent (Cinque Ports) Battalion, was made up of three companies which drew men from the towns of Dover, Folkestone and Deal and Walmer. The latter of these, D Company, was under the command of Major C. Barker, with their headquarters being at 87 Blenheim Road, Deal.

With the fall of France, the threat of a possible invasion of Britain suddenly became a very real possibility. With this in mind, large numbers of the civilian population were evacuated from the area along Kent's east coast and were replaced with British soldiers, who began constructing all manner of defensive structures just in case the threat of invasion changed to a reality. It subsequently came to light after the war that Hitler had intended an invasion of Great Britain due to commence on 17 September 1940 – Operation Sea Lion – but he cancelled it at the last minute. No doubt the Kent coastline would have included at least one of the German intended invasion points.

Within twenty-four hours of the announcement being made of the formation of the Local Defence Volunteers, Dover police station had received 600 men who had enrolled, many of whom were veterans of the First World War. The man in overall charge of the Kent LDV, was the Lord Lieutenant, John Pratt, the 4th Marquess of Camden. The man in charge of the Dover company of the 8th Kent (Cinque Ports) Battalion was Captain William Moore.

Dover, one of five platoons that made up the battalion, was kept extremely busy. Being so close to the French coast, it played an important role not only offensively, but defensively as well. Members of the Dover LDV along with regular soldiers, went about fortifying the town with barbed wire running uninterrupted along the coast. Gun batteries were built and sentry boxes put in place to assist with checkpoint duties. Trenches were dug and concrete and steel pillboxes were erected so as to be able to fight the enemy at close quarters and help defend the town for as long as possible. The reality of such an invasion would have required a fight to the death mentality for those tasked with defending the town.

Whilst researching this chapter I can across a photograph of No.9 Platoon, C Company 15th Kent (Cobham) Battalion, Home Guard. Unfortunately, I could not obtain permission to include it in this book, but it did provide a list of names of the platoon. The names of the men are in the order in which they appear in the photograph, running top to bottom, but unfortunately it is not dated.

Volunteer E.C. Stevens	Corporal W. Hall
Volunteer H. Taylor	Lance Corporal T. Medhurst
Volunteer A. Pealing	Lance Corporal R. Philbrick
Volunteer E.N. Bloggis	Lance Corporal A. Garwood
Volunteer F. Beard	Lance Corporal D. Palmer
Volunteer G. Marshal	Lance Corporal E Philbrick
Volunteer F.S. Preston	Sergeant G.B. Griffiths
Lance Corporal N.R. Patterson	Volunteer D.N. McWilliam

Volunteer R. Webb

Volunteer H. Maytum

Volunteer J. King

Sergeant H. Mills

Lieutenant W.S. Brooker

Major H.E. Laycock

Lieutenant J.A. Kersey

Sergeant N. Bull

Corporal D. Pointer

The 18th Kent (Dartford) Battalion came under the command of Captain E. Harrison.

The 32nd Kent (Edenbridge) Battalion didn't come into existence until November 1941 when the town was designated as a Nodal Defence Point. In 1940 it was decided that where a main road network ran through a town or a village, that location would be designated as a Nodal Point. Their object was to harass, impede and delay the advance of the enemy, and to deny roads on which Nodal Points were situated, to enemy armoured fighting and motorized vehicles. They could also be used as boundaries for the forward movement of reserve formations.

The manpower for these defences wasn't provided by regular soldiers or members of the Territorial Army, but by members of the Home Guard. This was a big responsibility because the men who were tasked with defending these locations were not expected to surrender and be taken prisoner, but to fight to the last man.

The 56th Kent (Erith) Battalion came under the command of Lieutenant Colonel Frederick William Briggs. He had been a soldier since 9 June 1921 when he was commissioned as second lieutenant in the 13th (Kent) Medium Brigade, Royal Garrison Artillery.

The 52nd Kent (Farnborough) Battalion came under the command of Lieutenant Colonel Lewis.

The 19th Kent (Farningham) Battalion was formed on 8 August 1940, with its headquarters at the local Lion Hotel, and its commanding officer Major O.H. Moseley. The battalion was originally made up of four companies. A Company were based at the Hartley Country Club at Longfield and came under the command of Brigadier General Andrus CMG. B Company were based at the Scout hut in Farningham, with Captain Buchanan Brown MC as commanding officer. C Company were based at the Drill Hall at Swanley with Mr J. Gordon in charge. D Company were based at Darenth Court, Darenth, and came under the command of Mr J. Langlands.

On 24 April 1942 E Company, which patrolled and looked after the Vickers Armstrong factory in Crayford, was added to the battalion, with its commanding officer Major G. Humphrey. The factory produced a range of machine guns, anti-aircraft predictors, naval gun-laying equipment, fuses and the casings for the bouncing bombs, invented by Barnes Wallace, and made famous by the bravery of the Dam Busters. Six months later, on 26 October 1942, another company was added, making six in total. This became F Company and was known as the Dartford Mobile Company. In charge was Major C.J. Ady.

The Farningham Home Guard had, at its peak, around 1,650 members who made up its ranks, twenty-six of whom were women, a phenomenal number of volunteers who gave up their time to defend their country, and they were certainly kept busy throughout the war. The German Luftwaffe dropped some 3,000 bombs on the district of Farningham, along with sixty-four V1 rockets and further twelve V2 rockets.

On 3 December 1944 all of the companies of the Farningham Battalion of the Kent Home Guard, had their official stand-down parade.

On 14 November 1944, His Majesty King George VI sent the following message to all Home Guard units across the country:

For more than four years you have borne a heavy burden. Most of you have been engaged for long hours in work necessary to the prosecution of the war or to maintaining the healthful life of the nation; and you have given a great portion of the time which should have been your own, to learning the skilled work of a soldier. By this patient, ungrudging effort, you have built and maintained a force able to play an essential part in the defence of our threatened soil and liberty.

I have long wished to see you relieved of this burden; but it would have been a betrayal of all we owe to our fathers and our sons if any step had been taken which might have imperilled our country's safety. Till very recently, a slackening of our defences might have encouraged the enemy to launch a desperate blow which could grievously have damaged us and weakened the power of our assault. Now at last, the splendid resolution and endurance of the Allied armies have thrust back that danger from our coasts. At last I can say that you have fulfilled your charge.

The Home Guard has reached the end of its long tour of duty under arms. But I know that your devotion to our land, your comradeship, your power to work your hardest at the end of the longest day, will discover new outlets for patriotic service in time of peace.

History will say that your share in the greatest of all our struggles for freedom was a vitally important one. You have given your service without thought of reward. You have earned in full measure your country's gratitude.

And with those royally spoken words of wisdom, the Home Guard was no more. A fine body of individuals who had answered their country's call to arms on the home front in its hour of need, an hour that had last for five long years.

One of the men of the 19th Kent (Farningham) Battalion, was Second Lieutenant Douglas W.M. Taylor. He served with them between 22 June 1940 and 31 December 1944.

19th Kent (Farningham) Battalion book cover.

The 9th Kent (Faversham) Battalion came under the command of Major H.S. Hatfield and in total was made up of ten companies. Some of those who served as officers with the battalion throughout the war, are as follows:

Lieutenant Colonel H.S. Hatfield, commanding officer.
Major R.C. Ching
Major R.K. Morrison
Major E.H. Wix
Major E.W.G. Robins
Major P.W. Silver
Captain D.W. Morgan-Kirby
Captain J.G. Jones (Adjutant)
Captain S.J. Selway, Quartermaster
Captain A.J. Stroud
Captain F.D. Harvey
Captain S.R. Rousell
Captain T.T. Jardine
Captain W.F.T. Adams
Captain The Lord Harris MC
Captain A.E. Darby
Captain R.A. Darney
Captain E.W. Gaskain
Captain E.T. King
Lieutenant W.D. Young
Lieutenant E.J.V.W. Davey
Lieutenant R.C. Alexander
Lieutenant G. Ivory
Lieutenant G.F. Pope DCM
Lieutenant C. Cook
Lieutenant P.A.V. Streatfield
Lieutenant G. Howlett
Lieutenant J.D. Ballantyne

Lieutenant A.C. Richardson
Lieutenant S.E. Dawes
Lieutenant T.P. Smith
Lieutenant F.A. Bennett
Lieutenant H.J.S. Neate DCM
Lieutenant A.L. Wildash
Lieutenant A.G. Philpott
Lieutenant W.J. Brown
Lieutenant H. West
Lieutenant C.S. Jones
Lieutenant F.A. Branchett
Lieutenant J.T. Witherden MM
Lieutenant J.R.R. Wells
Second Lieutenant B.E. Fridd
Second Lieutenant P. Ellis
Second Lieutenant P. Goodwin
Second Lieutenant A.E. Sedge
Second Lieutenant C.E. Barham
Second Lieutenant J.E. Evans
Second Lieutenant J.P. Reynolds
Second Lieutenant F.A. Chadwick
Second Lieutenant J. Ledger
Second Lieutenant W.H. Edwards BEM
Second Lieutenant G.W.R Link
Second Lieutenant J.R. Gilham
Second Lieutenant A.G. Hand
Second Lieutenant F. Woodward
Second Lieutenant C.B.W. Stevens

There is no suggestion that the above list is an exclusive one of all those officers who served with the battalion during the war. The names are laid out as they are, due to their position in a photograph of the battalion's officers.

The 23rd Kent (Goudhurst) Battalion, which consisted of sixty-one officers and men, came under the command of a naval man – Admiral Sir Reginald Tyrwhitt-Drake DSO.

The 16th Kent (Gravesend), along with the 17th Kent (Northfleet) and 18th Kent (Dartford) battalions, all being neighbouring towns that ran alongside the River Thames, were tasked with defending their collective stretch of the river against a surprise German naval or amphibious attack. Although highly unlikely that any German vessel would reach that point in the river without being detected, the

Goudhurst Home Guard.

eventuality still had to be catered for. With the route of the main London to Dover A2 road bypassing the three towns, the men of the same three Home Guard sections were also tasked with patrolling it and defending it in the event of a German invasion.

The 14th Kent (Hoo) Battalion were tasked with patrolling the Isle of Grain, which also had the luxury of a contingent of soldiers from the Royal Artillery who were based there, to man the district's anti-aircraft guns. They were part of the 34th Battery, Headquarters 12th Light Anti-Aircraft section, which was a Territorial Army unit.

The Hoo Home Guard contingent consisted of sixty-three men who had to protect and defend the entire Hoo peninsula, although they were far from being alone or isolated, with units from the Royal Artillery and the Royal West Kent Regiment stationed in the area. In fact, there was such a large concentration of military personnel that Kingshill Camp, where a hundred men of the 347th Searchlight Battery, Royal Artillery, were based, was classed as a 'designated defended locality'.

The 7th Kent (Lyminge) Battalion was under the command of Lieutenant Colonel S. Mildred DSO MC whose area of patrol included the flat lands of Romney Marsh as well as the forest at Lyminge.

The 11th Kent (Maidstone) Battalion, who were in part assisted by their colleagues of the Mid-Kent Battalion, came under the command of Captain W.A.N. Baker. Maidstone was an important town during the Second World War, because of its geographical location. Situated as it was half way between London and Dover, it was one of the main crossing points of the River Medway, which in case of a German invasion coming up from the direction of the Kent coast, was an key point to control.

As a result, Maidstone was classified as a Category A Fortress, although it didn't have any kind of medieval outer wall as an obvious perimeter, instead the outermost streets of the town had to be used for this very purpose. Concrete roadblocks were set up all round the town to slow down and thwart an invading German Army looking to cross the River Medway and continue their journey into London.

Although no German ground invasion ever took place on mainland Great Britain, that didn't stop the Germans from carrying out hundreds of air raids over Kent as a whole, but specifically over Maidstone which brought death, damage, and destruction, raining down on the town.

There was also a Captain F. Farmer who served with the Kent Home Guard, and although I could not determine which battalion he served with, there is every likelihood that it was with the Maidstone Battalion as his home address was 45 College Road, Maidstone. During the First World War he had served as a Private (3129) in the 6th Battalion, London Regiment.

One of those who served with the 24th Kent (Malling) Battalion was Captain Maurice Courtenay Vyvyan, who had been promoted to the rank on 1 February 1941. He had served during the First World War, initially from 8 May 1915 with the Natal Carbineers and the South African Machine Gun Corps in German South West Africa. He returned to England and enlisted as a private in the Duke of Wellington's Regiment on 13 March 1916. Five months later on 5 August 1916 he was commissioned as a second lieutenant with the Machine Gun Corps, before being further promoted to the rank of lieutenant on 5 February 1918. On 1 June 1918 he was wounded whilst serving on the Western Front, when he was shot in the right arm. His First World War experiences would no doubt have put him in good stead for his role with the Home Guard. He was 50 years of age when he began serving with them.

The 29th Kent (Mid-Kent) Battalion patrolled an area that stretched from Maidstone down as far as the Weald of Kent. It has to be remembered that the men of the Home Guard were not soldiers, some of them may once have been so, but they weren't any

Bofors Gun Maidstone Bridge.

more. They were working class men who earned their living in an office, a factory, a shop, a school, or a field, who had been called upon to serve and protect their country the best way that they could in its hour of need. The Home Guard had been formed due to the defeat of the British Expeditionary Force in France, which in turn had led to the strongly held belief that a German invasion of Great Britain would follow in the proceeding months. If that invasion had ever taken place the vast majority of men waiting to defend their nation and fight the German invaders would have been the brave and heroic men of the Home Guard.

It was therefore sad that in some quarters of society these men, the last line of defence, the men who would ultimately determine the success or failure of an invasion, were ridiculed and seen as nothing more than pipe-smoking, slipper-wearing old men who couldn't even bend over to tie up their own boot laces. Thankfully, such beliefs had no substance to them, and although they were never called upon to defend their nation in battle, they did a fine job, showed their doubters their true worth, and proved to be a very fine and effective body of men.

The 53rd Kent (Orpington) Battalion came under the command of Lieutenant Colonel A.J. Shepherd.

The 13th Kent (Rochester) Battalion was commanded by Captain H.S. Picking. One of the men who served in the battalion's C Company, was Cyril Norman Le Gassick, known to his friends as Sandy. He was born on 9 April 1925 in Gillingham and his father had served during the First World War. Sandy had lied about his age, and although only 15, when he had enlisted he had put 17. Being big and tall for his age, he 'got away with it'. It wasn't just his size that got him noticed, his abilities in basic soldiering hadn't gone unnoticed, especially by his company commander, who recognizing his leadership abilities, encouraged and convinced him to take the rank of company sergeant major, which was an amazing achievement, when taking in to account his true age.

The man in charge of C Company was Major Clive Anderson, who had previously held the lofty position of Mayor of Rochester and was a well-respected business man, just the calibre of man needed to hold such a position in the town's Home Guard. Major Anderson's second in command was Captain Charles Eldridge who was a plasterer by trade.

Two members of the 20th Kent (Sevenoaks) Battalion were killed by enemy action on Sunday 8 December. What made the tragedy even more poignant was the pair were father and son. Volunteer Herbert Gordon Ware Dabnor (46) and his 16-year-old son, fellow Home Guard volunteer, Gordon Dabnor, were buried in a joint grave in the Churchyard of St Botolph's Church at Chevening.

A search of the British Newspaper Archive produced an article which appeared in an edition of the *Sevenoaks Chronicle and Kentish Advertiser* dated Friday, 13 December, which provided some detail of the incident.

A village which has already experienced the effects of bombing, fortunately on past occasions without casualties, again suffered on Sunday night, when a father and son lost their lives. The father was killed instantly, the son dying some hours later in hospital. Other members of the family were injured.

The deceased man, Mr Dabnor, with his wife and 16-year-old son, resided in a cottage on a farm, together with a cousin of Mrs Dabnor's and her husband.

In the evening the little family party were about to leave the farm when a stick of high explosives came crashing down across the fields. One landed near the farm buildings, which were destroyed, and the male members of the party, who were in front of the women, sustained the full force of the blast. The two ladies escaped with shock and, in the case of Mrs Dabnor, a slight cut on one arm.

Mrs Dabnor attributed their escape to the fact that they were able to throw themselves to the ground just in time for the flying fragments of the bomb to miss them. They called to the others, she said, but got no reply, and then found them lying on the ground. She tried the telephone to seek help, but the wires had been severed, so she ran down to the farmhouse, from which help was summoned.

The article did not mention the name of village or its nearby town, but described it as being in the South-East of England, and went as far as saying that it was *'often acclaimed the prettiest in the county'*. It finished with the sentence: *'Even the Germans would be hard put to find anything in the village which could be described as a military objective.'*

The 30th Kent (Sheppey) Battalion came under the command of Lieutenant Colonel R. Hemmingway.

D Company, Sheppey Home Guard on disbanding at Sheerness in 1945. QMS Newman, PSM Dummott, PSM Body, CSM Fryer MM. PSM Harper, PSM Dwyer. Lieutenant Pole, Lieutenant Oldershaw, Second Lieutenant McMahon, Lieutenant Higgins, Captain Pearce, Major Barker, Lieutenant Crook, Lieutenant Dawes.

One particularly funny yet unfortunate incident took place late one evening when a car containing the Lord Mayor and his wife, being driven by their chauffeur, was challenged at a road checkpoint by a member of the Home Guard. 'Halt, who goes there?' the sentry called out. The chauffeur, convinced that the man must have known who his passengers were passed through the checkpoint without stopping. The sentry raised and aimed his rifle in the direction of the fleeing vehicle and opened fire. Luckily for the mayor, his wife and the hapless chauffeur, the single shot missed them all.

In 1942 the 334th Artillery Battery of the Royal Artillery was formed because the geographical location of the area made it vulnerable to air attack and therefore a potential enemy target.

The 33rd Kent (Short Brothers) Battalion was under the command of Lieutenant Colonel J.M. Prower DSO. The Short Brothers factory was situated in Rochester and was where Sunderland and Stirling bomber aircraft were built. Not surprisingly, Rochester not only became a legitimate military target as far as the Luftwaffe were concerned, but it was also on a direct flying route into London, which made life in the town even more dangerous.

The Imperial War Museum has in their archives a 16mm film that was taken in December 1940 of the 57th Kent (Sidcup) Battalion by Captain A. Scafe-Brown. It shows members of the Battalion undergoing training in Sidcup in preparation for the role that the men of the unit were expected to carry out.

The 10th Kent (Sittingbourne) Battalion was commanded by Lieutenant Colonel C.H.F. Metcalfe DSO TD. During the First World War he served as a major in the 5th Battalion Bedfordshire and Hertfordshire Regiment and was awarded the British War and Victory medals. He was also twice Mentioned in Despatches, the first of which was recorded in the *London Gazette* of 4 January 1917, page 199, whilst the latter appeared on 14 June 1918, page 7409. When he applied for his wartime service medals in February 1925, he was living at Court Lodge Farm, Harrietsham, Kent. For the men of the Sittingbourne Home Guard, it must have been quite inspiring to know that they had a man of Metcalfe's calibre and experience in charge.

The 4th Kent (St Augustine's) Battalion was formed by the men who lived in the villages on the outskirts of Canterbury. One of these villages was that of Blean. The photograph here is of the Blean Company, which was one of the areas that made up the St Augustine's Battalion. Eleven of the men in the photograph are displaying medal ribbons on their tunics, suggesting that they saw service in the First World War.

The men of this section patrolled the area between Whitsatble and Herne Bay, and came under the command of Major A.J. Gracie.

The 6th Kent (Thanet) Battalion was commanded by Major Charles Sydney Forster Witts, who served during the First World War with the 1st/4th Battalion, The Buffs (East Kent) Regiment, as both a lieutenant and a captain in the Asiatic theatre of war, where he first arrived on 15 August 1915. This includes such locations as South West Arabia, Aden, Muscat, and Mesopotamia, which is modern day Iraq. When he applied for his First World War service medals, he was living in Grove Road, Ramsgate.

Blean Home Guard.

The 21st Kent (Tonbridge) Battalion had an unnamed company quartermaster sergeant (14815329) as one of its members. He served with them in the early stages of the war, before transferring to the Royal Fusiliers on 14 September 1944 and on to the East Surrey Regiment on 13 December 1946. The battalion came under the command of Colonel H.H. Bateson CMG.

One of those who served with the 22nd Kent (Tunbridge Wells) Battalion was Lance Corporal George Wood. His commanding officer was the distinguished Brigadier General H.O. Knox CMG MC CIE OBE.

Tunbridge, along with the 21st Kent (Tonbridge) and the 24th (Malling) battalions, were tasked with defending what was known locally as the Ironside Line, a line of pillboxes and tank traps which ran across Kent and Sussex.

The men of the 5th Kent (Wingham) Battalion were under the command of Captain F.D.C. Newport and helped defend the Dover to Sandwich coastal area. These were hardy men, with the battalion made up mainly of miners and farm labourers who were used to long hours of hard, physical work.

The following four battalions were raised by major industries in the Kent area:

The 25th Kent (General Post Office) Battalion started out with four companies which eventually increased to six. The battalion suffered the sad loss of three of its officers, four days after the Home Guard had officially been stood down by the government. On 5 November 1944, 54-year-old Second Lieutenant John Neville Spellen, Lieutenant John Robert Garrod (42) and Lieutenant Lewin Alfred Palmer(51) were all killed in an accident at Bishopgate ranges, near Herne Bay. The men tragically lost their lives whilst destroying the battalion's remaining munitions. The slightly strange aspect of this incident was that there was a fourth victim, QAIMNS Sister Eileen M. Spellen, the 26-year-old daughter of Second Lieutenant Spellen. The obvious question to ask is what was she doing at Bishopsgate Ranges whilst the three men were engaged in destroying munitions.

John Spellen and his daughter Eileen were buried in Herne Bay cemetery, whilst John Garrod and Lewin Palmer were both buried in the churchyard at All Saints Church, Whitstable. Their funerals took place with full military honours on Saturday, 11 November 1944, the coffins draped with Union Jacks and flowers. John Garrod lived in Graystone Road, Tankerton, whilst Lewin Palmer lived in Albert Street, Whitstable.

In his address about the two men, the vicar said:

'I need hardly say that both for your sakes and my own, I would not add to the sorrow we all feel on this sad occasion, nor extend for one moment its strain. But it is fitting that something should be said as we lay to rest the mortal remains of Lewin Alfred Palmer and John Robert Garrod.

I must have known them both for a good many years, possibly seventeen… good fathers and good husbands both. Loyal friends, conscientious, trustworthy; men who loved their country and had served it well, the one in the last war, and the other later in the Regulars, and both in the current war as members of the Home Guard.

It is tragic to think that they, having run almost their full course, should have, on the eve of the 'stand down' suffered in this grievous accident. It reminds us that though the Home Guard was not called upon to engage our enemy, nevertheless its members were not always remote from danger, in the service they with others gave in our hour of need.

And now these lives have been cut off with a swiftness that, whatever our age or temperament, must make us pause, affronted as we are in its suddenness by the awe and mystery of life and death, of God's dealings with us, his children.'

The above words provide a flavour of the high esteem which both men were held in by those who knew them, as friends and relatives and colleagues.

The 26th Kent (Bus Company) Battalion was formed in June 1940, its purpose being to protect the numerous bus company depots across the county of Kent. The battalion's men were, not surprisingly, drawn from the staff of the different bus companies. Later during the war, the battalion, which came under the command of Lieutenant Colonel H.O. Hollas, was split into three companies, with each of them covering a separate geographical area of the county.

The 27th Kent (Electric Power Company) Battalion worked out of County House, situated at 178–184 High Street, Rochester. The manager of the Electric Power Company was Harold Knell, who also became the commanding officer of the Home Guard's 27th Kent Battalion.

The following two battalions were anti-aircraft batteries:

The 101st Kent 'Z' Battery was formed in Gillingham on 14 July 1942 and consisted of forty members of the Home Guard who were trained by Regular soldiers from the

Royal Artillery. The training to get the men up to speed in the use of the equipment they would be expected to use, took four months to complete.

Major P.T. Rogers was the Home Guard battery commander, who worked alongside Major M.W. Williams, who served with the Royal Artillery. The battery's first headquarters was in Beatty Avenue, Gillingham. In the two years that the battery was in existence it was active on more than 200 occasions, and opened fire on enemy aircraft fourteen times.

The 102nd Kent A Battery which was situated at Lodge Hill near Rochester, wasn't formed for nearly a year after the 101st Z Battery. It also saw action during its existence. The men of the Home Guard who served with A Battery, had on average, to undertake a duty once every eight nights, with each period of duty lasting for more than ten hours, from 8 pm to 6.15 am the following morning. Although the men could sleep during the time they were manning the battery, they also had to undergo training or receive relevant talks during their shift. The two batteries were amalgamated in June 1944 when they became the 5th Anti-Aircraft Regiment of the Home Guard.

Private Arthur James Tappin served with the Kent (1st Southern Railway) Battalion, Home Guard between 22 July 1940 and 31 December 1944. The battalion's men came from within the company, and their job was to provide protection across the railway network on which their trains travelled, especially at major rail junctions or railway sidings where the rolling stock was housed and maintained when not in use.

The Commonwealth War Graves Commission website records that a total of 1,065 men were killed or died whilst serving with the Home Guard during the Second World War of these, forty-nine were serving with Kent Battalions. I have randomly recorded the names of each of the Kent men below. They are in no particular order, either alphabetically or in the dates that they died.

Corporal Arthur **Chudley,** who served with the 55th Kent (Beckenham) Battalion, died on 6 June 1943 and is buried in the churchyard of St John the Baptist Church at West Wickham, Kent.

Volunteer Sidney Philip **Gregory**, who served with the 9th Kent (Faversham) Battalion, died on 20 July 1940. He is buried in the churchyard at St Peter's Parish Church, at Oare, Kent.

Sergeant Albert Edward **Rutherford**, who served with the 31st Kent (Dockyard) Battalion, lived in Rochester and died on 26 October 1943. He is buried in Aylesford Cemetery, Kent.

Volunteer George C. **Stevens**, who served with the 24th Kent (Malling) Battalion, died on 18 June 1940 and is also buried in the Aylesford Cemetery, Kent.

Volunteer George **Westbury,** who served with the 5th Kent (Wingham) Battalion, died on 3 July 1940 and is buried in the Aylesford Cemetery, Kent.

Volunteer James Alfred **Green**, who served with the 57th Kent (Sidcup) Battalion, died on 7 September 1940, and is buried in Bexleyheath Cemetery, Kent. He lived with his wife, Lily May Green, in Welling, who was killed in the same incident as her husband.

Private Sydney William George **Shove**, who also served with the 57th Kent (Sidcup) Battalion, died on 26 July 1943, and was buried in Bexleyheath Cemetery. Sydney was 65 at the time of his death and had previously served in the Second Boer War (1899 –1902) as well as the First World War, with the 8th/11th Hussars.

Corporal George Edward **Grinyer**, who served with the 12th Kent (Chatham) Battalion, died on 8 December 1944 and is buried in the Maidstone Road Cemetery in Chatham.

Lieutenant William John **Baker**, who served with the 17th Kent (Northfleet) Battalion, died on 5 August 1941 and is buried in the Stone Cemetery, in Dartford.

Volunteer Robert **Blakey**, who served with the 14th Kent (Hoo) Battalion, died on 3 December 1949 and is buried in Palmerston Road Cemetery, Chatham.

Volunteer Gordon **Dabnor**, who served with the 20th Kent (Sevenoaks) Battalion, died on 8 December 1940 and is buried in the Churchyard of St Botoplh's Parish Church, at Chevening.

Volunteer Herbert Gordon Ware **Dabnor**, who also served with the 20th Kent (Sevenoaks) Battalion, died in the same incident as his son Gordon on 8 December 1940. They are buried in the same grave. I have written about the circumstances surrounding the deaths of Herbert and Gordon Dabnor elsewhere in this chapter.

Lieutenant William Baird Charles **Brander**, who served with the 51st Kent (Bromley) Battalion, died on 7 September 1943 and is buried in Chislehurst Cemetery.

SergeantRobert George **Martin**, who served with the 14th Kent (Hoo) Battalion, died on 22 July 1942 and is buried in the Churchyard at St Helen church in Cliffe, Kent.

Volunteer Alfred E. **Pope**, who served with the 24th Kent (Malling) Battalion, died on 19 October 1940 and is buried in the New Churchyard at St Margaret's Church in Collier Street, Yalding.

Sergeant Thomas William Walter **Taylor**, who served with the 18th Kent (Dartford) Battalion, died on 11 July 1943 and is buried in the Churchyard of St Paulinus Church in Crayford.

Sergeant Henry James **Bardell**, who served with the 55th Kent (Beckenham) Battalion, died on 2 April 1943 and is buried in the Beckenham Crematorium and Cemetery.

Sergeant Charles Frank **Bridle**, who also served with the 55th Kent (Beckenham) Battalion, died on 23 September 1942 and is buried in the Beckenham Crematorium and Cemetery.

Volunteer Ernest Donald **Stagg**, who served with the 13th Kent (Rochester) Battalion, died on 17 October 1940 and is buried in Chingford Mount Cemetery.

Private William Albert Victor **Regan**, who served with the 6th Kent (Thanet) Battalion, died on 19 December 1940 and is buried in the Waltonwrays Cemetery at Sipton.

Volunteer Raymond Eric **Willey**, who served with the 51st Kent (Bromley) Battalion, died on 16 April 1941 and is buried in the Bromley Hill Cemetery.

Volunteer G. **Hibbert**, who served with the 20th Kent (Sevenoaks) Battalion, died on 15 January 1941 and is buried in St Micahel's Churchyard at East Wickham.

Lance Corporal Albert Eric **Kendall**, who served with the 57th Kent (Sidcup) Battalion, died on 14 May 1944 and is buried in the Churchyard at St Michael's Parish Church, East Wickham.

Private Christopher Samuel Alfred **Woods**, who served with the 16th Kent (Gravesend) Battalion, died on 4 March 1943 and is buried in Gravesend Cemetery.

Volunteer Charles Thomas **Ruse**, who served with No.3 Kent Zone, Home Guard, and who was 73 years of age, died on 1 July 1940 and is buried in the Woodlands Cemetery in Gillingham. During the First World War he had served as a captain in the Queen's Own (Royal West Kent Regiment).

Volunteer Walter James Victor **Axcell**, who served with the 16th Kent (Gravesend) Battalion, died on 31 January 1941 and is buried in the Gravesend Cemetery.

Private Charles Isaiah **Hooker**, who served with 16th Kent (Gravesend) Battalion, died on 4 March 1943, and is also buried in Gravesend Cemetery.

Volunteer William Horace **Taylor**, who served with the 23rd Kent (Goudhurst) Battalion, died on 30 October 1940 and is buried in the Churchyard at Christ Church at Kilndown, Goudhurst.

Volunteer William **Waters**, who also served with the 23rd Kent (Goudhurst) Battalion, died on 15 September 1940 and is also buried in Churchyard at Christ Church at Kilndown, Goudhurst.

Volunteer Harry Stephen **Amos**, who also served with the 23rd Kent (Goudhurst) Battalion, died on 2 June 1942 and is buried in the New Churchyard at St Peter & Paul Parish Church at Lynsted.

Private Reginald Alfred **Murthwaite**, who served with the 13th Kent (Rochester) Battalion, died on 4 July 1943 and is buried in St Pancras Cemetery in London.

Volunteer Walter **Mills**, who served with the 55th Kent (Beckenham) Battalion, died on 8 February 1942 and is buried in the Allerton Cemetery in Liverpool.

Volunteer Brian **Tunstall**, who served with the 53rd Kent (Orpington) Battalion, died on 25 October 1940 and is buried in the Beckenham Crematorium and Cemetery.

Private George Weightman **Ainsworth**, who served with the 31st Kent (Chatham Dockyard) Battalion, died on 3 November 1943 and is buried in the Eston Cemetery in Yorkshire.

Private Charles Arthur **Holman,** who served with the 8th Kent (Cinque Ports) Battalion, died on 29 May 1942 and is buried in St Mary's Churchyard at Capel-Le-Ferne.

SergeantAlfred Edward **Bush**, who also served with the 8th Kent (Cinque Ports) Battalion, died on 14 September 1944 and was cremated at the Charing Kent County Crematorium.

Lieutenant John Robert **Garrod**, who served in the 25th Kent (Post Office) Battalion, died on 5 November 1944 and is buried in the All Saints Parish Churchyard in Whitstable. He has been written about elsewhere in this chapter.

Volunteer Ronald George **Meager**, who served in the 4th Kent (St Augustine) Battalion, died on 9 September 1940 and is buried in the Churchyard at the All Saints Parish Church at Whitstable. Ronald's father was Wing Commander George Meager MBE.

Lieutenant Lewin Alfred **Palmer**, who served with 25th Kent (Post Office) Battalion, was killed on 5 November 1944 and is buried in the Churchyard at All Saints Parish Church. I have written about him and the circumstances surrounding his death, elsewhere in this chapter.

Private George Dunn **Bailey**, who served with the 4th Kent (St Augustine) Battalion, was killed on 9 June 1942 and is buried in Herne Bay Cemetery.

Second Lieutenant John Neville **Spellen**, who served with the 25th Kent (Post Office) Battalion, was killed on 5 November 1944 and is buried in the Herne Bay Cemetery. I have written about him in more detail elsewhere in this chapter.

Private Robert **Mays** who was only 18 years of age and who served with the 28th Kent (1st Southern Railway) Battalion, died on 21 May 1944 and is buried in Bromley Hill, Cemetery.

Lieutenant Colonel Charles **Kennedy-Crauford-Stuart** CVO CBE DSO, was 63 years of age when he died on 21 August 1942. At the time he was the commanding officer of the 8th Kent (Cinque Ports) Battalion. He is buried in Hawkinge Cemetery. He had also been awarded the Royal Order of George I, 4th Class and had previously served with the 127th Queen Mary's Own Baluch Light Infantry. He was a lieutenant colonel commanding the Hood Battalion, Royal Naval Division, at Gallipoli, the military secretary to the Viceroy of India between 1921 and 1923 and a member of the Royal Company of Archers. A more distinguished and eminently experienced individual to command a Home Guard battalion would have been hard to find.

Corporal Sidney Henry **Atkin**, who served with the Kent 52nd (Farnborough) Battalion, died on 7 December 1941 and is buried in the churchyard extension of the All Saints Church in Orpington, Kent.

Staff Sergeant Frederick George **Cullen** who served with the 14th Kent (Hoo) Battalion, died on 24 October 1943 and is buried in the Strood Cemetery, Rochester.

Volunteer Henry Charles **Smith** who served with the 6th Kent (Thanet) Battalion, died on 29 January 1941, and is buried in the Churchyard at St Peter's Parish Church in Thanet.

Volunteer R.D. **Maule**, who served with the 23rd Kent (Goudhurst) Battalion, died on 2 March 1942 and is buried in the churchyard at St Nicholas Church in Sandhurst, Kent.

Lieutenant Albert Joseph **Brittain**, who served with the 18th Kent (Dartford) Battalion, died on 5 July 1942 and is buried in the Watling Street

Private Thomas McClintock **Williamson**, who also served with the 18th Kent (Dartford) Battalion, died on 1 January 1945 and is buried in the Watling Street Cemetery, Dartford.

At least ten other men with connections to Kent, but who were serving with units elsewhere in the country, died or were killed whilst serving with the Home Guard during the Second World War.

The aptly named William Patrick **Kent** was a Volunteer with the 13th Essex (Post Office) Battalion of the Home Guard when he died on 17 September 1940. He was 40 years of age and lived in Welling, Kent with his wife, Daisy Rachel Kent, whilst his parents, Thomas and Charlotte Kent lived in Erith. William is buried in the Bexleyheath Cemetery.

Leonard Aubrey **Dupree** was a section commander with the 15th Staffordshire (Newcastle Boro) Battalion when he was killed on 11 October 1940. He was 44 years of age. His widow, Marguerite Dupree, lived at Sevenoaks in Kent, and he is buried in the Newcastle-under-Lyme Cemetery.

Robert **Mays** was 18 years of age and a private in the 28th Kent (1st Southern Railway) Battalion when he was killed on 21 May 1944. He lived with his parents, George and Kathleen Mays, in Hayes, Kent, and is buried in the Bromley Hill Cemetery.

Alfred James **Curtis** was a volunteer with the 36th County of London (Southern Railway) Battalion. He was 37 years of age when he was killed on 23 September 1940. His parents, Alfred and Eliza Curtis, lived in St Paul's Cray, Kent. He was cremated at the South London Crematorium in Mitcham.

Raymond Eric **Willey** was 34 years of age and a volunteer in the 51st Kent (Bromley) Battalion when he was killed on 16 April 1941. He left a widow, Lilian Gladys Willey, who lived in Bromley, Kent, and he was buried in Bromley Hill Cemetery.

Harry Charles Reynolds **Spillan** was a second lieutenant in the 179th (103rd County of London) Anti-Aircraft Z Battery, when he was killed on 1 June 1943. He was 50 years of age and was cremated at the South London Crematorium in Mitcham. Both his mother, Mrs N.F. Spillan and his wife, Maud Spillan, lived in Beckenham, Kent.

Frederick Arthur **Baker** was 45 years of age and a sergeant in the 17th Sussex (East Grinstead) Battalion, when he was killed on 5 October 1941. He lived his wife, Victoria Baker in Tonbridge, Kent. He is buried in the Mount Noddy Cemetery in East Grinstead.

Neville Blakeney **Wade** was 50 years of age and a corporal in the 17th County of London (Bermondsey) Battalion of the Home Guard, when he was killed on 21 June 1944. He was a married man who lived with his wife, Emily Alice Wade, in Welling, Kent. He is buried in the Plumstead Cemetery.

Charles Thomas **Ruse** was a volunteer in the 3rd Kent (Canterbury) Battalion of the Home Guard. Remarkably this man was 73 years of age when he died on 1 July 1940. He is buried in the Woodlands Cemetery in Gillingham, Kent. During the First World War he served as a captain in the Queen's Own Royal West Kent Regiment, first going out to France in May 1917. For some of his time at least he served with the regiment's 4th Battalion, where he was at one time their quartermaster. The 1911 Census shows Charles Ruse living at 144 Napier Road, Gillingham, Kent, with his wife Jeannie. His occupation was shown as being an Army Pensioner, which means he re-enlisted in the Army during the First World War. The 1901 Census records that he was a sergeant major in the Royal Engineers and that in 1907 he spent a week, between 11 and 18 July, as a patient at the Royal Hospital Chelsea.

Alfred John Patrick **Coghlan** was 60 years of age and a volunteer in the 6th Hampshire (Bournemouth) Battalion, when he died on 24 November 1940. He was a married man and the Commonwealth War Commission website shows that he was living with his wife Dorothea Annie Willars Coghlan, in Beckenham, Kent, although the National Probate Calendar Index for Wills and Administration, shows that at the time of his death, his address was 41 Leeson Road, Bournemouth. Maybe his widow Dorothea moved there after his death, which if this was the case, would remove him from having any connection with Kent. Alfred is buried in the Bournemouth East Cemetery. As a young man he served in the Second Boer war of 1899 – 1902, as well as the First World War, as both a corporal and a warrant officer 2nd Class (858) in the King Edward Horse, a cavalry regiment of the British Army. The regiment had four squadrons that were all sent out to fight on the Western Front. Alfred Coghlan first arrived in France on 22 April 1915, although it is not known with which squadron he served.

On 15 December 1944 King George VI bestowed the following awards on members of the Kent Home Guard in recognition of their wartime meritorious service.

CBE
Colonel R.H.V. Cavendish MVO

OBE
Lieutenant Colonel C.S.F. Witts TD. (6th Battalion)
Lieutenant Colonel H.S. Pickring (13th Battalion)
Lieutenant Colonel W.A.N. Baker MC (11th Battalion)

MBE
Major J.E. Vinson (8th Battalion)
Captain A.G White (12th Battalion)
Captain A.G. Walker (55th Battalion)
Captain J.B. Richardson (2nd Battalion)
Captain G. Pettit (3rd Battalion)
Major R.K. Morrison (9th Battalion)
Major B.L. Lelliott (14th Battalion)
Regimental Sergeant Major B. King (29th Battalion)
Captain S.M. Kew (28th Battalion)
Major H.E. Crouch (53rd Battalion)
Major C.W. Ashwell (5th Battalion)
Major H.A. Angier (20th Battalion)

BEM
Corporal E.S. Buck (1st Battalion)
Sergeant E.C. Heath (22nd Battalion)
Sergeant N.W. Dunk (31st Battalion)
Sergeant G.F. Fulcher (57th Battalion)
Sergeant A.J. Langridge (20th Battalion)
Private E. Lee (12th Battalion)
Sergeant L.W. March (18th Battalion)
Sergeant E.R. Marsh (8th Battalion)
Sergeant P.B. Martin (33rd Battalion)
Sergeant C. Ralph (14th Battalion)
Private C.F. Tomkinson (21st Battalion)

Company Quartermaster Sergeant C.H. Young (9th Battalion)
Company Quartermaster Sergeant G. Crump (3rd Battalion)
Company Quartermaster Sergeant A.E. Ashdown (11th Battalion)

The Battle of Britain

The Battle of Britain is one of those historic events that have gone on to define a nation. It showed a country with its back truly up against the wall, a country that had already been on the very precipice of defeat with the Dunkirk evacuations just months before, a country that was able to stare defeat squarely in the face and treat it with contempt.

To use the analogy of a boxing match, not only had Britain taken a savage beating in the first two rounds, it was extremely fortunate to still be on its feet. To survive one potential knock-out blow was an achievement in itself, but to survive two, so early in the fight and so close together, was truly remarkable, and showed a steely determination not to be beaten, self belief, resilience and the stamina required to go all the way to the end.

The British authorities were possibly not aware of the true significance of the Battle of Britain at the time. As far as Adolf Hitler was concerned, this was the beginning of Germany's planned invasion of Great Britain.

The German High Command knew the potential problems which they faced if they tried to invade Britain without a step by step structure to their planning. If Germany's invasion of Britain was to be purely a seaborne affair, then they were in trouble and they knew it. The Royal Navy ruled the waves, of that there was no doubt, and for Germany to send her ships laden with infantry and equipment, blindly across the English Channel, was only going to end in the loss of a great many men. If, however, Germany could control the skies by defeating the Royal Air Force before her ground troops and airborne soldiers invaded, then she had a more than fair chance of success. There was of course another option open to the German authorities if she was successful in knocking out the RAF, and that was to force Britain in to a negotiated peace settlement, a total surrender or an armistice, any one of which would effectively knock her out of the war.

The Battle of Britain lasted from 10 July to 31 October 1940, with what historians called the Blitz, a phrase coined by the press and which was simply an abbreviation of the German word blitzkreig, meaning lightning war, lasting from 7 September 1940 to 10 May 1941. Although industrial cities such as Birmingham, Coventry, Liverpool, Manchester, Sheffield, Belfast and Glasgow suffered, the primary target was London, which had to endure raids on fifty-six out of fifty-seven days and nights. Between November 1940 and May 1941, most of the raids took place at night, during which tens of thousands of British civilians were killed, but morale remained strong along with the determination not to be overcome by the enemy. Despite the damage caused by the continuous German bombing, war production was not overly affected.

Failure to defeat the Royal Air Force in the Battle of Britain along with the overall ineffectiveness of the Blitz on London and the bombing of industrial towns and cities, up and down the country, resulted in Hitler postponing Operation Sea Lion indefinitely.

This was the code name for the planned German invasion of the United Kingdom. Part of the plan was for elements of the 16th German Army under the command of General Karl Rudolf Gerd Von Rundstedt to carry out amphibious landings at both Ramsgate and Folkestone and parachute more troops slightly north of Dover, with the initial primary objective being a line running from Southampton on the south coast, running through Reigate in Surrey and on to Rochester on the east coast.

A large part of the Battle of Britain was fought in the skies over Kent, as aircraft from the RAF fought doggedly against the Luftwaffe for supremacy in the air.

Although by the end of the war Kent had some twenty airstrips, eleven of these were constructed after the Battle of Britain as part of the preparations for the invasion of Europe and were known as Advanced Landing Grounds. These were built at Great Chart, near Ashford, Brenzett, High Halden, Kingsworth, Lashenden, Lydd, Newchurch, New Romney, Woodchurch, Staplehurst, and Edgerton near Headcorn. Another was built at Swingfield, although it was never used.

Advanced Landing Grounds were only ever intended as a temporary measure and most were out of use within a matter of weeks after it had become apparent that the D-Day landings had been a total success. Heavy bombers such as Lancasters couldn't use the landing strips; they were only suitable for fighter aircraft such as Spitfires and Hurricanes as well as Mosquito light bombers.

The nine airfields in Kent during the Second World War which played their part in the Battle of Britain were Biggin Hill, Detling, Eastchurch, Gravesend, Hawkinge, Lympne, Manston, Rochester and West Malling.

Hermann Göring, the man in charge of Germany's Luftwaffe, had issued a directive on 19 August 1940 that his pilots were to carry out attacks on British aircraft factories. Then just four days later, on 23 August, he issued a further directive, which determined that his aircraft would concentrate their attacks on RAF airfields, in an attempt at reducing the effectiveness of Britain's Fighter Command. In the following two-week period following Göring's directive, there were twenty-four attacks on airfields across southern England.

Coastal Command's airfield at Eastchurch was bombed several times, whilst the sector station at Biggin Hill was hit four times, with Gravesend, Hawkinge, and Manston also being attacked.

Biggin Hill airfield came into being during the First World War when the Royal Flying Corps moved there on 13 February 1917, and it became part of the London Air Defence Area, its main purpose being defending London from Zeppelin and Gotha raids. The first operational fighting unit based there was No.141 Squadron of the Royal Flying Corps who flew Bristol Fighter aircraft, designed by Frank Barnwell and manufactured by the Bristol and Colonial Aeroplane Company.

Unlike many airfields used in the First World War, Biggin Hill wasn't one of those that was closed after the fighting had stopped. Initially it became home to a group of men employed in aircraft instrument design for future aircraft. During the years after the war and throughout the 1920s, it was used more as an aeronautical and ground defence system experimental location, than a flying field, although throughout the 1930s RAF squadrons were stationed there.

With the beginning of the Second World War, it once again became an operational airfield, but this time the aircraft were Spitfires and Hurricanes. There was nothing out of the ordinary about the airfield, much as would have been expected of an operational RAF base – a runway, mess room and living accommodation for both officers and men, hangers for the aircraft to be repaired and maintained by the overworked mechanics who had to ensure their air worthiness.

At the outbreak of the war the resident fighter squadrons were Nos.32 and 79, who were quickly joined by No.601, an auxiliary squadron which flew Blenheim 1Fs, all under the command of Wing Commander R. Grice. Members of No.601 Squadron comprised some very affluent young men, who were affectionately known as the 'millionaires mob' by their full time regular colleagues from Nos.32 and 79 squadrons.

On 21 November 1939 two Hurricane fighter aircraft stationed at Biggin Hill were sent to the forward operating airfield at Hawkinge, from there they took off, engaged and shot down a Dornier 17 aircraft this was one of the first actual 'dog fights' of the Second World War. At that time RAF squadrons didn't tend to remain in the same location for a long period of time. For example No.79 Squadron was moved from Biggin Hill in early May 1940, and sent to Merville in France to assist the beleaguered British Expeditionary Force. By 21 May 1940 they were back at Biggin Hill, before subsequently being replaced by No.610 (County of Chester) Squadron, a unit of the Auxiliary Air Force, which had been stationed initially at RAF Gravesend.

Bristol F28 Fighter aircraft.

No.610 Squadron Spitfire.

In addition to the fighter squadrons, there was the 90th Anti-Aircraft Regiment in place to help protect the base from German air attacks. There were also seventy-four soldiers from the Queen's Own (Royal West Kent Regiment). They were stationed at Biggin Hill just in case Germany decided to attack the base with paratroopers.

Spitfire Squadrons such as Nos.72, 74 and 92, along with Hurricane Squadrons Nos.79 and 242, were stationed at Biggin Hill, all of whom saw action during the Battle of Britain. It wasn't long before Biggin Hill became a target of the Luftwaffe, having been identified as an important part of the British air defence system. Not only did they carry out targeted attacks on the base, they did so on a dozen occasions, apparently determined to put it out of operational use once and for all. On 18 August 1940 a combination of Junkers Ju 88s and Dornier Do17 aircraft attacked Biggin Hill which resulted in large craters being blown in the runway. On 30 August 1940 the base suffered a further attack and a number of 1,000lb bombs were dropped causing severe structural damage to many of the airfield's buildings and aircraft, as well as killing thirty-nine personnel. At least one German pilot was also killed that day, Fritz Eckert, who is buried in Margate Cemetery which also contains the graves of sixteen other Luftwaffe airmen who were killed throughout the war.

In 1943 Biggin Hill had cause to celebrate, when along with its sector airfields, it claimed 1,000 enemy kills, which was no mean feat. It showed the flying skills and steely determination of the Allied pilots who flew for the RAF during the Second World War.

What was quite possibly the last time British forces had been involved in a fire fight against foreign troops on British soil took place in late evening of 27 September 1940 in what has become known as the **Battle of Graveney Marsh** and was fought between the four members of a downed German Junkers 88 aircraft and members of A Company, 1st Battalion, London Irish Rifles.

After having been involved in a bombing mission on London earlier that evening, one of the Junkers' engines had been damaged by anti-aircraft fire during the raid. As it turned tail and made for home, it was attacked by a combination of Spitfires and Hurricanes from Nos.66 and 92 squadrons, which managed to damage the aircraft's remaining engine, forcing the pilot, Unteroffizer Fritz Ruhlandt, to crash land his aircraft on Graveney Marsh in Kent.

Some London Irish Rifles soldiers were billeted at the Sportsman Inn at nearby Seasalter, having moved to Kent in May 1940 to undertake coastal duties, because of the possibility that the Germans might invade Great Britain. Just before the aircraft had crash landed, Temporary Captain Cantopher had arrived at the public house to inspect the men. It would appear that initially Sergeant Allworth sent some of his men to the scene of the crash but not taken their rifles. On discovering this, Captain Cantopher then told Sergeant Allworth to arm some of his men as they were to go with him to the German aircraft. One of the crew of the Junkers opened fire on the soldiers from the London Irish Rifles with the aircraft's two machine guns. The British soldiers returned heavy and sustained rifle fire, wounding one of the German airmen in the foot. Soon after the four men surrendered and were taken prisoner.

As Captain Cantopher, who was fluent in German, passed the prisoners, he heard one of them say that 'the aircraft would go up any time now'. Without hesitating, he immediately ran to the aircraft and after a feverish search, he found what appeared to be an explosive device placed under one of the wings. He quickly removed it before throwing it into a nearby dyke, saving the aircraft from destruction, which was later sent to Farnborough for a detailed examination to be carried out. The aircraft was only two weeks old and was discovered to have a new and accurate type of bombsight which proved to be invaluable information for the British.

The German airmen had initially been taken to the soldiers' billet at the Sportsman Inn, where they bought each of them a beer in exchange for insignia and bits of uniform, whilst waiting for the relevant authorities to arrive to take them in to captivity.

For his actions that day, Captain Cantopher, was awarded the George Medal which was announced in a supplement to the *London Gazette* on the 22 January 1941:

The King has been graciously pleased to approve the award of the George Medal, for conspicuous gallantry in carrying out hazardous work in a very brave manner, to Substantive Lieutenant (Temporary Captain) John Cantopher, The London Irish Rifles (The Royal Ulster Rifles).

During the Battle of Britain and what became known as the Blitz, there are numerous recorded incidents of death and destruction caused by the raids on towns and cities throughout the country. One such incident that caught my eye was in Gillingham, Kent on 27 August 1940. By the time the raid was over, many businesses and homes had been set on fire and destroyed, twenty people were dead and a further forty had been injured.

The Gillingham depot of the Maidstone and District Bus Company was hit by some of the bombs, destroying an estimated 50 of the depot's 120 buses. Due to the time of the raid at just after midnight, all the buses were off the road, having finished their day's work. Despite the carnage and disruption that the air raid caused, the Gillingham depot was able to provide a bus service just a few hours later.

CHAPTER 3

1941 – Defeats and Setbacks

With the war now in its third year, there was still no end in sight. According to the Commonwealth War Graves Commission website, 87,488 men serving with British and Commonwealth forces had been killed throughout the course of the year. Compare this with the losses of 1916, the third year of the First World War, where 237,168 – nearly three times as many – members of British and Empire forces were killed. The above mentioned website records that at least 1,110 people from Kent, or with direct Kent connections, were either killed or died of their wounds, injuries or disease, throughout 1941. This was split as follows:

Army: 248
Air Force: 206
Royal Navy: 396
Merchant Navy 51
Civilian: 207
Home Guard: 2
Total 1,110

The figures for the Air Force include all Commonwealth variations of the Royal Air Force, along with the Volunteer Reserve of those same nations. The figures for the Royal Navy, likewise include all Commonwealth variations, along with the Naval Reserve of those same nations._

The following is a list of incidents as well as battles or operations that took place throughout 1941. Most of these have no direct connection with towns and villages in Kent, but they help give the war a national as well as international perspective.

The year did not start off well for Britain on the home front. Germany's idea of celebrating New Year's Eve consisted of sending over a large number of their aircraft to bomb London. In the process, the Old Bailey, the Guildhall and at least eight churches designed by Sir Christopher Wren, the seventeenth and eighteenth century English architect, were either damaged or destroyed in the process.

Throughout January 1941, British and other Allied troops were involved in fighting with Italian forces throughout East Africa, culminating in the capture of Tobruk on 21 January, as part of Operation Compass. Soon British and German troops would be facing each other in North Africa for the first time.

With the Richborough refugee camp for German Jews in mind, two dates in the early part of the year become particularly relevant. The deportation of Austrian Jews to ghettos in Poland began on 20 February 1941 and on 4 March 1941, Adolf Hitler ordered the expansion of Auschwitz, which at the time was under the command of Rudolf Höss, who lived on the outskirts of the camp in a villa with his wife and five children.

The first weeks in March 1941 showed just how stretched Britain's military resources actually were.

On 4 March 1941 British forces from No.3 and No.4 Commandos, along with a section of Royal Engineers and men from the Royal Norwegian Navy, supported by a number of vessels from the Royal Navy, attacked fish oil facilities on the Lofoten Islands in Norway, as part of Operation Claymore. A number of German vessels were sunk, but the most significant result was the seizing of a spare set of rotor wheels for an Enigma cypher machine and its code books from the German armed trawler, *Krebs*. They were sent to Bletchley Park where ultimately the breaking of the German Enigma code led to Allied convoys being able to avoid U-boat concentrations.

During the operation the British also took more than 200 German prisoners along with some collaborators, destroyed eleven factories, 800,000 gallons of oil and five ships.

On 7 March 1941 – British troops landed at Piraeus, Greece. On 10 March 1941 British forces fought elements of the Italian Army in Eritrea. On 17 March 1941 there were high Allied losses of merchant shipping convoys in the mid Atlantic.

Between 14 and 27 April 1941, matters went from bad to worst in Greece, beginning with the 1st Panzer Division Leibstandarte SS Adolf Hitler (LSSAH), capturing Kleisoura Pass. They then began to cut off the retreat of the Greek Army in Albania. Two days later the Greek Army was completely cut off and surrounded. Fearing the worst, the Greek Prime Minister, Alexandros Koryzis, committed suicide in Athens by shooting himself in the head, and Britain began planning the evacuation all of its remaining staff from the country on 18 April 1941. The 223,000 Greek soldiers who had been cut off by German forces in Albania surrendered on 21 April 1941.

The British evacuation of Greece began on 22 April 1941 and the next day the Greek government was evacuated to Crete. By 24 April 1941, all British and Australian forces were evacuated from Greece and sent to Crete and Egypt. On 27 April 1941, Athens was occupied by German troops and Greece surrendered.

Throughout the early months of 1941 Britain had to deal with sustained and widespread bombing by the Luftwaffe. London was repeatedly bombed, and other locations such as Plymouth, Hull, Belfast, Liverpool and Glasgow were targeted.

However, in a four-day period at the end of May 1941, Britain had two pieces of good news. Firstly, on 27 May, the German Battleship *Bismarck* was sunk by the Royal Navy in the North Atlantic. Secondly, on 31 May, the Mayor of Baghdad surrendered his city to British forces, and in doing so ended the Anglo-Iraq war.

Thankfully for Britain, Hitler implemented Operation Barbarossa, the Axis invasion of the Soviet Union, on Sunday, 22 June 1941. This meant that Germany had opened yet another front which, with the benefit of hindsight, seems a strange decision, although one of Hitler's targets in the Soviet Union were the oil fields of the Caucasus. Hitler had committed his troops to fighting on the eastern and western side of Europe, as well as being heavily involved in North Africa; logistically it meant having to move men, food, equipment and ammunition to many different locations.

Although America had been sending aid to Britain, the Soviet Union and China through the Lend-Lease Act of 11 March 1941, she didn't actually enter the war until 7 December 1941, after the Japanese attack on Pearl Harbor in Hawaii, and declared war on Nazi Germany four days later. America's first intervention in the war was in North Africa as part of the Anglo–American Operation Torch on 8 November 1942, when US troops landed on the beaches at Algiers. The Battle of Kasserine Pass took place between 19 and 24 February 1943 during the campaign in Tunisia and was the first major engagement between American and Axis forces in Africa during the Second World War. It was a baptism of fire that so nearly went badly wrong for the determined, yet inexperienced American troops, who were poorly led by their officers.

July was a particularly interesting time for the UK. The British Government ruled out the possibility of a negotiated peace with Nazi Germany, which in itself is surprising that it was even a consideration. A similar situation had reared its head during the First World War, when a negotiated peace settlement with Germany was briefly considered in 1916. But Britain wanted Germany defeated once and for all and not hanging around in the shadows, waiting to come back and try again when she felt militarily strong enough to do so.

Just a few days later, on 8 July 1941, the government signed a mutual defence agreement with the Union of Soviet Socialist Republics (USSR), each nation promising not to sign any form of separate peace agreement with Germany. Britain needed all of her friends if she was to have any chance of victory in her fight to defeat the evil tyranny of Nazism.

On 31 July 1941 the process of the 'final solution' begins with the infamous words, 'submit to me as soon as possible a general plan of the administrative material and financial measures necessary for carrying out the desired final solution of the Jewish question'. The man who was given the task was SS General Reinhard Heydrich, the memo was sent by Hermann Göring.

Translated in to English, this is how the memo reads:

In addition to the task you received with the order of January 24 1939 to solve the Jewish question of emigration or evacuation in a manner feasible according to the current circumstances, I hereby command you to make all necessary organizational, functional, and material preparations for a complete solution of the Jewish Question in the German sphere of influence in Europe.

In case this affects the responsibilities of other central organisations, these shall participate as well.

I further instruct you to submit to me in the near future an overall concept of the organizational, factual and material measures to carry out the desired final solution of the Jewish question.

Der Reichsmarschall des Großdeutschen   Berlin,den   7.1941
            Reiches
Beauftragter für den Vierjahresplan
         Vorsitzender
des Ministerrats für die Reichsvertei-
           digung

        An den

           Chef der Sicherheitspolizei und des SD
           -Gruppenführer H e y d r i c h

               B e r l i n.

        Jn Ergänzung der Jhnen bereits mit Erlaß vom

24.I.39 übertragenen Aufgabe,die Judenfrage in Form der

Auswanderung oder Evakuierung einer den Zeitverhält-

nissen entsprechend möglichst günstigsten Lösung zuzu-

führen, beauftrage ich Sie hiermit,alle erforderlichen

Vorbereitungen in organisatorischer,sachlicher und

materieller Hinsicht zu treffen für eine Gesamtlösung

der Judenfrage im deutschen Einflußgebiet in Europa.

        Soferne hierbei die Zuständigkeiten anderer

Zentralinstanzen berührt werden, sind diese zu betei-

ligen.

        Jch beauftrage Sie weiter,mir in Bälde einen

Gesamtentwurf über die organisatorischen,sachlichen

und materiellen Vorausmaßnahmen zur Durchführung der

angestrebten Endlösung der Judenfrage vorzulegen.

Final Solution letter.

Victims of the Blitz

In the *Thanet Advertiser* dated 9 September 1941 there was a short article filled with both fact and humour, both of which had absolutely nothing to do with the war. The paper's statistical correspondent managed to work out the amount of rain the town of Ramsgate experienced for the month of August 1941. The total was 1,793,880 tons. The statistician was kind enough to share how he had managed to arrive at that figure. The rainfall for the month had officially been measured as 5in, and with the total area covered by Ramsgate being 3,624 acres, and with 1in of rain per acre having a calculated weight of 99 tons, that added up to 1,793,880 tons. He went on to explain that the rainfall for August 1941 had been phenomenal, (or hideous, depending on which way you interpret such matters) as it was approximately 500 times as much rain as had fallen in August 1940.

The total yearly rainfall for Ramsgate had been measured at 22in. The figure for August 1941, alone was almost a quarter of the average figure for the year. It was also a record (or the worst weather, depending on which way you look at it) for 29 years, going back to 1912 when the August figure was 5.76in of rain.

The unnamed correspondent finished his article with humour, informing the readers that a consoling thought on the matter was that Ramsgate had no visitors to grumble about the weather in 1941.

The *Advertiser & Echo* which incorporated the *Thanet Advertiser* and the *Broadstairs & St Peter's Echo*, covered Ramsgate, Margate, Broadstairs, St Peter's, Minster, Westgate, and Birchington, in essence the Thanet area in its entirety. The edition of the newspaper dated Tuesday 9 September carried the front page headline 'Dive Bombing Moonlight Raiders'. Under that were two sub-headings: 'Husband and Wife Among Seven Dead' and 'Cinema and College Hit, Mother and Son Killed'. Unfortunately neither article mentioned the name of the town where the incidents took place, using the title of 'south-east coast town'.

On Sunday 7 September there were two German air raids on an unnamed Kent coastal town. Although casualties were comparatively light, the damage caused was immense. By the time the raids were over, two public houses, along with several shops and a number of private houses, had been destroyed. Good fortune was shining on the town, because one of the public houses received a direct hit, just minutes after it had emptied at the end of the night's drinking. If the pilot of the German aircraft had dropped his bombs five minutes earlier, the death toll would have been very high as the inn had been packed with drinkers.

The landlord and his wife were both casualties. Mr William P. Evans was conveyed to the local hospital by ambulance to have his injuries, which were not deemed to be life threatening, treated. His wife was killed by the explosion. Her sister, Miss Sarah Richards, aged 67, was discovered amongst the rubble, with a few minor cuts and bruises, suffering from shock. In a nearby house badly damaged by the blast, a husband and wife were both killed. Mr and Mrs Bowles had only recently returned to the town, Mr Bowles, a miner, having managed to secure employment in one of the nearby collieries. The body of Mrs Bowles was discovered first, followed shortly afterwards by that of her husband.

Mr William Landi and his 17-year-old son Billy were both killed when one of the bombs wrecked their home. When they were discovered the father had his arms wrapped round the body of his son, as if he had been trying to protect him from the blast. A friend of Mr Landi's, who was a serving soldier home on leave, had spent the evening with them and luckily for him he had left about five minutes before the bomb struck the house. Mrs Landi had left home earlier in the evening to spend the night with neighbours in a public air raid shelter.

Martin Carr had an extremely lucky escape. He was sitting in an easy chair in an upstairs front room when he heard the sound of the German aircraft as the pilot prepared to make his attack. He rushed into an adjoining room and dived under the eiderdown on the bed. After the bombs had exploded Mr Carr returned to the room he had been sitting in to discover a mass of brickwork had come through the ceiling on to the chair he had been sitting in. If he hadn't moved, he undoubtedly would have been seriously injured if not killed.

There was the remarkable experience of Mr J.W. Woods who, together with a group of friends, had been watching the bombing by the RAF of the Channel ports. As the aircraft began to dive, Mr Woods suggested that Mr James Simpson aged 74, Mr Albert Setterfield, a trawler skipper, and Mr James Tomlin, aged 72, should take shelter on his front porch. Mr Woods was helping Mr Simpson up on to the porch when a German bomb struck the rear of his premises and exploded, the force of which killed Mr Simpson instantly, while Mr Woods was still holding on to him.

As the interior of the building came crashing down, Mr Woods was hurled to the ground and found himself among a mass of rubble in the bottom of the cellar. Once he had come to his senses he remembered that his wife and their 13-year-old daughter Pamela had taken themselves off to the family shelter which he had built at the back of the property. He clawed his way through the wreckage of his home to the garden. He immediately thought the worst when he discovered the partly demolished shelter but after clearing away a pile of bricks and timbers, he found both his wife and daughter alive. He pulled his daughter out first and then his wife who was lying just a few feet away. Quickly checking them both over he could see that other than a few scratches and abrasions, and being shocked, they appeared to be OK. He then ran to the front of the house to try and locate Mr Setterfield and Mr Tomlin, who had both being seriously injured. Mr Woods had escaped with nothing more than a few cuts and abrasions but his home had been wrecked. Mr and Mrs Woods then went to the nearby rest centre which they managed and saw to the well being of others, who like them, had been left homeless by the German attack.

Mr Woods, who kept a number of canaries at his home, returned there the following morning with his daughter. Miraculously, the canaries were alive, although a couple of them had escaped. Meanwhile his daughter Pamela made her way through the rubble to the basement to rescue her dog who was still alive, if a bit dusty.

Mr George Cossons, the brother of a War Reserve Police Sergeant, had earlier in the evening helped his wife, who was wheel chair bound, into the basement of their home. It was fortunate that he did, as during the raid their house was totally wrecked. He had been at Mr Woods' home with him and the other men watching the evening's events unfold in the skies above them, but had started to make his way home before the raid had began. Unfortunately, he never made it, as he was killed on the way by an exploding bomb.

In another unnamed south-east coastal town that had also been attacked, the cinema, a college and a number of 'working class' houses, were damaged. The victims included a woman, her son and a baby.

One of the town's residents, Mrs Maud Denton, and her 14-month-old son, went to the home of her neighbour, Mrs Katie Pilcher, and along with her two sons, they all took refuge in the front basement, just before the house took a direct hit and collapsed on top of them. Police officers, wardens and members of a rescue party descended on the scene and immediately heard a baby crying and the voice of a woman calling for help. The large amount of debris made it difficult at first to determine which room the woman and baby were trapped in. After some of the wreckage had been removed, the door to the basement was found, but once opened it was discovered that there was nobody inside. Still the noise of a baby crying and a woman's voice could be clearly heard, which made it apparent that what they could hear was coming from an adjoining basement, but not one that it was easy to get to. Despite the obvious dangers from falling bricks and timbers above them, the rescuers began tunnelling their way forward, their actions making matters even more precarious for themselves. One woman called out that she was trapped underneath a gas stove, but after about an hour's digging the voice of the second woman could no longer be heard.

It was nearly dawn before the rescuers made it to the door of the basement and crawled inside, but they still had to move very slowly and show caution with each movement to make sure that they did not dislodge anything around them and end up trapping themselves along with those they were trying to rescue. Mrs Pilcher and her 16-year-old son Edward, were both dead, along with Mrs Denton's 14-month-old baby, although Mrs Denton and 22-year-old Alan Pilcher were both alive and taken to hospital for treatment.

The town's cinema received a direct hit, which blew out all the windows and one of the doors at the front of the building. George Atkins was the official fire watcher on duty at the cinema, along with two youths, who were under his instruction. When the German bombs started exploding, they ran from the vestibule, towards the front of the premises and threw themselves to the ground as they heard the sound of one of the German aircraft begin its attack. All three of them escaped injury, although George Atkins had the soles of his boots blown off, so powerful was the blast.

Other buildings were also damaged and destroyed during the attacks, leaving each of the locations resembling a battle scene. No longer was the war something that was out of sight the other side of the English Channel. The residents of these Kent coastal towns might not have been able to see the whites of the eyes of the attacking German pilots, but the attacks were acts of war all the same. The sad thing about it was that the Germans had decided to target areas that were quite clearly civilian populated and had no military significance whatsoever.

Throughout October 1941 German forces continued their push into the Soviet Union. Their fight wasn't just in a military sense against the Soviet Army, but the civilian population as well. They brutally murdered Jewish civilians in their tens of thousands. The Odessa Massacre began on 22 October and continued for two days. Before it was over an estimated 30,000 people had been either shot or burnt alive.

On 17 November 1941 Justin Clark Grew, the then United States Ambassador to Japan, sent a secret message to the State Department in Washington, warning them of a surprise attack on Pearl Harbor in Hawaii that was being planned by Japan's military. This was passed to Admiral Harold R. Stark, Chief of Naval Operations, and Admiral Husband Kimmel, Commander-in-Chief of the US Pacific Fleet. Both men dismissed the report and the rest, as the saying goes, is history.

The attack on Pearl Harbor by the Japanese Imperial Navy took place on 7 December 1941. The same day Japan declared war on both the United States of America and the United Kingdom, as well as invading Thailand and Malaya. Aerial attacks were also initiated on Singapore, Hong Kong, Guam, Shanghai, Philippines and Wake Island, an American territory in the western Pacific. The same day, both Australia and Canada declared war on Japan.

Ambassador Grew was interned by the Japanese and not released until July 1942, when Japan and American carried out an exchange of prisoners, mainly diplomatic and civilian personnel.

The British battlecruiser HMS *Repulse* and the battleship HMS *Prince of Wales* were sunk in the South China Sea by Japanese aircraft on 10 December 1941. A total of 840 officers and men were killed in the attack, 513 from the *Repulse* and 327 from the *Prince of Wales*.

On 14 December 1941 HMS *Galatea* was torpedoed and sunk close to Alexandria in Egypt by the German submarine *U-557*, with the loss of 469 officers and men. There are two asides that relate to this story which are also worthy of mention. Firstly, the *U-557* was attacked and rammed and sunk by the Italian torpedo boat, *Orione* two days later. Her entire crew perished.

Earlier on 7 September 1940 the *Galatea* was on patrol throughout the night in the Straits of Dover, on the look out for German shipping, as a result of the issuing of the code word 'Cromwell'. This meant it was believed there was an imminent threat of a German amphibious landing somewhere in Kent. Whilst returning to port the following morning she struck a mine off Sheerness. The damage she sustained was not sufficient to warrant her being scrapped, but it took three months before she was seaworthy again.

On the world stage the last ten days of the year were brutal by anybody's standards. What was taking place in some of these far-flung parts of the world made any troubles that communities in Kent were having, pale almost into insignificance. Here is a flavour of just how tragic, brutal and inhumane some of these occurrences were.

On 19 December 1941 HMS *Neptune*, a Royal Navy cruiser, was sent to intercept an Allied convoy and escort her to Tripoli. As she approached the Libyan city she struck three mines, which had been freshly laid by an Italian vessel. The third mine, which she struck as she was reversing out of the mine field, blew off her propellers, and although still afloat, she had no propulsion. She subsequently struck a fourth mine as she floated with the tide, capsized and sank. Of a crew of 767 only about 30 survived the initial sinking, but after spending five days bobbing aimlessly around in the sea, they too perished before being discovered by other vessels. One man survived, Able Seaman Norman Walton, who spent 18 months in an Italian PoW camp before being repatriated.

On 20 December the Vilna Ghetto was established in the Lithuanian city of Vilnius, by the Nazis. It is estimated that 400 Jews were killed inside the ghetto by Lithuanian militias. German troops first arrived in Vilnius on 26 June 1941. They were quickly followed by the murderous *Einsatzgruppe B* death squad, and between the date of their arrival and 6 September 1941, approximately 21,000 Jews were executed.

On 25 December Hong Kong surrendered to Japan and on 28 December Japanese paratroopers landed on the island of Sumatra, in western Indonesia.

Looking at what life was like for the people of Kent during the same period, here is at least one story for each month of the year from different towns.

An inquest took place at Chatham on Friday 10 January in relation to the death of Lieutenant Commander Walter Edmund Fletcher, who died on 5 January 1941.

He was in command of the trawler HMS *Haslemere* that had gone to the rescue of pilot Amy Johnson whose aircraft had crashed in the Thames Estuary, after she had bailed out. By then, she was already an international celebrity for her flying achievements, in particular when she became the first woman pilot to fly solo from England to Australia. Having left Croydon, Surrey on 5 May 1930 in her second-hand de Havilland Gypsy Moth aircraft, she arrived in Darwin, Australia on 24 May, a journey of 11,000 miles which had taken her nineteen days.

In 1940 during the Second World War, Johnson, who by then was 36 years of age, joined the newly formed Air Transport Auxiliary, whose job it was to fly Royal Air Force aircraft to different airfields around the country. On 5 January 1941 she was flying an Airspeed Oxford twin engine monoplane, which was predominantly used in a training capacity, from Prestwick, Scotland en route to RAF Kidlington near Oxford. She encountered adverse weather conditions and was reportedly out of fuel when she took the decision to bail out.

Amy Johnson.

She was spotted by the crew of HMS *Haslemere* descending by parachute and landing in the Thames estuary near to their position. At that time, she was alive in the water, calling for help. Despite the rough seas and inclement weather, made worst by falling snow and extreme cold, Lieutenant Commander Fletcher dived into the water to try and save her. He failed in his attempt, made it back on to his ship but later died in hospital. The Commonwealth War Graves Commission website records the date of his death as 5 May 1941.

Amy Johnson's body was never recovered but her name is commemorated on the Runnymede Memorial in Surrey.

Amy Johnson's death, and the accident that led up to it, is still shrouded in mystery, and as of July 2017, the reason for the flight Johnson had undertaken was still a government secret. Her entry in Wikipedia includes the story that in 1999, Tom Mitchell from Crowborough, Sussex, who during the Second World War had been an RAF pilot, claimed to have shot down Johnson's aircraft because she twice failed to provide the correct identification code when challenged to do so over the radio. Believing it to therefore be a German aircraft, he opened fire on it. Mitchell further claimed that he was told by senior officers not to tell anybody about what he had done.

Commander Fletcher was posthumously awarded the Albert Medal for his gallant attempt to recue Amy Johnson. The medal was subsequently replaced by the George Cross in 1971. A post-mortem showed that his death was due to exposure and shock following immersion in the icy cold waters of the Thames Estuary. As evidence of identification had not been provided to the court due to Fletcher's mother having been delayed and the crew of the trawler *Haslemere* being at sea, the inquest was adjourned until both parties were available.

On 30 January 1941 Leading Seaman Harry Lucas and Stoker Thomas L. Phillips, of the Royal Navy, were the crew of a motor boat, which capsized in rough seas some 700 yards out to sea at Sheerness. Phillips was not a strong swimmer and Lucas knew this and so gave him his inflatable life belt and fastened it to him. He also gave him an empty oil drum to hold on to for more buoyancy. Lucas remained with his colleague for about ten minutes, whilst offering him support and encouragement. Realising the precarious situation the two men were in, Lucas ensured, as best he could, that his colleague was as safe as he could be, then swam ahead as he made his way back to the beach, offering his continued support as he went.

When Lucas reached the safety of the shore he immediately went for help. He ran across two open fields covered it thick snow, despite cutting his feet on barbed wire while scrambling through hedges, he continued his run to find help. On reaching the military authorities at the Isle of Grain Tower, he collapsed with exhaustion, but because of his efforts Phillips was located on the beach where he had finally come ashore after bobbing around in the sea for nearly one and a half hours, unconscious, but alive.

For his efforts that night and on the recommendation of the Admiralty, Lucas was awarded the Stanhope Gold Medal by the Court of the Royal Humane Society for the bravest deed of 1941.

Two soldiers appeared at Canterbury Police Court on Monday 3 February accused of breaking and entering at the premises of Messrs. Field and Jordan at 51 Peter's Street, Canterbury, and stealing £1 and 30s worth of items. Laurence F. Boxall, from Canterbury and Ernest F.C. Leak, of London, were the two men in question.

Police Constable Russell told the court that he examined the premises at 10.30 pm on 14 January and noticed that the lavatory window at the rear of the premises had been forced open and two iron bars fitted into the window frame had been ripped out and were lying on the ground outside.

Mr Ernest L. Jordon, who was the owner of the premises, lived at 54 Mandeville Road, Canterbury. He said that when he had left the premises at 6 pm on 14 January, all the doors and windows at the shop, had been shut and secured. At 11 pm later the same evening he had been called to the shop by the police and discovered that the rear window had been broken and forced open. On checking the premises he discovered that £1 had been removed from the till, a desk in an upstairs office had been forced open, but nothing had been taken. Several pieces of plate goods, a glass salt cellar and a blue glass sugar bowl had been removed from one of the display cases.

Detective Constable Croome gave evidence that whilst in company with Detective Sergeant Webb, he saw Boxall and told him that he had reason to believe that he knew something about the incident at 51 Peter's Street, Canterbury. Boxall replied that he didn't know what Detective Constable Croome was talking about. Despite his protestations, he was conveyed to Canterbury and later interviewed concerning a jam dish, and a spoon and sugar bowl that had been discovered at his place of abode, which were identical to those stolen from Mr Jordon's shop. After initially denying having committed or being involved in the offence, he admitted what he had done.

The next day Detective Croome attended a house in Edgar Road, Canterbury, where he saw Ernest Leak. He searched the premises and discovered a salt cellar and a butter dish. Leak was also arrested and taken to Canterbury police station to be interviewed about the same crime. He too admitted his involvement and both men were committed for trial at the Tenterden Quarter Sessions, which took place on 7 February 1941.

It was a long day for Laurence Boxall at Canterbury police court on 3 February, as he was further charged with a similar offence of breaking into Messrs. Fagg, 87-88 Northgate Street, Canterbury, on 17 January whilst in company with an unnamed 16-year-old soldier. On this occasion he stole cash from the till, a quantity of cigarettes and a typewriter.

Throughout March 1941 in Canterbury, two offences in particular were repeatedly dealt with at the town's police court. The first offence of failing to black out windows during the hours of darkness was understandable because of the potential danger it caused, not just for the person who was letting the light escape from their windows, but for other residents in the area.

The other offence seems slightly harsh when compared with today's standards – riding a bicycle during the hours of darkness without displaying a front or rear light. Today, a large number of cyclists don't have lights anywhere on their bikes, let alone having them switched on. With the country at war, massive demands were being placed upon everybody, and time was of the essence. For those on the home front it was work as usual, or as usual and normal as that could be in the circumstances. For most, especially the men, on top of their work and family time, there would also be a commitment of a voluntary nature to allow for, as an ARP Warden, a Member of the Home Guard, a Special Constable or an Auxiliary Fireman. With so many people giving so much, prosecuting somebody because they didn't have a light on their bicycle does appear somewhat extreme.

Reported in the local newspapers on Saturday 1 March was the story of Sapper Robert William Hymers, who had appeared at Canterbury police court on 28

February, charged with stealing 10s 9d from a meter, belonging to the owner of the house, Elizabeth Stock of 347 Sturry Road, Canterbury.

Mrs Stock told the court that Hymers had been a lodger at her house for more than twelve months and that on the afternoon of 29 January 1941, Hymers, his wife, Sergeant Humphries, her daughter and herself, were all in the house. Hymers and Humphries were in the kitchen at the back of the house when Mrs Stock walked in and saw Hymers tampering with the lock on the gas meter. She asked him what he was doing, but he did not answer. She went back to the living room at the front of the property, followed shortly afterwards by the two men. She again asked him what he had been doing. He replied, 'What are you talking about, I haven't been to your f***ing meter.' Without any warning Hymers then grabbed her by the throat and threatened to 'bash her face in'.

Mrs Stock explained to the court that on previous occasions both her gas and electricity meters had been short of money.

Sergeant Humphries, an army colleague of Hymers, gave evidence that he went into the kitchen, followed by Hymers. He saw the gas coin container and saw Hymers locking up the meter. He decided to say nothing as it was 'not his business', but he did tell Mrs Stock's daughter that he had known Hymers to commit similar offences. Humphries' reaction was strange, as not only did he know what Hymers was doing was wrong, and a criminal offence, but he was a sergeant in the army, at a higher rank than Hymers, making it incumbent on him to deal with somebody of a lower rank, in an appropriate manner, having witnessed a blatant act of criminality.

Police Inspector Port was not impressed with Humphries' lack of action against Hymers, explaining to him in clear and precise language that even though he was in court as a prosecution witness, he was lucky that he did not also find himself in the dock, charged with an offence.

Ethel Dorothy Best, a meter inspector, told the court that she had examined Mrs Stock's meter on 11 February and found that it contained 3s 4d instead of 3s 1d. The lock was intact, but the seal was missing.

Detective Constable Soutan gave evidence that on 19 February he saw Hymers when he was detained at Chatham police station. Found in his possession at the time of his arrest was a bunch five keys, all capable of opening gas and electricity meters. When charged with the offence of stealing monies from the meter he replied, 'I am guilty.' He also admitted committing two other similar thefts from meters.

Before a decision was made on how best to deal with Hymers, the court was informed that he had one previous conviction for an offence of cruelty to children dating back to May 1939. Prior to enlisting in the Army the previous year, he had worked for Kent Concrete Products at the Chislet Colliery and the concrete works at Chartham. His military record was poor, especially for a man who had less than a year's service; he already been arrested several times for being a deserter.

Mr F. Sendall, the local Probation Officer, commented that Mr G. Blaiklock, the Chairman of the Petty Sessional Bench had remarked that Hymers and his wife were both lazy individuals and dirty in their habits. Their home had been in a filthy condition. It was also noted that he had returned late from periods of leave on at least two occasions, and that he had been allowed what some might class as somewhat over-generous leave on account of what could only be described as trivial sickness.

Hymers was sentenced to two month's imprisonment with hard labour. The Mayor also addressed some of his comments directly at Sergeant Humphries, saying that he and the other magistrates regarded his evidence as being of a very unsatisfactory standard, and as a sergeant he would have known perfectly well that Hymers was misbehaving. Humphries was also told by the Mayor that he had come very close to being treated as an accessory to the fact in the matter, and that in future he needed to be much more circumspect in his conduct.

On Friday 4 April the commissioner for the South-Eastern region of England, determined that the Civil Defence Duties Compulsory Enrolment Order, 1941, should be allied to certain towns in Kent, which included Ashford, Broadstairs, Chatham, Dartford, Deal, Dover, Gillingham, Gravesend, Herne Bay, Hythe, Maidstone, Margate, Northfleet, Queenborough, Ramsgate, Rochester, Sandwich, Sheerness, St Peters, Swanscombe, Tenterden, Tonbridge, and Tunbridge Wells. This was implemented due to the special conditions which existed throughout Kent because of its geographical location, and it being the nearest point of the British mainland to German occupied France.

The order empowered the local authorities in each of the towns to direct men between the ages of 18 and 60 to register for the performance of pre-prevention duties for a total period of 48 hours throughout each month of the year. The new powers allowed the local authorities to supplement those men and women who had already volunteered to carry out this important role. In evoking these powers, the regional commissioner was keen to highlight the importance of the role, and that the continued efforts of those who had already volunteered was very much appreciated.

Many Kent towns had been on the receiving end of German air raids, each attack bringing with it death, damage and destruction or a combination of all three. There was a real need for people to be in place to deal with the aftermath of such attacks. So far in many of the Kent towns there had been insufficient numbers of volunteers to ensure an effective response when air raids took place.

On Thursday 19 June news was reported in British newspapers in relation to offensive actions by the RAF against the Germans on the French side of the English Channel that had taken place on 18 June.

Bombers escorted by fighter formations made an offensive sweep across the Straits of Dover. Once over French soil explosions could be clearly heard for some time in Kent. The exact target of such large quantities of munitions was not known, but it appeared to have been aimed at coastal areas rather than further inland. One particular explosion was so loud that not only could it be heard in Kent, but it actually shook some of the buildings as well.

The following official announcements were released by the Air Ministry News Service about the same day:

A German supply ship of 1500 tons was bombed and hit by a Coastal Command aircraft off of Brest yesterday. Making two attacks, the pilot flew over the ship and dropped a stick of bombs. He saw two of the bombs hit the ship amidships below the waterline and immediately afterwards a great rush of steam belched from the funnel as though the bombs had exploded in the engine room.

The Air Ministry also made this announcement later the same day about other RAF offensive operations:

The RAF again carried out large scale offensive operations over the Channel and Northern France during the daylight on Tuesday. Many squadrons of our fighters provided escorts for aircraft of Coastal Command attacking enemy shipping in the Channel and for Bomber Command aircraft attack.

An industrial plant at Béthune, the plant which supplies fuel and power for the occupying forces, received direct hits, and was left burning.

No aircraft of Coastal or Bomber Command are missing from these operations, although our fighters encountered many enemy fighters and numerous combats took place. Thirteen of the enemy were destroyed and ten of our fighters are missing.

Further attacks by the RAF which took place on 17 June were also reported by the Air Ministry:

Bomber Command were once again out in force during Tuesday night over industrial areas in Western Germany. Their principal objectives were at Cologne and Dusseldorf, and as on the previous night many fires were started and much destruction was caused.

Subsidiary attacks were also made during the night on the docks at Rotterdam, Ostend, Boulogne and Cherbourg, and on enemy shipping by aircraft of Bomber and Coastal Commands, and aircraft of the Fleet Air Arm, operating with Coastal Command. One aircraft from Bomber Command is missing from these night operations.

The attack on the industrial plant near Béthune was described by one of the bombers' crew:

As I watched the smoke curling up, I imagined that there would be no more to see, but evidently the flames had touched off chemicals in the works, for there were sudden bright explosions. They must have caused much destruction in the curious onion-shaped cooling towers, for the clouds of smoke immediately increased and thickened.

As the aircraft made for home, their path was lined with the black puffs of exploding anti-aircraft shells. Overhead the fighters were busy beating off yellow nosed Messerschmitts, in a continual series of encounters. When one

Messerschmitt got among the bombers, four of the latter opened fire at close range. The enemy was hit, and broke off the fight with black smoke pouring from the root of his port wing.

The newspapers had to be extremely careful of what and how they reported matters, so as to not get in to trouble with the authorities. Despite their desire to print the news of what was going on they had to be mindful not only of public morale but to make sure that they did not breach the provisions of the Emergency Powers (Defence) Act 1939.

All of the aircraft, regardless of whether they were part of either Bomber or Coastal Command, took off from and returned to their bases in Kent.

On Friday 18 July it was reported in the *Dover Express* that Lady Violet Astor had begun a Kent Prisoners of War Fund in conjunction with the British Red Cross Prisoners of War organization. The aim of the fund was to obtain support from every town and village throughout Kent, by getting them to join in the scheme, so that the county could play its part in the collection of much needed funds to pay for food parcels for the men of Kent who were prisoners of war, and no matter where they were being held.

The cost of one such food parcel was approximately 10s and in order to ensure uniformity and standardization of the parcels, the contents were purchased and packaged by the staff who work at the Headquarters, Prisoners of War Department, St James's Palace, London, SW1.

One parcel of food per week was despatched to each British prisoner of war. The International Red Cross in Geneva, Switzerland was responsible for the delivery of the parcels to the prison camps. The parcels were very much appreciated and the men were grateful that they were being remembered by their friends and relatives back home in the UK.

So keen was the Mayor of Dover, Mr J.R. Cairns, to support the appeal that he wrote a letter to the editor of the *Dover Express*, appealing for readers to support Lady Astor's appeal. Any such donations were to be sent to him at Dover Town Hall, or to the Borough's Treasurer at Brook House, Dover.

There had been a similar country-wide scheme during the First World War. The concern then was how much of the parcel actually got through to the prisoners and wasn't stolen by the prison guards. There was a distinct lack of available food in Germany especially during the latter stages of the war, so food stuffs arriving at prisoner of war camps, where the guards were often just as hungry as the local population, had an added attraction. How many food parcels, intended for prisoners of war, were stolen and how many were delivered as intended, is not recorded. During the war Red Cross food parcels are accepted by historians as having greatly helped in prisoner survival, as the food that was provided by the Germans was often meagre in its content. The sight of a delivery of Red Cross food parcels would have been a massive morale booster.

In early August 1941 a presentation took place in the Old Hall of Lincoln's Inn, London. The purpose of the presentation was to honour the 'little ships' that had taken part in the rescue from the beaches of Dunkirk. The award, in the form of a gold

Kent Red Cross Parcel.

medal, was issued by the Cruising Club of America. The Blue Water Medal, as it was officially known, was awarded annually for the most meritorious act of seamanship by an amateur yachtsman. The medal for 1940 was conferred upon the Royal Cruising Club of Great Britain to commemorate all the British yachtsmen who took part in the Dunkirk evacuations.

The medal was presented by Captain Charles Lockwood, who was the United States Naval Attaché in London. Also in attendance was Sir T. Vaughan-Phillips, who was representing the Board of Admiralty, and Vice Admiral Muselier, representing the Free French Navy.

Before reading the citation for the award, Captain Lockwood commented that this award was 'not a tale of one voyage, but of many men and a nondescript fleet acting in a great emergency to perform a patriotic service'. This was about the civilian crews of some 600 vessels of all shapes and sizes, who were collected at Sheerness, Ramsgate and Dover, before making their way across the English Channel to rescue as many British, French and Belgian soldiers, as they could. The citation read:

> They arrived without charts, without fuel and without food. All had to be supplied and given instructions. In the end they proceeded to the beaches of Dunkirk, where their crews acted mostly on their own initiative. There were open boats, and motor cruisers, auxiliaries and ships' lifeboats, barges with brailed sails, river launches, pinnaces and picket boats, drifters and dinghies, beach boats, tenders and tugs, yachts and fishing boats.
>
> They acted under almost incessant attack by bombs, machine guns and shell fire, in areas that were mined, in shallow waters, narrow channels, and strong tidal currents. Naval forces, fishermen, yachtsmen, shipyard workers, men of all callings left their shops or their desks, some without change of clothing, and joined in this gallant effort to evacuate the apparently doomed Army.
>
> To the British yachtsmen who took part in this rescue, both those who survived the hazardous undertaking and those who gave their lives in the attempt, the Cruising Club of America awards its Blue Water award for 1940.

An article appeared in the *Thanet Advertiser* dated Friday, 22 August 1941, concerning the death of five firemen who had been killed during an air raid. The report had obviously been censored to a degree as the exact location was not given and only referred to as 'a south coast town'.

On 16 August a chief fire officer, along with three other firemen were killed by a bomb which landed in the grounds of the men's sleeping quarters, where they were standing. A fifth fireman died of his wounds two days later.

The five men were, Mr A. Bates, Chief Fire Officer, Percy C.R. Spice (39), William D. Hammond (54), Robert W. Pemble (35) and Frank White (35).

A second bomb was dropped by the apparent 'lone ranger' which landed in the road. The blast of the exploding shell was such that it caused severe damage to the adjacent homes and businesses.

On 16 August 1941, Mr Bates was walking up the road with one of his junior officers, Second Officer Leonard Lowings, when he happened to remark to him that he wasn't as young as he once was, and that he, Mr Lowings, should go on ahead. Taking Mr Bates at his word, Mr Lowings quickly made his way up the hill at a somewhat faster pace. As he reached the top of the road, he stopped to look back down the hill just as the bombs exploded, killed Mr Bates and his colleagues. Mr Lowings survived, escaping with just minor cuts and bruises. Mr Bates had escaped from a previous wartime bombing incident, but only by chance and good fortune. The room in which he would have normally been resting was destroyed in an air raid. Luckily for Mr Bates he was away at the time visiting his son, who was a police officer in a neighbouring town.

AFS L. Spice, the son of Percy Spice, who was one of those killed, survived with minor injuries. But the experience of seeing his father killed must have scarred him for the rest of his life.

AFS Frank White, who survived the blast but was badly injured, died two days later, whilst still in hospital.

Chief Fire Officer Bates joined the London Fire Brigade shortly after leaving school. After completing sixteen years service as a fireman, he was posted to Richborough Fire Brigade, where he continued to serve throughout the First World War. In 1920 he joined the Ramsgate Fire Brigade and was appointed as their chief officer the following year. Mr Bates was a Freemason, affiliated to his local lodge. He left a widow and three sons.

Sub Officer Percy Spice, had been a voluntary fireman before the war. Before going to work on that fateful evening, he made sure that his wife, two sons and a daughter were safely ensconced in an Anderson shelter. Sadly, for them, he never came to pick them up the following morning.

At the outbreak of the war Mr Hammond joined the Auxiliary Postal Service, but later transferred to the Auxiliary Fire Service.

The evening could have been much worse when another German bomb exploded nearby causing extensive damage to a building that was being used by a group of fifteen firemen. Fortunately, the building stayed intact under the power of the blast and debris and none of the firemen were injured.

A house which adjoined the firemen's sleeping quarters didn't fair so well. Mr Fred G. Reader, aged 52, and his two sisters were at home in a downstairs room when the ceiling collapsed and an outside wall was blown in. Remarkably, all three of them only received superficial injuries and walked out of the ruined building.

The *Thanet Advertiser* for Tuesday 9 September included an interesting article concerning a family from Ramsgate. Mr and Mrs Paddy Brough of 36 Allenby Road, Ramsgate, received a letter from their son, Private P.A. Brough who was somewhere in the Middle East serving in the Army. Mr Paddy Brough worked for Ramsgate Corporation, and was well known locally for his prowess at darts, winning many local tournaments.

The letter was brief and didn't provide much in the way of specifics, perhaps due to war time censorship. Private Brough's Christian name is not given, nor the regiment in which he was serving.

I have a little excitement to tell you now. Since I have been out here I've travelled thousands of miles and to top it all I became a prisoner of war, but I am glad to say it was for one week only. I am pleased to say I'm safe and well and back with my unit again.

With his letter Private Brough enclosed a copy of 'The Message', a poem written by a comrade, which reads:

'Here in the desert, midst the sand and blood,
The soldier bravely struggles on, his lot is one which is,
In common good, to rid the world of the Devil's son.
But whilst he fights with all his will, and hardly stops for rest,
His heart is with his loved ones still; a message he sends with zest.
It is good health to all, good cheer, till peace shall reign once more;
Keep smiling through the coming year, there are happier days in store.'

Friday 3 October saw the sudden death of Corporal Malcolm W. Brodie at Sheerness. He was the third son of the late Mr George Brodie of Salthaven, Joy Lane, Whitstable. He was out and about in Sheerness when he collapsed and died a short while later. It was at Sheerenss that Malcolm Brodie enlisted in the Royal Naval Air Service during the course of the First World War, and within six weeks he found himself in France. He remained with the Royal Air Force for just over four-and-a-half years.

Shortly after the Munich Conference of 30 September 1940, Brodie was encouraged to join the Royal Air Force's ground staff, where he could put his skills as an engineer to good use.

The funeral took place at Old Seasalter Churchyard on 1 October. His brother, sister, an uncle, and his fiancée, Mrs V. Sills, were the chief mourners.

On Friday 31 October Mr George Pain died at the home of his daughter at 13 Castlemount Road, Dover aged 74. Mr Pain had served as a police officer for 30 years between 1888 and 1918, joining Ramsgate police when he was 21 years of age. He had been promoted to the rank of detective sergeant towards the end of the nineteenth century and was further promoted to chief inspector, just prior to the start of the First World War, by which time he was 51.

Not satisfied with having been a police officer at Ramsgate for so many years, and feeling that he still had something to offer, he took charge of the police at Richborough before retiring in 1918. For a number of years, he had lived at Buckland Avenue, Dover, before returning to living in Ramsgate. He took an avid interest in local affairs and regularly attended Sunday conference meetings as well as those of the old Isle of Thanet Parliamentary Debating Society. He also took an active interest in the early years of the Ratepayers' Association. The theme that appeared to have run through his entire life was one of service to others, a desire to serve his community and the people who lived in it.

In 1935 when Ramsgate Town Council increased in size, he stood for election as a councillor in the ward of Southwood and won. He was not afraid to speak his mind, or to be direct and blunt when those traits were required. When in full flow in the council chamber at Albion House, he was a formidable presence, as well as being a splendid adversary for anybody who was prepared to take him on. It was like a boxing match, but with words.

Due to poor health he was unable to see out his term of office and had to resign from his council position. His funeral took place on 4 November at Charlton Cemetery, Dover. There was an excellent turn out with family, friends, and ex-colleagues from both the police and the council.

An unusual matter was before the Canterbury police court on Boxing Day 1941. It involved George E. Beard, a postman and driver for the Post Office in Margate. He had received a notice in the post, on three separate occasions, instructing him to attend for a medical examination which would determine if he was fit enough to be conscripted into His Majesty's armed forces. He ignored each of the letters and never presented himself at the relevant time, date and location.

Beard's wife told the court he had informed her only that morning that he had feared he was suffering from some kind of disease, what exactly that might be, he didn't know. He hadn't told her about his concerns as he didn't want her to know and he was afraid if he took the medical the ailment would come to light.

The Mayor, Alderman C. Lefevre, told the man that one way or another the medical examination would set his mind at rest, and if it transpired that if he was suffering with an illness, he would at least know what the issue was and he could then consult with his doctor. Beard agreed to attend for his medical examination the following Tuesday.

The year did not end on a high note for the United Kingdom. After attacks by the Japanese on Malaya, Singapore and Hong Kong, the government of the United Kingdom was left with no option but to declare war on the Empire of Japan. The declaration was made on 8 December 1941, and although protocol decreed that such a declaration should come from the British Secretary of State for Foreign Affairs, Anthony Eden, who held the post, he was en route to Moscow at the time, and in his absence, the Prime Minister, Winston Churchill was in charge of the Foreign Office, so the responsibility fell to him.

His letter to the Japanese Ambassador in London was as follows:

Sir,

On the evening of December 7th His Majesty's Government in the United Kingdom learned that Japanese forces without previous warning either in the form of a declaration of war or of an ultimatum with a conditional declaration of war had attempted a landing on the coast of Malaysia and bombed Singapore and Hong Kong.

In view of these wanton acts of unprovoked aggression committed in flagrant violation of International Law and particularly of Article 1 of the Third Hague Convention relative to the opening of hostilities, to which both Japan and the United Kingdom are parties, His Majesty's Ambassador at Tokyo has been instructed to inform the Imperial Japanese Government in the name of His Majesty's Government in the United Kingdom that a state of war exists between our two countries.

I have the honour to be, with high consideration,

Sir,
Your obedient servant
Winston Churchill.

In relation to the wording and style of the letter of declaration of war against Japan, Churchill later wrote in an article which appeared in *Life Magazine* on 27 September 1954:

Some people did not like this ceremonial style. But after all when you have to kill a man, it costs nothing to be polite.

CHAPTER 4

1942 – Seeing it Through

The war was into its fourth year and still there was no end in sight. Britain and her allies now had two enemies to fight – Germany, mainly throughout Europe and North Africa, and Japan in the Far East and the Pacific. It would be an interesting year with both highs and lows for Britain and her Allies, but the important ingredient of the equation, and with the help of a sporting analogy, by the end of the year, they were still in the game.

Although America had declared war on Japan on 8 December and Germany on 11 December 1941, the latter declaration being just hours after Germany had declared war on the USA, it wasn't until 8 November 1942 that American troops experienced their first real fighting, when taking part in Operation Torch in North Africa.

It was now a case of whether the combined forces the United Kingdom and the USA could beat those of Germany and Japan. The Allies had an advantage in that on more than one occasion during the war their soldiers fought either side by side or at least in the same battles. There is no recorded instance of Japanese and German soldiers ever having done the same, although submarines of the Imperial Japanese Navy and the German Kriegsmarine did work together.

According to the Commonwealth War Graves Commission website, British and Commonwealth losses for the year 1942 stood at 113,740, and a number of these individuals came from Kent. The county would lose at least 1,357 of its young men as a result of the fighting during the course of 1942. Since the outbreak of the war on 3 September 1939 and the end of 1942 Kent had seen at least 3,600 of its men killed, and before the end of the war they would lose thousands more.

One of those killed was Corporal 118646 Greta Ball, a nurse with the Voluntary Aid Detachment from Rochester, Kent, who was married to Captain E.P. Ball. She died on 15 February 1942 and is buried in the Heliopolis War Cemetery, in Cairo, Egypt. Those buried in the cemetery came mainly from the numerous military hospitals that were situated in the area whose patients were in the main the wounded and sick from the Western Desert campaigns, although after the war 125 graves were moved into Heliopolis from Mena Military Cemetery.

The year 1942 was undoubtedly a time of consolidation for the Allies; with America now on their side it certainly provided Britain with some much needed breathing space as well as renewed vigour, and no doubt inspired the Russians into believing the war wasn't a lost cause after all. The first American troops arrived in Europe from the United States when they landed in Northern Ireland.

What Winston Churchill called one of the worst defeats in British military history was undoubtedly the total capitulation at Singapore, which resulted in an estimated

80,000 British and Commonwealth soldiers being taken prisoner, when Lieutenant General Arthur Percival, General Officer Commanding Malaya Command, decided that his only option was to surrender to a much smaller Japanese army on 15 February 1942.

A number of men from Kent were casualties of the fighting at Singapore. For the men mentioned below, who are shown as serving with the Royal Army Medical Corps and having died between 14 and 15 February 1942, it is more than likely that they were killed during the attack, or massacre, as it has also been described, by Japanese soldiers at the British Military Hospital, Alexander, Singapore.

All of these individuals are commemorated on the Singapore Memorial, unless otherwise stated.

Volunteer George **Powell** of the Special Operations Executive was killed between 10 December 1941 and 15 February 1942. He has no known grave. He was a married man from Old Brompton. The Special Operations Executive (SOE) was formed on 22 July 1940 to conduct espionage, irregular warfare, sabotage and raiding operations, as well as reconnaissance in occupied countries and to aid local resistance groups.

Private 7521581 Reginald Samuel John **Hayward** (24) was serving with 32 Company Royal Army Medical Corps when he died between 14 and 15 February 1942. His mother, Mrs E. Hayward, lived at Ashford.

Private 7538035 Sydney Mark **Brooker** (24) of the Army Dental Corps was killed in action between 14 and 15 February 1942. His parents, William and Edith Brooker lived at Maidstone.

Private S/5629690 Henry Thurston **Whiting** (33) died on 13 February 1942 when serving with the Royal Army Medical Corps. He lived with his wife, Olive Whiting at Rochester.

Private 7521282 Charles James **Williams** (26) was serving with the Royal Army Medical Corps at the time of his death between 14 and 15 February 1942. His home was in Downham, Bromley.

Private 7392641 Douglas Stanley **Nicholls** (34) was serving with the 198 Field Ambulance, Royal Army Medical Corps, when he was killed between 14 and 15 February 1942. He was a married man who lived his wife, Minnie Nicholls, in Ramsgate.

Sergeant 3851935 William Charles Henry **Grant** (40) was serving with the 18th (5th Battalion The Loyal Regiment) Regiment, Reconnaissance Corps, when he was killed between 5 and 15 February 1942. He lived with his wife Clarissa Grant in Gravesend.

Private NX35873 Louis Donald **McPherson** (31) was serving with the 2nd/19th Battalion, Australian Infantry, when he was killed on 15 February 1942. He is buried in Kranji War Cemetery. His parents, Edward and Edith McPherson, were from Hadlow.

Sergeant Henry McIntyre **Shepton** (51) was a member of the Local Defence Corps (Malaya) when he was killed on 30 December 1941. His wife Joan Shepton, lived at Chislehurst.

Lieutenant 99739 Dennis Keith **Smith** (26) was serving with the 2nd Battalion, East Surrey Regiment, when he was killed on 20 December 1942. His parents, Keith and Mary Smith, lived in Bromley.

Flight Sergeant 365210 Stanley Thomas **Childs** (36) from Gillingham was killed in action on 14 February 1942 whilst serving with No.258 Squadron of the RAF. He had previously been Mentioned in Despatches.

Private S/244484 Ronald Frederick **Peer** (27) was serving with 'Z' Combined Motor Transport Depot, Royal Army Service Corps, when he was killed in action on 14 February 1942. His parents, Frederick and Cicely Peer, lived in Gravesend.

Lance Corporal 6169 James Wallace **Cameron** (34) was a married man from Biggin Hill. At the time of his death on 15 February 1942, he was serving with the 1st (Perak) Battalion, Federated Malay States Volunteer Force.

Gunner 6345522 Leonard Victor **Gardner** (20) was serving with the 3rd Battery, 6 HAA Regiment, Royal Artillery. He was killed in action on 13 February 1942. No.6 HAA Regiment Royal Artillery was equipped from stocks in Singapore as its original equipment had been sent to the Middle East. It was then deployed to gun positions around Singapore, including the golf course over looking Keppel Harbour. No.3 Battery was the only Battery of 6 HAA Regiment to remain in Singapore, as the rest had left Singapore in a convoy of small ships on 30 January 1942. Leonard had also previously served with The Queen's Own (Royal West Kent) Regiment. His parents, Ernest and Alice Gardner lived at West Wickham. His father, Ernest, was a holder of the Military Cross.

Corporal 13232 Leslie **Best** (33) was a married man who before the war lived with his wife, Cicely Judson Best, in Maidstone. He served with the Armoured Car Regiment of the Federated Malay States Volunteer Force and was killed on 13 February 1942.

Private 578010 Patrick Joseph **Beard** (20) served with the 4th Battalion, Royal Norfolk Regiment, which was a Territorial unit, and part of 54 Infantry Brigade, which in turn was part of the 18th Infantry Division, when he was killed on 13 February 1942. His parents, Sidney and Ann Beard, lived at Coney Hall, West Wickham.

Lance Corporal 766735 Alexander Walter **Barton** (27) lived with relatives in Otford, Kent. He served with the 6th Battalion, a Territorial unit of the Royal Norfolk Regiment. He was killed in action on 26 January 1941.

Private S/244514 Ernest John **Eastman** (29) was serving with the Royal Army Service Corps when he was killed in action on 13 February 1942. He was a married man, who before the war lived with his wife, Rita Winifred Eastman, at Gillingham.

Corporal NX73197 Frederick Clifford **Sharp** (22) was serving with the 2nd/30th Battalion, Australian Infantry when he was killed on 10 February 1942. His parents, James and Florence Sharp, lived in Gillingham.

Aircraftman 1st Class George Leonard **Everett** (21) was serving with the Royal Air Force Volunteer Reserve when he was killed on 14 February 1943. His parents, Walter and Rose Everett, lived at Gravesend.

Private 6141833 Tom **Smith** (24) lived with his parents, Samuel and Florence Smith, in Thanington. His father Samuel was a holder of the Military Medal, for his military service in the First World War.

Private Tom **Smith**, who served with the 2nd Battalion, East Surrey Regiment, was killed on 15 December 1941.

Gunner 964196 Douglas Allen **Wright** (24) was serving with the 118th Field Regiment, Royal Artillery, when he was killed on 15 February 1942 in Singapore. He is buried in the Kranji War Cemetery in Singapore. Before the war he had lived with his parents, William and Alice Wright, in Bexley.

Aircraftsman 1st Class 1360504 Hayes William **Morgan** (31) was serving with No. 36 Squadron, Royal Air Force Volunteer Reserve, when he was killed on 31 January 1942. His parents, Percy and Etehel Morgan, lived at Anerley, Kent.

Corporal 957096 Arthur Henry Francis **Sparkes** (23) was serving with No. 243 Squadron, Royal Air Force Volunteer Reserve, at the time of his death on 15 February 1942. Before the war he had lived with his parents, Charles and Annie Sparkes, at Barrow Hill.

Aircraftman 2nd Class 1284112 Spencer Charles **Clampin** (29) was serving with No. 243 Squadron, Royal Air Force Volunteer Reserve, when he was killed on 14 February 1942. His parents, Alfred and Edith Clampin, lived in Tunbridge Wells.

Aircraftman 2nd Class 1375889 Thomas Edward **Davis** (29) was from Gravesend. He was killed on 14 February 1942, whilst serving with No. 243 Squadron, Royal Air Force Volunteer Reserve.

Aircraftman 1st Class 1285998 Donald William **Dimon** (21) had lived with his parents, Arthur and Dorothy Dimon, at Ashford. He was killed on 14 February 1942, whilst serving with the Royal Air Force Volunteer Reserve, as part of No. 243 Squadron.

Sergeant 6134726 Sidney William **Roche** (39) was serving with the 2nd Battalion, East Surrey Regiment, when he was killed on 15 December 1941. He was a married man, who before the war lived with his wife, Kathleen Roche, in Tunbridge Wells.

Lance Corporal S/227628 Aubrey Charles **Lambert** (31) was killed on 13 February 1942. During the latter stages of the fighting on Singapore the Headquarters of the Malaya Command was ensconced in what was known as the Battle Box, an underground bunker, located nearly 30ft beneath the hill at Fort Canning. He was a married man who before the war had lived with his wife, Beryl, in West Wickham.

Lance Corporal 6019410 Frederick William **New** (24) was, at the time of his death on 13 February 1942, serving with 1st Battalion, Cambridgeshire Regiment. He was a married man who before the war lived with his wife, Ellie, at Downham. The 1st Battalion, Cambridgeshire Regiment were located at the Sime Road Camp in Singapore, and defended it stoically for two days before being ordered to surrender by Lieutenant Colonel Arthur Percival. During the two days of fighting, the Cambridgeshire Regiment lost 105 of their number, who were either killed or who died of their wounds.

Lieutenant John Evelyn Desmond **Darwall** (24) was serving with the Royal Navy at HMS *Sultan*, a shore establishment in Singapore, when he was killed on 26 January 1942. His parents, Captain (RN) William Henry and Edna Darwall, lived in Rochester.

Sapper 1277 Edward Watts **Ellaby** who served with the Johore Volunteer Engineers, was killed on 21 January 1942 and is buried in the Kranji War Cemetery in Singapore.

His parents, Christopher and Gertrude Ellaby, lived at Shortlands. The volunteers were only 258 men in total of these, 16 were killed during the war.

Major AI/852 Edward Lionel Wakefield **Fox** MC (43) was killed on 11 January 1942, whilst serving with the 18th Battalion, Royal Garhwal Rifles. He is buried in the Kranji War Cemetery. The Rifles paid a high price for their involvement in the war, with some 708 killed and approximately 1,400 wounded. He was a married man, who had previously lived with his wife, Marion, at Hadlow.

Gunner 1110134 George Henry **Hadlow** (33) was serving with 5th Field Regiment, Royal Artillery, when he was killed on 9 February 1942 during the fighting at Singapore. His parents, William and Mary Hadlow, lived at Faversham.

Sister 213310 Margory Eveline **Gale** (34) was serving with the Territorial Army Nursing Service, when she was killed on 14 February 1942. She had been working at the 1st Malaysian General Hospital in Singapore and was evacuated on board the SS *Kuala* on 14 February 1942. Just twelve hours later it was bombed and sunk by Japanese aircraft, just off Pom Pong island. Having sunk the SS *Kuala*, the Japanese then started bombing survivors in the water. Of those who did survive, some were picked up by SS *Tanjong Pinang*, which three days later was also attacked, as it made its way to the island of Sumatra. Margory's parents, John and Georgina Gale, were from Sevenoaks.

Private 6141002 Derek Reginald **Coombs** (27) was serving with 2nd Battalion, East Surrey Regiment, when he was killed on 13 February 1942. The regiment lost 155 men during the fighting in Malaya and Singapore. His parents lived in Herne Bay.

Private 6027022 William Ernest **Mitchell** (29) was serving with the 2nd Battalion, Cambridge Regiment, when he was killed on 24 January 1942. Before the war he had lived his wife, Daisy Gwendolyn in Tonbridge.

Bombardier 1425263 William **Mudge** (37) died on 8 February 1942, whilst serving with the 80th Anti-Tank Regiment, Royal Artillery in Singapore. Prior to the war he had lived in Gillingham with his wife, Lillian.

Lance Corporal 6020927 Albert George Francis **Keep** (25) was killed on 13 February 1942 whilst serving with the 1st Battalion, Cambridgeshire Regiment. His parents Albert and Sarah Keep lived in Beckenham.

Major 50007 Arthur Denis **Martin** (34) was killed on 14 February 1942, whilst serving with the 259th Battery, 118 Field Regiment, Royal Artillery. He was buried in Kranji War Cemetery. A married man, prior to the war he lived in Tunbridge Wells with his wife, Heather.

Lance Corporal 2318902 Frederick Hart **Dyason** (32) was serving with the 34th Fortress Company, Royal Engineers, when he was killed on 15 February 1942, the day that Percival surrendered to the Japanese. Dyason had also previously served with the Royal Corps of Signals. His parents, Fred and Sybil Dyason lived in Gillingham.

Battalion Sergeant Major 909539 Alan Bradshaw **Pethybridge** (29) was a relatively young man to have reached such a rank. He was serving with the 188th Field Regiment, Royal Artillery when he was killed on 10 February 1942. He is buried in the Kranji War Cemetery. Prior to the war he lived his wife, Nellie, at Mottingham.

Leading Aircraftman 573063 Victor John **Deverson** (19) was serving in the Royal Air Force, when he was killed on 29 January 1942. Before the war he lived with his parents, Ernest and Edith Deverson, in Gillingham. Victor's brother, Ernest, was also killed during the war, meaning another sad loss for their parents.

Captain AI/529 Foster Abney **Giles** (30) was serving with the 8th Punjab Regiment, when he was killed on 16 December 1941. He was a married man and prior to the start of the war, he lived with his wife, Eleanor Clarissa Giles, in Rochester. Two of the regiment's battalions, the 1st and 7th, were serving in Singapore at the time of the British surrender on 15 February 1942, so it was one of these that Captain Giles was serving with at the time of his death.

Lance Corporal 7262366 Jack Valentine **Lewis** (25) was serving with the 32nd Company, Royal Army Medical Corps, when he was killed on 14 February 1942. He is remembered at the Singapore Civil Hospital Grave Memorial. His parents, James and Elsie Lewis, lived at Anerley. They lost another son, Victor Turney Lewis, in the war.

Sister 209317 Lorna Sybil **Symonds**, was serving with the Queen Alexandra's Imperial Military Nursing Service at the 17th General Clearing Hospital in Singapore. Along with other medical staff, she had been evacuated on board the SS *Kuala* when it was attacked and sunk by Japanese aircraft on 14 February 1942. Lorna was on the top deck of the ship with other nurses, when it was struck by one of the bombs and exploded and was killed in the blast. She was the daughter of John Henry Gale, and of Georgina Eleanor Gale, of Sevenoaks, Kent. Her uncle was Lieutenant Colonel H. Bertram Foster, who had previously lived at Dry Hill Park, Tonbridge, Kent.

Corporal 569643 Eric John **Datson** was 23 years of age and serving with the Royal Air Force when he died of his wounds on 16 February 1942. His grandfather, Mr H. Mitchell, lived in Dartford, Kent.

Throughout March 1942 the RAF increased its missions into the very heartland of Germany, carrying out raids on both Essen and Lübeck. During the latter over 30 per cent of the city was destroyed. The same month saw a Commando raid on the French port of St Nazaire, which possessed the largest dry dock on the Atlantic coast. Operation Chariot, although deemed a success from a military perspective, came at a high price as 168 of the men who took part in the operation were killed. A further 214 were taken prisoner, with five managing to escape to Spain. As a result of the action, five men were awarded the Victoria Cross, the most for any operation in the Second World War.

Whilst the Japanese continued to run amok throughout the Far East and the Pacific, Britain kept up her bombing raids on Germany cities, Hamburg being one of the targets for the RAF's aircraft of Bomber Command. Later the same month, so impressed was King George VI with the heroic defensive actions of those tasked with keeping Malta out of the clutches of the enemy, that he awarded the island the George Cross.

In May all Jews living in France were ordered to wear the Star of David. On the night of 30/31 May the first thousand bomber raid on the German city of Cologne was carried out by the RAF. June saw heavy fighting in the Pacific, mainly between

Japanese and American forces. The first news of atrocities against the Jews, with gas being used to carry out cases of mass killings, reached the West. The British Coal industry was nationalized, and the bombing of the industrial cities throughout Germany continued. Things were not going well in North Africa for the British, in particular, the 8th Army, as Rommel's Afrika Korps continued their dominance of the region. The opening of Treblinka II extermination camp in Poland took place on 22 July 1942.

The Battle of Stalingrad went on for over five months, beginning on 23 August 1942 and finally ending on 2 February 1943. Germany had not been on her own fighting the Russians. She was fighting alongside Hungarians, Italians and Romanian forces, but still lost the epic battle, suffering over 400,000 casualties in the process.

Work on the Atomic bomb began in America on 4 September 1942. The following day Australian and American forces inflicted the first defeat on Japanese forces at Milne Bay, Papua New Guinea, during the Pacific War. Hitler issued an order to his commanders on 18 October 1942 that any captured British Commandos are to be executed immediately. The same month saw the age of conscription in Britain lowered to 18, and the Second Battle of El Alamein began. In November 1942 Rommel's Afrika Korps was forced to retreat during the night at El Alamein, and the Americans gained a victory over the Japanese during the action at Koli Point on Guadalcanal. As the month drew to a close the British Eighth Army retook Tobruk. The Russians were close to defeating the Germans at Stalingrad, and the RAF carried out raids on Berlin with little in the way of resistance.

The year ended on a high for the Allies, with the Royal Navy winning a strategic victory in the Battle of the Barents Sea on 31 December. Rommel was surrounded in Tunisia, while German forces suffered the same fate at Stalingrad, and the Japanese were close to evacuating Guadalcanal.

'On the enemy's doorstep'

Although Dover had never been 'blitzed' like London, Coventry, Liverpool, or Plymouth, it certainly had seen its fair share of German aircraft in the skies above its towns and villages. To many, it was seen as the front line in the defence of the nation against the Nazi-led threat of the German nation.

In January 1942 a reporter from a newspaper in Scotland paid the town a visit to see what all the fuss was about, and whether the belief was a reality. The reporter had no name, just a title 'war correspondent' and there wasn't a hint as to whether the journalist was male or female although most reporters during the time of the Second World War were men, so we can assume the reporter was a male. He stayed in Dover for four days in the early part of January 1942. The weather was bitterly cold, though clear and sunny.

As he stepped out of the railway station onto the streets of Dover, on Saturday lunchtime he was surprised to hear the sound of shell fire coming from across the Channel heading in the direction of Dover. He couldn't help but notice that there was no panic, just a surreal calmness as people went about their business. Even though the afternoon was relatively hazy, it was still possible to see the flashes of the enemy's long range artillery guns along the French coastline, which became even more pronounced as the grey afternoon gave way to the darkness of the evening.

He was taken with how it was possible to clearly make out the French coastline, albeit with the help of a telescope, although he couldn't see any vehicles moving about. He commented on how fascinating it was to be able to sit having a meal one evening in a cosy little restaurant in Dover within sight of 'enemy country'. Despite there being a war on he was able to enjoy a meal consisting of soup, followed by a main course of liver, bacon, scrambled eggs, although not fresh farm eggs, but palatable nevertheless, baked beans and chipped potatoes, washed down with a glass of wine. The meal was followed with a pastry and a coffee. As he enjoyed a pleasant evening, he was left contemplating whether there were people on the French side of the English Channel, sitting in a restaurant enjoying a similar well cooked meal like the one he had eaten.

On the Sunday evening he went to the cinema, and whilst taking in the film, the words 'Shelling Warning' came up across the large screen, superimposed over the picture so that the audience didn't miss any of the film. Once again there was no panic, no rush for any of the exits, just a group of people calmly enjoying an evening's entertainment, and paying little if any attention to the warning, whilst the distant sound of shelling continued to be heard throughout the rest of the screening.

One evening, just before leaving the house he was staying at in Dover, the reporter saw a German aircraft passing overhead whilst he and his hosts stood in the front garden and watched a spectacular display of anti-aircraft fire directed towards the enemy plane. The aircraft made good its escape, no doubt in possession of a few souvenirs from its visit to Dover. This was an experience that the reporter would witness again before his visit was over.

One of his strangest impressions of Dover was witnessing an exercise that took place one evening along the area of the harbour front and the beach, both of which were lit up by a number of searchlights, right under the nose of the enemy and without any apparent response. He compared this to being back home in Edinburgh, some 350 miles away from the front line with the enemy, yet being bellowed at extremely loudly by a passing Warden or Police constable to 'put that light out' if he dared show a light during a blackout.

He returned to his home in Edinburgh with a degree of admiration for the towns people, who as he put it, 'lived on the enemy's doorstep'.

In February 1942 Flight Lieutenant G.F.L Coates the officer commanding the RAF high speed launch base at Dover, received the Distinguished Service Cross from King George VI at Buckingham Palace. The award was for his continued zealous service during the seven months he was in charge of the RAF air sea rescue service launches at 'Hell's Corner'.

During his time in charge the men under his command rescued large numbers of pilots and aircrews whose aircraft had been shot down in the English Channel or the Dover Straits, both allied and German alike. What made these rescues even more remarkable was the fact that on many occasions this involved having to brave the dangers of minefields, enemy aircraft and surface vessels.

By the age of 24, Coates had gained his Master Mariner's certificate, and in 1937, aged 32, he was the navigating officer aboard the British research ship *William Scoresby* which sailed to the Antarctic on a whale marking and scientific observation research expedition in the South Polar waters. In April 1939 he returned to Britain and joined the RAF a few months before the outbreak of war.

The St Nazaire Raid

On 28 March 1942 what has gone down in military history as one of the most daring raids of the Second World War, took place at St Nazaire in France, the site of the biggest dry dock on the Atlantic coast. The facility allowed the Germans to repair some of their biggest ships which meant they could be back in use much quicker than if they had to use other locations.

Code named Operation Chariot, this joint venture between the RAF and the Royal Navy aimed to put the dry dock at St Nazaire out of action. A combined force of 611 men took part in the operation. Of these 169 were killed, 215 were captured, some of them wounded, and the remaining 227 made it back home. So valiant were the actions of all those who took part in the raid that five men were awarded the Victoria Cross, fifty-one were Mentioned in Despatches, whilst a further eighty received other gallantry medals. Approximately 23 per cent of those who took part in the raid received awards for their bravery.

One of those honoured for his actions at St Nazaire that day, was Sergeant 1874047 Thomas Frank Durrant of the Royal Engineers and No.1 Commando, who was born on 17 October 1917 in Farnborough, Kent, now part of Greater London. He had enlisted in the Corps of Royal Engineers on 1 February 1937. In 1940 the British Prime Minister, Winston Churchill, ordered the formation of specially trained troops who would 'develop a reign of terror down the enemy coast'. Durrant applied and was accepted to serve with this unqiue band of brothers, which after its involvement in the Norway campaign, became No.1 Commando.

During the raid Durrant was on board HM Motor Launch 306, manning a twin Lewis gun which came under heavy fire from shore-based German units. The launch was unable to land its band of brave commandos and as it started to withdraw it was attacked by a German destroyer. Durrant, who continued to fire his Lewis gun, was wounded several times, in the head, both arms, both legs, the chest and stomach, but still would not leave his post, remaining in an exposed position and only able to remain standing by supporting himself by holding on to the mounting of his gun.

Durrant died of his wounds later that day in a German military hospital in St Nazaire. He was buried in the Escoublac-la-Baule War Cemetery, just outside the town.

A week after the raid in a prisoner of war camp in Rennes, Kapitanleutnant F.K. Paul, the commander of the German destroyer which engaged Durrant's motor launch, met Lieutenant Colonel Augustus Charles Newman, who commanded the

Above: *Thomas Frank Durrant VC.*

Right: *Victoria Cross.*

British Commandos. Paul fully apprised Newman of Durrant's actions and bravery, suggested to him that he might like to recommend Durrant for a high award, which he did. This is quite possibly the only time a member of the British or Commonwealth military has been awarded a Victoria Cross on the recommendation of an enemy officer. It is also the only time a Victoria Cross has been awarded to a soldier because of his involvement in a naval action. For his part in the raid Lieutenant Colonel Newman was also awarded the VC.

The award of Durrant's Victoria Cross was announced in the *London Gazette* on 15 June 1945 and was presented by King George VI to his mother at an investiture at Buckingham Palace on 29 October 1946.

The citation for the award read as follows:

The King has been graciously pleased to approve the posthumous award of the Victoria Cross to No.1874047 Sergeant Thomas Frank Durrant, Corps of Royal Engineers (attached Commandos) (Green Street Green, Farnborough, Kent).

For great gallantry, skill and devotion to duty when in charge of a Lewis gun in HM Motor Launch 306 in the St Nazaire raid on 28th March 1942.

Motor Launch 306 came under heavy fire while proceeding up the River Loire towards the Port. Sergeant Durrant in his position abaft the bridge, where he had no cover or protection, engaged enemy gun positions and searchlights on shore. During this engagement he was severely wounded in the arm but refused to leave his gun.

The Motor Launch subsequently went down the river and was attacked by a German destroyer at 50-60 yards range, and often closer. In this action Sergeant Durrant continued to fire at the destroyer's bridge with the greatest coolness and complete disregard of the enemy's fire. The motor launch was illuminated by the enemy searchlights and Sergeant Durrant drew on himself the individual attention of the enemy guns, and was again wounded, in many places. Despite these further wounds he stayed in his position, still firing his gun, although after a time only able to support himself by holding on to the gun mounting.

After a running fight, the commander of the German destroyer called on the motor Launch to surrender. Sergeant Durrant's answer was a further burst of fire at the destroyer's bridge. Although now very weak, he went on firing, using drums of ammunition as fast as they could be replaced. A renewed attack by the enemy vessel eventually silencing the fire of the motor Launch but Sergeant Durrant refused to give up until the destroyer came alongside, grappled the Motor Launch and took prisoner those who remained alive.

Sergeant Durrant's gallant fight was commended by the German officers on boarding the Motor Launch. This very gallant Non-Commissioned Officer later died of the many wounds received in action.

An extremely brave young man, but mention must be made of the actions of the German naval officer Friedrich-Karl Paul for bringing Durrant's actions to the attention of his commanding officer when he saw him at the prisoner of war camp at Rennes. A truly honourable individual, on 4 March 1945 Paul was awarded the Knights Cross of the Iron Cross.

A meeting took place at Dover Town Hall on Wednesday 1 April concerning prisoners of war from Kent being held in camps throughout Germany, Japan and the Far East. There were about eighty people in attendance who were either next-of-kin or relatives of prisoners of war. They were there to listen to a talk given by Miss Christine Knowle OBE, the founder and Honorary Director of the British Prisoners of War Books and Games Fund.

The Mayor of Dover, Alderman J.R. Cairns, thanked Miss Knowles for what she had done and continued to do for Kent's prisoners of war. Miss Knowles gave a detailed explanation as to what the organization did, and how its efforts helped British prisoners of war in a practical sense.

After the meeting many of the audience remained behind to take the opportunity to speak to Miss Knowles on a personal level, to see if she could help or offer any advice about difficulties they were experiencing in trying to make contact with prisoners. The wife of a prisoner of war from Dover made a collection during the course of the afternoon and raised two guineas which she later presented to Miss Knowles, who promised that the monies would be spent on providing cigarettes for prisoners of war from Dover.

One can only guess at the stress involved in having been the wife, child, parent, etc. of a loved one who was being held as a prisoner of war in a foreign country, wondering if they were ever going to meet again, not knowing if they had they been wounded or were being mistreated. The only thing that could really put their mind at rest was to receive a letter or a post card.

On Wednesday, 6 May a young man appeared at the Bungay police court in Suffolk for an offence he had committed at Dover two days earlier. He was 17-year-old Frederick Charles Stewart, who as well as being a farm labourer, was a member of the Home Guard in Bungay, and the reason for his arrest was for being in possession of a Thompson submachine gun and ammunition. He was trying to get across the Channel and 'use it'. After being detained, he was escorted back to Bungay by train.

He told the court that he knew it was no use going with a rifle so he took the tommy-gun. He went to London first and then on to Dover. Once he had arrived in the town he went into a pub and had a drink before going off to look for a small boat. He spotted one and got to within about 150 yards of it when he was stopped by the police. He had never fired a tommy-gun but he had read all of the instructions. What he really wanted was to get into the Army. He had tried the previous year (1941) but wasn't accepted as he was too young.

After having been found guilty of stealing the gun and ammunition, he was put on probation and ordered to pay £2 8s 6d in costs. If it hadn't been a time of war and Master Stewart hadn't been on his way to try and take part in the fighting, he would have no doubt been sent to prison for a lengthy period of time.

After being released from the court he told a reporter: 'I fully intended to make for Paris and find Laval and Darlan [French politicians of the Vichy regime]. I was going to kill them and return to England. They are traitors. I should have shot up a few Germans on the way and destroyed as much stuff as I could.'

He was obviously a keen young man who just went about it the wrong way. I would imagine it must have been a bit of a shock for the two policemen when they stopped him.

'Ok, son, what have you got in the bag?'

'Would you believe me if I said a Thompson Machine Gun?'

(Laughter from the two policemen) 'Of course you have, son....'

The *Thanet Advertiser* included an article in its edition of Tuesday 9 June. The story entitled 'Margate Man's Adventure' told the story of one man's escape from the soon to be occupied island of Singapore.

The son of the late Mr and Mrs David Cox, from Margate, and the brother of Mrs E. Kennard of Victoria Avenue, Margate, Mr Charles D. Cox, who was the manager of the P&O Bank in Singapore, was one of the last civilians to leave the island before it was captured by the Japanese.

The boat on which Mr Cox left, was attacked by Japanese aircraft and sunk, leaving him wounded in three places, but despite this and along with other survivors, he managed to make his way to an uninhabited island, where they were without food or water. After walking for many miles, they were spotted and picked up by a Royal Navy vessel and taken to Bombay in India. After having his wounds treated, he returned to England. Mr Cox had worked and lived in Singapore for many years. He had served in the Army during the First World War as a lieutenant, both in Singapore and France.

By the outbreak of the Second World War, the National Service (Armed Forces Act) imposed a liability for all men aged between 18 and 41 years of age to be conscripted into His Majesty's Armed Forces. There were always exemptions to the rules; men could be rejected on medical grounds, as not physically fit enough for military training. Those who were employed in vital industries or occupations were also exempt.

In 1942 with the war having continued for longer than had at first been expected, all British men aged between 18 and 51 years of age, and all women aged between 20 and 30 years were liable to be called up, with the following exemptions:

British subjects from outside Britain and the Isle of Man who had lived in the country for less than two years.

Northern Ireland

Students

Clergy of any denomination.

Persons employed by the government of any country of the Briish Empire except the United Kingdom.

Those who were blind or who had mental disorders.

Married women

Police, medical and prison workers.

Women who had one or more children 14 years or younger living with them. This included their own children, legitimate, illegitimate, step-children and adopted children, as long as the child was adopted before 18 December 1941.

In 1939 men under 20 years of age were exempt from being sent overseas, but by 1942 this exemption was lifted.

An article in the *Thanet Advertiser* dated Friday 31 July reported that Gunner Rodney Hawkins RA, the son of Alderman W. Hawkins and Mrs Hawkins, of 123 Crescent Road, Ramsgate, had been reported missing. Alderman and Mrs Hawkins received an airgraph letter from their son dated 15 June 1942, and the date from which he was officially reported missing was five days later.

Gunner Hawkins, who was 23 years of age, was an old boy of Chatham House School, where he gained high marks in the Civil Service examination and entered the income tax department. He enlisted in the Army just after the outbreak of war and in 1940 he was sent out to serve in the Middle East.

A check on the Commonwealth War Graves Commission website records a Gunner 959054 Rodney William Hawkins who was 26 years of age and serving with the 234th Battery of the 68 Medium Regiment. He died on 20 July 1945 and is buried in St Laurence-in-Thanet, Churchyard in Kent, and his parents were William and Annie Louise Hawkins of Ramsgate.

As he was buried locally it suggests that he was either wounded while fighting abroad and then sent home, or he was in the UK and had an illness from which he subsequently died.

In 1942 the August Bank Holiday was at the beginning of the month rather than at the end as it is today. It stretched from Saturday to Monday 1-3 August, but because of wartime restrictions, it was the third August Bank holiday that the people of Thanet had spent the weekend enjoying themselves rather than catering for the leisure time and enjoyment of others. With wartime restrictions still prohibiting visitors from entering the district, the Bank Holiday was a relatively quiet affair. Despite the threat of air raids, some of the children and mothers who had been moved out for their own safety, came back to spend a few days in the area.

The tennis courts and bowling greens at Ramsgate, Margate and Broadstairs, were kept particularly busy for most of the weekend and there were the fetes at both Ramsgate and Margate. Once the daytime family entertainment and festivities had finished, it was time for the adults to enjoy themselves in the evening. On the Saturday and Monday evenings there were dances at the West Cliff Theatre in Ramsgate, when young couples and a few hopeful singletons danced the night away to the sounds of Fred Hargreaves and his band.

On Friday 25 September Mr Walter Ian Medcalf from Louisville Avenue, Gillingham, appeared before the Chatham police court, charged with failing to enrol in the Home Guard when instructed to do so by a National Service officer. He told the court that he was doing enough as a civilian because he was fire watching and was cultivating a piece of ground approximately 70ft by 280ft. He added that he did not want to be a 'part time' soldier and was more than willing to enlist in the Army. He was found guilty of the offence and fined £5.

That month also saw an interesting story about Frank Henry John Baker from Margate who was fighting the Germans in North Africa. Before the war he had been a grocer's assistant. His parents, Mr and Mrs Frank Baker, lived at 45 Orchard Road, Margate.

Baker was a sergeant serving with The Buffs Regiment as part of the British Eighth Army and involved in fighting in and around El Alamein. During an Allied night operation, aimed at Rommel's flank, in the first stage of a German Panzer withdrawal, Baker and eleven of his comrades found themselves occupying a number of abandoned enemy trenches, but once the Germans found out they began shelling them. Initially Baker and his men returned fire with rifles and machine-guns, but rather than continue with the shelling, the enemy attacked their position and overran it, forcing Baker and his men to surrender. But things were about to get a lot stranger one of the German officers told Baker, in broken English, that they wanted him to go forward on a mission for them. Baker explained:

They shoved a white towel into my hands, and it became clear that they wanted me to go through their lines to some Maoris still worrying their position and call on them to surrender or be blasted out by shell fire.

I went along with it and they sent one or two shots after me to make sure I went in the right direction. When I approached the Maoris' position, they thought I was an Italian and that this was an enemy ruse, but I managed to make them understand I was English and they took me to their commanding officer.

The Maoris just grinned when they learnt about my mission, so I said, 'Well, do I go back or do I stay with you?'

I stayed, and although the Jerries opened up with all they had, when they saw I was not returning, the New Zealanders held their position and returned fire until they received the order to withdraw.

That was surely one of the shortest periods of time that any soldier had ever spent as a prisoner of war, and how surreal that the German officer was even thinking about the wellbeing of the New Zealand soldiers and giving them the option to surrender, by sending forward a captured British soldier to get them to do so.

Mr Robert Edgar Pointer and his wife, Mrs Ada Pamela Pointer of 34 Magdala Road, St Peter's, Kent, were informed that her son, Arthur George Pointer, aged 23, had been killed in action in the Middle East on 3/4 September 1942 whilst serving as a Corporal (6288915) in the 2nd Battalion, The Buffs (Royal East Kent Regiment).

During the early months of the war he had taken part in the fighting in France as part of the BEF, and was one of those evacuated at Dunkirk in May 1940. In March 1942 he had married Miss Joan Hatherway, the daughter of Mr and Mrs Hatherway of 57 Westover Road, St. Peter's, Kent, but the following month he was sent out to the Middle East. After having been informed by her daughter-in-law of the death of her son, Mrs Pointer, received a letter from him dated 2 September 1942, the day before he was killed. He has no known grave, but his name is commemorated on the Alamein Memorial in Egypt.

Monday 12 October saw the beginning of the fire-watching registration for women at Ramsgate, after they were officially called upon for the first time. By the end of the week 2,507 had completed their registration. Of these, 970 made no claim to be exempted. At the time there were 239 women living in Ramsgate who had no fixed abode, their homes being in the town's tunnels. Of these only 106 had taken it upon themselves to register as they were not exempt from having to register because they were of no fixed abode.

All of the women who registered and claimed no exemption from having to serve, were trained accordingly, but it was not the intention of Ramsgate Council that these women would then be sent to a prescribed fire guard post to undertake their duty. Instead they carried out their fire-watching duties from their own homes and were only required to report to their nominated posts in the case of an emergency, although some women expressed a desire to carry out their duties at a fire guard post.

A similar registration took place at the same time in Margate, which was for both men and women. A total of 2,025 people registered, the majority women. Of these only about 500 were available for duty at that time, with more than half of those who had registered, 1,015, claiming an exemption as they had children who were under the age of fourteen. A further 250 claimed exemptions on other grounds, whilst some were already carrying out voluntary fire-watching duties at businesses or in locally arranged street groups.

Once the registration scheme began, there were quite a number of women who volunteered to carry out part time Civil Defence work, rather than do fire watching duties.

Strange as it might seem, it was not the job of fire watchers to watch for fires, but to watch for incendiaries dropped from enemy aircraft in large numbers during air raids and extinguish them before a fire could take hold on the ground. In September 1940 a law required factories and businesses to appoint a number of their employees to watch for incendiary bombs dropped near their premises outside their normal working hours.

Civil Defence was the responsibility of local authorities, who ascribed volunteers to different roles depending on their experience or training. It included ARP wardens, firemen, fire watchers, rescuers, first aid posts and stretcher parties. Nearly two million people served in Civil Defence throughout Britain during the Second World War; nearly 2,400 of them were killed as a result of enemy action. It was a major commitment with a massive responsibility which covered so many different areas of civil defence requirements.

The funeral took place at Margate Cemetery in early November 1942 of 20-year-old Robert William Powell, who lived with his parents, William and Helen Isabel Powell, at 31 Addiscombe Gardens, Margate.

Robert was a Private (5781693) with the Royal Norfolk Regiment. Although he died on 25 October 1942, he had been injured nearly a year before that, not on the battlefields of Europe, North Africa or the Far East, but on the streets of Norwich, in Norfolk.

Robert's regiment was stationed in Norwich when he was caught in an air raid in August 1941. A steel girder fell on his shoulder, an injury that he never recovered from, so much so that he was discharged from the Army in October 1941 as no longer physically fit for military service and had been seriously ill until the time of his death. He had joined The Buffs (Royal East Kent Regiment) before the outbreak of the war but was discharged just six months later because of a foot injury. Not to be deterred from serving his country, he re-enlisted in early 1940, when he joined the Royal Norfolk Regiment.

Margate Cemetery.

On Christmas Eve 1942 the following was reported in newspapers up and down the country, once again bringing home the real tragedy of war, and highlighted how deadly it was in ways that were least expected.

Four children of Mr and Mrs F. Fruin of Dane Hill Row, Margate, who were between 2 and 15 years of age, were killed in their home by an explosion. It is believed that the explosion was the result of a mortar bomb which had been found by the eldest child and brought home to show his siblings.

The inquest into the deaths which took place the same day in Margate, heard how the eldest of Mr and Mrs Fruin's children, their 15-year-old son, had been working on a firing range for a Ramsgate-based contractor, and whilst there had found the unexploded shell, taken it home with him, where sadly, it exploded, killing him, his two younger sisters and younger brother.

The foreman of the company told the inquest that only the week before the tragedy he had taken an unexploded bomb away from the boy and put it in a place of safety. Three days later he found the boy in the workshop with another bomb in a vice. He told him to put it back where he had found it, and the boy replied that he wanted to take it home.

The coroner for Margate, Mr J.H. Robinson, said the fatality was primarily due to the boy's curiosity, but that it could and should not have happened, and wouldn't have, if the foreman had recognized that it was his duty, when he had knowledge of the bomb, to report the matter to the police or military authorities. Instead he acted in a way that most people would have done, and didn't tell anybody, but it wasn't the right decision. The coroner went on to say that there was a moral and legal duty upon people to report the finding of such objects.

Despite highlighting the part that the foreman had played, a verdict of accidental death was returned and no action was taken against the foreman or the company for whom he worked. Whether the man kept his job, was not recorded.

As the year drew to an end the nation was in a relatively good state of affairs, and certainly in a much better place than it had been at the same time the year before. For the first time in three years Britain and her Allies, despite setbacks, appeared to be militarily on the front foot. The question was, could they now consolidate that position and move forward towards victory.

CHAPTER 5

1943 – Turning the Corner

The Commonwealth War Graves Commission website records that a total of 114,525 British and Commonwealth military personnel lost their lives throughout 1943. Of these, approximately 1,530 men were either from, or had connections to the county of Kent. These were split as follows:

Army: 736
Navy: 240
RAF: 522
Merchant Navy: 30
Miscellaneous: 2

One of the two men who are included under the miscellaneous heading was 59-year-old Stuart Isles Buck, a married man who lived with his wife, Emma, in Gravesend. He worked for the Lighthouse and Pilotage Authorities, Trinity House Service, SS *Norhauk* (Norway) and died on 21 December 1943. He has no known grave, but his name is commemorated on the Tower Hill Memorial in the City of London.

The SS *Norhauk* had started out as the *Waban* in 1919 and had been renamed the *Empire Sambar* in 1940, the *Empire Beaver* in 1941, and finally the SS *Norhauk* on 5 April 1942, when the Norwegian government took ownership of her. She was a general cargo ship and spent most of her time sailing between America and the United Kingdom bringing in supplies of food stuffs and military equipment.

Part of a convoy that had sailed from Halifax in Nova Scotia on 2 December and arrived in Liverpool on 16 December 1941, she unloaded her cargo of 236 tons of aircraft equipment and guns; 727 tons of aluminium; 863 tons of cheese; 111 tons of flour; 627 tons of military vehicles; 60 tons of tank spares, 95 tons of wireless sets, as well as 1,000 tons of zinc. From there she travelled to Loch Ewe in Scotland and then on to London. She left London in the early afternoon of 21 December 1943 as part of a coastal convoy and struck a mine in the Thames Estuary soon afterwards, sinking almost immediately. Eleven crew members, including Stuart Buck, were killed.

An enquiry into the sinking of the *Norhauk* on 6 January 1944, heard that the vessel had degaussing equipment fitted, which was being used at the time she struck the mine. In essence degaussing is a means to stop magnetic mines being able to attach themselves to steel hulled ships.

From the figures for the Army, 373 of these were men serving with The Buffs (Royal East Kent Regiment); of these only sixty-seven were either born or lived in Kent. The biggest loss of life on a single day experienced by The Buffs during the year was 116 men from the 4th Battalion, who were all killed on the night of 23/24 October 1943.

The 116 men of the 4th Battalion were in Alexandria, Egypt when, without any prior warning, they were told to get their kit together as they were on the move. They were then taken to the city's docks and put on board two Royal Navy destroyers, HMS *Eclipse* and HMS *Petard*. Where they were going, they didn't know, but being soldiers they didn't need to, they would find out soon enough when they got there. They were actually on their way to the Greek island of Leros, which is part of the Dodecanese Islands, in the Aegean Sea, between the islands of Patmos and Kalymnos but sadly, they never reached their intended destination.

On the night of 24/ 25 October, HMS *Eclipse*, while carrying part of 4th Battalion, along with HMS *Petard*, struck a mine, burst into flames and sank with the loss of 253 men –119 of the ship's company and 134 troops. About 100 men were picked up by an air-sea rescue launch of the RAF dispatched from Leros and boats from HMS *Petard*, after spending over three hours in the water. Those who died are commemorated on the Athens Memorial.

The following are the sixty-seven men from Kent mentioned above who were killed throughout the course of the year. They served with the 4th Battalion unless otherwise indicated.

Private 14404912 Ronald George Johnson **Aldis** (21) was from Gillingham. At the time of his death on 9 August 1943, he was serving with the regiment's 5th Battalion. He is buried in the Catania War Cemetery in Sicily.

Catania War Cemetery, Sicily.

Leros War Cemetery, Greece.

Private 6287711 Charles George Hubert **Ashdown** (26) lived with his parents, Herbert and Charlotte Ashdown, in Ickham. He was killed between 16 and 17 November 1943, and is buried in the Leros War Cemetery in Greece.

Private 6290357 Albert Ernest **Baker** (23) lived with his parents James and Emily Baker in Cheriton. He was killed on 5 October 1943, and is buried in the Sangro River War Cemetery in Italy.

Lance Sergeant 6286792 Donald James **Baitup** (20) was serving with the 5th Battalion, The Buffs (Royal East Kent Regiment) at the time of his death on 27 March 1943. He is buried in the Medjez-el-Bab War Cemetery in Tunisia. His parents, Frederick and Rosie Baitup, lived in Cranbrook.

Private 6287239 Albert George **Bartlett** was serving with the 5th Battalion, The Buffs (Royal East Kent Regiment) when he lost his life on 2 July 1943. He is buried in the Enfidaville War Cemetery in Tunisia. Albert's mother lived at Milton Regis.

Private 6288033 George Frederick **Bartlett** (26) lived with his parents, George and Harriett Bartlett, in Hastingleigh. He was killed between 23 and 24 October 1943 and is commemorated on the Athens Memorial.

Private 6288183 Joseph John **Barton** (22) was killed on 22 November 1943 serving with the regiment's 5th Battalion. He was a single man who lived with his parents, Albert and Ellen Frances Barton in Lyminge. He is buried in the Sangro River War Cemetery, in Italy.

Private 6288340 Edward **Beard** (21) was serving with the 5th Battalion, The Buffs, (Royal East Kent Regiment) at the time of his death on 9 April 1943. He is buried in the Beja War Cemetery in Tunisia. He lived with his parents, James and May Eva Beard, at Beaver.

Lance Sergeant 6285942 James Robert **Bligh** (24) served with the 5th Battalion, The Buffs (Royal East Kent Regiment). He died on 26 April 1943 and is buried in the Medjez-el-Bab War Cemetery in Tunisia. His parents, William and Elizabeth Bligh, lived at Upper Stourmouth.

Private 6286151 Jacob Charles **Boxall** (36) was one of the oldest in the battalion. He served with the 1st Battalion, The Buffs (Royal East Kent Regiment) and was killed on 4 April 1943. He is buried in the Sfax War Cemetery in Tunisia. His parents, William and Hilda Boxall, lived at Eastchurch.

Private 6096449 James **Burrough** (28) lived with his parents, Herbert and Florence Burrough, of Whitstable. He was killed between 23 and 24 October 1943 and his name is commemorated on the Athens Memorial.

Sergeant 6297988 Leonard **Burt** (39) was a married man who lived with his wife at Cranbrook. He was killed on 6 January 1943 whilst serving with the 5th Battalion The Buffs (Royal East Kent Regiment) and is commemorated on the Medjez-el-Bab Memorial, Tunisia.

Private 6296064 William Henry **Burton** (33) was serving with the 5th Battalion, The Buffs (Royal East Kent Regiment) when he was killed on 18 November 1943. He is buried in the Minturno War Cemetery in Italy. William's parents lived in Milton Regis.

Private 6300487 Robert William **Butcher** was only 19 years of age when his young life came to a tragic end on 19 June 1943. He is buried in the Bone War Cemetery in Algeria. His parents, Robert and Edith Butcher, lived in Staple.

Private 6096453 Ernest Edward **Castle** (28) was a married man who lived with his wife, Lily, at Sutton Valence. He was killed between 23 and 24 October 1943 and is commemorated on the Athens Memorial.

Sergeant 6286309 Reginald Frank **Champs** (21) was serving with the 5th Battalion, The Buffs (Royal East Kent Regiment) when he died on 30 January 1943. He is buried in the Massicault War Cemetery in Tunisia. He lived with his wife, Phyllis Queenie Anne Champs, in Ramsgate.

Lance Corporal 6288418 Frederick Thomas Walter **Coleman** (25) lived with his parents, Robert and Emma Jane Coleman at Willesborough, Ashford. He was killed between 16 and 17 November 1943 and is buried in the Leros War Cemetery.

Private 6287435 Arthur Robert **Cooper** (28) was killed between 13 and 14 November 1943. He is buried in the Leros War Cemetery. He lived with his parents Robert and Ann Cooper in Littlebourne.

Private 6287227 Stanley Alfred **Cooper** (24) lived with his parents at Littlebourne. He was killed between 23 and 24 October 1943. His name is commemorated on the Athens Memorial in Greece.

Private 6289177 Thomas William **Daffurn** (23) was a single man who lived with his parents at Swanley. When he was killed on 23 April 1943, he was serving with the regiment's 5th Battalion. He is buried in the Medjez-el-Bab War Cemetery, in Tunisia.

Private 6292397 George William **Dartnell** (30) was a single man who lived with his parents at Strood in Kent. He was killed in action between 14 and 16 November 1943, and is buried in the Leros War Cemetery in Greece.

Private 6289689 Eric Booth **Dawson** (25), was another who was serving with the 5th Battalion at the time of his death on 9 April 1943. He had lived at home with his parents, Tom and Mary-Ann Dawson, and is buried in the Medjez-el-Bab war cemetery in Tunisia.

Warrant Officer Class II 6286391 Harry Joseph **Day** (33) was a Company Sergeant Major in the 5th Battalion. He was a married man and lived with his wife Eunice Muriel Day at St Michael's, Tenterden. He was killed in action on 8 December 1943 and is buried in the Ancona War Cemetery in Italy.

Lieutenant 281159 Frank Thomas **Downe** (27) was killed in action on 2 December 1943. He is buried in the Bone War Cemetery, at Annaba, Algeria. His parents, Thomas and Alice Downe lived at Faversham.

Private 6288436 Lewis David **Fagg** (25) lived with his parents at Alkham. He was killed between 23 and 24 October 1943. His name is commemorated on the Athens Memorial.

Corporal 6289845 Stanley Norman **Fitzsimons** (24) was serving with the 5th Battalion, The Buffs (Royal East Kent Regiment) when he was killed on 9 October 1943. He is buried in the Sangro River War Cemetery in Italy. His wife, Winifred Hilda Fitzsimons, lived at Gravesend.

Private 6288323 Frank Henry **Foreman** (36) was a married man who lived with his wife, Minnie, at Whitstable. He was killed on 23 October, has no known grave, and his name is commemorated on the Athens Memorial.

Corporal 6284597 John Edward **Fosbraey** (30) was a married man who lived with his wife, Rose, in Sittingbourne. He was killed between 13 and 14 November 1943 and is buried in the Leros War Cemetery.

Corporal 6289649 John Hedley **Gwyther** (24) was serving with the 5th Battalion, The Buffs (Royal East Kent Regiment) at the time of his death on 22 February 1943. He has no known grave but his name is commemorated on the Medjez-el-Bab Memorial, Tunisia. His parents were from Cudham.

Lance Corporal 6292417 Charles Sidney **Hadlow** (28) was a married man who lived with his wife May Francis Hadlow, at Kemsley. He was killed between 23 and 24 October 1943. His name is commemorated on the Athens Memorial.

Private 6291148 Philip Ethelbert **Hales** (22) was serving with the 1st Battalion, The Buffs (Royal East Kent Regiment) when he was killed on 16 January 1943. He has no known grave and his name is commemorated on the Alamein Memorial. His parents, Ethelbert and Frances Hales, lived in Tenterden.

Corporal 6288454 Thomas Charles **Harber** (25) lived with his parents at Dartford. He was killed between 23 and 24 October 1943, and his name is commemorated on the Athens Memorial.

Lieutenant 184672 Reginald John **Heaton** (22) was at the time of his death on 9 September 1943, attached to 2nd/6th Battalion, The Queen's Royal Regiment (West Surrey). He is buried in the Salerno War Cemetery in Italy. His parents, Captain Arthur Reginald and Clara Daisy Heaton lived at Beckenham.

Private 6295108 Alfred Richard **Heldt** (29) was a married man who lived with his wife in Bromley. He was serving with the 5th Battalion, The Buffs (Royal East Kent Regiment) at the time of his death on 1 August 1943. He has no known grave and his name is commemorated on the Cassino Memorial in Italy.

Private 6286943 Alfred **Hinder** (27) was a married man who lived with his wife, Joan, in Chartham Hatch. He was killed between 23 and 24 October 1943, has no known grave and is commemorated on the Athens Memorial.

Corporal 6286585 Victor Charles **Hollingsbee** (23) was a single man who lived with his parents, Horace and Bertha Hollingsbee. He was killed between 23 and 24 October 1943, has no known grave, and his name is commemorated on the Athens Memorial.

Private 5503064 Frank Robert **Horsnail** (26) was at the time of his death on 9 August 1943, serving with the 5th Battalion, The Buffs (Royal East Kent Regiment). He is buried in the Catania War Cemetery in Sicily. He was a married man who lived with his wife, Alberta Agnes, at Four Oaks.

Sergeant6285931 Harry George **Hughes** was serving with the 1st Battalion, The Buffs, (Royal East Kent Regiment) when he was killed on 29 March 1943. He was a holder of the Military Medal which had been awarded for an individual act of bravery. He is buried in the Sfax War Cemetery in Tunisia. His parents George and Emily Hughes, lived at Acol.

Lieutenant 237874 David John **Lyons** (23) was serving with the 1st Battalion, The Buffs (Royal East Kent Regiment) at the time of his death on 26 March 1943. He is buried in the Sfax War Cemetery in Tunisia. His parents, David John and Janet Parker Lyons, lived at Welling.

Private 6288052 William Frederick Henry **Mantle** (23) was a single man who lived with his parents, Ernest and Annie Mantle in Ramsgate.

Private 6292476 Fred Arthur **Martin**, lived with his parents at Swanscombe. He was killed on 14 November 1943 and is buried in the Leros War Cemetery, Greece.

Private 6299439 Victor Charles **Merritt** (22) lived with his parents, Alfred and Emma Merritt, at Whitstable. He was killed on 23 March 1943 and is commemorated on the Medjez-el-Bab Memorial in Tunisia.

Private 6291176 Albert John **Morley** (30) was a married man from Welling where he had lived with his wife, Catherine. He was killed on 8 April 1943 whilst serving with the 5th Battalion, The Buffs (Royal East Kent Regiment) and is buried in the Oued Zarga War Cemetery in Tunisia.

Private 6287758 Horace William **Newby** (28) lived his parents, Horace and Augusta Newby, in Ramsgate. Horace was killed between 13 and 16 November 1943 and he is buried in the Leros War Cemetery in Greece.

Private 629915 John **Newman** (19) was serving with the 5th Battalion, The Buffs (Royal East Kent Regiment) when he died on 8 April 1943. He is buried in the Oued Zarga War Cemetery in Tunisia. He lived with his parents in Biggin Hill.

Private 6299688 James Robert **Ponsford** (18) years of age was a member of 5th Battalion, The Buffs (Royal East Kent Regiment) when he was killed on 5 October

1943. He is buried in Sangro River War Cemetery. His parents Alfred and Edith Ponsford, lived at Gillingham.

Private 6292489 Ernest Elijah **Porter** (28) was a married man from Dartford, where he lived with his wife, Rosie Eleanor. He was serving with the 5th Battalion, The Buffs (Royal East Kent Regiment) at the time of his death on 8 April 1943, and he is buried in the Med-el-Bab War Cemetery in Tunisia.

Corporal 6289176 Royston Robert **Poynter** (24) was serving with the regiment's 5th Battalion at the time of his death on 9 April 1943. He is buried in the Beja War Cemetery in Tunisia. Beja is a market town situated about 100 kilometres west of Tunis.

Lieutenant 245295 Norman Philip **Reeves** (20) was married and lived with his wife, Letitia Gwendoline at Bickley. He was killed on 13 November 1943 and is buried in the Leros War Cemetery in Greece.

Private 6292016 Dennis Gordon **Richardson** (21) was serving with the 5th Battalion, The Buffs (Royal East Kent Regiment) at the time of his death on 27 April 1943. He is buried in the Oued Zarga War Cemetery in Tunisia. He lived with his parents, David and Mabel Richardson, in Herne Bay.

Private 14284946 Wesley John Charles **Saker** (19) was killed in action on 27 August 1943, whilst serving with the regiment's 5th Battalion. He was a single man who lived with his parents Josiah and Harriet. He is buried in the Florence War Cemetery.

Lance Sergeant 6290374 Reginald William **Santer** (26) was serving with the 5th Battalion, The Buffs (Royal East Kent Regiment) when he was killed on 8 October 1943. He is buried in the Moro River Canadian War Cemetery in Italy. He was married and lived with his wife, Joyce Ina, at Whitfield.

Lance Sergeant 6289963 Gordon Charles George **Sewell** (26) was serving with the 5th Battalion, The Buffs (Royal East Kent Regiment) at the time of his death on 26 April 1943. He is buried in the Oued Zarga War Cemetery, Tunisia. His parents, Hedrick and Edith, were from Queenborough.

Private 6282898 Ernest Henry **Smith** (36) was a married man from Sandwich. He was killed between 23 and 24 October 1943. His name is commemorated on the Athens Memorial.

Private 14284958 George Walter **Steele** (20) lived with his parents, Lionel and Rosetta in Bromley. He was serving with the 5th Battalion when he was killed on 9 October 1943, and is buried in the Sangro River War Cemetery in Italy.

Private 6283458 George William **Strand** (35) lived with his wife Mabel, in Herne Bay. He died between 23/24 October 1943 and is commemorated on the Athens Memorial.

Private 6288274 Victor Suitters **Taylor** (24) was the son of Harry and May Taylor of Biddenden. He died on 3 January 1943 and is buried in the Imtarfa Military Cemetery in Malta.

Private 6288515 Norman **Thomas** (25) and a single man who lived with his parents, Edley and Mary Ellen Thomas, at Hersden, Kent. He was killed between 23 and 24 October 1943 and is commemorated on the Athens Memorial.

Athens Memorial.

Private 6294760 Frederick **Thomsitt** was serving with the 5th Battalion, The Buffs (Royal East Kent Regiment) at the time of his death on 27 April 1943, and he is buried in the Oued Zarga War Cemetery in Tunisia. His parents, Frederick and Elizabeth Thomsitt, lived at Dartford.

Private 14527623 Charles **Turner** served with the regiment's 5th Battalion and was killed in action on 3 November 1943. He lived with his parents in Belvedere, Kent. His final resting place is at the Sangro River War Cemetery in Italy.

Sergeant 6288524 John Raymond **Welburn** (25) was a single man who lived with his parents, George and Fanny Welburn, in Worth. He was killed on 14 November 1943 and is buried in the Leros War Cemetery in Greece.

Private 6290311 Tommy **White** (25) was killed on 7 October 1943. He is buried in the Bari War Cemetery in Italy. His parents were Harry and Alice White.

Private 628825 Fred William **Whorlow** (25) lived with his parents, Frederick and Sarah Whorlow, in Whitstable. He was killed on 17 November 1943 and is buried in Leros War Cemetery.

Private 6289985 Percy Clement **Williams** (26) was from Lydd in Kent. At the time of his death on 9 April 1943, he was serving with the regiment's 5th Battalion. He is buried in the Oued Zarga War Cemetery in Tunisia.

Warrant Officer Class II or Company Sergeant Major, Oliver **Wood** (29) was killed on 9 April 1943. He is buried in the Heliopolis War Cemetery in Egypt. His wife, Olive Laurel, lived at Faversham.

Alamein Memorial Egypt.

Private 6288531 Percy Thomas **Woodward**, (24) was a single man who lived with his parents, Thomas and Edith Woodward, in Ramsgate. At the time of his death on 19 January 1943 he was serving with the regiment's 1st Battalion. He has no known grave and his name is commemorated on the Alamein Memorial in Egypt.

Lance Sergeant 6290625 Edwin Alfred **Wyborn** (26) was serving with the 5th Battalion, The Buffs (Royal East Kent Regiment) at the time of his death on 15 April 1943. He is buried in the Medjez-el-Bab War Cemetery in Tunisia. He was a married man, who lived with his wife Vera Emily Mary, in Ramsgate,. He had previously been Mentioned in Despatches for his bravery.

Sunday, 17 January 1943 saw the death of Margate soldier, Private Cyril Martin Bishop, aged 21, the third son of Mr and Mrs Bishop of Victoria Road, Margate. Private Bishop, 5th Battalion, The Buffs (Royal East Kent Regiment), had just begun a 14-day period of leave. He was staying in London with a friend, 21-year-old Gunner 6296973 Harry Derry of the 98th Anti-Tank Regiment, Royal Artillery, when both men were killed as the result of an air raid. Private Bishop was killed instantly whilst Gunner Derry died the following day of his wounds in hospital.

Before the war Private Bishop had worked for a Margate printing company. Two of his brothers and a step-brother were all in the Army, whilst another had joined the 4th (Thanet) Cadet Battalion, The Buffs (Royal East Kent Regiment). His funeral took place at Margate Cemetery on 22 January.

On Wednesday, 3 February 1943 Mrs Elizabeth Ann Powell of 42 Helena Avenue, Margate received the news that her son, 28-year-old Sergeant 1158838 George Thomas Kennington, of the Royal Air Force Volunteer Reserve, had officially been reported as missing in action, after the aircraft in which he was serving as a gunner, with 218 (Gold Coast) Squadron, had failed to return from a night raid over enemy territory.

Sergeant Kennington had enlisted in the RAFVR in June 1940 and after completing his basic training, went on to complete more than forty operational missions in a year, including some on cities such as Cologne in Germany and Turin in Italy.

He has no known grave and his name is commemorated on the Runnymede Memorial, in Surrey. At the time of his death, 218 Squadron were based at RAF Downham Market and the Gold Coast connection to their Squadron name was to do with the Governor of the Gold Coast, modern day Ghana, and so its people officially adopted the squadron.

Before the war Sergeant Kennington had been employed as a baker's roundsman. He was a married man with three children. His father Mr A. Kennington had served as a Private (G/5422) with the 1st Battalion, The Buffs (East Kent Regiment) during the First World War and was killed on 8 June 1917 aged 27, and is buried in the Philosophe British Cemetery, Mazingarbe, in the Pas de Calais.

It was 24 March 1943 when aircraft from the Luftwaffe targeted Ashford for one of their raids. It was a very short affair, the time that it takes to boil an egg, just three minutes, but in that short space of time the Primary School in Victory Road suffered a direct hit as did the town's Southern Railway works. There were no deaths or injuries sustained at the school as the staff and young children were safely in their shelter. Sadly, those at work inside the Southern Railway works were not all so lucky. Nine of the men working there were killed along with two women, one of whom was a fire watcher.

Damage, some of it severe, was caused to several of the streets, where thirty-eight more people were killed.

The attacking aircraft were Focke-Wulf Fw 190s, one of which was shot down in the attack by an anti-aircraft battery. The pilot was Oberleutnant Paul Keller, whose aircraft was hit just as it was about to drop a bomb, causing it to explode. Keller's body was discovered in fields between Barrow Hill Terrace and St Mary's Primary School. His body was laid to rest at Hawkinge Cemetery.

The Commonwealth War Graves Commission website records the names and addresses of 47 people from Ashford who were killed on 24 March 1943, and a further two who died of their wounds the following day.

Esther **Ades** (60), 15 Hardinge Road, Ashford.

Mary **Ades** (33) 17 Hardinge Road, Ashford.

Victor John **Ades** (3) 17 Hardinge Road, Ashford.

William **Allen** (65) 61 Beaver Lane, Ashford, died at Godinton Road, Ashford.

Henry **Andrews** (54) 2 Kither Road, Ashford, killed at the Southern Railway Works, Ashford.

George Thomas **Baber** (68) 50 Francis Road, Ashford, Died at Stanhays Agricultural Engineering Works, Godinton Road, Ashford.

Gerald **Barton** (21) 98 The Street, Willesborough, Ashford. He was injured at Stanhays Agricultural Engineering Works, Godinton Road, Ashford, and died at Ashford Hospital the same day. He was also a despatch rider for the Home Guard.

Seaman **Beale** (40) 191 New Town, Ashford, died at the Southern Railway Works, Ashford.

John **Brown** (53) 5 Marlowe Road, Ashford, died at the Southern Railway Works, Ashford.

Frederick **Brown** (14) 11 Provident Place, Ashford. He was injured at Stanhays Agricultural Engineering Works on 24 March 1943, and died of his injuries at Ashford Hospital, the following day.

Clement **Corke** (43) 18 Church Road, Willesborough, Ashford was a member of the Home Guard, and killed at the Southern Railway Works, Ashford.

Eleanor Barbara **Court** (30) 'Woodlands' Bislington, Ashford was killed at the Southern Railway Works, Ashford.

Frederick Hubert **Fox** (59) 66 Cudworth Road, South Willesborough, Ashford was killed at the Southern Railway Works, Ashford.

William Frederick **Hawkins** (49) 'Roseleigh' Westenhanger, Hythe, died at Ashford Hospital. He was a company sergeant major in the Home Guard.

Doris Lillian **Heddle** (23) Heddles Stores, 21A New Rents, Ashford.

Jessie **Hogben** (33) Repton Cottages, Chart Road, Ashford. She was killed whilst visiting 11 Hardinge Road, Ashford, with her daughter Mary.

Mary Rose **Hogben** (5) Repton Cottages, Chart Road, Ashford. She was killed whilst visiting 11 Hardinge Road, Ashford, with her mother Jessie.

Frederick Charles **Holness** (23) 8 Council Houses, Smarden, Ashford, died at Stanhays Agricultural Engineering Works, Godinton Road, Ashford.

Gwendoline **Hutchings** (16) 1 Mead Road, South Willesborough, Ashford, died at Stanhays Agricultural Engineering Works, Godinton Road, Ashford.

John Ambrose **Johnson**, (37) 8 East Hill, Ashford was injured at Stanhays Agricultural Engineering Works, and died later the same day at Ashford Hospital. He was also a member of the Home Guard.

Clara **Jones** (65) 10 Star Road, Ashford.

Letitia **King** (71) 13 Hardinge Road, Ashford.

Peter **King** (74) 13 Hardinge Road, Ashford.

Ada Maria **Laker** (88) 10 Star Road, Ashford.

Margaret Isabel Bella **Law** (17) 2 Milton Road, Ashford, was killed at Stanhays Agricultural Engineering Works, Godinton Road, Ashford.

Leonard Edward **Lawrence** (31) 1 Denbigh Place, Torrington Road, Ashford, died at Snashalls, Kent Avenue, Ashford. I believe this actually refers to Mr and Mrs Snashall, of 85 Kent Avenue, Ashford. He was also a member of the Home Guard.

John Alfred **Lunn** (49) Musgrove, Kingsnorth, Kent, injured at Stanhays Agricultural Engineering Works, and died at Ashford Hospital later the same day.

Albert Samuel **Milton** (21) 21 Dane Road, Ramsgate, died at Stanhays Agricultural Engineering Works, Godinton Road.

Clara Elizabeth **Morris** (19) 12 Godinton Road, Ashford, initially injured in the attack, but died later the same day at Ashford Hospital.

Ernest John **Morris** (18) 69 Francis Road, Ashford, a member of the Home Guard who was killed at the Southern Railway Works, Ashford.

John **Newington** (14) 135 Favershan Road, Kennington, injured at Stanhays Agricultural Engineering Works, but died later the same day at Ashford Hospital.

Ernest **Powell** (58) 'Oakcrest' Charing Heath, Ashford, killed at Haywards Garage, New Street, Ashford.

Stephen **Rand** (85) 4 Station House, Godinton Road, Ashford, died of his injuries the day after the attack in Ashford Hospital.

Lydia Charlotte **Roberts** (41) 10 Aylesford Green, Willesborough, Ashford, died at the Southern Railway Works, Ashford.

Lewis **Russell** (79), 10 Hardinge Road, Ashford.

Robert Frank **Salmons** (54) 263 New Town, Ashford, killed at the Southern Railway Works, Ashford.

Clarissa Daisy **Sexton** (54) 12 Star Road, Ashford.

George William **Snashall** (73) 85 Kent Avenue, Ashford.

Mary Selina **Snashall** (62) 85 Kent Avenue, Ashford.

Rowland Owen George **Snashall** (44) 85 Kent Avenue, Ashford.

Edward Cyril **Soper** (39) 136 Beaver Road, Ashford, killed at Stanhays Agricultural Engineering Works, Godinton Road, Ashford.

Charles William **Stevens** (52) 2 Forge Lane, Ashford, died at Stanhays Agricultural Engineering Works.

Anthony John **Stone** (18) Hill View, Brabourne, Ashford, injured at Haywards Garage and died later the same day at Ashford Hospital.

Cicely Ethel **Tolhurst** (33) 42 Kent Avenue, Ashford, died at Snashall Bakery, Kent Avenue.

Edward Joseph **Turner** (47) 38 Norfolk Road, Tonbridge, died at Ashford Hospital.

Joseph Stanley **Tye** (18) Police Station, Lydd, died in New Street, Ashford.

Catherine **Walker** (84) 10 Birling Road, Ashford, died in Star Road, Ashford.

Arthur **Ward** (41) 20 Providence Street, Ashford, initially injured at the Southern Railway Works, Ashford and died later the same day at Ashford Hospital.

Sydney **Wiles** (59) 33 Barden Road, Tonbridge, died at Ashford Hospital.

It was interesting to note the number of people who were killed at both the Southern Railway Works, nine outright and two who were injured there and died of the injuries later that day in hospital, and eleven at the Stanhays Agricultural Engineering Works. There were also six members of the Home Guard and a fire watcher who were killed in the incident, four of whom died as a result of their presence at the Southern Railway Works.

In a global sense the war definitely turned in favour of the Allied forces from 1943 onwards. There was a notable change in the fortunes of the two sides, one from which Germany and Japan never really recovered from. It began on the very first day of the year when the 1st Panzer Division, an elite armoured division of the

German Army, was forced to withdraw from the Terek River, in southern Russia, to avoid being surrounded and cut off by advancing Soviet forces. The division had been formed in 1935 and had been involved in the pre-war invasions of Austria and Czechoslovakia, the invasions of Poland and Belgium, and had been on the Eastern Front since 1941.

The following day a combined American and Australian force captured Buna in Papua New Guinea from the Japanese Army.

Soviet forces began an offensive to retake Stalingrad on 10 January 1943.

The ten-day conference of Allied leaders in Casablanca began on 14 January where, besides other matters, they openly discussed both the invasions of Sicily and the eventual invasion of German-occupied Europe. This highlights the strong position which the Allies knew they are in, a position they wished to fully galvanise to bring the war to an end and impose a crushing defeat on both Germany and Japan, along with their Axis partners. The conference came to an end on 24 January and the Allies informed Germany that they wanted her unconditional surrender.

As a result of Hitler's refusal to surrender unconditionally at that time, between 24 January 1943 and by the end of 1947, when official figures for war-related deaths stopped, a further 383,554 British and Commonwealth servicemen and women, died. On top of this number a further 16,256 British civilians also died. These figures include approximately 4,200 service personnel from Kent along with 265 civilians from the county. These figures do not of course include those casualties from France, Belgium, America, Germany and any of the other Axis nations.

Whilst the Casablanca conference was taking place, Britain began an offensive to capture the oil-rich area of Tripoli. Iraq belatedly declared war on Germany and her Axis powers and the RAF carried out a two-night bombing raid on Berlin. Soviet forces recaptured the last airfield at Stalingrad, preventing the Luftwaffe from delivering much needed supplies of food, equipment and ammunition to her ground troops.

The last day of January 1943 made Germany's situation much worse. Despite Hitler's order to the man in charge of the German Sixth Army, Generalfeldmarschall Friedrich Paulus, to fight to the last man at Stalingrad, he surrendered. He knew that his position was untenable and to continue the fight against a rejuvenated Soviet Army would only result in the deaths of thousands more of his men. Despite informing Hitler that his men were out of food and ammunition and some 18,000 of his men required immediate medical attention, he was told on two occasions to hold Stalingrad to the death. In a somewhat warped final 'communication' between the two men Hitler promoted Paulus to the rank of General Field Marshal, not for his dedication to duty and good work, but to prevent his surrender, saying to senior aides that there had never been an occasion when an officer of such high rank in either the Prussian or German armies had ever surrendered. He expected Paulus to commit suicide. In Soviet captivity Paulus became a vocal critic of the Nazi regime. He died in East Germany in 1957.

It was clear to see just in the first month of 1943 how the direction of the war had changed so drastically in favour of the Allies, an advantage that they would maintain.

Adrift for ten days

An article in the *Thanet Advertiser* dated Thursday 22 April described the circumstances of the abandonment of the crew of a British merchant ship, who were adrift in an open life boat for ten days before they were finally rescued, after having being left to their fate hundreds of miles from land by the commander of a German submarine.

One of the crew was Bombardier Eric Glanfield of the Maritime Regiment, Royal Artillery. Before the outbreak of the war he had been a member of staff at the Margate corporation borough treasurer's department. Bombardier Glanfield was on watch on the ship's bridge when the first torpedo struck bringing her to a standstill. Soon afterwards orders were given to abandon ship, and within twenty minutes the life boats were in the water. They were still alongside the merchant ship, waiting for the last of the men to climb in, when the second torpedo struck just aft of the boat deck and only about 12 yards away from the boat that Bombardier Glanfield was in with some of his comrades, on the starboard side of the vessel. He was standing by the falls in the stern of the boat when there was a hiss and a lurid red flash. He later told a reporter:

I've no distinct recollection of the next few seconds, but evidently I let go my fall and ducked. I heard nothing but felt the lifeboat lurch high and thought it was smashed, but it wasn't, although it might easily have done so as it dropped back down to the water.

Despite everything, there was only one casualty, a seaman in the bow of the boat who was hit by a piece of shrapnel and died later that day.

A few minutes after the second torpedo had done its job the crew in the lifeboats had pulled safely away from their stricken vessel, just before the stern of the ship slid below the waves in a vertical position. The life boats hadn't got far when without any warning the German submarine that had just sent their ship to the bottom of the sea, broke the surface and sat menacingly in their path. The commander of the ship appeared and asked a few general questions before moving off and once again disappearing beneath the waves. He did not offer any assistance or advice as to which direction they should take, but much to the relief of the men, neither did he do them any harm. The worry of what they should do next was balanced by the feeling of relief that they were still alive.

When dawn came the following morning the crew managed somehow to work out that they were some 750 miles from the nearest land, slightly north of the Equator. One of the four boats was badly damaged, so the men and supplies from that boat were shared out amongst the remaining three boats. Although one of the life boats had an emergency portable radio set stored on board, it had been completely soaked before it had been noticed, so now they had no way of calling for help. The ten days at sea not knowing whether they were going to survive were the worst of Bombardier Glanfield's young life. To be so close to hungry man-eating sharks was not a pleasant experience. On the first night, one of the three remaining life boats became separated from the other two.

A ship was sighted on the horizon on the afternoon of the tenth day, and the boats were able to place smoke distress signals over the side of their small craft. The ship altered its course and headed straight towards them while they prayed it wasn't an enemy vessel that might think it easier just to blow them out of the water and in doing so, eradicate any evidence of the German commander's decision not to provide any assistance to the stricken men.

By four o'clock that evening twenty-one of the abandoned crew were safely on board the rescue vessel, but none of them ate any food that evening, instead they just drank copious amounts of water and tea, whilst some indulged in a cigarette or two. They were eventually landed at Rio de Janeiro on 22 December 1942, where they would spend the next two months. They also discovered that their other life boat had already been picked up and that the crew were all safe and well in another part of Brazil.

Eric Glanfield eventually made it back to Margate and appears to have survived the rest of the war.

It was announced in the pages of a local newspaper dated Tuesday 4 May that Pilot Officer William Edward Lanchberry, the eldest son of Mr and Mrs Lanchberry of 10 Barnes Avenue, Margate, and a member of the Royal Air Force, and serving with No.150 Squadron, had been awarded the Distinguished Flying Medal. He took part in the first of the 1,000 bomber raids on Cologne, and had been involved in other operations over Germany, Italy and Tunisia.

The official citation for his award stated that he had always shown great devotion to duty, coolness and courage, combined with a fine fighting spirit. At the time of the award he was 28 years old and an old boy of Woodford House School Birchington. In 1938 he acquired a job working for the government of Sudan, before returning to England in April 1940.

Pilot Officer Lanchberry's younger brother Sergeant Pilot Roe Lanchberry, the pilot of a Lockheed Hudson aircraft of Coastal Command, was reported missing in January 1942. A check on the Commonwealth War Graves Commission website does not have a record for the death of either brother during the course of the war.

In June 1943 William Verrals and Victor Taylor, who had previously served as Margate policemen and joined the RAF in 1941, gained their pilots wings and were commissioned into the South African Air Force. Others who volunteered at the same time were Bernard Holman who went on to become a pilot-officer observer on operations. Jack Cornhill and Maurice Turner became sergeant bomb-aimers. Frank Bremner qualified as a pilot, Len Adlington was a sergeant pilot instructor in America and Frank Corke joined the RAF for air crew duties, shortly after hearing that his brother who had previously enlisted in the RAF had become a prisoner of war and was being held in Germany.

That month also saw the announcement that Mrs Norah Jackson, aged 45, of George Vth Avenue, Margate and a leading aircraftwoman, has been mentioned in despatches for her devotion to duty while serving as a cook in the Women's Auxiliary Air Force. The daughter of Mr and Mrs L. Woodward, of 8 Oxford Street, Margate, during the year leading up to her award, she served as a rigger as well as becoming a lance corporal whilst stationed at Westgate. In 1942 her husband, Jack, was killed during an air raid on RAF Manston, but despite this personal and emotional setback she continued with her role in the WAAF.

She was a local girl born in Margate where she attended St John's School. She married in 1924 and they had a son, who in June 1943 was a member of the Margate Sea Cadet Corps. Mr Jackson had served in the RAF during the First World War, and at the time of his death was the Thanet's section secretary to the Comrades of the Royal Air Force Association, to which he had belonged since its formation in 1935. Before taking a job with the Air Ministry, he was the manager of the Albert Garage at Westgate.

Mrs Jackson had two brothers serving in the armed forces. One, Leading Aircraftman Henry Woodward, had been in the RAF since 1941, and after completing his basic training was sent out to the Middle East. Before enlisting he worked for a photography company in Margate, skills which he utilized in the RAF, where he carried out similar work. The other brother, Harold Woodward, aged 35, joined the Army in March 1943. It appears that Mrs Jackson and her two brothers all survived the war.

Monday 27 July saw a case brought before the Cinque Ports police court, which was of a despicable nature. George Francis Goodman (28) who lived in Prestedge Avenue, Ramsgate, Kent, was a serving soldier in the Coldstream Guards. He, along with his wife, Jean Mary Dorothy Goodman, and another young woman, 20-year-old Vera Mary Brett of Ashcombe Road, Wimbledon, were charged with the large-scale thefts of furniture and household items from either bombed-out buildings or houses which had been left unoccupied as a result of the war.

They faced four charges, two of which were under the Defence Regulations Act, and directly related to acts of looting from insecure, bomb damaged properties. The other two charges were thefts.

The first of the thefts took place in April 1943 at the Southcourt Nursing Home, in Swinburne Avenue, Broadstairs, a property owned by a Miss Florence Elizabeth Widdop. Guardsman Goodman allegedly stole four towels from the premises, which had a value of 12s. The other theft involved the theft of six black-out curtains, a dustpan, a screwdriver, a kitchen clock, a fly sprayer, two boot brushes, a gardening trowel, a small gardening fork, a bar of soap, and an enamel jug, the total value of the items being £7 10s.

The two women were charged with breaking and entering the property of Mr John Attwood, Tillingbourne, St George's Road, Broadstairs, and stealing carpets, linen, crockery and other items, valued at £130.

Councillor B.J. Pearson, an estate agent of the High Street, Broadstairs, told the Court that he was the agent for Southcourt Nursing Home as the owner, Miss Widdop, was now living in Sussex. In April that year, the premises were occupied on a part furnished basis. Councillor Pearson identified the towels as belonging to Miss Widdop.

Leonard Smith, of Westover Road, St Peters, was a War Reserve police constable, and the caretaker of the Forelands property owned by Mr Royds. He told the court that the property was empty except for a few black-out curtains and some items from the kitchen. He visited the property on 19 June on one of his regular visits just to make sure everything was as it should be, and to open the windows to let in some fresh air, and must have omitted to have closed the toilet window on the ground floor. He further told the court that on 28 June the police showed him some articles which he identified as belonging to Mr Royds.

Detective Constables Self and Oram went to Goodman's home at 46 Prestedge Avenue, Ramsgate on 23 June, to execute a search warrant. As a result of what was discovered at the premises Detective Constable Self arrested Goodman. When interviewed later that same day he admitted stealing all of the articles that had been mentioned at Southcourt and Forelands. He explained how the windows at Southcourt had been smashed by a bomb blast, whilst at Forelands he entered the premises via an open window at the rear of the property. In his statement he added:

'I have had no money to start off married life with. I could not borrow any. My wife had a baby and the woman with whom we were staying was going to have a baby, so my wife and I decided to build up a home of our own. That's why I took the things and I have not sold any of them. They are all at home.'

Even during a time of war, the temptation to unlawfully possess property and belongings that did not belong to them was simply too strong a desire for some people.

News was received by Mrs M.L. Walker of 133 Canterbury Road, Margate, at the beginning of August that must have been bitter sweet for her. First she heard that her son, 31-year-old Henry Frederick Walker, a Petty Officer in the Royal Navy had been reported missing due to the presumed loss of the submarine, HMS *Turbulent*. No sooner had Mrs Larkins been informed of this than she was told that he had been awarded the Distinguished Service Medal, whilst not knowing if he was alive or dead.

His was one of eleven similar medals awarded to members of the submarine's crew. The citation for his award included, 'for bravery and devotion to duty in many highly successful war patrols in the *Turbulent*. Always cool in the face of the enemy, at one period he carried out not only his own duties but those of the torpedo gunner's mate, with outstanding skill and success.'

Commander J.W. Linton, captain of the *Turbulent*, was awarded the Victoria Cross, three officers were awarded the Distinguished Service Order, and eight of the crew were mentioned in despatches.

Petty Officer Walker had also been mentioned in despatches in December 1942, for displaying outstanding skill and zeal while serving on the submarine during her first four patrols in the Mediterranean, when she was responsible for the sinking of eight enemy vessels. She also attacked and damaged a further six ships.

The *Turbulent* was also involved in controversy when she attacked and damaged the Italian cargo ship, the *Nino Bixio*, named after a nineteenth century Italian soldier and politician. The attack took place on 17 August 1941 and resulted in the deaths of 336 British and Allied prisoners of war, who were on board at the time being transported from Benghazi in Libya to Brindisi in Italy.

HMS Turbulent.

It is believed that HMS *Turbulent* was lost on 12 March 1943, sunk either by a Junkers Ju-88 aircraft, an Italian torpedo boat named the *Ardito*, or that it struck a mine whilst preparing to attack an enemy convoy out of Naples. Despite the above date, the deaths of the crew members, have officially been recorded as being 23 March 1943. This is the date that the *Turbulent* was due back from her patrol, from which she never returned.

In August 1943 it was announced that Sergeant Albert Thomas Larkins of the Royal Air Force, serving with No.10 Squadron, has been awarded the Distinguished Flying Medal. He was the son of Mr and Mrs A.L. Larkins of 18 Osborne Terrace, Margate. He enlisted in the RAF in 1941 and became an air gunner and had taken part in numerous operational sorties. The aircraft which he flew had been damaged on many occasions by the machine-gun fire of enemy aircraft, flak and anti-aircraft guns, which also resulted in two of his colleagues being injured. Despite this he had continued to do his job with relentless enthusiasm and efficiency, consistently displaying gallantry of the highest order as well as an unrivalled devotion to duty.

In September 1943 an article appeared in a local newspaper which highlighted the stoic approach and determined attitude of British families towards the war. The Fish family – mother, father, son and daughter – of 2 Claremont Cottages, Upper Drumpton Park Road, Ramsgate, were certainly committed to the cause. Father, son and daughter were all serving in the forces, whilst the mother had been a member of the WRNS during the First World War.

Mr Albert Fish was an aircraftman in the RAF, joining in September 1942, and attached to the police at the camp where he was stationed in Scotland. Prior to enlisting he was a pavier for the Ramsgate Corporation. Prior to that, and in the immediate aftermath of the First World War, he was employed in building aerodromes.

Albert's only son, Albert Victor Fish, was an air mechanic in the RAF. In September 1943, he had just turned 20 years of age. From just after his eighteenth birthday he had been serving with the Fleet Air Arm. Prior to enlisting he was employed by

Messrs. Howard & Sons, cycle dealers in Ramsgate, and before starting with the Fleet Air Arm, he served as a member of the Ramsgate Home Guard.

Daughter Rose, a year older than her brother, followed in her mother's footsteps and became a member of the WRNS in March 1941, after having been in domestic service in Devonshire. In September 1943, Rose was an officer's steward, stationed somewhere in the north of England.

Mr and Mrs Tompkins had been officially informed that their 24-year-old son, Private 6289023 George Frederick Tompkins, who had been serving with the 5th Battalion, The Buffs (Royal East Kent Regiment) was on his way home as a repatriated prisoner. This suggests that he had been wounded, as it would be unlikely that the Germans would have returned him to England knowing that he was a fit and healthy young man, who would then more than likely be sent back to fight against them again. Sadly, Private Tompkins died during the voyage back on 21 October 1943 and was buried in sea. He had joined the Buffs in the early part of 1940 and was sent out to France in April of that year. He was captured by the Germans during the British Expeditionary Force's retreat at Dunkirk. His name is commemorated on the Dunkirk Memorial.

Mr and Mrs Albert and May Pitcher, the parents of Leonard Valentine Pitcher, of 67 Winstanley Crescent, Ramsgate, had received news from their daughter-in-law and Leonard's wife, Kathleen Pitcher, that he had died whilst having his wounds treated in a North African hospital. He had initially been severely wounded in the legs and chest during fighting in Italy. He was buried in the Bone War Cemetery in Annaba, Algeria.

He had married Miss Kathleen Cosgrove in 1936 and they had a son, who was seven years of age at the time of his father's death. Before the war Leonard had been employed by Mr E. Pettitt, who ran a butcher's shop in the High Street, Ramsgate. He enlisted in June 1940 as Private 5389571 in the 7th Battalion, Oxfordshire and Buckinghamshire Light Infantry. After finishing his basic training, he was sent out to Persia in August 1942, and later fought with the British Eighth Army in Tunisia.

Sergeant Thomas Huckstep of the Royal Artillery had some interesting stories to tell a reporter from one of Thanet's local newspapers in November 1943, when he was home on leave in Margate. He had served in the Middle East for three years from 1940, in such places as Syria, Cyprus and throughout the victorious Allied advance from El Alamein to Tunisia, and in Sicily as well. He had many interesting stories to pass on about the bravery, and determination of the British and Indian soldiers. Sergeant Huckstep also commented on how well equipped the men of the British Army were, and how good was the support from the RAF.

He had met General Montgomery, who showered him and his colleagues with a supply of cigarettes, and he had also bumped in the Prime Minister, Winston Churchill, on the outskirts of Tripoli, but unfortunately, there was no shower of Cuban cigars on that occasion.

He had seen a Royal Artillery sergeant and his battery shoot down six German aircraft, but another one landed right on one of the artillery pieces, killing several of the crew, before exploding and setting fire to the surrounding cornfields. Even though the sergeant was mortally wounded, he stayed at his post and supervised the evacuation of the remaining guns and all of the ammunition, whilst helping to beat out the flames, before then calmly walking unaided to a field dressing station.

On another occasion he witnessed six Indian troops, who were sent to silence a German 88mm artillery piece. They climbed up an exposed rock face, so as to reach the enemy position, killed the German crew and then brought back the captured gun, which taking into account the size of it, was no mean feat, even across level ground.

Sergeant Huckstep paid particular tribute to three men from a light infantry regiment. They performed a deed which in his opinion showed unsurpassable, cold, calculating courage and deliberate self-sacrifice. The men's unit had been held at bay for some considerable time, which resulted in them incurring some heavy casualties from another German 88mm gun. When volunteers were asked for to try and silence the gun, three brave men stepped forward and did just that. They climbed on board a Bren gun carrier and drove full speed at the offending weapon, ramming the gun as hard as they could, and destroying it in the process, but at the cost of their own lives to secure the lives of their comrades. It was bravery of the highest order.

It was another case of the war being a family affair. Sergeant Huckstep's wife, Irene, worked in London as a nurse. His brother William was a petty officer in the Royal Navy, and Irene Huckstep's brother was serving in the Army.

On Friday 26 November Walter and Amelia Hazlewood of 18 Goodwin Road, Ramsgate, Kent, received the sad news that their son RAF Aircraftman 2nd Class 1219747 Arthur Stanley Hazlewood, had died whilst being held captive in a Japanese prisoner of war camp. Mr and Mrs Hazlewood received a telegram from the Air Ministry informing them that information had been received via the International Red Cross. They had been informed in June 1943 that he was a prisoner of the Japanese in Java.

Arthur Hazlewood was 22 years of age at the time of his death, which had actually been some five months earlier on 25 June 1943. Prior to enlisting in the RAF in April 1941, he had worked for Messrs. G. and A. Clarke Ltd, nurserymen. The last time he had been in Ramsgate was in November 1941, when he was home on leave on a 48-hour pass. That was the last time that his parents would see him alive. It would appear that at the time of his capture, Arthur had been stationed at Kalidjati Airfield, north of Bandung on the island of Java, which fell to the Japanese on 1 March 1943, soon after they had successfully invaded. He was more than likely held at one of the camps in Tjimahi, which between May and June 1943 is where the 30,000 Dutch, Australian, British, and American PoWs were held.

Letters received by Mr and Mrs R. Sherred of 72 Boundary Road, Ramsgate, from their 20-year-old son, Corporal Edgar Sherred of the Royal Marines, in December 1943, recounted a lighter side of the war in the central Mediterranean area of Europe.

Edgar had enlisted in the Royal Marines in November 1942 and after basic training he was sent out to North Africa in July 1943. He later moved on to Sicily where he spent a short time in a field hospital due to a mild bout of malaria. The tented accommodation was ideal with the weather being as warm as it was, and the luxury of having his meals served to him whilst he relaxed in his warm, comfortable bed, was what dreams were made of.

'We are seeing the world anyhow,' he wrote from his hospital bed. 'There is plenty of fruit, nuts and wine, and the Italians make almond toffee. We also get quite a bit of chocolate. It is hotter here than in Tripoli, but fortunately there is no sand here.'

Whilst in Sicily, Corporal Sherred saw a large group of Italian prisoners, as many as a hundred, repairing the roads on their own, with not a single British soldier guarding them. The Italians had surrendered to the Allies on 8 September 1943, with most more than happy to do so. In the circumstances the need for guarding their defeated soldiers was not a high priority for the Allies. Whilst he had been in hospital there were one or two who used to work there, keeping the wards clean and tidy, as well as washing crockery and carrying out other odd jobs. For them the war was over and they were happy.

Before the war, Edgar had been a member of the Ramsgate National Fire Service. His elder brother, Ruben, had worked on the local buses for many years before the war, as a conductor, driver and ticket collector for both the East Kent Road Car Company and the Maidstone and District Omnibus Company. He joined the RAF in December 1942 and by December 1943 was stationed in Oxfordshire, where he worked as an RAF policeman.

As 1943 came to a close with the Allies in the ascendancy, the future was looking decidedly brighter than it had done in previous years, there was a glimmer of light at the end of the tunnel and hope had been replaced with a steely determination.

CHAPTER 6

1944 – Hitting Back

Operation Pluto involved the laying of a pipeline across the English Channel, to help provide the much-needed fuel supplies in support of Allied forces fighting their way across Europe in the aftermath of the D-Day landings in Normandy.

Pluto actually stood for 'Pipe Line Underwater Transportation of Oil', although some referred to it as standing for 'Pipe Line Under The Ocean', but as the English Channel is technically a sea and not an ocean, the latter of the two descriptions is actually not factual. The idea of such a proposal had been in consideration since 1941, even though at the time the war had only been going on for a couple of years. The Allied military authorities had known right from the start of the fighting that to win the war, sooner or later they would have to deploy troops into Europe and take the fight direct to the Germans. To be able to sustain such an offensive required fuel and lots of it.

The obvious way of sending oil across the English Channel was in large tankers, but there were obvious issues with this, one of them being the weather. The route, although only 21 miles across at its shortest point, was notorious for sudden and unexpected bouts of inclement weather, as was highlighted with the postponement of the original date set for the the the D-Day landings. The other risk with sending large quantities of fuel across the English Channel in a tanker, was the potential threat from either German submarines or aircraft.

This was a matter which the Allied powers had to effectively address, because without guaranteed constant supplies of oil for tanks, vehicles and aircraft, Allied troops would be stuck along the Normandy coast, which in turn would allow the Germans to bring up reinforcements and stop the invasion of Nazi-occupied Germany, before it even got started.

Operation Pluto came about through the co-operation of the British Armed Forces, civil engineers and the Anglo-Iranian Oil Company. Although the final approval for the operation was given by the Chief of Combined Operations, Admiral Louis Mountbatten, this only happened after a series of high powered meetings between British Government ministers, senior military personnel, and representatives from the oil industry. The idea of laying an oil pipeline and its development was down to Arthur Hartley, a civilian engineer, and the chief engineer of the Anglo-Iranian Oil Company. In 1954 this company was renamed the British Petroleum Company and today it is universally known by the two letters, BP.

The initial idea was for the pipeline to be three inches in diameter, with a lead core, but it quickly became apparent that such a large amount of lead would render the idea prohibitive. After giving the idea more thought, it was decided to go with a pipe of a similar diameter, but to make the core out of flexible steel. The pipe was laid with the help of a conundrum (cone-ended-drum), or what looked like a giant cotton reel, running across the English Channel at two separate locations. One ran from Shanklin on the Isle of Wight for a distance of approximately 75 miles, coming ashore again at Cherbourg in north-west France. The other line ran from Dungeness in Kent to Ambleteuse on the coast of northern France in the Pas-de-Calais.

Even though the D-Day landings in Normandy had begun on 6 June 1944, the first of the oil pipelines – the one from Shanklin on the Isle of Wight – wasn't actually laid until 12 August 1944. The one from Dungeness went live later the same year. At their peak the pipelines were collectively pumping some one million imperial gallons across the English Channel each day, but this was still only a small amount of the overall fuel needs of the Allied push across Europe.

The pipeline that travelled across the English Channel from Dungeness, started out in the nearby Kent town of Romney Marsh before being piped down the coast to its neighbouring town. The actual pumping station at Dungeness which was used to send the oil across the English Channel to its destination in France, was built to resemble an ordinary cottage so as not to draw unwanted attention to its real purpose. The building still exists to this day and is now a bed and breakfast establishment, with many of its guests no doubt oblivious as to the important part it once played in the Allied victory in the Second World War.

Another feather in Kent's cap for the county's involvement in Operation Pluto, was that the first testing of the laying of the oil pipeline, took place across a stretch of the River Medway. Other locations across the country were also used, but the River Medway was the first.

After the war, and with the Allied victory against Germany secured, the oil pipeline was no longer needed, so between September 1946 and October 1949, nearly all of the pipeline was recovered from the floor of the English Channel as salvage.

A Conundrum laying the oil pipeline.

V1 and V2 Rockets

This year would also see the county of Kent bombarded by V1 and V2 rockets. Most were intended for London, but many fell short of their intended target, and when this happened, some fell on towns throughout Kent.

Although only first used by the Nazis on 12 June 1944, just six days after the D-Day landings, their development had begun in the early years of the war, with the first test launch of a V1 rocket in December 1942. If it hadn't been for successful airstrikes by the RAF on locations such as Peenemunde, an island in the Baltic Sea but part of Germany, in August 1943, where the development and production took place, and four months later on launch sites in the Pas de Calais, they would have been used by Germany a lot earlier in the war.

In the following pages are just some of the accounts of V1 and V2 rockets that landed in the county of Kent. This is by no means a comprehensive list of each rocket attack, but an abridged account of the devastating effect that these indiscriminate weapons had on the towns and people of Kent during the second half of 1944 and the early months of 1945.

The V1 rockets were often referred to as 'buzz bombs', 'doodlebugs' or 'flying bombs' by the British public, the first of which landed in Swanscombe in Kent on 13 June 1944. A newspaper article of the time recorded the following.

The Flying Bombs

It was on the morning of Tuesday, June 13, that an aeroplane flying very fast and in flames, was reported to be heading for London over the Maidstone area. This machine which crashed in Swanscombe, was established as the first pilotless aircraft. Three-quarters of an hour later a second one crashed at Crouch. The following night and early morning passed quietly, but shortly before midnight on the Thursday (15th), flying-bombs were reported in considerable numbers, 26 being shot down over Kent during the first 24 hours. The flying bomb was with us and was to continue with us for some 80 days.

The week commencing 25 June 1944 was the worst week for V1 rocket attacks. The area of south London which immediately borders Kent, saw 125 V1s hit the area with a staggering 357 people killed.

There were approximately 6,725 V1 rockets sent to wreak havoc on the British mainland. Of these 2,340 struck London, killing 5,475 civilians and military personnel and injuring another 16,000.

The first of the V2 rockets was launched against Britain in September 1944. More than 1,400 would land on different areas of London, although in total an estimated 3,000 were launched towards different targets including Antwerp and Liège. It is estimated that some 9,000 civilian and military personnel were killed by the rockets with a further 12,000 labourers and concentration camp prisoners who died as a result of forced participation in their production.

What made the V2 rocket even more dangerous wasn't just its size. It could travel faster than the speed of sound, which meant that it was nearly impossible to see and it didn't make a noise. The first most people would know anything about one of these rockets is when they exploded and by then it was too late.

The V stood for *Vergeltungswaffe*, or Vengeance Weapon. Often referred to as 'Hitler's last throw of the dice'.

One of the most tragic V1 attacks of the war happened on 30 June 1944, when the satisfaction of one of the V1s being shot down by a ground-based anti-aircraft battery quickly turned to sadness when the downed rocket, which hadn't exploded, landed on Weald House in Crockham Hill, Kent. At the time Weald House was occupied by a group of school children and their teachers who had been evacuated from a London school, which had been destroyed in another air raid. There were eleven female members of staff and thirty young children, all under the age of five. Of the members of staff, eight were killed along with twenty-two of the children and everyone else was injured. For those who died, the only saving grace was that it had just turned 3.15 am, when everybody would no doubt have been asleep, thus not having any idea of what was happening, with death no doubt being instantaneous. All of those who were killed, were buried in the churchyard of Edenbridge Parish Church.

On 3 August five men were killed in Maidstone in a V1 rocket attack, when one dropped on the town's West Goods Station, whilst loading coal on to a horse drawn cart. All of the men were buried in Maidstone Municipal Borough Cemetery. They were:

Ebenezer Hammond
Henry Albert Highams
Frederick Charles Selves
Henry Albert George Smith
Bert Tomlin

On Wednesday 16 August a V1 rocket inadvertently derailed the London Victoria to Ramsgate express train at Newington near Sittingbourne, killing ten people. The tragic incident was made even sadder as it came about from an act of heroism by a Canadian born pilot of the Royal Canadian Air Force, Flight Lieutenant John Alfred Malloy, who had been chasing the rocket as it came in over the English Channel. He had manoeuvred his aircraft right up next to the V1 rocket and then using one of the wings of his aircraft, managed to tip it, so that it headed downwards to the ground. Instead of crashing harmlessly into a field below, on this occasion it landed close to the Oak Lane railway bridge near Upchurch in Kent, the subsequent explosion destroyed the bridge just before a train was due to pass over it. Despite the efforts of the train's driver and fireman, it was unable to stop in time and crashed into the gap where the railway line should have been. Ten people were killed with a further fifty-eight injured. The driver and the fireman, both survived. The casualties were:

Ethel Emily **Beadle** (51) of 111 Pemdevon Road, Croydon. She was buried in Swale Rural District Cemetery.

Arthur Edward **Naylor** (61) of 26 Turton Road, Rainham, Kent. He was a railway worker and not actually on the train. He was buried in Swale Rural District Cemetery.

Frank Albert **Snazell** (56) of 112 Lennard Road, Beckenham, Kent. He was buried in Swale Rural District Cemetery.

Ivy Maud **Smith** (37) of Dovedale, Herne Bay Road, Swalecliffe, Whitstable.

George **Skinner** (60) of Upper Brents is named on the list of those who were killed in the crash. There is a George Skinner mentioned on the Commonwealth War Graves Commission website, but it was his father, William A. Skinner, who lived at 22 Upper Brents, Faversham. George Skinner was married to Louisa Alice Skinner, and they lived at 24 Aldeburgh Street, Faversham, which is where he died on 23 November 1944. If it is the same person, I can only assume that he subsequently died of his injuries which he had sustained in the crash. He was buried in the Greenwich, Metropolitan Borough Cemetery.

Able Seaman C/J 45268 Charles William **Cummins** (44) was a married man from Welling in Kent. He was buried in Plumstead Cemetery, London.

Able Seaman C/J 67510 Albert Edward **Eley** (42) was serving on board HMS *Queen of Kent*. He had also served during the First World War. He was a married man who lived with his wife, Ethel, in Faversham, Kent and was buried in the town's borough cemetery.

Private 6300499 Geoffrey Herbert **Gallop** (20) was serving with the 30th Battalion, The Queen's Royal Regiment (West Surrey). He was from Faversham and buried in the town's Borough Cemetery.

Private W/246571 Vera Barbara **Martin** (19) was serving with the Auxiliary Territorial Service. She is buried in St Peter and St Paul Churchyard in Shoreham, Kent.

Blanche May **Daniels** (66) is shown on some websites as being one of the passengers on the train who was killed. This is open to some debate, as although she died on 16 August 1944, the Commonwealth War Graves Commission website shows that she was injured at Frindsbury and died later the same day at St Bartholomew's Hospital.

On Friday 18 August an article about the crash appeared in the *Daily Record* newspaper.

Eight Dead in Train Crash

Seven passengers, including an unidentified woman and a workman on the line, were killed and 35 seriously injured, when a crowded train travelling between Gillingham and Sittingbourne, Kent, left the rails after rounding a bend on Wednesday night. About 100 other people were treated for minor injuries.

Among the dead are two seamen, a soldier, and an ATS private.

The engine overturned, bringing the train to a stop. Men and women from the undamaged rear of the train, among them a number of doctors and nurses, holiday makers, and servicemen and women, helped the injured with the train's first aid kit. Doctors hurried to the scene from the surrounding district.

A stretch of roadside was converted into a dressing station, seats and doors from the train being used as temporary stretchers. Among the injured was the train's fireman (David Humphreys) who, dazed and bleeding, walked along the line to the next station to keep the rail clear.

Interestingly, there is no mention in the article of a V1 rocket, Doodlebug or the like, being forced down by an RAF aircraft, exploding on impact, and knocking out the bridge. This would have been censored so as not to inform the enemy of the success of their missile attack.

Another article about the crash which appeared in the *Manchester Evening News* on Thursday 17 August included the following:

> *The driver helped in rescue work until he himself was taken to hospital.*
>
> *Mr W. Loft, a railway guard, of Cambridge Road, Rochester, who was on duty, was travelling in the guard's van. With him were a party of ATS girls who had been unable to get accommodation in the compartments. Mr Loft said, 'Everybody worked magnificently to rescue the injured, some of whom were pinned in the coaches crying for help. Nobody thought of themselves.'*

Yet again, there was no explanation of how the bridge had been damaged, or even mention of the fact that it had been damaged, let alone it being as a result of a V1 rocket having been forced to earth by an RAF pilot.

Among those passengers on the train who were injured, a number came from the Thanet area:

Miss Mary **Leveridge** (42) of St Mildred's Road, Ramsgate. She had previously worked as a driver for Ramsgate Police.

Henry **Taylor** (44) of 14 Approach Road, Ramsgate, a railway clerk.

Harry **Brooks** (59) of 32 Whitehall Road, Ramsgate, also a railway clerk.

Frederick **Padbury** (63) of 18 Alexandra Road, Broadstairs.

Dr Olga M. **Sainsbury**, a resident medical officer at the Three Counties Hospital, Arlesey, Bedfordshire, was admitted to Margate General Hospital with suspected fractured ribs. She was on her way to spend a holiday with her parents. During the crash she was thrown from the train, and landed on soft ground in a cherry orchard, but fractured several of her ribs. Remarkably once she had recovered from the shock, she hitched a lift on a fruit cart to Sittingbourne Railway station, where she calmly caught a train to Margate. On arriving in the town and by now in obvious discomfort, she was taken directly to Margate General Hospital for treatment.

Sergeant Ernest Charles **Allen** of All Saints Avenue, Margate was returning to his home on leave, but instead ended up in hospital at Chatham.

Miss **Yeomanson** of 4 West Field Road, Margate.

George **Glover** of 43 Rancorn Road, Margate.

Petty Officer Reginald **Stokes** RN of 4 Victoria Road, Margate, was detained in hospital.

Leslie **Knight** of Alpha Road, Birchington, an Admiralty Inspector, was taken to Chatham Hospital with head and leg injuries.

Mr Percy **Mount**, a farmer from the Isle of Sheppey was badly injured, losing part of a leg.

Two members of staff from Messrs. Bobby and Co. of Margate, Mr W. Langton, the local manager and Miss Swingler, one of the firm's buyers, were unaware they were on the same train and were in separate carriages. Other than being shocked by their experience, both were uninjured.

Mr W.J. Hawkins, a Margate Sanitary Inspector, was travelling in the train's second carriage, and apart from being thrown around by the sudden jerking of the train, was uninjured.

Flight Lieutenant John Alfred Malloy of No.274 Squadron, stationed at West Malling airfield, who was responsible for bringing down the V1, repeated the same wing tip feat later that same evening when he brought down another V1 over the Isle of Sheppey. On that occasion the rocket fell harmlessly into the sea. Flight Lieutenant J/11008 John Malloy was killed in action during an operation over Germany on 13 January 1945. He is buried in the Reichswald Forest War Cemetery, in the Nordhein-Westfalen region of Germany. This is not where he was originally buried, as Reichswald was not created until after the end of the Second World War, so he was initially buried elsewhere in the surrounding area and his remains moved there some time after the war.

The City of Rochester had five V1 rockets land within its boundaries during that year.

25 June 1944 – 7 injured.
30 July 1944
14 August 1944

V2 Rocket.

16 August 1944 – 4 killed, 44 injured.

8 November 1944 – 7 killed, 44 injured.

A number of people from Kent were killed by V2 rockets throughout 1944. In the list below I have included their names and the date they died:

17 September 1944 – Lilly **Johnson**; Doreen Elizabeth **Todd**; Frank **Wakeling**.

28 October 1944 – James Thomas **Goldsmith**

11 November 1944 – Kathleen Florence **Angel**; Margaret Charlotte **Jacobs**; Alfred Charles **Watson**

15 November 1944 – Albert Edward **Maskell**

22 November 1944 – Joyce Grace **Hibben**; Albert Horace **Tickner**; Marie Alice **Tassie**

23 November 1944 – Mary Anne **Lockyer**; Kathleen Olive **Stratton**; Ernest Robert **Wilson**

25 November 1944 – Frank Moyle **Burroughes**; Reginald Bradford **Calder**; Doris Eileen Edith **Card**; Mary **Carroll**; Winifred **Farnish**; Thomas James **Gushlow**; William Herbert **Hastings**; Winifred Phyllis **Messenger**; Constance Dora **Newell**; Ellen Irene **Smith**; Emma Louise **Thatcher**; Lillian May **White**; George Frederick **White**; George Ellis **Wincott**; Barbara **Woodland**; Violet Kathleen **Woodland**; Phyllis Ethel **Woods**

26 November 1944 – Maud Louise Archbell **Branton**; John Richard **Siegert**

27 November 1944 – George William **Gregory**; Frank Percy **Loveday**

15 December 1944 – Ethel Mary **Ferguson**

The above list is for the year 1944 only. There were other people in Kent killed by V2 rockets throughout 1945, who are not included here. The last V2 rocket to be fired at mainland Britain was launched on 27 March 1945, and landed in Kynaston Road, Orpington, killing Mrs Ivy **Millichip**.

Throughout 1944 an estimated total of about 180 Kent civilians were killed as a result of air raids by the Luftwaffe, and the devastating effect of both the V1 and V2 rockets. It wouldn't be until the early months of 1945 that the rocket attacks finally came to an end, as the Allied armies advanced across Europe towards Germany, defeating all in their path.

Operation Bodyguard

Operation Bodyguard was the codename given to a Second World War deception plan, deployed by the Allies, immediately before the invasion of Europe in Normandy on 6 June 1944. The main element of the plan was intended to make the German High Command believe that the invasion of Europe was going to take place in the Pas de Calais region of France, with Allied forces coming across from Kent, although there were other aspects to the operation.

Supreme Headquarters
ALLIED EXPEDITIONARY-FORCE,
Office of the Secretary General Staff

3 February 1944

MEMORANDUM FOR: Chief of Staff.

Subject: Precise of Plan "BODYGUARD"

1. Plan "BODYGUARD" is an overall deception policy for the war against Germany, approved by the Combined Chiefs of Staff (TAB A). Its object is to induce the enemy to make faulty strategic dispositions in relation to operations by the United Nations against Germany.

2. This overall deception policy is presented to induce the enemy to believe that the allied plan for 1944 is as follows:

Long range bomber reinforcement is delaying ground forces build-up;
An attack on Northern Norway with Russia is to be concerted in the Spring;

The main Allied effort in Spring 1944 should be against the Balkans. Operations in Italy would be continued, augmented by amphibious operations.

3. In regard to Allied strength and dispositions, we should induce the enemy to believe the following:

Shortage of manpower has obliged cannibalisation within the British Army in UK;
Number of divisions in UK is less than is in fact the case;
Personnel of certain allied divisions in Mediterranean are being relieved by fresh divisions from U.S.;
Shortage of landing craft exists until Summer, 1944;
Forces in Mediterranean are greater than is, in fact, the case;
French forces are taking over responsibility for defense of North Africa, relieving Anglo-American forces for Spring operations elsewhere;
British divisions and craft are being transferred from India to Middle East;
Fresh divisions from U.S. are expected to arrive in Mediterranean.

4. Means of implemenation of plan "BODYGUARD" include movement of forces, camouflage devices, W/T deception, diplomatic approaches to Sweden and Turkey, leakage and rumours, and political warfare.

ROBERT E. BAKER,
Major, G.S.C.,
Asst. Sec. General Staff.

Memorandum of Operation Bodyguard.

The idea for the operation came about during the Teheran Conference in November 1943, at a meeting of the leaders of America, Britain and Russia, Roosevelt, Churchill and Stalin. It was originally called Operation Jael, which was a reference to an Old Testament heroine, who by using the art of deception, managed to kill an enemy commander.

The part of the operation that involved Kent, was Operation Fortitude South, which was a crossing from Dover to the area of the Pas de Calais. Part of the success of making the enemy believe that this would be where the invasion would take place, was because in Hitler's aborted 1940 plan to invade Britain, part of his Operation Sea Lion, was an amphibious landing in the Dover areas, having set out from the Pas de Calais, based on its being the shortest route across the notoriously difficult waters of the English Channel.

Secrecy was absolutely crucial. To mislead the Germans, the British devised ingenious deception plans, notably Operation Fortitude. They deliberately transmitted and broadcast all the radio traffic generated by US forces in south-west England, and British and Canadian forces in south central England, from radio stations in Kent. Vast, fake army camps appeared around Maidstone and Canterbury, with thousands of partly concealed dummy tanks and aircraft.

Part of what convinced Hitler that the expected invasion of Europe by the Allies would be coming across the English Channel from Dover, was the presence, seen throughout Kent of US General George Patton, who was in command of the fictional 1st US Army Group. Other elements of the deception included wireless transmissions, the use of German agents who had been turned, and controlled leaks of information via diplomatic connections. The other main aspect of the deception was the use of dummies.

There were dummy aircraft, landing fields, tanks, lorries, army camps, and most impressive of all, full-scale landing craft, many of which were strategically placed in Dover Harbour.

One of the double agents, Juan Pujol Garcia, code name Garbo, was so good at what he did that he was awarded the Iron Cross by the Germans and the MBE by the British. German agents turned by MI5 leaked the news that the Allies' most powerful assault formation, the US Third Army, was destined to assault the Pas de Calais region of France, making its way across the English Channel from Kent.

The Allies developed floating 'Mulberry' harbours, meanwhile Operation Bolero, codename for the American build-up in Britain, transformed southern England into one big army camp. By early June 1944 more than 2 million Americans had arrived in the United Kingdom in preparation for D-Day and beyond, along with 250,000 Canadians.

Insignia of the fictitious 1st US Army Group.

Dummy Lorry and unknown soldier.

To German reconnaissance aircraft, it all would have all looked very real, even down to the attempts at camouflage. Knowing that German intelligence would be trying to find out as much as they could concerning an invasion which they knew was coming, double agents planted stories and documents with known German spies. Pretend radio transmissions were broadcast, just as if a large army was being organised. By the time that the Germans realised what was actually happening, it was too late; the Normandy bridgehead had been secured and Allied troops had fought their way off the beaches and were advancing across northern France.

Many of the German radar stations on the French coast were destroyed in preparation for the landings. In addition, on the night before the invasion, a small group of Special Air Service (SAS) operators deployed dummy paratroopers over Le Havre and Isigny.

In the early hours of 6 June 1944, RAF bombers from No. 617 Squadron, dropped strips of aluminium foil over the area of the Pas de Calais, to simulate a radar profile of a massive invasion fleet. The illusion was bolstered by a group of small Allied vessels towing barrage balloons. A similar deception was undertaken near Boulogne-sur-Mer in the Pas de Calais area by No.218 Squadron of the RAF in Operation Glimmer.

The D-Day planners had done all that they could to ensure a successful amphibious assault on the beaches of Normandy. By spring 1944 all of the divisions that were taking part in the initial seaborne landings on 6 June 1944, had previously taken part in extensive training exercises in Scotland and Devon, including Slapton Sands near Lyme Regis.

Thankfully Hitler believed that the invasion was going to occur in the Pas de Calais, and because of this he left his 15th Army Group in the area and did not move them down to the Normandy coast, to bolster up his 7th Army Group. If he had, the outcome could have been a very different and might well have resulted in a major defeat for the Allies, which would have set them back months, if not years, before they were in a strong enough position to carry out a similar attempt in the future. The worst case scenario was if Hitler hadn't fallen for the ruse, an Allied defeat on the beaches of Normandy leaving with both Britain and America, literally dead in the water.

Hitler was convinced that the early reports from his senior officers of an invasion taking place in Normandy, was a diversion for the real invasion force that would be amassing and then crossing the English Channel from the Kent coastline. That one wrong decision by Hitler was quite possibly the major factor in determining the final outcome of the war.

The planners for the invasion of occupied France, had determined a set of ideal conditions which involved the phase of the moon, the tides, and the time of day. These different facets would only be satisfactory on a few days in each month. A full moon was desirable, as it would provide illumination for aircraft pilots and also have the highest tides. The Allies wanted to schedule the landings for shortly before dawn, midway between low and high tide, with the tide coming in. This would improve the visibility of obstacles on the beach, while minimising the amount of time the men would be exposed in the open. Eisenhower had tentatively selected 5 June as the date for the assault. However, on 4 June, conditions were unsuitable for a landing; high winds and heavy seas made it impossible to launch landing craft, and low clouds would prevent aircraft from finding their targets.

Group Captain James Stagg of the RAF met Eisenhower on the evening of 4 June. He and his meteorological team predicted that the weather would improve enough for the invasion to proceed on 6 June. If this date was missed, then the next available dates after this, with the required tidal conditions, but without the desirable full moon, would have been, from 18 to 20 June. But the problem for Eisenhower was that once the bulk of his invasion vessels set out on their journey across to France and the beaches of Normandy, there could be no turning back. Calling a postponement after those first ships had left was not really an option, as it would have required recalling men and ships already in position to cross the Channel. This would have increased the chances of the invasion plans being detected by the Germans. After much discussion with his senior most commanders, Eisenhower decided that the invasion should go ahead on 6 June.

D-Day 6 June 1944 had finally arrived and involved 160,000 Allied troops, as well as 5,000 vessels of differing descriptions. The amphibious landings had been preceded by an airborne assault which had involved 1,200 aircraft and gliders. The invasion of Europe had begun – a moment in history that would ultimately lead to victory for Britain and her Allies over Nazi Germany. With her involvement in Operation Fortitude South, Kent was at the very forefront of ensuring that the landings on the beaches of Normandy, had every opportunity to succeed.

The operation was officially declared as having come to an end on 30 August 1944, when German forces had retreated back across the River Seine. By this time there were more than two million Allied troops in France.

Below are some relevant and interesting facts about the D-Day landings:

(1) Planning for Operation Overlord began in earnest in 1943. Dwight D. Eisenhower was made Supreme Allied Commander. British General Bernard Montgomery, hero of the Eighth Army in North Africa, was put in charge of the ground troops.

(2) Approximately 3,200 reconnaissance missions were launched in the run-up to the invasion, specifically to take photos of vital locations along the Normandy coastline where the invading troops would land on D-Day.

(3) In the summer of 1943 an early copy of the plans for Operation Overlord, blew out of a window in Norfolk House, London. They were found by a member of the public who just happened to be passing by. Thankfully he handed back them in, having not been able to read them due to his poor eyesight.

(4) Normandy was chosen instead of the Pas-de-Calais area for an invasion of occupied France, because although it was a longer journey across the English Channel, the defences there were fewer, and once troops had made their way off the beaches, they would have had fewer rivers and canals to cross.

(5) Five landing locations had been identified along a 50 mile stretch of Normandy coastline. The Americans would attack at what had been code named, Utah and Omaha beaches, the British at Gold and Sword, with the Canadians being allocated Juno beach.

(6) D-Day was originally set to go ahead on June 5, but it had to be postponed for 24 hours because of bad weather in the English Channel, which was notoriously bad at that time of the year.

(7) The 'D' in D-Day actually stood for Day. The title was used as it was believed that it would help preserve the operation's secrecy.

(8) On 28 April 1944 at Slapton Sands in Devon, a total of 946 American servicemen were killed during a dress rehearsal for the D-Day landings, when German torpedo boats sank a convoy of tank landing ships involved in the training exercise. The death toll was compounded by a mix-up in radio frequencies between the Americans and British, life jackets worn incorrectly and 'friendly fire' from shore gun emplacements using live ammunition. The tragedy was covered up and military and medical personnel ordered not to speak about it.

(9) In May 1944, crucial code words for the D-Day landings, which included the name of the operation and the names of the allocated beaches, began appearing in the *Daily Telegraph* crosswords. An MI5 investigation apparently failed to find any evidence of foul play, I am not actually sure I believe that.

(10) Hitler's Atlantic Wall, which had been built all along the French coastline using 100,000 enforced labourers, was a formidable defence, for Allied troops to have to overcome.

(11) The Allied High Command had estimated a successful landing at Normandy would cost them 10,000 men dead and a further 30,000 wounded. With this in mind, the medical teams in operation across the Normandy beaches on D-Day were issued with 30,000 stretchers and 60,000 blankets to care for the wounded.

(12) New gadgets were designed for D-Day, which included a swimming tank, and a flame throwing tank called the 'crocodile'. There were even collapsible motorbikes.

(13) Lieutenant Colonel Terence Otway, the commanding officer of the 9th Battalion, Parachute Regiment, whose unit was tasked with taking the vital Merville Gun Battery, as part of the Normandy landings, decided to test security among his men. He sent thirty members of the Women's Auxiliary Air Force into the local pubs near to where his men were staying, to see if any of his troops would divulge the top-secret plan. This was one mission he failed, as none of his men said a word.

(14) The evening before the landings, a nervous British Prime Minister Winston Churchill, turned to his wife, Clementine, and said: 'Do you realise that by the time you wake up in the morning 20,000 men may have been killed?' A passion killer of a bedtime comment to make, if ever there was one.

(15) On the eve of the D-Day landings, the Supreme Commander of the Allied Expeditionary Forces, General Dwight D. Eisenhower, sent a letter to all military personnel who were taking part in the operation. The first paragraph of the letter contained the following sentence: 'You are about to embark upon a great crusade, toward which we have striven these many months. The eyes of the world are upon you.'

(16) Eisenhower also wrote a draft statement in case the landings failed which in part read: 'Our landings in the Cherbourg-Havre area have failed to gain a satisfactory foothold and I have withdrawn the troops... If any blame or fault attaches to the attempt it is mine alone.' Thankfully for the free world, it was one that he never had to send.

(17) Coded radio messages were sent to alert French Resistance fighters to begin a programme of acts of sabotage, so as to hinder German movements near to the intended Normandy landing sites. Phrases that were used included 'the dice is on the carpet', this was an instruction to destroy trains and railway lines. Who came up with such eloquently thought out phrases, is not clear.

(18) The naval operation part of the invasion, was codenamed Operation Neptune, and involved an armada of 6,939 vessels including 4,126 landing craft. This was the largest single day amphibious invasion of all time. On 5 June 1944, they had assembled at a point off of the Isle of Wight, that was referred to as Piccadilly Circus.

(19) From 2300 hours on 5 June some 24,000 airborne troops were delivered behind the German lines to secure important roads and bridges. Along with more than 2,000 aircraft there were 867 gliders. Dummy paratroopers were also dropped near to the area of Pas de Calais, to try and convince the Germans that the real landings would take place there.

(20) The first British casualty on D-Day was Lieutenant 237676 Herbert Denham 'Den' Brotheridge, of the 2nd (Airborne) Battalion, Oxfordshire & Buckinghamshire Light Infantry, who was shot in the neck shortly after landing in a glider at just after midnight on 6 June. His unit had been tasked with taking the crucial target of Pegasus Bridge. Despite his death, it was an objective that they successfully achieved. He is buried in the churchyard, at Ranville in the Calvados region of France.

(21) Many paratroopers that day were dropped in the wrong place including US Private John Steele. His parachute famously became snagged on the church steeple at Sainte-Mère-Eglise. He was trapped for two hours before being taken prisoner by the Germans.

(22) At 0300 hours on 6 June 1944, a total of 1,900 Allied bombers attacked German lines along the Normandy coastline. A staggering seven million pounds of bombs were dropped that day. A total of 10,521 combat aircraft flew a total of 15,000 sorties on D-Day, with 113 aircraft being lost to enemy fire.

(23) The defences on the beaches at Normandy that Allied troops stormed on D-Day, included concrete gun emplacements, wooden stakes, mines, anti-tank obstacles, barbed wire and booby traps. There were around 50,000 German troops waiting for the Allied forces.

(24) Field Marshal Erwin Rommel, who was in charge of defending northern France from the expected Allied invasion, was at home in Germany on 6 June 1944, celebrating his wife's fiftieth birthday, having been told that the sea in the English Channel was too rough for an amphibious landing.

(25) Adolf Hitler was asleep when word of the invasion arrived at his location in Salzburg but no one would dare to wake him, which led to vital time being lost in sending reinforcements to Normandy.

(26) The newly developed drug penicillin was sent to Normandy with troops on D-Day and helped save the lives of thousands of wounded men.

(27) Total Allied casualties on D-Day were much lighter than had been anticipated. The number was around 10,000 with 4,572 of those killed. This included 1,641 British military personnel. The Germans are estimated to have lost about 9,000 men.

(28) The well-known actor Richard Todd starred in the hit movie *The Longest Day*, a 1962 film about the D-Day landings. He played the part of Major John Howard. Todd was involved in the real landings as an officer in the 7th Parachute Battalion.

(29) The actor James Doohan, who went on to find fame as Scotty in the TV programme Star Trek, was a lieutenant in the Royal Canadian Artillery on D-Day, and lost a finger during the fighting.

(30) The stunning Omaha Beach scene in the 1998 movie *Saving Private Ryan*, starring Tom Hanks, cost £7million to film and used 1,000 extras.

(31) The famous Hungarian war photographer Robert Capa, real name Endre Friedmann, captured some of the most memorable images of the action during the Normandy landings, although only a handful of the frames he took survived. The others were accidently destroyed by a lab technician. Ironically, Capa died in 1954 in Vietnam, after stepping a landmine.

CHAPTER 7

1945 – On to Victory

The final chapter of the war had arrived, although that was not immediately apparent at the beginning of the year. Now in its seventh year, people were tired and wanted a victory. There had been too many sacrifices paid for in blood and the loss of loved ones, especially with the shadow of the First World War still in the minds of many.

On 8 May 1945 Prime Minister Winston Churchill, announced Victory in Europe. The war was over at long last, at least in Europe. Four months later on 2 September 1945, General Douglas MacArthur accepted the Japanese surrender aboard the deck of USS *Missouri*.

Between 1 January and 8 May 1945, at least 516 people with Kent connections were killed or died of their wounds, illness, disease or as the result of an accident. These included:

Army: 302
RAF/RAFVR: 131
RN/RNVR: 45
Merchant Navy 6
Civilians: 32

Between 9 May, the day after Victory in Europe, and 2 September 1945, the date of the surrender of all Japanese forces, a further 144 people with Kent connections lost their lives.

Army: 87
RAF/RAFVR: 38
RN/RNVR: 16
Merchant Navy: 1
Civilians: 2

Between 2 September 1945 and 31 December 1947, when deaths could still be officially attributed to war time involvement, whether that was as part of an occupying force, or injuries received that were connected to the war, at least 266 people from Kent or with connections to the county, lost their lives.

An interesting article appeared in the *Kent & Sussex Courier* dated Friday 26 January which gave a snapshot of the cost in financial and social terms which the war had brought to just one town.

The Surveyor to the Tonbridge Rural Council reported that the cost of repairs from the outbreak of the war, up to and including 7 September 1944, to properties damaged by enemy action, stood at £56,000, a great deal of money at the time. All properties that had been damaged and did not require being demolished, had been suitably repaired. The number of builders and labourers employed by the council to carry out the required repairs, was around 300. Although that figure might at first appear somewhat high, compare it with the number of homes in the town that were damaged. Some 548 were slightly damaged, which could be some or all windows blown out; another thirty-eight were severely damaged, which meant a wall or the roof of a property had come down, due to a bomb exploding nearby and nine had been totally destroyed, which usually meant a direct hit.

It was also reported that for the same period of time Tonbridge had experienced 969 air raid warnings. This had resulted in 429 actual air raids on the town along with a hundred V1 and V2 rockets. There had been 592 high explosive bombs dropped and exploded as well as a number that had failed to detonate on landing. The Luftwaffe had dropped 42 oil bombs, they were known to the Germans as *Flammenbombe* and contained an oil mixture and a high explosive bursting charge. Originally they weighed 250kg but later in the war the Germans made a 500kg version. Each bomb was fitted with an impact fuse that quite often failed to go off, making it an unreliable piece of ammunition. It was a fault that the Germans never fully overcame and so it was withdrawn from general use by the Luftwaffe as early as January 1941.

A total of 3,400 incendiary devices were dropped, along with eleven heavy incendiary bombs, and fifty-three unexploded anti-aircraft shells. Twenty-four German aircraft had been shot down and crashed in the town. On sixteen occasions, Luftwaffe pilots had fired their machine guns on the town's unsuspecting population. Four mines had been dropped along with three High Explosive SD1 bombs.

All of these attacks had resulted in eleven deaths, ten who had been killed instantly and one who died later in hospital.

Below are listed some of the civilian population of Tonbridge who were killed during the period mentioned above, although this is not exclusive to the year 1945. Their names are listed in the date order of when they died rather than alphabetically.

Lucie **Harris** (57), a married woman of 16 Dernier Road, Tonbridge, who died at the County Hospital, Sandhill, Pembury on 25 October 1940. She was buried in Tonbridge Rural District Cemetery.

Edward Joseph **Turner** (47) of 38 Norfolk Road, Tonbridge, who died at Ashford Hospital on 24 March 1943. He was buried in Ashford Urban District Cemetery.

Sydney **Wiles** (59) of 33 Baron Road, Tonbridge, who died at Ashford Hospital on 24 March 1943. He was buried in Ashford Urban District Cemetery.

Michael William **Osbourne** (12), of 30 Danvers Road, Tonbridge, who was injured at Tonbridge Sports Ground on 19 June 1944, and subsequently died at the County Hospital, Sandhill, Pembury, on 22 June 1944. His father was William Patrick Osbourne, a sergeant in the RAF. He was buried in the Rural District Cemetery, Tonbridge.

Elizabeth Maud **Baker** (53), who lived at The Oaks, Quarry Hill, Tonbridge. She was injured at home on 3 July 1944 and died at the County Hospital, Sandhill, Pembury, on 17 August 1944. She was buried in the Tonbridge, Rural District Cemetery.

George Clifford **Locke** (18), who lived at 76 Pembury Road, Tonbridge. He died at the County Hospital on 10 September 1944 and was buried in the Municipal Borough Cemetery, Dover.

James Thomas **Goldsmith** (46), who lived at 88 Pagnell Street, Tonbridge, which is also where he died on 28 October 1944. His parents, James and Ann Goldsmith, lived at 28 Harlow Road Tonbridge. He was buried in the Metropolitan Borough Cemetery, Deptford.

On Monday 5 February Leonard John Margetts of Lansdown, Foley Road, Claygate, Surrey stood before the magistrates at Kingston County Magistrates Court in Surrey. His crime was that he had left his employment with the Kent War Agricultural Executive, at Benenden, Kent on 8 August 1944, without the permission of the National Service Officer. He pleaded guilty, was fined £10 or six week's imprisonment and was allowed two months in which to pay.

Margetts was a conscientious objector who had been put to work on the land by the Kent Agricultural Committee, during 1944. In August that year he applied for permission to be allowed to leave his work in Kent so that he could enrol in an art course near to his home address in Surrey. Permission was refused, a decision which he appealed against, which was also rejected, but in fairness to Margetts he continued to work on the land until the hostel where he was living was destroyed by a V1 rocket. He was injured as a result of the raid and received a cut to his forehead, but not one that required him to be off work. It was at this time that he demanded his release, when this request was again refused, he made it known that he was leaving and had not been seen at his place of work since that time.

Margetts told the magistrates that he had worked on the land at Sheppey for more than three years and had become very tired and depressed as a result of it and that he wanted to be nearer his home and family. He had told the National Service Officer that he was determined to leave his job in Sheppey, no matter what the consequences of his actions were. Even though he was repeatedly denied the right to do this by the Kent authorities, he told the magistrates that he was under the impression that after being interviewed in relation to the matter that had caused his attendance at court that day, that they would not stand in his way if he left.

Conscription had been brought in on 3 September 1939 when all men aged between 18 and 40, became eligible to be called up under the new National Service Armed Forces Act. At the end of 1941 the age limit was raised to 51, and for the first time, single women aged between 20 and 30 were required to do some kind of home-based war work.

People who did not wish to fight on conscientious grounds, usually because of religious beliefs, had to attend a tribunal to argue their case as to why they should not be made to undertake military training. The tribunal had the power to exempt people from having to undergo military service, but could recommend an alternative civilian service in support of the war, by suggesting they join such organisations as the non-combatant corps of the armed forces. During the Second World War, some 60,000 men and 1,000 women applied for exemptions for having to undergo military service, on the grounds of being a conscientious objector. About 3,000 conscientious objectors were given unconditional exemptions, whilst 18,000 applicants were dismissed, and others were either recorded on the military service register as being military personnel, but in a non-combatant role.

For these individuals the type of work they were expected to carry out, was bomb disposal or working for medical units such as the Royal Army Medical Corps.

As the war was fast drawing to a close in Europe an interesting talk took place on the evening of Tuesday 13 March at the Victoria Hall, Tonbridge, which went some way to reminding people that the war in the Far East and the Pacific, against the Japanese, was far from over.

Brigadier J.G. Smyth VC MC, who commanded the 17th Division in Burma, told an enthusiastic audience of friends and families of members of the 14th Army, the immortal story of British heroism on the jungle front line of the Far East. The talk was given under the watchful eye of the Minister of Information.

Brigadier Smyth explained that in the fighting, no quarter was asked or given on either side; it was that brutal, the most bitter imaginable. He captivated his audience, not only with his words and presence, but his chest full of medals that had been won during thirty years of military service.

He continued by explaining that two British fleets were currently based in Australia and Ceylon, and that operations of a more amphibious nature might be expected as the campaign against the Japanese in the Far East and Pacific, progressed.

'We had made a wonderful comeback in Burma in a short space of time, and in our feelings of pride and satisfaction at the present situation, we should not forget the British and Indian soldiers who fought one of the grimmest rearguard actions in our history.'

The evening came to a most unexpected yet interesting end, when Major T. Hepburn, the deputy County ARP Controller, proposed a vote of thanks to the brigadier for his interesting talk, before going on to recall how in 1919 he had been engaged in a bitter struggle out east, when a convoy led by Brigadier, then Captain, Smyth, had come to his aid. By a remarkable coincidence he had never again set eyes on Brigadier Smyth until that evening.

The Brigadier had been awarded his Victoria Cross during the First World War, whilst serving on the Western Front on 18 May 1915 when he was a lieutenant. He was also mentioned in despatches on six occasions as well as being awarded the Military Cross.

Any and all of the war time deaths were sad occasions, and especially difficult for the friends and relatives who were left behind to have to deal with, but when those deaths happened near the war's end, they were tinged with an element of poignancy.

Brigadier General John G. Smyth, VC, MC.

The edition of the *Kent and Sussex Courier* dated Friday 27 April carried an article about such a story:

Mrs Doris Eames of 3 Douglas Road, Tonbridge, had received news through official channels that her 23-year-old husband, Flight Lieutenant 141706 Kenneth Horace Eames, had been reported missing whilst on active service. He had joined the Royal Air Force Volunteer Reserve in July 1941 and had then been sent out to America to undergo his training and gain his wings, qualifying as a military pilot, after which time he spent some time acting as an instructor, teaching other keen and enthusiastic young men, the same skills that he had been taught by others. He later returned to England and ended up with No. 626 Squadron, a heavy bomber squadron, that was stationed at RAF Wickenby, in Lincolnshire. During the war the squadron, which had only been formed on 7 November 1943, flew 2,728 sorties with the loss of 49 of its aircraft. Kenneth Eames was on board one of those aircraft, when it was lost on 5 April 1945.

The following is taken from an entry on *www.626-squadron.co.uk* which is an excellent example of how to keep alive the memories and actions of the men who both served and died whilst flying with the squadron and ensuring that these men are never forgotten.

On the evening of 4 April 1945, Kenneth was the pilot of Lancaster PD295UMB2, which took off from RAF Wickenby, Lincolnshire at 2101 hours to take part in a mission by 258 Lancasters and 14 Mosquitos of Nos.1 and 8 Groups, Bomber Command, to bomb a synthetic oil plant near Lutzkendorf. Some time after take off the aircraft crashed in to the sea just off of the French coast. The reasons for the crash are not known. Only five bodies of the seven crewmen were found, these being washed ashore at various times and locations following the crash.

Kenneth Eames was one of the two members of the crew whose body was never found. Three weeks after Kenneth's death, Lancaster bombers from No.626 Squadron, bombed Hitler's mountain retreat at Berchtesgaden in Germany.

On Saturday 19 May there was an interesting article in the *Whitstable Times and Tankerton Press*, about a man from Whitstable who had been held as a PoW in Germany since October 1942.

Rifleman Charles W. Olive was the youngest son of Mr and Mrs R. Olive of 53 Reservoir Road, Whitstable. He had been involved in fighting in the Adriatic sector of the Italian battlefront when he was captured by the Germans on 26 October 1942. Allied troops had attacked enemy-held positions but had quickly been forced to retreat and ended up jumping into the icy waters of a river, in full battle dress, in an attempt to escape. A combination of the coldness of the water and a strong current towards the middle of the river, forced them to quit trying to reach the safety of the opposite bank, and make their way back to the German-held side of the river. Soaked through and extremely tired from their exertions and realising that their situation was futile, they surrendered to the Wehrmacht soldiers who were waiting for them. After he was pulled out of the river, he was searched by his captives and his details were taken before he was marched off to be interrogated by an English-speaking officer. After the questioning he was treated by a German medic for shrapnel wounds to his face and hands.

Conditions at the Italian prison camp where Charles and his comrades were held for the first two days of their captivity, were not the worst but all they had to eat each day was one meal of soup and four slices of bread. From Italy they travelled by rail in filthy cattle trucks, fifteen men crammed into one truck, with not enough room to sit down. The five-day journey was not a pleasant one. There was no stopping so that the men could stretch their legs and the food consisted of ersatz sausage, bread and water.

Eventually they reached their destination, Stalag V11-A, near Moosburg, north of Munich. The camp held British, Polish, Russian, Czechoslovakians, and Americans, and was the largest PoW camp in Germany. The conditions were extremely cramped and food was scarce. Meals consisted of what passed for a soup in the morning, with hot water, potato peelings and swedes. That would be followed later in the day by four potatoes and a thin slice of bread.

Charles Olive was tasked as part of a daily work detail, to be taken to the centre of Munich and with the help of a shovel and a broom, he had to clean up the streets of the debris caused by Allied air attacks the previous evening. He was in Munich when the Allies delivered a crushing air attack on the city, which was nearly flattened by the end of it. He remembered that as being a difficult time, happy in the knowledge that if the air raids were anything to go by, then freedom couldn't be that far away. The problem was what would their guards do, would they panic, would they react aggressively towards them, but thankfully both sides held their nerve. Even the German civilians offered them no violence and simply went about their lives as best they could in the circumstances.

Each day the prisoners were woken up at 5.30 am and they had chores until 1.30 pm, and then the rest of the day was their own. He only saw one act of brutality by a German guard towards another prisoner, which took place when the man, consumed by the extreme cold refused to work and was beaten ceaselessly by the guard with the butt of his rifle.

As liberation drew nearer they experienced three days and nights of distant artillery fire which drew nearer and nearer as the days passed by. Their longed-for freedom finally arrived on 29 April 1945 in the shape of Combat Command A of the 14th Armoured Division. The 240 camp guards did not put up a fight and laid down their weapons with none of them attacked by any of the prisoners, by which time there were more than 76,000.

Bored and impatient with waiting around to be repatriated Charles and a few of his friends 'borrowed' a German car, filled it up with Red Cross parcels and set out to drive from southern Germany, halfway across Europe, and home to Whitstable. But just 40km up the road, the exuberant, now ex prisoners of war were halted at Augsburg, by American soldiers, put into a US Army car and taken to Luxembourg. After that the journey was continued by train to Paris where they spent a day sightseeing, and from there it was by air to an undisclosed RAF station in southern England, to be met by a wonderful reception committee, and finally home to Reservoir Road, in Whitstable.

On 30 April Hitler committed suicide in his underground bunker in Berlin and one week later on 7 May 1945, the new German Reich President, Grand Admiral Karl Dönitz, agreed to an unconditional surrender of all German forces. Finally, the war in

Europe was over. Hitler and Nazi Germany had been soundly beaten into submission, with the hope that in 1966, the world wouldn't be embroiled in another global wide war. That was the year of course that England defeated Germany yet again, but thankfully on this occasion it was only at a game of football.

With Germany well and truly defeated, it was now time to put another hostile nation to the sword, this time Japan. Britain and America now had to concentrate their joint efforts on ridding the Far East and the Pacific of the Japanese who had terrorized the region for the previous three and a half years.

Heavy bombing of Japanese cities by American B-17 and B-29 aircraft had been taking place since the beginning of the year and on 6 August the American B-29 bomber, called *Enola Gay* dropped the first atomic bomb 'Little Boy' on Hiroshima. On 9 April the final death knell for the Japanese Empire came when the American B-29 bomber *Bockscar* dropped the second atomic bomb, known as 'Fat Man' on the Japanese city of Nagasaki. The bombs resulted in the deaths of 90,000–146,000 people in Hiroshima and 39,000–80,000 people in Nagasaki although many more died from burns and radiation sickness in the following months.

Emperor Hirohito announced over the radio on 15 August 1945, news of the Japanese surrender. The following day he ordered all Japanese forces to lay down their weapons and surrender. The war was finally over.

Friday 1 June saw a special occasion at the Café Royal in Tankerton. Mrs M.B. Reeves, the chair of the Café Royal Prisoners of War Cigarette Fund in Europe, and her committee, had arranged a welcome home party for some seventy repatriated local men who had been held as prisoners of war in Germany. The party was to be the final act of the fund. Mrs Reeves was everywhere, moving from table to table offering kind words of thanks for a job well done to all of the men present. When she introduced Sergeant Major Darwood of the Grenadier Guards, an ex PoW, he was met with a hearty round of applause.

Although the khaki battledress of The Buffs (Royal East Kent Regiment) predominated amongst those present, other services were represented as well, such as the blue of the Royal Air Force, with Warrant Officer Harding representing them. His had been a fleeting visit, as he had only just been home to Chestfield after flying home from Germany, before dropping in at the Café Royal. Others had missed the celebrations as they were away on holiday. One unfortunate man had missed the party because he had to return to his unit.

It was a memorable day, with lots of reminiscing going on amongst the many groups of men, telling their stories about what each of them had done and been through during their wartime captivity. Camps were high on the agenda with talk about the treatment they received, the food they were given, Red Cross parcels, and how many cigarettes they received from the Café Royal. For many, just the ability to talk to other men who had been through what they had was more than enough. They were kindred spirits who understood what their comrades had lived through, each man having experienced and witnessed very stressful, frightening and distressing events, which would have left many of them with nightmares, flashbacks and feelings of guilt.

It was first documented during the First World War, when it was more commonly referred to as 'shell shock'. This was at a time before post traumatic stress disorder had become a commonly used phrase by the medical profession. It wasn't officially recognized as a mental health condition until as recently as 1980, when it was included in the Diagnostic and Statistical Manual of Mental Disorders, which had been developed by the American Psychiatric Association.

As the men chatted, dance music was playing peacefully in the background, then it was time for tea, and what a spread it was, better than anything they had eaten or could have dreamt of in any of their Stalag camps in Germany. There was a selection of tomato sandwiches, sausage rolls, cakes, trifle, Kentish cherries and strawberries. But the *pièce de resistance* was the large, two tiered, multi coloured, iced cake, with the words 'Welcome Home' iced across the top. It was a grand occasion for well deserving, returning men who had endured testing times during their captivity in the German camps, many of whom had been incarcerated for three and four years, never knowing when and if they would ever return home to their loved ones.

Many of them had friends and comrades who were still involved in the fighting in the Far East, no matter what branch of the military they were serving in. Knowing the danger which these brave souls faced, didn't make it easy for those who had already returned from Europe. Only when the war was completely over and the fighting had stopped, could they relax and start to enjoy themselves.

A poignant reminder that there was still a war going on came in the shape of an article which appeared in the edition of the *Whitstable Times and Herne Bay Herald* dated Saturday 28 July.

People of Whitstable, Herne Bay, and Kent as a whole, could now hurry along the streets of their towns, as they had spent the previous five years doing, but now there was a difference. Besides the obvious spring in their step that had maybe been missing in the previous years, for obvious reasons, there was now a new feeling, and a positive one at that. The air raid shelters which had become an integral part of everyday life were now padlocked and deserted. The sandbags and barbed wire had disappeared. The large public water tanks were empty, not needed anymore in post war Kent. Lights could be switched on with the curtains wide open without the sound of a whistle from an irate warden, or the worry of being dragged off to court to pay a fine. These were just a few of the things in people's daily lives which were a reminder that the fighting was at an end in Europe, but it wasn't the end of the war.

Just because places like Burma, Singapore, Malaya, the Philippines, the Pacific, and hundreds of small islands in between, were a long way away, didn't mean the war wasn't still going on. Sons, husbands and brothers of families in Kent, were in some of these places continuing the fight, which wouldn't be over until the Japanese had been finally defeated, only then could people start to properly smile again.

With the war in Europe over, men no longer had to spend their evenings standing a guard duty because of their commitment to the Home Guard, whilst the women no longer had to rush off to spend some time at the warden's post. People could start organizing social gatherings without having to worry about cancelling them at the last minute. They could go to the cinema or visit a restaurant without having to worry about the dreaded sound of an air raid warning abruptly cancelling their night out. After five years without a social life, such niceties could once again be woven back in to the very fabric of society and fully enjoyed.

There had been the lifting of certain restrictions and prohibitions and people were once again planning for the future, for a better tomorrow, for a return to a life that had previously existed. The people of Whitstable and Kent were politely reminded that to truly appreciate all such aspects of society, the world had to be returned to its previous state and that could only be achieved when Japan had been defeated and the war was finally over.

During the first week of August, the Surveyor for Dover, Mr P.V. Marchant, presented a report to the local council, concerning the amount of damage that had been caused to the town's homes since the outbreak of the war. It was split into four categories;

(a) Destroyed or subsequently demolished A or B category – 957
(b) Seriously damaged, uninhabitable, C (b) category – 1,158
(c) Seriously damaged, but inhabitable, C (b) category – 1,756
(d) Less seriously damaged, D category – 7,095 (does not include houses where window glass only was damaged.)

The above figures only related to 'dwelling houses' that had been damaged and did not include business premises. They also only related to the numbers of dwellings that had been damaged and did not take in to account how many times each of those properties had been damaged, which was a relevant factor, as many had been damaged on more than one occasion. There were records of some having been damaged thirteen or fourteen times, with one property having being hit by the Luftwaffe on an incredible twenty-seven occasions.

Faced with having to continuingly carry out urgent repairs on so many of its properties, drastic measures had to be taken if the houses concerned were to be repaired to an acceptable standard, and those made homeless as a result of enemy air raids rehoused as quickly as possible. With this in mind, arrangements were made, with the approval of the Ministry of Works and the Ministry of Health, as well as the co-operation of local house agents and builders, to place all building labour in the hands of the local authority. Having this work centralized and with one body in charge, made the process more productive, as well as guaranteeing that all work carried out was done to the exact same specification.

The main problem before the centralization of the workforce was that although there were 346 men engaged in undertaking the work, they worked for sixteen different firm, and even that amount of men wasn't enough. To counter this, assistance for extra labour was also requested from the Army, Navy and the Fire Brigade, who were able to collectively provide between 100 and 500 men on a weekly basis, depending on what their other commitments were. On top of these additional numbers, a further 250 men from the Ministry of Works Special Repair Service were drafted in to the area for the same purpose.

With the end of the war in Europe, and air raids nothing more than a historical footnote, no more homes and businesses were being damaged, which meant that not only was the repair work going along unhindered, more and more homes were being repaired at a much quicker pace, which in turn saw a sharp upturn in the numbers of local residents returning to the town – in August 1945 approximately ninety per week. To this end it was deemed to be just as important to carry out work on repairing shops and business premises as it was homes, to sustain the residents of the town being able to earn a living when they returned to Dover.

At the start of the war Dover Council was given advances totalling £428,100 by the War Damage Commission to cover the cost of war damages and repairs, but that did not include the cost of any wages. Between 26 September 1944 and 30 June 1945, the expenditure incurred on the repair of war damage, once again exclusive of staff wages, amounted to £231,214, a staggering amount of money for the time. Multiplied for every town across the county of Kent, and the rest of the country, the War Damage Commission would have paid tens of millions of pounds. By the end of the war Britain was close to bankruptcy. The war had cost her $120 billion, which by 2005 prices, was $1.26 trillion. The Lend-Lease programme with America, cost Britain £31.4 billion alone, and was exacerbated by the fact that because America expected Germany to defeat the Britain no later than 1940, she wanted paying in dollars, then gold, before she would even consider pounds sterling. The debt was finally paid back as recently as 2006.

Whatever the cost was in financial terms, and whether it was deemed to be excessive or not, it certainly allowed Britain to stay in the war and continue the fight. The cost of the war committed Britain to a period of austerity and comparative poverty and was why petrol was rationed until 1950 and food was rationed until 1954. A cost, that in my opinion was worth every penny, and ensured that the loss of British, Commonwealth and Allied military personnel was not all in vain.

On Friday 7 September 1945 the *Dover Express and East Kent News* announced the sad news of the death of the Mayor of Dover, Councillor John Parker Fish. He died at his home at 165 Buckland Avenue, Dover, aged 75 and had been in poor health for a couple of weeks before he passed away.

It was said that there is little doubt that the assiduous manner in which he conducted himself and carried out the many duties associated with the office of mayor had contributed to his illness. His last official duty was to light the huge bonfire on Whinless Down on VJ (Victory over Japan) night, as part of the town's celebrations, before the many thousands of residents who had turned out to mark the occasion. The next day he had a seizure whilst returning home, one that he sadly never recovered from.

Mr Fish had first been elected as a councillor for the Barton Ward of Dover in 1931, having lived in the area for many years. He was elected mayor in November 1944, a fitting tribute and recognition of his thirteen years loyal service as a councillor.

Celebrations took place in towns and villages all over Kent to mark the end of the Second World War, an occasion that was bitter-sweet for many people. Some were happy of course that after six long, bloody years of war, the fighting was over at last, and they could finally begin to rebuild their lives and move on to a better tomorrow. The sadness came for those who had lost loved ones, many of whom were never brought back to Britain, but buried close to where they were killed, or lost to the depths of the sea.

On 1 January 1939 the total population of the United Kingdom and her Colonies was 47,760,000. Of these, some 383,700 were military personnel who died as a result of their involvement in the Second World War. A further 67,200 were civilians who were killed as a result of enemy military activity.

According to the Commonwealth War Graves Commission website, approximately 7,000 military personnel and 1,000 civilians from Kent lost their lives in the war, and thousands more were injured and wounded. These figures included around 250 individuals who died between 2 September 1945 and 13 December 1947.

The last two people from Kent to die as a result of the war died on the same day and were the same age. They were:

Gunner 19056915 Gerald A. **Taylor** (19), serving with the 1st Regiment, Royal Horse Artillery, who died on 13 December 1947 and is buried in Khayat Beach War Cemetery, in Israel. Before enlisting he lived with his mother, Gladys Lucy Taylor, in Edenbridge, Kent.

Private W/337750 Minnie Maude **Davis** (19), serving with the 721st Car Company, 1st Continental Group, Auxiliary Territorial Service, died on 13 December 1947 and is buried in Munster Heath War Cemetery, in the Nordhein-Westfalen region of Germany. She was the daughter of Charles and Violet Davis, of Cheriton, Kent.

On Sunday 16 September, two weeks after Japan had formally signed the documents of unconditional surrender which brought an end to the hostilities of the Second World War, over 2,000 members of the Kent County Special Constabulary, from all parts of the county, attended a 'stand down' parade and church service at All Saints' Church in Maidstone. It was conducted by Canon A.O. Standen, with an address being given by the Bishop of Rochester who pointed out that God needed men like those sitting before him, so that he could build a new and better world.

After the service the men paraded at the County Police Headquarters, where they were addressed by the Lord Lieutenant of Kent, Lord Cornwallis. He told them that it was appropriate at the same time they were celebrating one of the greatest days in Kent's history, that they should hold a stand down parade from war duties of the Kent Specials. He said that it was most heartening to know that a great many of them had volunteered to continue their service. Few of them had realised at the start of the war, the important nature of their duties. When the country had been threatened with invasion by the might of the German army, they were asked to stand their posts unarmed, except for a wooden truncheon, to succour people in distress, to deal with disorganised traffic, whilst maintaining law and order, with nothing more forceful than a policeman's uniform, 'which every Englishman respected'. He continued:

'There are countless unknown warriors in this country, and I am sure that many of them are to be found in your ranks, and, through me, the county thanks you, not only for your efficiency as policemen but for your tact and forebearance, your understanding and your friendship, and for the way you have carried out your difficult tasks.'

For a large part of the war, Lord Cornwallis had been the Chairman of the Standing Joint Committee which was responsible for police matters, and on behalf of the regular police force, he wished to pass on their heartfelt thanks for the way they had assisted them when depleted in numbers.

As the month of September 1945 drew to a close, there were many celebrations in the towns and villages of Kent, marking the end of the war. At long last they could get on with their lives.

October 1945 saw the interesting story of Company Quartermaster Sergeant Jack Lock, whose home was at 106 St John's Hill, Sevenoaks, Kent. He had the distinction of being the senior non-commissioned officer in the detachment of the Royal West Kent Regiment, which formed part of the guard-of-honour for Admiral Mountbatten in Rangoon when he handed Burma over to the civil administration. Before the war he had worked in the office of the South Suburban Gas Company at Sevenoaks. Lock, having enlisted in the 4th Battalion, Royal West Kent Regiment in May 1939, had served throughout the war and was part of the British Expeditionary Force that was evacuated from Dunkirk in May 1940. The unit was part of the Territorial Army and was predominantly made up of men from the Tunbridge Wells area of Kent.

He had served in France, the Middle East and Burma, with the Eighth and later the Fourteenth Armies. He was involved in the Battle of Kohima in North West India, against the Japanese between 4 and 22 April 1944, this was the same battle that saw one of his colleagues in the 4th Battalion, Lance Corporal John Pennington Harman, win a posthumous Victoria Cross for his actions. Lock escaped at Dunkirk with nothing more than a tattered uniform hanging from his body. During the crossing back home to England, the ship he was on was attacked by aircraft from the Luftwaffe. A bomb exploded so close to his ship that the man standing right beside him was killed instantly.

In early November 1945 the return of local men from Japanese prisoner of war camps was reported in the *Sevenoaks Chronicle and Courier*. Gunner W.E. Cosby of 14 Grove Road, Sevenoaks, Kent, returned home after having been held by the Japanese for three and a half years, after being captured during the fall of Singapore on 15 February 1942. Mr Cosby who returned home during the first week of November, was initially thought to have been killed, with his wife not knowing that he was alive until he had been a prisoner of the Japanese for more than a year. One of the postcards that he had been allowed to write could only contain a certain number of words, and had finally reached his wife back home in England.

He had joined the Royal Artillery in December 1940 and had arrived in Singapore on 13 January 1942. After being taken prisoner he remained there for the next nine months, until 11 October 1942, when he was sent to Thailand with other PoWs to clear a way through the jungle for the Thailand railway that the Japanese wanted to build. Throughout his entire captivity, Mr Cosby saw only one Red Cross parcel, and although intended for one person, it had to be shared between fourteen men. Before the war he had been a coalman in Sevenoaks.

In the same batch of repatriated PoWs was Lieutenant Patrick H. Fuller of the Loyal Regiment. He was reunited with his parents, Mr and Mrs H. Fuller of 40 Granville Road, Sevenoaks, after three and a half years as a prisoner of the Japanese.

Lieutenant Fuller was 30 years of age, and before he had enlisted he was a teacher at a school in Reigate, Surrey. He also became a prisoner of war when the British surrendered Singapore to the Japanese on 15 February 1942, and he then spent the next four months being held at the Changi camp. From there he was sent by cargo ship to Korea, a journey which took two months. He remained a prisoner at the Keiji camp in Korea for the remainder of the war, before being liberated by the Americans on 9 September 1945.

Lieutenant Fuller explained that being a PoW had been a tough time, made worse due to the treatment that they received from the guards. Following his release, he was taken by an American naval ship to Manilla, where he stayed for eight days. From there he boarded HMS *Implacable* and was taken to Vancouver in Canada, via Honolulu. From there it was a rail journey across Canada, and the final leg was by ship, the SS *Isle de France*, home to Britain. On the train journey across Canada, Lieutenant Fuller and his fellow returning PoWs were given a rousing reception at every town they stopped in. They received a civic reception on each occasion, whilst members of the Red Cross distributed chocolates and cigarettes amongst them. At each stop there were parties and dances given in their honour. In Vancouver, where they stayed for eight days, the celebrations were so intense, twenty-eight of the men stayed behind and married local Canadian girls.

On Monday 3 December members of the 4th Battalion, Royal West Kent Regiment, who had just returned home from Burma, were entertained at the Chequers Inn, by the licensee, Mr C. Chittenden. This was a prelude to the welcome and entertainment that was due to be provided to the entire battalion at the Medway Hall in January 1946. Many of those who were present included those who had been with the battalion in the pre-war days, when it was a Territorial unit. One of the men, Private Frank Foster, was Mr Chittenden's son-in-law.

A number of the men joined the battalion soon after the outbreak of the war, and although they did not serve with the British Expeditionary Force, every one of them present had served in the Burma Campaign. At the time of the evening's entertainment, the 4th Battalion was still stationed in Burma, but most of those out there were recently recruited men, which allowed the war veterans to return home for a well-earned break. It was a most enjoyable evening, with complimentary drinks, and dancing to music by the GBS band.

Among the battalion's officers who had recently returned from Burma was Captain A.J. Wiles, of 7 Park Crescent, Tonbridge, who had attended Cambridge University before the war. He joined the battalion in 1941 and served with them in Egypt, El Alamein, India and Burma, taking part in numerous actions along the way.

It was good to see the year ending on such a high note, one of celebration for the fighting being finally over, and for many, a first Christmas at home for seven years, whilst remembering those friends and comrades who were not so lucky and who paid the ultimate price. They were absent in a physical sense but never forgotten in the hearts and minds of those who lived on to see a better tomorrow.

CHAPTER 8

Kent's Police Officers

Many men who were called up into the armed forces in both the First and Second World Wars, were serving police officers, who were still on the Army Reserve, having served in the Army before they had become police officers. This was the main reason for the invention of Special Constables at the outbreak of the First World War. They were ordinary members of the public who had daytime jobs, but who were prepared to police their communities so that those serving policemen who were also Army reservists, could go off and fight in the war. Even though there was a war going on, a nation still needed its police service to maintain law and order and keep the king's peace, otherwise there might be mass unrest, civil disobedience and the potential for the government and the monarchy to be overthrown.

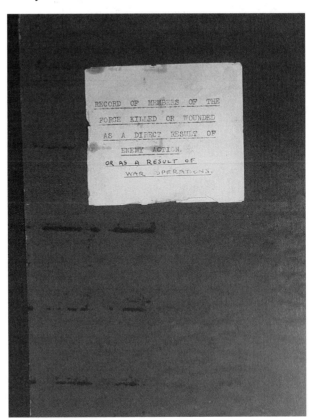

Kent Police Register of officers who were either killed or wounded during the Second World War.

The following list remembers Kent police officers who were either killed or injured as a direct result of enemy action during the Second World War in the Kent area whilst carrying out their policing duties.

Each entry in the register includes the date when the officer was killed or injured, their name and rank, the circumstances of how they were killed or injured, the Chief Constable's comments and any ancillary remarks that were recorded.

The first recorded injuries took place on 18 August 1940. There were two. The first was Report No.S 3054/40 which concerned the injuries caused to Special Sergeant SA 149 **Holt**, which at first glance is somewhat confusing. The circumstances of the incident were that Holt was attempting to free chickens from a chicken coop that was on fire, when an enemy aircraft crashed near his home at Mill View Garage, Barham, Kent, yet he wasn't injured by flying debris from the German plane, but from a bullet wound to his right leg. On hearing of the incident, the Chief Constable said, 'I am sorry to read of Special Constable Holt's wound and I hope his business will not suffer unduly.'

The other incident which occurred on the same day involved Police Constable 745 **Kitney**, who was on duty during an enemy air raid on Biggin Hill aerodrome at 1315 hours on 18 August 1940, when he was struck by flying shrapnel, causing injuries to his face and abrasions to his lower back. He did not return to duty for nearly two months, such was the extent of his injuries, his first day back being 7 October 1940.

The first fatality of a Kent police officer during the war took place on the night of 27/28 August 1940, when Special Constable C 199 **Olive** was on duty during an air raid at Gillingham. He was attempting to assist an injured person who was partly buried under some fallen debris from a shell blast, when another shell fell near by, burying him under even more rubble, which resulted in him receiving injuries, one of which was a wound to his groin from which he subsequently died at St Bartholomew's hospital in Rochester. He left a widow and a young son. The Chief Constable wrote a letter of condolence to Special Constable Olive's widow. Further research shows that this was John Olive, who was 55 years of age and lived at 89 Beatty Avenue, Gillingham. He is buried in the Rochester Municipal Borough Cemetery.

Higher Special Constable S 391 **Bennett** was on duty guarding an enemy aircraft which had crashed at Brasted on 1 September 1940. He was wounded in the right forearm by cannon shell.

Special Sergeant C 82 **Scannel** was on duty on the night of 2 September 1949 in Burnham Road, Wouldham, Kent, during an air raid. He was hit in the right shoulder by a piece of falling anti-aircraft shell. In essence he was shot by one of his own side, albeit not intentionally.

On 7 September 1940 the first deaths took place of full-time serving Kent police officers when Police Constable 396 **Parker** and Police Constable R 280 **Kettle** were on duty taking cover in a private shelter at Mill Lane in Hawkinge, during a German air attack on RAF Hawkinge. Whilst in the shelter with several civilians, one of the German shells scored a direct hit killing everybody inside.

Further research shows that it was Police Constable Ronald Parker who was 23 years of age and who lived at Cornerway, Canterbury Road, Hawkinge. He was buried in the

Elham Rural District Cemetery. His father, Henry Parker, lived at 7 Rothesay Road, Oldham, Lancashire. The other officer was Police Constable Henry Kettle who was 30 years of age and who lived at Rose Cottage, Mill Lane, Hawkinge. He was a single man who lived with his parents, Henry and Annie Kettle and his twin sister, Helen.

It is quite possible that the shelter that the police officers were in at the time of their deaths was the one that belonged to the parents of Henry Kettle. The added sadness to this incident, which isn't recorded in the Police Register, is that Henry's mother, Annie Kettle and his sister Helen Kettle, were also killed in the same attack. All three of them were buried, side by side, in Elham Rural District Cemetery.

The others who were killed in the attack, alongside the Kettles, and buried in the same cemetery, were Beatrice Maude Green (43) and her 17-year-old daughter, Bessie Florence Green, who both lived at 5 St Denys Road, Hawkinge.

On 10 September 1940, Police Constable 1 **Robinson** was off duty and resting on his bed at home at 37 Wickenden Road, Sevenoaks, when his house was demolished by a bomb dropped by a German aircraft during an air raid on the town. Fortunately, he survived the attack suffering only relatively minor wounds, which included shock, bruising to both shoulders, a contused wound to his right side, along with a sprained ankle. He was off sick from work recovering from his injuries until 16 October 1940. Sadly, his 53-year-old mother, Edith May Robinson, was killed in the attack and was buried in the Sevenoaks Urban District Cemetery.

On 15 September 1940 Police Constable 279 **Albon** was assisting his colleagues in guarding a downed Dornier 17 German bomber aircraft that had crashed at Staplehurst in Kent about 2.30 pm that day. At about 4.15 pm an incendiary bomb on board the aircraft, suddenly and without any warning, exploded, causing PC Albon to be burnt by molten magnesium. Despite sustaining a burn to his left hand, bruises on his right shoulder and slight deafness, he carried on working and did not report sick.

Police Constable 58 **Tibble** was also injured as a result of the same incident and received bruises to his back and right side, when he was blown into the air as a result of the incendiary device exploding. Like PC Albon, he remained on duty.

Another officer hurt in the same explosion was Police Constable R 341 **Relf**, who sustained slight cuts to his left arm and wrist, as well as bruises and abrasions to his right leg and right arm, and the hearing in his right ear was slightly affected, when he was thrown to the ground by the force of the explosion.

Police Constable R 350 **Bromley** was hit on the back of the head when a bomb exploded in the wreckage of a crashed German aircraft which had come down at Paddock Wood on 15 September 1940. The explosion occurred at around 7.40 pm, and although he received a bruise to the back of his head, he remained on duty. This was the second time that a crashed German aircraft had a bomb of some description explode after it had been downed. Maybe it was a delayed attempt at totally destroying the aircraft so that it couldn't be properly examined by the British.

On 16 September 1940, Police Constable 19 **Hopper** received a slight wound behind his right ear as the result of being struck by a piece of shrapnel, whilst he was on duty during an air raid at Sittingbourne. Despite what could have proved to be a fatal injury, he remained on duty and carried on regardless.

On 18 September 1940, Special Constable SK 93 **Rogers** who lived at 'Journeys End', Lebanon Gardens, Biggin Hill, was killed when the Anderson shelter he was in, at the bottom of his garden, took a direct hit from a bomb dropped from a German aircraft. His wife was also killed in the explosion. Their deaths left their four young children orphaned. The Commonwealth War Graves Commission website records the couple as being killed on 19 September 1940, and him as being Reginald John Rogers, and her as Daisy Alexander Rogers. They were both buried in the Orpington Urban District Cemetery.

Police Constable R 279 **Hawkins** who was stationed at Sittingbourne in Kent, was on duty on 29 September 1940 outside Sittingbourne police station during an air raid. Two of the bombs that were dropped during the raid landed within just fifteen yards of the police station, blowing PC Hawkins off his feet. As a result of the blast he sustained a badly fractured right leg and severe abrasions and lacerations to his head and body and was lucky to be alive.

On 4 October 1940 Special Constable E 134 **Dearling** is recorded as having sustained severe bruises to his chest and face, along with multiple injuries and shock, as a direct result of enemy action, but the report does not explain in any detail how that came about.. I can only assume that his injuries were the result of an air raid.

Special Constable E 301 **Potten** was killed on 5 October 1940 whilst off duty, but as a direct result of enemy action whilst going about his normal employment, at the junction of The Leas with Earls Avenue in Hythe. The particular entry in relation to SC Potten is sparse and does not include what he did for a living or the circumstances of his death, but once again it is assumed that it was a result of the actions of a German aircraft. Further research shows that SC Potten was 43-year-old Arthur Edward Potten, a married man who lived at The Street, Postling, in Hythe, with his wife, Helen Grace Potten, and that he was buried in the Folkestone Municipal Borough Cemetery.

Arthur had served during the First World War as a Gunner (14753) in the Royal Artillery, Royal Horse and Royal Field Artillery. He had enlisted on 7 September 1914 at Dover, when he was just one month past his nineteenth birthday, and was posted to the 73rd Brigade Royal Field Artillery. But having served for just a total of forty-eight days, he was discharged from the Army for being medically unfit for wartime military service. There is no explanation on his Army Pension Record about exactly what it was that had warranted his medical discharge. This is somewhat at odds with the medical which he had undergone on the day of his enlistment, when he was considered to be fit for the Army, the doctor's report stating: 'I have examined the above named man and find that he does not present any of the causes of rejection specified in the Regulations of the Army Medical Services. He can see at the required distance with either eye; his heart and lungs are healthy; he has the free use of his joints and limbs, and he declares that he is not subject to fits of any description.'

His elder brother Frederick George Potten, had served as a Gunner (76312) with the Royal Garrison Artillery during the First World War and had been killed in action whilst serving in France on 25 November 1917. The family home had then been 2 May Field Terrace, Lyminge, Folkestone, Kent.

Police Constable 199 **Roberts** was carrying a live enemy cannon shell, which had been dropped from a German aircraft, back to his police station at Stelling Minnis, when it exploded. He lost the top joint of the forefinger of his left hand; the top joint of his forefinger and the top joint of his thumb on his right hand, as well as sustaining superficial injuries to both hands, his face and right leg. Presumably the cannon shell PC Roberts was carrying was a relatively small one, because if it had been of a large calibre, it would have killed him.

Special Constable E 218 **Bates** who lived at Lydd in Kent, was at home on 5 October 1940 when his home was hit by a bomb dropped from a German aircraft during an air raid. He sustained a broken leg, a wound to his head and severe shock. Sadly, Mrs Bates was killed, her body was discovered amongst the wreckage. The Chief Constable of Kent, Captain J.A. Davison wrote the following in the register next to the entry for SC Bates: 'I am extremely sorry to read the attached. My sympathy to be conveyed to SC Bates if he is well enough to be seen. I should be very glad to know, incidentally, how he is.'

The Commonwealth War Graves Commission website shows that 36-year-old Isabel Ruth Bates, of The Haven, Skinner Road, Lydd, was killed on 5 October 1940, and that her husband was Graham Henry Bates. Isabel was buried in the Lydd Municipal Borough Cemetery.

Police Constable R 269 **O'Farrell** was on duty during an air raid at Biggin Hill on 12 October 1940 when a bomb dropped from a German aircraft, landed near to where he was. Although not physically injured, he was knocked over and dazed by the concussion blast but remained on duty.

Special Constable SK 15 **Spencer-Hawkins** was on his way to report for duty at Knockholt police station on 15 October 1940, when he heard the sound of German bombs falling from the skies above him. He took shelter at the home of Special Constable 31 Horncastle who happened to live on the route he took to work. One of the bombs exploded close to the house which was severely damaged in the resulting blast. SC Spencer-Hawkins received minor injuries to his head, legs and ankles, whilst SC Horncastle appears to have been unscathed.

Special Constable M 238 **Heine** and Special Constable M 197 **Hunt** were on duty on 16 October 1940 at Wrotham Heath when they entered the Royal Oak public house to purchase some tobacco, when a bomb landed on the premises during an air raid. SC Heine, who was a married man with three children was killed in the blast. The Commonwealth War Graves Commission records that Frederick Walter Heine (40) was killed on 15 October 1940, and that his wife, Lilian Mary Heine, was living at Heathfield, London Road, Addington. It is not clear if that was where the couple were living at the time Frederick was killed or whether that was where Lilian was living at the time that the Commission began collating its records.

Even though Frederick was with his colleague, SC Hunt, at the time of the Royal Oak being bombed, Hunt not only survived but wasn't, it would appear, injured, as he does not appear in the Kent Police Register of those were injured and killed during the Second World War. The following people were however killed in that explosion:

Edith Caroline **Arrogan** (61) of Meadow Cottage, Wrotham Heath.

Harriet **Fread** (80) of the Royal Oak Inn in Wrotham Heath. She initially survived, but died later that day at the Preston Hall Emergency Hospital in Aylesbury.

Margaret **Breeds** (15) of Hill View, London Road Wrotham. She was the daughter of Mr and Mrs John Breeds.

Frederick George **Whiteman** (30) of 1 Ford Bungalows, Ford Place Farm, Wrotham Heath. He was the husband of Marie Yvonne Whiteman.

All of the above, as well as Frederick, were buried in the Malling Rural District Cemetery. An interesting aside to this story, and the question around whether Frederick was killed on either 15 or 16 October 1940, was that figures compiled by the Commonwealth War Graves Commission, record that 654 civilians across the United Kingdom, were victims of the war on 15 October, with a further 531 the following day.

Frederick had come from a big family. His parents, Dalton and Emily Heine, had ten children, although by the time of the 1911 Census only nine of them were still alive. Besides Frederick, there were four other sons and four daughters. Two of Frederick's brothers, Leonard Frank Heine and Leslie Heine, both served in the Army during the First World War, whilst Frederick missed the fighting by about a year.

Leonard enlisted in the Army on 21 February 1912 and became a Private (2030) in the Royal Army Medical Corps, he survived the war and was finally discharged on 2 May 1919, having served for seven years and 71 days. During his wartime military service, he was part of the Mediterranean Expeditionary Force between 17 July 1915 and 16 October 1915, and the Egyptian Expeditionary Force between 13 August 1916 and 20 April 1919.

Leslie Heine was a Private (G/21751) with the 10th Battalion, East Kent Regiment, and was killed in action on 8 December 1917, whilst serving in Palestine and is buried in the Jerusalem War Cemetery.

Special Constable WS 138 **Shearn** was off duty, and visiting Dover Castle on 21 October 1940, when he was struck by shrapnel, which caused injuries to his right arm and thigh.

Special Constable M 196 **Farrow** was off duty and on his way to his job as a baker's delivery man when a bomb from a German aircraft landed in front of his van and exploded. He was conveyed to the West Kent General Hospital at Maidstone, but died the following day. The Commonwealth War Graves Commission shows an Ernest Albert Farrow, a married man who was 51 years of age. He was buried in the Maidstone Municipal Borough Cemetery.

It has to be remembered that the reason for such a large number of casualties in such a relatively short period of time was because this was during the Battle of Britain when there were not many days when the Luftwaffe didn't send aircraft over to Britain to carry out attacks and bombing raids in specific targets, most of which resulted in enemy aircraft having to fly across the skies of Kent.

Police Constable 276 Thomas James **Farrell** was on duty on 1 November 1940 in the London Road in Riverhead, during an air raid. Despite having his steel helmet on for added protection, a splinter of shrapnel from an exploding German bomb, pierced it, killing him instantly. Constable Thomas James Farrell was 38 years of age and a married man who lived at 106 Chipstead Lane, Riverhead, Kent, with his wife, Liliam A. Farrell. He was buried in the Sevenoaks Rural District Cemetery.

Police Constable 155 **Nash** was on duty on 4 November 1940 during an air raid at East Malling, Kent, when ironically he was hit by shrapnel from an anti-aircraft shell, which exploded high in the sky and fell back down to earth, hitting him on the left hand and causing a bad cut to his knuckles.

Police Constable R 532 **Bullock** was on duty on 12 November 1940 at Dartford during an air raid, when a high explosive bomb landed close to where he was. He was taken by ambulance to the County Hospital at Dartford, where an operation was hastily carried out to remove shrapnel splinters from the area of his front upper groin close to the femoral artery.

Next was the extremely sad story of Police Constable R533 **Boorman** who on 12 November 1940 was off duty at home with his wife and young son at 25 Westgate Road, Dartford, when a bomb landed in the back garden of his property and exploded, causing the house to partially collapse. He was buried under the debris before being discovered and taken to the County Hospital at Dartford where he was treated for shock and facial abrasions and detained overnight. His wife, Hettie Margaret Boorman and their 19-month-old son, John Richard Boorman, were killed in the same explosion. They were both buried in the Dartford Municipal Borough Cemetery.

Police Constable R 640 **Reeves** was on duty at the Shepherds Lane barrier in Dartford on 27 November 1940, when a high explosive shell landed about 30 yards away from his location. The force of the subsequent explosion knocked him off his feet, and he was conveyed to the County Hospital at Dartford suffering with shock. He was detained overnight for observations and discharged next morning with a recommendation from the doctor who treated him, that a few day's rest in the circumstances would be appropriate, a decision with which PC Reeves would have no doubt concurred.

Higher Special Constable Captain W.A. **Brown**, proved that even those of rank were not exempt from the dangers of the numerous German air raids that had beset his county. On 8 December 1940 he was on duty near to his home at Shoreham-on-Sea during an enemy air raid, when a high explosive bomb dropped by a German aircraft landed and exploded close to where he was and he was struck by flying glass which resulted in cuts to his hands and face.

Police Constable R 682 **Kemp** was on duty on 21 November 1940 when a German Heinkel 111 bomber aircraft crashed and exploded at Stone. The blast of the subsequent explosion threw him to the ground, causing a slight injury to his right shoulder and left him suffering with shock.

After more than two months passing by without any similar incidents, Special Constable SA 196 **Shaw** was injured on 5 February 1941, as he was attempting to extinguish a number of incendiary bombs which had landed near to his home at Blean, when he was struck by one. He was conveyed to the Kent and Canterbury Hospital where he was treated for injuries to both legs, which included removing a sliver of shrapnel from one of his thighs. He remained in hospital for a number of days.

Police Constable R 707 **Featherstone**, who at the time of this incident on 10 March 1941 was off from work having reported himself sick, was on his way home after visiting a friend when he was struck by shrapnel from an exploding German bomb. He was treated at a nearby First Aid Post. He was fortunate that it turned out to be nothing worst than a flesh wound, marking him just above his right kidney.

Special Constable T 475 **Fowler** was on duty and attempting to remove an incendiary bomb which had landed in the guttering of a property when he sustained wounds to his left hand.

Police Constable R 371 **Bristol** was on duty at the North Foreland Radio Station at Rumsfield, which had been official designated as a Category A Vulnerable Point. It was 1.45am on 12 May 1941, when an air raid began of a particularly heavy nature in the skies over nearby Broadstairs. As the air raid continued it moved nearer and nearer to his location, but before he could get to the safety of a shelter, a high explosive bomb landed close by and he was struck on the left calf by a flying brick which had been dislodged as a result of the explosion and sustained bruising to the muscles of his left leg.

On the night of 4 and 5 June 1941, a large number of incendiary bombs were dropped by German aircraft, which landed in a pea field belonging to Tile Barn Farm at Hoo, but not all of them were discovered at the time. Many were not discovered until the peas were actually picked on 30 July 1941, when Police Sergeant **Lambden**, who was on duty at the time, went to collect them from the farm. Whilst he was examining them and preparing them for transportation to the divisional headquarters, one of them exploded. He received burns to his eyes, face and both arms and was fortunate not to have sustained more serious injuries. He was off work for a number of weeks after the accident.

Police Constable R 363 **Gosbee** was on duty at 9.35 pm on 16 August 1941 making his way to the Broadstairs Control Centre at Pierremont Hall. He had just reached the

Group of Special Constables.

steps leading down to the control centre when a high explosive bomb went off nearby in the High Street. PC Gosbee was blown down the stairs, such was the force of the blast. His injuries, which consisted of bruising to his buttocks, left shoulder and left thigh, along with grazes to the knuckles of both hands, were only of a superficial nature and he did not deem it necessary to seek the assistance of a doctor or report himself sick.

Police Constable R 640 **Williams** was cycling past the Welsh Harp public house at 7.05 pm on the evening of 18 November 1941, when he heard the whistling noise associated with the sound of a falling parachute mine. As he hastily approached the entrance to the public shelter at Banks Yard, pedalling for all he was worth, the mine exploded a short distance behind him, the blast knocking him off his bike, down the steps and into the bottom of the bunker. The record shows that he injured the lower part of his back, but obviously not that badly as he remained on duty.

Higher Special Constable E 52 **Charman** was at home on 23 March 1942 when, just as he opened his front door a bomb exploded outside in the street. The force of the blast knocked him back into the house, and the plaster from the ceiling fell on his face and chest. He suffered from shock, had head and face lacerations and bruising, as well as cuts and abrasions to both hands and wrists.

Police Constable 195 **Constable** was Cecil George Constable, a Kentish man born in Tonbridge, 41 years of age and a married man who lived at 91 Canada Road, Walmer, Kent, with his wife, Irene. It was 6.26 am, he had just finished working a night shift and had arrived home, when in a matter of minutes his home was demolished by a high explosive bomb. He was killed in the blast, but miraculously his wife, Irene, survived. Cecil was buried in the Deal Municipal Cemetery.

Police Constable 173 **Huggins** was Stephen George James Huggins, 37 years of age and a single man of 96 Spencer Road, Herne Bay. At 5.10 pm on the evening of 31 October 1942 he was on duty, standing at the junction of Canterbury Road and Eddington Lane, Herne Bay, when German aircraft strafed Canterbury Road with machine-gun fire. One of the bullets struck him in the forehead. He wasn't killed outright but died later that day at the town's Queen Victoria Memorial Hospital. Stephen was the only serving Kent police officer to be killed during the war by a bullet.

Police Constable 63 **Groombridge** was on duty at about 8.25 am on 3 February 1943 in the High Street, Ashford, when a 500kg bomb was dropped from a low flying German aircraft, landing nearby. The blast from the explosion knocked him through a shop window, shredding his uniform trousers and leaving him with a cut to his left hand. Undeterred, he changed his trousers and calmly went straight back to work, with an 'its all in a day's work' attitude.

The entry in the register for Women's Auxiliary Police Corps member **Palmer** is sparse on detail. All it says is she was in Folkestone at 6.30 pm on 9 April 1943, when there was a low-level attack presumably from a German aircraft. The outcome was that Palmer, her first name or details of whether she was single or married, are not recorded, was left with severe lacerations to both legs. An addition to the entry for Palmer has been added in pencil and reads as follows: 'Not included on monthly returns. Not on actual police duty.'

Women's Auxiliary Police Corps (WAPC) Badge.

In August 1939 the Women's Auxiliary Police Corps was established and catered for women aged between 18 and 55. During the Second World War, women police officers dealt with enemy aliens, evacuees, and refugees. By the end of the war there were an estimated 3,700 members of the Women's Auxiliary Police Corps across the country, along with a further 400 women who were members of the regular police.

Police Constable 167 **Webster** was on patrol duty at 4 am on 19 April 1943 at Ratling Bridge in Aylesham, when he was struck on the left hand by a bomb splinter dropped by an enemy plane causing a minor cut. Despite this, PC Palmer continued his patrol and did not report sick.

Police Constable 682 **Bridges** was off duty at his home address of 11 Arness Road, Swanscombe, when a high explosive bomb fell in the street outside at 1.30 am on 18 May 1943, resulting in PC Bridges suffering from shock and superficial cuts to his face and left leg.

Chief Inspector **Fleet** was on duty just past midnight on 18 August 1943, when he was assisting other police officers and members of the Fire Service in the removal of homeless people in Kingsgate, when a high explosive bomb landed and exploded in nearby Percy Avenue. In an effort to avoid injury Chief Inspector Fleet threw himself to the ground and struck his chest on the kerb which resulted in bruising and soreness to his chest and lower ribs.

Higher Special Constable **Tainton** was carrying out an inspection of the ARP Warden's post at George Hill Road, Broadstairs on 18 August 1943, when a German aircraft dropped a bomb which landed nearby and exploded, the blast of which blew him into the warden's shelter. As a result HSC Tainton received a cut to his right leg, numerous bruises and shock.

At just after midnight on 18 August 1943, a bomb landed in the rear garden of Fairfield, Foreland Avenue, Margate Police Constable 12 **Bannister** having been informed of the incident, immediately turned out from his home to investigate, but as he ran along Foreland Avenue he caught his left foot in some roadside debris, and twisted it, causing a bad sprain.

Women's Auxiliary Police Corps member **Thorogood** was on duty at 2 am on 21 December 1943, when a high explosive bomb dropped at Park Avenue, Northfleet, which was the same street in which WAPC Thorogood lived. She wasn't physically hurt by the resultant explosion but was left suffering with shock.

At 9.30 pm on the evening of 29 January 1944 a German aircraft dropped a high explosive bomb which scored a direct hit on the property at 5 School Avenue,

Gillingham, the home of Police Constable 725 **Russell** a 37-year-old married man. He was killed in the explosion and buried a few days later at Gillingham Municipal Borough Cemetery. His wife, Henrietta Louise Russell, survived the attack.

Sergeant **Wood** and Police War Reserve Constable 29 **Woodland** were on duty at 2 pm on 5 February 1944 when a Flying Fortress of the United States Air Force, crashed on bungalows in Lyndhurst Road, Dymchurch. The entry in relation to the incident isn't detailed, but I can only assume that they were close by at the time of the crash, as both men were shown as having suffered with shock, whilst PWR Woodland, also suffered minor injuries to his right ankle.

At 11.15 pm on the evening of 14 March 1944, Police War Reserve Constable 190 **Tong** was on duty and trying to rescue the occupants of a café, in an un-named Kent town, that had been hit by a high explosive bomb dropped by a German aircraft. Whilst sifting feverishly through the rubble, looking for people who were trapped, he sprained his ankle.

Police War Reserve Constable 378 **Sellen** was on duty on 25 February 1944 when he was carrying pieces of an exploded phosphorous bomb to a place of safety and in doing so suffered a burn to his left forearm.

On 5 August 1944 Police Sergeant 248 William George **Braddick**, aged, 37 and a married man, was killed whilst off duty, when a 'flying bomb' landed on his home at 2 Elmfield Villas, Malling Road, Snodland. His wife, Alice Olive Braddick, was also killed in the blast. Both William and Alice were buried side by side at Malling Rural District Ceremony.

Police War Reserve (PWR) Badge.

By flying bomb, I am assuming the register is referring to the German Luftwaffe's V-1 Rockets or flying bombs, the first of which was launched on 13 June 1944 and targeted London, just a week after the D-Day landings. Between the firing of the first V-1 Rocket and October 1944, more than 9,500 were launched across the Channel towards the south-east of England, which at its peak was more than one hundred per day.

Police Constable **Miller** suffered a bruised back when he was blown off his bicycle by an exploding German shell on 6 September 1944.

Police War Reserve Constable 248 Frederick **Chapman** was off duty at 8.50 pm on 20 June 1944, when a bomb landed on his home at Lillys, Chelsfield, which resulted in the 49-year-old constable receiving a severe head wound from which he died at 11 pm at the County Hospital, Farnborough, the same day. Frederick's wife Edith Mary Chapman, who was eleven years his senior, was also killed in the blast. They were both buried in the Orpington Urban District Cemetery.

Special Constable D 90 Harry Thomas Redvers **Pankhurst** was 43 years of age, and lived with his wife, Mabel Kathleen Pankhurst, at The Bungalow, Ingress Abbey Estate, Greenhithe, when he was killed on 16 June. He was on duty when he was killed by an exploding British anti-aircraft shell, at Rochester Way, Greenhithe. He was buried in the Bexley Municipal Borough Cemetery.

On 15 September 1944 Police Sergeant 308 William George **Dickinson** aged 49, had returned to his home at 29 Walton Gardens, Folkestone, where he was a member of the Folkestone Borough Police Force, when he heard a shell burst close by. He opened his front door to go and see if his colleagues in the area needed any help, and had almost reached his front garden gate, when another shell exploded 20 yards away from where he was, killing him instantly. Such was the force of the blast, his head was nearly severed from his body.

William had served during the First World War, having enlisted on 28 October 1914 at Dover, just a month before his twentieth birthday, and was initially allocated to the Household Cavalry as a Trooper (3382). With the war just six months from its close, he transferred to the Life Guards, where he became a Trooper (3456) in the Guards Machine Gun Regiment. Before joining up he had worked as a hotel porter in Folkestone. He served in France with the British Expeditionary Force for nearly four years from 18 May 1915 until 6 March 1919, and was awarded the 1914-15 Star, the British War Medal and the Victory Medal for his wartime service.

On 10 January 1918 he faced a Field General Court Martial, having been charged that, when on active service on the nights of 30 and 31 December 1917, he did neglect to the prejudice of good order and military discipline as he was not alert when acting as one of a detached post. He was found guilty as charged and his punishment was 56 days Field Punishment No.1. The ultimate sanction that a Field General Court Martial could administer was the death penalty. Field Punishment No.1 consisted of the guilty individual being shackled in irons and secured to a fixed object, a gun wheel or something similar, for up to two hours in every twenty-four hours and not for more than three days out of four. It was an extremely humiliating experience for a man to have to endure.

Having served for four years and 158 days, he was eventually demobilized on 4 April 1919 in London. His home address at the time was 29 Watkin Road, Folkestone, where he lived with his parents, George and Bessie Dickinson, along with his sister Ethel.

There was a degree of irony in William's death. He had served in France for nearly four years and survived, having not been touched by either bullet or bomb, yet twenty-six years later, whilst still serving his country, albeit in a different uniform, he was killed by an untargeted German bomb just yards from his own front door.

There wasn't much detail for the entry concerning Detective Constable 938 **Lowe**, other than on 10 August 1944 he had cut a finger as a result of flying glass from an explosion at Ely and did not seek medical attention.

Police War Reserve Constable 53 **Boon** suffered a finger wound on 23 August 1944, when his left hand was struck by shrapnel during anti-aircraft fire against German parachute bombs.

On 6 September 1944 Police Constable E.F.S. **Miller** suffered a bruised back when a high explosive shell dropped from a German aircraft blew him from his bicycle whilst he was patrolling his patch. He got back on his bike and continued his patrol but five days later he reported sick with anxiety neurosis brought on by the earlier incident. Anxiety neurosis is described as leading to panic disorder where a person suffers from brief attacks of intense terror and apprehension, frequently marked by trembling, confusion, dizziness, nausea and a difficulty in breathing.

On top of these brave officers, there were a number of other police officers who were killed in different, and unrelated accidents, which did not come about as a direct result of enemy related actions, so they are not included in this section.

During the Second World War Kent Constabulary had three different Chief Constables. The first of these was Major Harry Ernest Chapman CBE DL who was in charge of the force between January 1921 and 1940.

He was born at Telega on 19 February 1870, in what was then Austro-Hungary, but is now Romania. His military career began when he was commissioned as a second lieutenant in the Border Regiment on 9 April 1892 and served in the Waziristan Field Force between 1894–95, as part of the continuous fighting throughout the North West Frontier region of what was then the British Indian Empire. He was promoted to the rank of lieutenant on 1 July 1895 and further promoted to captain on 8 June 1902. He died on 12 January 1944 at the age of 73 at Bembridge, Isle of Wight.

The man who took over from Major Chapman and became the new Chief Constable of Kent in 1940 was Captain John Arthur Davison, aged 43, who was born in Sevenoaks, Kent in 1897. He died in hospital on 13 October 1942 from a bullet wound to the head. He had been found in a wood near Maidstone, with a revolver by his right hand, by Police Inspector F. Wood, who had followed him after he had left the Kent County Police Headquarters just after midday on 10 October 1942. The inquest into his death took place on 15 October, with the county coroner for Kent, Mr W.H. Whitehead recording a verdict of suicide, in that Captain Davison took his own life, and at the time he did so, his mind was deranged.

Evidence presented to the coroner showed that late on the morning of Saturday 10 October a female dispatch rider from County Hall delivered a letter personally to Captain Davison as she had been instructed to do. After having opened and read the letter he immediately left his office. The letter in question was subsequently discovered on Captain Davison's desk by Chief Superintendent Shepherd, who in turn handed it over to the coroner. It was from the Kent County Standing Joint Committee and was an acceptance of the Chief Constable's resignation with effect from the time that the letter was delivered. Chief Superintendent Shepherd also informed the inquest that he had received a phone call from Captain Davison asking him to go to his office and deal with his letters. Amongst the correspondence was a letter addressed to him.

Thus do I say farewell to the unhappy world, leave of which should have been taken as a soldier in Libya. I said after surviving the last war, which I ought never to have done, that I did not expect to reach the age of 40, but there it is. When everything goes wrong there is but one court, as Dean Inge had it, 'To declare the innings closed.'

Matters between the Standing Joint Committee and the Chief Constable had been on-going since July 1942, and were believed to have been of a monetary nature and in relation to certain undisclosed disciplinary matters. Captain Davison was directed by the committee to attend a meeting with them on 9 October 1942, but he failed to do so.

His widow told the inquest that she knew of no monetary troubles that her late husband might have had. In his Will he left the sum of £1,118. 2s. 6d to his wife Dorothy Mary Davison.

He had served and seen action during the First World War, initially going out to France on 5 December 1916 as an acting captain with the 1st Battalion, Rifle Brigade. During his wartime service, he was awarded the Military Cross for bravery.

The third wartime Chief Constable of Kent was the distinguished, Sir Percy Joseph Sillitoe. He was born at Tulse Hill in London on 22 May 1888. His career had seen him join the British South Africa Police in what was then Southern Rhodesia, today's Zimbabwe, when he was 21 years of age in 1909. During the First World War he served in both Northern Rhodesia and Nyasaland, today's Zambia and Tanzania.

He returned to Britain in 1922, to recover from rheumatic fever which he contracted during his time in Africa. Having recovered from his illness, his long and illustrious police career in England began. In 1923 at 35 years of age and with no previous policing experience in the United Kingdom, he acquired a job with Chesterfield Borough Police, based in Beetwell Street, not as a lowly police constable, but as the man at the top, the Chief Constable. By nature, he must have been a restless character, because two years later he

Sir Percy Joseph Sillitoe.

moved on, this time becoming Chief Constable of the East Riding Constabulary, and the following year, on 1 May 1926 he became the Chief Constable of Sheffield Police.

After the death of the Chief Constable of Glasgow, Andrew Donnan Smith, on 19 June 1931, Percy Sillitoe, along with more than thirty other candidates, applied for the job. On 22 December 1931 it was he who was appointed as the city's new Chief Constable, and whilst in post was responsible for many innovative ideas that were ground breaking for their time, including being the man responsible for police officers wearing chequered cap bands.

He was knighted in the 1942 New Year's Honours list and, after resigning from Glasgow Police on 28 February 1943, he became the new Chief Constable of Kent soon after. This was his fifth and final appointment as a Chief Constable.

In 1946 Sir Percy left the Kent Constabulary and was appointed the Director General of MI5, a position he held for seven years until he retired in August 1953. In 1951 as the head of the agency he became embroiled in the Burgess and Maclean spy case, when both men managed to escape to Russia before they could be fully exposed for what they were. It was the only time that Sir Percy had attracted negative press, as in the subsequent investigation it was highlighted how MI5 were unaware of their activities, and when they eventually did discover what was happening, they were slow to act in response.

Without a doubt Sir Percy was the most enigmatic and influential Chief Constable that Kent Police has ever had at its helm.

During the Second World War twenty-six members of the Kent Constabulary, left the force to serve with His Majesty's Armed Forces. Some of these men were wounded and others were killed.

Police Constable 420 Charles Phillip **Stammers**, who served in the Canterbury Division, left to join the Royal Navy as a Signalman (C/J75151) and served on HMS *Kelvin*, a K-Class destroyer, which was commissioned on 27 November 1939. He was 38 years of age when he died in a drowning accident on 10 February 1940. He was buried in Romford Cemetery.

Police Constable 58 Kenneth Amos **Cradduck**, who served in the Ramsgate Division, left to join the 2nd Field Squadron, Royal Engineers where he held the rank of corporal (1870089). He was 26 years of age when he died on active service on 3 October 1941, having been awarded the Military Medal. He was buried in Khayat Beach War Cemetery which is in Tel-Aviv, Israel.

Police Constable 54 John **Nicholson**, who served in the Gravesend Borough Police, left to join the Royal Naval Patrol Service as an able seaman. He served on the crew of HM Drifter *Rosebud*, and was killed on active service on 23 December 1942. The Commonwealth War Graves Commission website records Ordinary Seaman (LT/JX382575) John Nicholson (27), a married man, whose wife, Beryl Monica Nicholson, later lived at Langdon Hills. John is buried there in the churchyard of St Mary and All Saints Church. The church has for many years existed as a private residence, although the cemetery is still available for members of the public to visit.

Police Constable 45 Ronald Frank **Thain**, who served in the Dover Borough Police, before joining the Royal Air Force Volunteer Reserve as a Flying Officer (124843).

John Nicholson's Headstone.

He died on 27 March 1943 in a flying accident, and left a widow, Ellen Dorothy Thain. He is buried in the Charlton Cemetery at Dover.

Police Constable 1247 John George **Watkins** served in the Folkestone Constabulary, before leaving to join the Royal Air Force Volunteer Reserve as a Sergeant Air Bomber (1390906) as part of No.166 Squadron, whose motto was 'Tenacity'. It had originally been formed at Bircham Newton in Norfolk on 13 June 1918 during the First World War but was disbanded only a matter of months later on the signing of the Armistice. The unit was reformed in November 1936 as a heavy bomber squadron but lost its individual identity when it was subsequently merged with other units. It didn't regain its full independence until January 1943 when it was reformed as a bomber squadron and found its new home at Kirmington, Lincolnshire. The aircraft flown by its crews were Wellingtons and Lancasters.

John Watkins died on 26 May 1943 and is buried in the Woensel General Cemetery in Eindhoven, Holland.

Lancaster Bomber.

Police Constable 1129 George James **Mitchener**, who served with the Tunbridge Wells police, also left to join the Royal Air Force Volunteer Reserve; as a sergeant navigator (1389928) he also served with No.166 Squadron and also died on 26 May 1943. John Watkins and George Mitchener were either part of the same crew or were on the same raid when they were killed, with Mitchener also being buried in the same Woensel General Cemetery in Eindhoven in Holland.

The Operations Record Book for No.166 Squadron, No.1 Group, shows the following entry for 25 May 1943, which was initially marked as SECRET.

14 Aircraft took off to attack Dusseldorf. 12 aircraft dropped 3,240 x 4lb bombs, 270 x 4lb, 316 x 30lb, and 27 x 500 lb bombs on the target. Eight enemy aircraft were seen but no combats developed. Moderate to intense flak was encountered over the target area, but no searchlights were seen. M/166 and H/166 failed to return. The operation was carried out in conditions of poor visibility with much haze and was a very successful effort.

The following day the squadron was stood down from operations, but the men and aircraft were back to work as usually, carrying out more bombing raids on the night of 27 May 1943.

Police Constable 953 Cyril Ernest **Wellard**, who served in the Swale Division, left to join the Royal Air Force as a Flying Officer (131125), serving with No.100 Squadron. He was a married man who lived with his wife, Betty Margaret Wellard, at Boughton, Kent.

No.100 Squadron Royal Air Force was reformed on 15 December 1942 and was stationed at RAF Grimsby as a night time heavy bomber squadron and was part of No.1 Group, Bomber Command. From March 1943, flying Avro Lancasters, the squadron was involved in Bomber Command's targeted raids on German cities.

Lancaster Bomber Crew.

On the evening of 21 April 1943 he was involved in a night operation, and his aircraft never returned, he was officially reported as being missing presumed dead from that date. His body was subsequently discovered and he was buried in the Lemvig Cemetery, a coastal town in Western Jutland, Denmark.

Police Constable 928 Jack Dighton **Bennett** (27) was a single man who served in the Thames Division of the Kent Constabulary, and left to join the Royal Navy as an Able Seaman C/JX 332202. He was reported as missing presumed dead as of 24 April 1943, according to the Kent Constabulary's Register which lists its men who left the force to enlist in the armed forces. The Commonwealth War Graves Commission has his date of death as 27 March 1943, but it is definitely the same man.

Jack Bennett was serving on board HMS *Dasher* which was a Royal Navy Avenger class aircraft carrier. On 27 March 1943 she was in the Firth of Clyde, with one of her Swordfish planes practising taking off and landing from her deck. Suddenly and without warning, there was a violent internal explosion, and in only five minutes the ship was beneath the waves. There were 149 survivors who were plucked from the sea, including 36 officers and 113 ratings, whilst another 379 men lost their lives. Rescue attempts were not helped by the gallons of oil which had leaked from the ship and then caught fire.

An official board of enquiry that was convened just two days after the *Dasher* sank, concluded that an internal petrol explosion because of leaking fuel pipes was ultimately what led to the devastating explosion. Many other reasons and theories have been put forward as to how HMS *Dasher* met her end. These range from her having struck a mine, to being torpedoed, to one of the aircraft crashing into it, to sabotage. No one is absolutely certain what happened on that fateful day. What is clear, is the government of the day did not want anything about the incident getting out. Even the documents from the Board of Enquiry were not made public until 1972.

Police Sergeant 254 Rodney Sydney **Bowden**, aged 30 and a married man, served in the Ramsgate Division of the Kent Constabulary. He left to join the Royal Air Force Volunteer Reserve as a Flying Officer Navigator (142347) with No.576 Squadron, during the early years of the war. He was killed on 4 December 1943 and is buried in the Berlin 1939-1945 War Cemetery. Approximately 80 per cent of the British military personnel who are buried there, are airmen who lost their lives whilst on bombing missions over the city of Berlin and towns in eastern Germany.

The motto of No.576 Squadron was 'Carpe diem' or 'Seize the day'. It came in to being on 25 November 1943, a heavy bomber squadron that flew Lancaster Mk I and III aircraft, which was based at Elsham Wolds, Lincolnshire. It had only been in existence for nine days when Rodney Bowden was killed.

Police Constable 1176 George Edward O. **Milham** (28) was a married man who served in the Folkestone Division of Kent Constabulary and left to join the Royal Artillery as a Gunner (14253879). He served with the 142nd (The Royal North Devon Yeomanry) Field Regiment and was killed in action in Italy on 15 January 1944.

At the outbreak of the war the 142nd Field Regiment was a home defence unit, before being sent out to Sicily and Italy from July 1943, where it took part in the landings in Sicily and Anzio as well as the Battle of Monte Cassino. George Milham is buried in the war cemetery at Minturno about 50 miles north of Naples.

Police Constable 1117 Arthur J.W. **Upton** (28) was a married man who lived in Strood, Rochester, with his wife, Evelyn Peggy Upton. As a member of Kent Constabulary he served in the Medway District, but he left to join the Corps of Military Police at the rank of lance corporal (14249660) in the early years of the war. He died on 29 January 1944 and is buried in St Margaret's Churchyard, Rochester.

142nd Field Regiment.

Above left*: RAF Recruitment Poster.*

Above right*: No. 467 Squadron (Kangaroo).*

Police Constable 1110 John Frederick **Cusworth** (31) was a married man who lived in Pudsey with his wife, Grace Edna Cusworth. He was another who served in the Medway Division of the Kent Constabulary, but who left to join the Royal Air Force Volunteer Reserve as a Pilot Officer Navigator (148746). He was killed in action on 31 January 1944. His name is commemorated at the Lawnswood Crematorium, Leeds.

Police Constable 864 Maurice **Turner** (38) was a married man who lived at Margate with his wife Rosetta Florence Turner, he also served in the Margate Division of the Kent Constabulary, and left to join the Royal Air Force Volunteer Reserve as a Sergeant Pilot (1389695) during the early years of the war.

He was part of No.467 Squadron, a Royal Australian Air Force bomber squadron, whose theatre of operations was Europe. Although an Australian squadron it came under the command of the Royal Air Force and included personnel from different Commonwealth nations, Maurice Turner being proof of that. The squadron's base was initially at RAF Scampton in Lincolnshire, having been formed there on 7 November 1942. Flying Avro Lancaster heavy bombers, it was part of No.5 Group, Bomber Command. But by the time it flew its first operations on 2 January 1943 laying mines off the French coast near Furze, the squadron had moved to RAF Bottesford.

The squadron's aircraft left their home base on the evening of 5 January 1944, to carry out night time operations over Europe, but sadly Maurice Turner and his crew mates never returned. He has no known grave and his name is commemorated on the Runnymede Memorial in Surrey, which includes the names of more than 20,000 airmen who were lost during the war who flew from bases either in the United Kingdom or in north or western Europe.

Police Constable 1134 Frederick Ernest **Greenstreet** (29) was a married man who lived with his wife Joan Elizabeth Sylvester Greenstreet, in Folkestone. He served in the Folkestone Division of the Kent Constabulary, but with the beginning of the war he left to join the 53rd Divisional Provost Company, Corps of Military Police as a lance corporal (14245460).

He was killed in action on 21 July 1944 and is buried in the Brouay War Cemetery, in the Calvados region of France. Most of those buried there were from Commonwealth forces who were engaged in attempts to encircle the city of Caen.

Police Constable 796 John **Hands** (32) was a married man and lived with his wife, Marjorie, in Hythe, Kent. He served in the Tunbridge Wells Division of the Kent Constabulary, before leaving to join the Royal Air Force Volunteer Reserve as a sergeant pilot (1390983), and became part of No.415 Squadron, which was formed on 20 August 1941 at Thorney Island, Hampshire. By July 1944 it was part of No.6 Group of Bomber Command, with its crews flying Halifax Mark III aircraft.

John Hands was killed in action whilst engaged in night time operations on 12 July 1944, the very day that the squadron had officially changed from being part of Coastal Command to Bomber Command. He was initially reported as being missing in action, which was then changed to death presumed, as of 13 July 1944. He has no known grave, but his name is commemorated on the Runnymede Memorial in Surrey.

Brouay War Cemetery.

Pilot 1944.

Police Constable 779 Frank Ernest **Mitchell** was a married man and a policeman who served in the Folkestone Division of the Kent Constabulary, but with the outbreak of the Second World War, he left to join the Royal Air Force Volunteer Reserve as a flying officer and bomb aimer (129679). He joined No.431 Squadron, which was part of the Royal Canadian Air Force, although it came under the control of Bomber Command. By the time Frank Mitchell met his death, the squadron was flying out of RAF Croft in County Durham, which had been opened in 1941. His aircraft did not return from a bombing operation on 18 July 1944 and he was presumed dead as of that time. He is buried in the Communal Cemetery in the village of Cramoisy, in the Oise region of France.

Police Constable 1197 John Edward **Harling**, aged 27 years of age and married served in the Thames Division of Kent Constabulary, but left to join the Royal Air Force Volunteer Reserve as a sergeant (1399617) at the beginning of the war, serving as part of No.515 Squadron.

The squadron, which was equipped with de Havilland Mosquito Mk VIs, and had been formed on 1 October 1942, was famous for the first use of Electronic Counter Measures (ECM) technology, which allowed for the jamming of enemy radar installations. Its motto was *Cleriter ferrite ut hostes nacesit,* which means 'Strike quickly to kill the enemy'. The squadron had been part of Bomber Command since December 1943 and moved to Little Snoring in Norfolk at that time.

He was reported as missing presumed dead after failing to return from an operation on 27 August 1944. His grave is located in the town of Amersfoort General Cemetery, which is in the Utrecht region of Holland.

Police Constable 1194 Frederick George **Ovenden** aged 26 and a married man who served in the Thames Division of the Kent Constabulary, left to join the Royal Air Force Volunteer Reserve in the early months of the war, when he became a leading

RAF Croft.

aircraftman (1626444). He was on a training flight in Canada when his aircraft went missing on 6 December 1944, and did not return to its base. Frederick has no known grave, but his name is commemorated on the Ottowa Memorial in Toronto, Canada.

Police Constable 924 William Edward Heaton **Barty** was born in Thanet, Kent, and went on to serve with the County Constabulary in the Thames Division. He enlisted at Cardington, Bedfordshire, in March 1943 into the Royal Air Force Volunteer Reserve as pilot officer 187752, with No.429 Squadron, based at Leeming, North Yorkshire and flew Halifax MK IIs.

He was killed in action on 6 December 1944 and has no known grave, but his name is commemorated on the Runnymede Memorial in Surrey. The memorial was unveiled by Her Majesty Queen Elizabeth II on 17 October 1953.

Police Constable 1024 Edgar James **Wilmot** served at Sevenoaks police station before leaving to join the Royal Air Force Volunteer Reserve as a sergeant navigator (1801568), early on in the war. He was killed in a flying accident on 10 January 1945 and is buried in the Greatness Park Cemetery in Sevenoaks, Kent.

Police Constable 1144 Clifford **Jackson** left to join the Army and became a Gunner (14668280) in the 28 Field Regiment, Royal Artillery. He was 29 years of age when he died of his wounds on 16 October 1945 and is buried in the Taukkyan War Cemetery in what is now Myanmar, but in 1945 was known as Burma. Although the war in Europe had finished in May 1945, the fight against the Japanese in Burma was still in full swing in October that year, with the enemy having either not been aware of their country's surrender or chosen to ignore it. The cemetery was not completed until

1951 when the remains of men who had initially been buried in Akyab, Mandalay, Meiktila, and Sahmaw were moved there. The original locations were hard to access and difficult to maintain.

Police Constable 1256 Arthur Thomas **Mullard**, who served in Gravesend, left to join the Royal Navy as a temporary sub-lieutenant. He was initially reported missing on active service from 12 April 1945, this was subsequently changed to the presumed date of his death. I could not however find a match for him on the Commonwealth War Graves Commission website for those who lost their lives during the Second World War.

Police Constable 1077 Alfred William **Stapleton** who served in the Tonbridge Division of the Kent Constabulary, left to join No.5 Royal Marine Commando. He also served with the Queen Victoria Rifles, before ending up as a rifleman (14311519) with the King's Royal Rifle Corps, with which he was serving at the time of his death on 31 January 1945. He is buried in the Taukkyan War Cemetery in Burma, now called Myanmar.

Police Constable 1061 Neil **McGaw**, who served in the Gravesend District of the Kent Constabulary, left to join the Royal Air Force as a pilot officer (173338) and was with No.625 Squadron at the time of his death on 4 May 1944. He is buried in the churchyard of the parish church at the village of Trouan-le-Petit in the Aube region of France.

No.625 Squadron, whose motto was 'We avenge', was based at Kelstern, Lincolnshire between October 1943 and April 1945, and was a heavy bomber squadron equipped with Lancasters, carrying out bombing missions on German towns and cities. Kelstern had only become fully operational on 18 August 1943 and was officially opened by Air Commodore Arthur 'Hoppy' Wray.

Police Constable 1088 William Johnston **Tawse**, who served in Gravesend District, was a single man whose parents, William and Helen Tawse, lived in Tunbridge Wells. He left the police to join the Royal Navy, where he became a chief motor mechanic, 4th Class (C/MX 11626PK) and was a holder of the Military Medal. He died on 4 May 1945 and is buried in Tunbridge Wells Cemetery. At the time of his death he was serving at HMS *Pembroke II*, a shore-based establishment.

The next group are the six members of the Kent Constabulary who left the force to enlist in His Majesty's Armed Forces, but who then were captured by the Germans and became prisoners of war. The information contained in the Register of the Kent Constabulary, concerning these men, is sparse.

Police Constable 467 John **Fail** of the Medway policing district, joined the Royal Artillery and acquired the rank of battalion sergeant major. He was initially reported missing in action, but it was subsequently confirmed that he had become a prisoner of war some time in early 1942 and was being held in Japan. This would suggest that he had been serving in either Singapore, Malaya or Burma at the time of his capture. There was no further information about which unit of the Royal Artillery John Fail was serving with.

Police Constable 1002 H **Edmondson** served in the Wingham Division of Kent Constabulary, before becoming a lance corporal in the Corps of Military Police. He became a prisoner of war on 15 July 1941, but the entry in the register does not provide any further information apart from that he was 'released and returned to England'.

However, on the list of UK British Prisoners of War 1939-1945, which can be found by searching the records on the Ancestry.co.uk website, I discovered the following information: Lance Corporal (819747) H. Edmundson. Corps of Military Police. PoW No: 16723. Camp: Stalag 344. Camp Location: Lambinowice, Poland.

Police Constable 1000 J.G. **Pilkington** served in the Wingham Division of Kent Constabulary before enlisting in the Armed Forces and becoming a flying officer in the Royal Air Force Volunteer Reserve. He was initially listed as missing presumed dead on 11 November 1943, after his aircraft failed to return from an operation. It was subsequently ascertained that he had been captured and held as a prisoner of war.

The listings for UK British Prisoners of War 1939-1945 provided the following information: Flight Lieutenant (135888) J.G. Pilkington. Royal Air Force Volunteer Reserve. PoW No: 5107. Camp: Stalag Luft L3. Camp Location: Sagan and Belaria, Poland.

Police Constable 1202 J.W.G **Dorrell** served in the Ashford district of the Kent Constabulary, before enlisting as a lance bombardier in the Royal Artillery. He became a prisoner of war late on in the war, not being captured until 16 January 1945 and liberated less than three months later on 2 April 1945 by US Forces and returned to England.

The listings for UK British Prisoners of War 1939-1945 provided the following information: Lance Bombardier (14248525) J.W. Dorrell. Royal Artillery. PoW No: 93209. Camp: Stalag Vlll-C. Camp Location: Konin Zaganski, Poland.

Police Constable 1127 H.D. **Burwash** served in the Maidstone division of the Kent Constabulary, but like many of his colleagues, once the war had begun he wanted to do his bit. He was commissioned as a lieutenant into the Parachute Regiment and was captured just twenty days before the official unconditional German surrender on 7 May 1945, confirming the end of the Second World War. He was liberated by American troops on 10 May 1945 and returned to England.

The listings for UK British Prisoners of War 1939-1945 provided the following information: Lieutenant (251647) H.D. Burwash. Army Air Corps. PoW Number: 2196. Camp: Oflag Lx-A/Z. Camp Location: Rotenburg as der Fulda, Hesse.

Police Constable 1160 N **Bradley** served in the Tonbridge division of the Kent Constabulary, but he enlisted and became a sergeant in the Grenadier Guards. Like Lieutenant Burwash, Sergeant Bradley was captured, became a prisoner of war on 17 April 1945 and was released by US Forces on 10 May.

The listings for UK British Prisoners of War 1939-1945 provided the following information: Sergeant (2614584) N. Bradley. Grenadier Guards. PoW No: 127753. Camp: Stalag Vll-A. Camp Location: Moosburg an der Isar, Bavaria, Germany.

The Kent Constabulary Register also contains the names of a further twenty-two of its officers who were injured or reported sick as an indirect result of enemy action. An example of what constitutes inclusion in this particular category is as follows.

At 0345 hours on 31 July 1941 a British Hampden Bomber crashed on East Hill, Dartford. The rear portions of five houses were demolished and resulted in what remained of the properties, catching fire. Sergeant **Halls**, a member of Dartford police managed to rescue two of the people who were trapped in the ruins of the buildings, but in doing so strained his back whilst helping to lift two large and heavy joists that had trapped a woman.

The only other individual from this category is Special Constable S514, **Bazley-White**. On 17 November 1940, he saw a British aeroplane crash in a field near his home. He rushed towards the chaotic scene on foot but collapsed and died a few minutes after reaching the location of a suspected heart attack.

The last category that has been recorded in the register is a list of five names of members of the force who became disabled as a result of the injuries or wounds they received as a result of the war. The entry does not clarify if the men concerned incurred these disabilities as a result of their wartime police service, or whilst members of His Majesty's Armed Forces.

Police Inspector 99 A. **Gray**. J Division.
Police Constable 1085 G.F.H. **Jenney**. E Division.
Police Constable 983 H. **McLaughlin**. C Division.
Police Sergeant 1059 D. **Parking** DSO. R Division
Police Constable 702 P.C.A. **Saville**. K Division.

There were also no individual descriptions of what disabilities each of the men had. All in all, the register is an interesting and informative historical document that has been saved for future generations of historians and other interested parties to view, in their quests to find answers and information to previously unanswered questions concerning those who had served the county of Kent before and during the Second World War.

CHAPTER 9

Dover Castle

Dover Castle dates back to 1066 and was one of the first Norman castles in the country. The tunnels which lie beneath it were cut out of the soft white chalk that make up the cliffs of Dover and were part of the reason that it played such a significant part in the Second World War. The tunnels had been there since before the Napoleonic Wars, 1803 to 1815, and were part of the defensive systems that were put in place to defend the county against the potential threat of a French invasion from directly across the English Channel.

There are in fact three tunnels. Casement, which was the original one, with work beginning on it in 1797 was further extended in 1941. In the same year, the highest of the three tunnels, Annex was built, before the final one, the unusually named, Dumpy, was excavated in 1942. It was from these tunnels that one of the most important British operations of the entire war was developed and directed. Operation Dynamo was where the planning and co-ordination for the evacuation of Dunkirk took place in 1940. The man responsible for the operation was Vice Admiral Sir Bertram Home Ramsay.

Ramsay and his team, worked for nine straight days implementing and overseeing the operation to safely repatriate as many British soldiers of the British Expeditionary Force as possible, along with Belgian and French troops who were being hounded by German combined land and air forces.

Ramsay had served in the Royal Navy for 40 years, enlisting in 1898. During the First World War he was part of the Dover Patrol with which he served in August 1915 as officer in command of HMS *M25*, a small monitor vessel. For two years his duties saw him carrying out patrols off the Belgian coast. On 30 June 1916 he was promoted to the rank of commander. He remained with HMS *M25* until October 1917 before transferring to another Dover Patrol vessel, the destroyer HMS *Broke*. He was mentioned in despatches for his actions during the second Ostend raid.

He retired in 1938, the year before the outbreak of the war and it was Winston Churchill who managed to entice him back into the Royal Navy on 24 August 1939, just ten days before Britain declared war on Germany. His return to navy life also came with a promotion to the rank of vice admiral, with the additional title of commander-in-chief, Dover. His new job was threefold: to provide protection to cross-Channel military traffic; to deny German submarines the ability to travel through the Straits of Dover; to oversee the defence against possible German destroyer raids on ports and other similar facilities along the south and south east coastline.

King George VI asked Ramsay to give him a personal report on the operation. For his achievement in securing the recovery of so many British and Allied soldiers from the beaches of Dunkirk he was made a Knight Commander of the Order of the Bath.

Ramsay was to play further important roles before the war was over, although not just from the chalk cliffs beneath Dover Castle. The tunnels were initially designated as an air raid shelter for members of the public to go to in the case of a German air raid, surely one of the safest locations to have such a shelter. As the tunnels still exist to this day and are open to the public, it is possible to transport oneself back to those bygone days to get a feel of what it must have been like to work there or have been one of the patients. One of the six tunnels, named Annexe, was transformed into an underground dressing station in 1941, complete with an operating theatre, for wounded troops returning from Europe.

In July 1943, during the Allied invasion of Sicily, Operation Husky, Vice-Admiral Ramsay was the Naval Commanding Officer, Eastern Task Force, and was responsible for the amphibious landing part of the operation.

On 27 April 1944 he was promoted to the rank of admiral, having once again being placed back on the active list, the day before, and appointed as the Naval Commander-in-Chief of the Allied Naval Expeditionary Force for the invasion of Europe, Operation Neptune. His skills in leadership and diplomacy were shown at their best, when he reportedly managed to refuse a request by both the Prime Minister, Winston Churchill and King George VI, who had both determined that they were going to observe the D-Day landings from on board HMS *Belfast*. His decision to refuse both men's request was based on the potential danger he knew it would have placed them in by being on board. Their loss, should anything untoward have happened to the ship, could have not only had an effect on the nation's morale, but on the final outcome of the entire war.

There cannot have been too many individuals throughout history, who would have dared to say no to a Prime Minister and their King, but Ramsay did. In doing so he showed the difference between being in charge, simply because of a rank that had been bestowed upon him and being a natural born leader who could instinctively make decisions in difficult circumstances, because he knew it was the right thing to do at that time. He did not allow any potential effect it could have had on him personally, to sway his decision-making process.

CHAPTER 10

Kent's Commonwealth Connection

During the Second World War there were a number of men from the county of Kent, or with Kent connections, who ended up serving in the Australian armed forces. The research into this particular topic was carried out by Andrew Bratley, himself a man of Kent and a supporter of Gillingham Football Club, who now lives in Perth, Western Australia – yet another Kent man who left these shores to venture off 'down under'. Many of these men were killed in the service of their adopted country for the good of Britain and the Commonwealth.

Here is Andrew's list of those men of Kent who served with the Australian forces and who lost their lives. Apologies if I have missed anybody off the list, if I have done so it is purely an oversight on my part.

Private WX807 Albert **Beck** (32) served with the 2nd/11th Battalion, Australian Infantry, Australian Imperial Force. He died on 29 May 1941, has no known grave but his name is commemorated on the Athens Memorial. His parents, Edwin and Jane Beck, lived at Whitstable in Kent.

Lance Corporal (VX8959) Robert **Brundrett** (33) was serving in the 2nd/5th Battalion, Australian Infantry, Australian Imperial Force, when he died on 3 January 1941. He is buried in the Halfaya Sollum War Cemetery, which is twelve miles inside the Egyptian border with Libya. His parents, Walter and Ada Brundett, lived in Rolveden, Kent.

Private (391407) Albert **Crayden** (56) of the 13th Garrison Battalion, Australian Infantry, died on 25 January 1944. He was buried in the Sydney War Cemetery. His parents, George and Ellen Crayden, lived in Sittingbourne, Kent.

Sergeant (QX 1530) Jack **Edwards** (27) of the 2nd/1st Army Field Workshop, Australian Army Ordnance Corps, was killed in action on 23 April 1941. He is buried in the Tobruk War Cemetery in Libya. His mother, Mrs H.F. Rule, lived in Bickley, Kent.

Flying Officer (400276) Peter Thomas Leeds **Hallett** (26) of the Royal Australian Air Force, a holder of the Distinguished Flying Cross, was killed in action on 5 November 1943. Sadly, his body was never recovered, but his name is commemorated on the Runneymede Memorial, in Surrey. He was a married man, and his widow, Isobel Joan Hallett, lived at Horsmonden, Kent.

Private (VX47600) Dennis Claude **Hawkins** (21) of the 2nd/4th Battalion, Australian Imperial Force, Australian Infantry was killed in action on 18 December 1944 and is buried in the Lae War Cemetery, in Papua New Guinea, which was begun by the Australian Army Graves Service in 1944. Out of the 2,828 burials of Commonwealth military personnel at the cemetery, 444 of them remain unidentified; thankfully for

Tobruk War Cemetery.

the family of Dennis Hawkins, he was not one of them. His parents, George and Ethel Rebecca Hawkins, lived at Erith, Kent.

Flight Sergeant (420566) Henry Outred **Hillier** (21) of the Royal Australian Air Force, was killed in action on 30 July 1943. He has no known grave, but his name is commemorated on the Runnymede Memorial. His parents, Henry and Margaret Hillier, lived at Gravesend in Kent.

Lieutenant George Mainwaring **Hills** (60), of the Royal Australian Navy, was serving as part of the crew of HMAS *Penguin*, when he died on 26 July 1943. He is buried in the Sydney War Cemetery.

Wikipedia records HMAS *Penguin* as having originally been built as a submarine depot ship for the Royal Navy. The ship was renamed HMAS *Platypus*, which had been its original name in 1941. HMAS *Penguin* was also the Royal Australian Navy's primary naval base and was situated on Garden Island in Sydney, on the east coast of Australia, but that was renamed HMAS *Kuttabul* in January 1943, six months before George Hills died. His parents, Charles and Matilda Hills, had lived in Sittingbourne, Kent.

Craftsman (NX82669) Edward Charles **Jolly** (38) of the Australian Corps of Electrical and Mechanical Engineers, Australian Imperial Force, which was part of 129th Brigade Workshops, died on 16 March 1944 and is buried in the Lae War Cemetery in Papua New Guinea. His parents, Herbert and Louise Jolly lived in Lewisham, which at the time was part of Kent, but which is now a borough of London.

Private (WX9214) George **Lee** (36) of the 2nd/4th Machine Gun Battalion, Australian Infantry, Australian Imperial Force, died on 26 August 1943. He was buried in the Thanbyuzayat War Cemetery, which is now Myanmar, but during the Second World War was Burma. His parents, William Henry and Elizabeth Lee, lived in Bromley, Kent.

Corporal (NX77696) Lloyd George **Marsh** (21) was in the Corps of Signals Warning Wireless Company, part of the Australian Imperial Force, when he died on 8 November 1943. The corps was formed at Port Moresby, Papua New Guinea in January 1942 to provide early warning of Japanese air attacks, and surveillance of Japanese shipping and troop movements. By the end of the war the Corps was Australia's most highly decorated signals unit. His name is commemorated on the Singapore War Memorial, and his parents, George and Louise Marsh, lived in Kent.

Warrant Officer (411226) Hugh George **Murray** (23) of the Royal Australian Air Force, died on 22 October 1943. He is buried in the Cambridge City Cemetery in England. His parents, George and Amy Murray, lived at Tunbridge Wells in Kent.

Able Seaman (S3905) Sydney **McCulloch** (20) of the Royal Australian Naval Reserve, died on 20 November 1941. He has no known grave, but his name is commemorated on the Plymouth Naval Memorial. His parents, Sydney and Jessie McCulloch, lived in West Rochester, Kent.

Louis Donald **McPherson** (31) was a private (NX35873) in the 2nd/19th Battalion Australian Infantry, Australian Imperial Force, when he was killed in action on 15 February 1942, which was the day that Singapore fell to the Japanese, and tens of thousands of British and Commonwealth forces became prisoners of war. He was buried in the Kranji War Cemetery in Singapore. His parents, Edward and Edith McPherson, were from Hadlow in Kent.

Pilot Officer (2678) Sean Wrist **Nielson** (30) of the Royal Australian Air Force was killed in action on 7 March 1945 over Germany. He is buried in the Berlin War Cemetery in Germany. His widow, Dorothy May Nielson, lived in Sevenoaks, Kent.

Driver (VX35455) Alfred Leonard **Obee** (37) of the Australian Army Service Corps 4th Reserve Motor Transport Company, Australian Imperial Force, died on 23 April 1945. His name is commemorated on the Labuan Memorial, in Malaysia. His parents, Alfred and Edith Obee, were from Chelsfield in Kent.

Warrant Officer (415679) Arthur William **Pryor** (21) of the Royal Australian Air Force, was killed in action whilst on operations over Germany, on 6 July 1944. He is buried in the Klagenfurt War Cemetery in Austria. His parents, Leslie and Enid Pryor, lived at Horsmonden in Kent.

Corporal (NX73197) Frederick Clifford **Sharp**, who served under the surname of Sharpe, of the 2nd/30th Battalion, Australian Infantry, Australian Imperial Force was killed in action on 10 February 1942 during the fighting to defend Singapore. He has no known grave and his name is commemorated on the Singapore Memorial. His parents James and Florence Sharp lived in Gillingham, Kent.

Private (SX2176) Reginald Frank **Shepherd** (34) of the 2nd/10th Battalion, Australian Infantry, Australian Imperial Force, was killed in action on 29 April 1941.

He is buried in the Tobruk War Cemetery in Libya. His foster-parents, Michael and Emily Killian, lived in Canterbury, Kent.

Petty Officer (15018) Stanley George **Silk** (43) of the Royal Australian Navy was serving on board HMAS *Sydney* at the time of his death on 20 November 1941. He was a holder of the Distinguished Service Medal. He has no known grave but his name is commemorated on the Plymouth Naval Memorial. Stanley's parents, James and Alice Silk, lived at Sevenoaks, in Kent.

The story of HMAS *Sydney* is an intriguing one. It was lost with all hands on 19 November 1941 after it was sunk by the German naval vessel, HSK *Kormoran* in the Indian Ocean off the coast of Western Australia. With the loss of its entire crew of 645 officers and men, it is still to this day the worst naval disaster in Australian history. What made the situation worse was the apparent cover up into its sinking.

Sailors from HMAS Sydney who were awarded the Distinguished Service Medal for gallantry during the action with the Italian cruiser Bartolomeo Colleoni, off Cape Spada on 19 July 1940.

Left to right; Chief Petty Officer 10745 Alfred Percival Prior; Chief Petty Officer 15018 Stanley George Silk, who was subsequently killed in action on 20 November 1941; Chief Ordnance Artificer 19440 Walter John Keane, who was also killed in action on 20 November 1941; Chief Stoker 13814 Joseph Ernest Beaumont; 19251 Able Seaman 19251 Geoffrey Rosevear, who was another who was killed in action on 20 November 1941; and Stoker 16069 Eric Charles Evans.

The Australian Government made the decision to withhold announcing the *Sydney*'s fate for twelve days, before the Australian Prime Minister, John Curtin, finally made the announcement on 1 December 1941. Despite the loss of both the *Sydney* and her entire crew, no formal or public enquiry was ever undertaken in to the reasons behind it. This just added to the public held belief that there had been an official government cover up.

The loss of the *Sydney* continued to cause controversy throughout Australian society, and culminated in an official enquiry into the disaster, the results of which were eventually released in June 2000, placing on record for the first time the official findings concerning the loss of the *Sydney*.

The truth of what actually happened is difficult to ascertain due to a lack of real evidence. None of *Sydney*'s crew survived and there was a notable disinclination of the crew of the HSK *Kormoran* to become embroiled in the controversy.

In 1981 Michael Montgomery, whose father was one of the officers on board the ship at the time of her sinking, wrote a book entitled *Who Sank the Sydney?* In essence Montgomery's theory was that Captain Detmers, the man in charge of the *Kormoran* had acted contrary to international maritime law by sailing under a Norwegian flag and pretended to be in distress, and by doing so drew the *Sydney* close to her, then opened fire from an extremely short distance, which resulted in the *Sydney* being sunk. Montgomery also asserts that when the survivors from the *Sydney* took to the boats they were machine gunned by the crew of the *Koromoran* on the orders of Captain Detmers.

If Montgomery is correct in his claims, then this would explain why not a single man from the *Sydney* survived the encounter, whilst more than 300 men from the *Kormoran* did, and could at the time, if proven, have resulted in Detmers and his crew being treated as pirates and therefore facing summary execution, rather than being treated as they were, as prisoners of war. It would also further explain the reluctance of the latter's crew to effectively assist with Australia's attempts at trying to discover the truth of what happened on that fateful day.

Montgomery made other allegations in his book concerning the involvement of a Japanese submarine and the reasons behind why there was a cover up by the Royal Australian Navy to hide its own inadequacies in the matter. Others have also written about the incident, including the Parliamentary Joint Committee on Foreign Affairs, Defence and Trade, some of whom do not concur with Montgomery's findings.

Able Seaman Ernest Basil **Simpson** (36), of the Australian Merchant Navy and on board HMAHS *Centaur*, was killed in action on 14 May 1943. He has no known grave, but his name is commemorated on the Sydney Memorial. His parents, Arthur and Amy Simpson, were residents of Kent.

HMAHS *Centaur*, a hospital ship of the Royal Australian Navy, was attacked and sunk by a Japanese submarine off the coast of Queensland, on 14 May 1943. Out of a crew and medical staff of 332, 268 were killed, including sixty-three of the sixty-five Army personnel who were on board.

In the somewhat surreal way that events can connect with each other, HMAHS *Centaur* had some 18 months prior to her sinking, picked up survivors from the

Kormoran who had been in a lifeboat for seven days. The *Centaur's* captain, who was concerned that the German sailors might try to gain control of his ship, decided to keep them in the lifeboat for safety, although he did allow those who were obviously wounded on board for treatment. An interesting fact about this rescue, taking into account the controversy surrounding the loss of the *Sydney*, was that the man from the lifeboat who was initially allowed to board the *Centaur* to explain who they were, claimed to be a Norwegian merchant navy officer, before revealing his true identity and that of his rescued comrades.

Gunner (QX16280) George **Strachan** (45), of the 2nd/10th Field Regiment, Royal Australian Artillery, Australian Imperial Force, was killed in action on 6 April 1945. He is buried in the Labuan War Cemetery. Labuan is a Malaysian island off the coast of north-west Borneo. His parents, George and Alice Strachan, lived in Gillingham, Kent.

Corporal (QX16718) Charles Henry **Alpin** (33) of the 2nd/7th Independent Company, Australian Infantry, Australian Imperial Force, died on 17 March 1943. He is buried in the Lae War Cemetery in Papua New Guinea. His parents, Frederick and Miriam Alpin, lived in Bromley, Kent.

Warrant Officer (415921) John Ernest Stuart **Thompson** (20) of the Royal Australian Air Force, was killed in action on 20 December 1944. He is buried in the Ambon War Cemetery in Indonesia. His parents, David and Adelaide Thompson, lived in Bromley, Kent.

Lieutenant John Stewart **Wink** (32), of the Royal Australian Naval Volunteer Reserve, was stationed at HMAS *Moreton*, when he died on 23 March 1943. He has no known grave, but his name is commemorated on the Plymouth Naval Memorial. HMAS *Moreton* was a shore-based establishment in Brisbane. His parents, Dr Charles and Maud Wink, lived in Hythe, Kent. John Wink had previously been the Assistant Commissioner of the Sarawak Police, and also served with the Royal Canadian Mounted Police.

The following men who were either born in Kent or who had connections with the county also served with Australian forces during the Second World War and survived.

Private (QX25535) Raymond **Tyrrell**, Australian Infantry, Australian Imperial Force. He was born in Ashford, Kent in 1921.

Petty Officer (J10268) Joseph Richard **Buss** served in the Royal Australian Navy. He was born in Aylesford, Kent on 14 May 1894.

Gunner (N467219) John Cyril **Johnson** was in the 8th Battalion, Volunteer Defence Corps, part of the Australian Army. He was born in Bromley, Kent on 17 November 1905.

Sergeant (S20639) Geoffrey Orr **Young** born on 9 October 1912 in Bromley, Kent, enlisted in the Australian Imperial Force.

Able Seaman (32847) Desmond Hubert **Beazley** was born in Bromley, Kent on 5 January 1927 and enlisted in the Royal Australian Navy on 29 August 1944.

Lance Sergeant (WX26015) Edwin James **Bennett** was born in Bromley, Kent on 22 February 1922. He enlisted in the Australian Infantry, Australian Imperial Force, on 16 January 1941.

Corporal (20386) Thomas Eric **Davis** was born in Bromley, Kent on 13 August 1911. He enlisted in the Royal Australian Air Force on 10 December 1940 serving in No.5 Airfield Construction Squadron.

Squadron Leader (034411) Esmond Walter Cecil **New** was born in Bromley, Kent on 22 August 1900. He enlisted in the Royal Australian Air Force on 1 January 1942.

Able Seaman (14836) Victor Ernest Charles **Eley** was born in Bromley, Kent on 18 December 1909. He enlisted in the Royal Australian Navy on 30 September 1924 at the age of 14, and went on to serve for 21 years before being discharged.

Private (N270096) Henry Thomas **Whitehead** was born in Bromley, Kent on 25 August 1896. He enlisted in the 2nd Garrison Battalion, Australian Infantry, Australian Imperial Force on 6 May 1941 when he was 44 years of age.

Staff Sergeant Frank **Durbin** was born on 2 April 1886 in Brompton, Kent. He enlisted in the Australian Infantry, Australian Imperial Force on 9 May 1940.

Gunner (N99008) Ernest Alfred **Gumbrill** was born in Bromley, Kent and enlisted in the Australian Infantry, Australian Imperial Force, on 18 October 1940.

Corporal (18244) William Charles **Norton** was born in Canterbury on 3 July 1906. On 26 August 1940 he enlisted in the Royal Australian Air Force.

Sergeant (3025) Archibald William **Tucker** was born in Canterbury on 12 August 1903. He enlisted in the Royal Australian Air Force on 25 October 1937, before being discharged on 9 March 1950, having served for over twelve years.

Private (S12687) Wilfred Harold **Cook** was born in Chatham, Kent on 17 April 1889. He enlisted in the 18th Garrison Battalion, Australian Infantry on 8 November 1939. On page 463 of 'The South Australian Police Gazette' dated 4 December 1946, there is an entry that shows Wilfred had been arrested on 26 November 1946 for assaulting his wife, Katherine Mabel Cook. He was fined £5 with costs of 7s 6d. Failure to pay would have resulted in 14 days' imprisonment.

Private (Q226685) Horace Norman **Rowles** was born in Chatham, Kent on 30 September 1906. He enlisted in the 8th Battalion, Volunteer Defence Corps, Australian Army, on 11 April 1942.

Lance Corporal (WX28867 – W43775) Harry **Graham** was born at Chatham, Kent on 17 July 1908. He enlisted in the 7th Australian Army Troops Company.

Private (N474422) Percy Noel **Self** was born in Dartford, Kent on 25 December. He enlisted in the 10th Battalion Volunteer Defence Corps of the Australian Army on 16 May 1944 at Cockatoo Island, New South Wales.

Aircraftman 1st Class (8921) Cyril Walter **Lynds** was born in Dartford, Kent on 26 November 1902. He enlisted in the Royal Australian Air Force on 12 February 1940 at Laverton Victoria.

Private (WX13037) Frederick Harley **Rooke** was born in Deal, Kent on 27 August 1910. He enlisted in the 101st General Transport Company of the Australian Army on 16 May 1941 at Claremont, Western Australia.

Petty Officer Fred Archer **Claringbould** was born in Deal, Kent on 2 February 1884. He enlisted in the Royal Australian Navy on 25 August 1925 at Chelsea in Victoria.

Corporal (9377) Frank Ernest Sutherland **Hicks** was born in Deal, Kent on 2 May 1911. He enlisted in the Royal Australian Air Force on 26 February 1940 at Laverton, Victoria.

Flight Sergeant (3303) Charles Edward **Nicholas** was born in Deal, Kent on 22 October 1910. He enlisted in the Royal Australian Air Force on 19 April 1938 at Laverton, Victoria.

Corporal (11131) Percival John **Peterson** was born on 5 May 1905 in Deal, Kent. He enlisted in the Royal Australian Air Force on 19 July 1940 in Melbourne, Victoria.

Warrant Officer (3532) William Charles **Branchett** was born in Faversham, Kent on 17 May 1919. He enlisted in the Royal Australian Air Force on 20 June 1938 at Laverton, Victoria.

Sergeant (11223) William Henry **Branchett** was born in Faversham, Kent on 23 June 1980. He enlisted in the Royal Australian Air Force on 23 July 1940 in Melbourne, Victoria.

Flight Sergeant (A35551) (13348) Thomas Edward **Coleman** was born in Folkestone, Kent on 3 August 1906. He enlisted in the Royal Australian Air Force on 5 March 1941 in Melbourne, Victoria.

Able Seaman (PM7995) Alexander Earl **Fowler** was born in Gillingham, Kent on 1 November 1927. He enlisted in the Royal Australian Navy on 6 February 1945 in Melbourne, Victoria.

Chief Engineering Mechanic (R24000) Arthur James Frank **Beavan** was born in Gillingham on 29 April 1920. He enlisted in the Royal Australian Navy on 12 February 1940.

Constable (R23422) Cecil Edwin Allaby **Bell** was born in Gillingham, Kent on 20 November 1904. He enlisted in the Royal Australian Navy on 12 July 1939 in Kings Cross, New South Wales.

Flight Sergeant (8859) Leonard **Cavender** was born in Gillingham, Kent on 1 November 1907. He enlisted in the Royal Australian Air Force on 6 February 1940 at Laverton, Victoria.

Corporal (15825) John Harold **Stevens** was born on 26 March 1913 in Gillingham, Kent. He enlisted in the Royal Australian Air Force on 18 June 1940 in Sydney, New South Wales.

Flight Sergeant (9065) Bernard **Topley** was born in Maidstone, Kent on 7 October 1919. He enlisted in the Royal Australian Air Force on 13 February 1940 at Laverton, Victoria.

Warrant Officer Gregory **Deeble-Rogers** was born in Maidstone, Kent on 10 May 1904. He enlisted in the Royal Australian Air Force on 2 April 1942 in Melbourne, Victoria.

Flight Sergeant (4373) Maurice **Mighall** was born in Rainham, Kent on 15 January 1911. He enlisted in the Royal Australian Air Force on 22 May 1939 in Laverton, Victoria.

Bombardier (NX29490) Alfred Edward **Carroll** was born in Sheerness, Kent on 28 August 1908. He enlisted in the Australian Infantry, Australian Imperial Force on 10 June 1940, in Paddington, New South Wales.

Private (NX47749) Eric Charles **Williams** was born in Sittingbourne on 29 October 1907. He enlisted in the Australian Infantry, Australian Imperial Force, on 3 September 1940 at Newcastle, New South Wales.

Sergeant (S221) Stephen Henry **Towner** was born on 24 November 1890 in Tonbridge, Kent. He enlisted in the Australian Infantry, Australian Imperial Force on 4 July 1940.

Private (NF410310) Mercy **Lines** was born 23 June 1915 in Tunbridge Wells, Kent. He enlisted in the Australian Infantry on 6 August 1942 at Paddington, New South Wales.

Stoker (F2913)William George James **Bridger** was born on 23 February 1899 in Tunbridge Wells, Kent. He enlisted in the Royal Australian Navy on 2 December 1939 at Freemantle, Western Australia.

Richard **Batty** was born on 12 February 1897 in Whitstable, Kent. He enlisted in the Royal Australian Navy on 14 May 1942 at Freemantle Western Australia.

Having looked at Andrew Bratley's research on men with Kent connections who served with Australian forces during the Second World War, it seems only fair to also take a brief look at other Commonwealth countries that had a similar wartime Kent connection.

Kent's Canadian connection

There are at least seventy-one men who had Kent connections, who served in the Canadian Armed Forces during the Second World War, and were killed in action or died of their wounds. They are in no particular order, other than how they appear on the Commonwealth War Graves Commission website.

Albeni Camille **Vautour**
Victor Taylor Louis **Harvey**
Raymond James **Pain**
Nigel **Coombes**
Omer Herve **Bouchard**
Robert J. **Adair**
Robert Ferguson **Lockerbie**
William **Armstrong**
Roy Littlewood **Couves**
John Charles **Stone**
Hector **Doiron**
Eric Crowe **Loughead**
Raymond Woods **Hughes**
Sidney George Foster **Barnes**
Thomas Clinton **Beers**
Joseph Martin **O'Leary**
Alfred Barish **Levene**
Isaac Lincoln **Bloodsworth**

Donald Verdun **Brewster**
Frederick K. **File**
Aurele Joseph **Leger**
Joseph Alcide Edmund **Maillet**
Livain **Richard**
Gerrard Joseph **Roy**
Francis Condolly **Burns**
Frederick John **Joyce**
William **Willis**
Norman George **Shirlaw**
Alphonse Joseph **Caissie**
William Hume **Mather**
Charles Arthur **Gouch**
Emile **Mazerolle**
Patrice **Daigle**
Joseph John **Guimond**
Gordon Douglas **Spearman**
Frederick Enslie **Elward**

Arthur Gregory **Carter**

Roy Littlewood **Couves**

Hector **Doiron**

Robert Alexander **Faulafer**

Aldei **Jaillet**

Dolphe **Richard**

Everest Walter **Tindall**

Robert Gunn **Nicoll**

Earl **Rupert**

Albert Edward **Roberts**

Saul Alphie **Arsenault**

Harold Lyne **Purcell**

Bruce Ivan **Hillman**

Jean Baptiste **Boucher**

Albert Arthur **Moore**

William Angus **Vautour**

Joseph Romauld Alcide **Boissonnault**

Arthur Boyson **Slee**

Edward Joseph **Cormer**

Jacques **Richard**

Samuel **Way**

James Burnett **Mann**

Augustin Joseph **Cormier**

George Bryan Noble **Sparks**

Kent's Indian connection

There were thirty-nine young men with Kent connections who died or were killed whilst serving in the Indian Armed Forces during the Second World War. They are listed below, with a few personal notes.

Peter Frederick Whitaker **Penny**

Sidney Robert **Layton**

Robert Charles **Edgar**

John George **Gibson**

Eric James Clark **Posgate**

Ronald Ellis **Johnstone**

Peter Carey Stuart **McDowell**

Keith Alexander **Jameson**

Robert **Paine**

Douglas Crawford **Howard**

Walter Robert **Stevens**

John Hassall **Gardner**

Edward Lionel Wakefield **Fox**

Leslie Charles **Martin**

Kenneth Charles **Townsend**

Percival John **Fennell**

Norman William Elliot **Manning**

L.W. **Entwistle**

George **Palmer**

Frederick Horstead **New**

Kenneth Charles Howis **Cornwell**

Margaret Eileen **James**

Ronald Cecil **Malham**

John Russell **Greave**

Leopold Francis **Burns**

Reginald Fairman **Bonham**

Dalton Godfrey Stuart
Alan **Tuite**

Richard William **Scanlon**

Frederick Joseph **Cubitt**

George Peter **Howland**

Harold Victor **Lewis**

George Douglas Chamberlain
Dunmore

Gordon Brook **Neale**

Archibald Willoughby **Gwatkin**

Robert Anthony **Vernon-Betts**

Frederick Charles Nicol **Gwatkin**

Lieutenant Colonel (AI/849) Skipwith Edward **Tayler** (42) was a married man who before the war had lived with his wife, Freda Fortescue Tayler, at Brenchley, Kent. At the time of his death on 17 March 1941, in Eritrea, he was the holder of the Distinguished Service Order and had also been Mentioned in Despatches for his actions, which he had been awarded six weeks before his death. He was the commanding officer of the

3rd Battalion, 18th Royal Garhwal Rifles and had served during the First World War with the same regiment, commissioned as a second lieutenant in the Indian Army at just 17 years of age on 29 June 1916, and promoted to a full lieutenant a year later. It took him just four years to get to the rank of captain when he was still only 21. He then had to wait fourteen years for further promotion to the rank of major, and a further six years before he was promoted temporary lieutenant colonel.

He is buried in the Keren War Cemetery in Eritrea. Three years after his death, his widow, Freda, married Lieutenant Colonel Thomas Ivor Stevenson.

Captain A1/529 Foster Abney **Giles** (30) served with the 8th Punjab Regiment. He died on 16 December 1941, and his name is commemorated on the Singapore Memorial. His parents were the Reverend Abney and Mary Giles. His wife Eleanor Clarissa Giles, lived at Rochester, Kent.

Major Reginald William Hargrave **Cary-Grey** (44) was serving with the 1st Battalion, 7th Rajput Regiment when he died on 22 June 1942. He is buried in the Delhi War Cemetery in India. He was a married man whose wife, Noray Phyllis Cary-Grey lived at Walmer, Kent.

Kent's New Zealand and South African Connection

As far as we know there were twelve men either from Kent or with connections to the county, who died whilst serving in the military forces of New Zealand during the Second World War.

John Robert **Kent**
Stephen Bryan **Goord**
James Walter **Strood**
Eric Charles **Inder**
James Boardman **Venning**
Charles **Wilson**
Norman Roland **Reed**
Wilfred Gregson **Sola**
Percy Henry **Brooks**
Richard Teri Kaipara **Mason**

There were also two men from Kent who served with South African Forces during the Second World War.

Private 589475 V.F.R **Goldsmith** (30) served with the Royal Natal Carbines. He died on 17 June 1944 and is buried in the Bolsena War Cemetery on the eastern side of Lake Bolsena, in Italy. His parents, George and Ellen Goldsmith were from Tunbridge Wells, Kent.

Lieutenant (Observer) 205576 Eric W. Dave **Airey** (29) of No.12 Squadron, South African Air Force died on 10 February 1943. He is buried in the Tripoli War Cemetery in Libya. His parents, Robert and Eleanor Airey, were from Welling in Kent.

CHAPTER 11

The Human Touch

Here is a brief look at the war through the eyes of two people in love – the typical war time scenario of the man fighting overseas whilst his fiancée is back home doing her best to cope with the situation, never quite knowing if she was ever going to see her man again. If they were both destined to survive the pain and suffering which any war brought with it, would he still be the same person that he was when he departed?

Envelope of letter sent from Major Webb.

Here are two letters written by Major R.H. Webb of the Royal Army Ordnance Corps to Miss Gena Dawes, who lived at 2 Sussex Avenue, Ashford, Kent. The letters are dated 6 and 16 July 1944.

The first of the two letters is very short, but that may be a reflection of the state of his health at the time rather than anything else. I am guessing because of the reference to flies that he was suffering with a bout of malaria.

6 July 1944
My Dear Gena,
Thanks for your lovely letter. I shall be writing soon. On sick list at present and absolutely no energy. I am just leaving the office and off to bed. Three of my boys have the same complaint. It is carried by the blasted flies. Thousands of them and they will get on the food despite precautions. Thought I must drop you a short note in between the moments of great personal distress.
Do write soon. Thank you, my dear.
Ever yours sincerely
Reg.

In the second letter it would appear that Major Webb had recovered from his bout of illness as it was quite a long correspondence written in quite a cheerful manner. Although he doesn't say in the letter where he is stationed, I am guessing from his references to flies and an item he had posted, taking six weeks to reach England, Major Webb was stationed either somewhere in the region of North Africa or Palestine. He also makes a slightly unintentional whimsical remark about the plastic thing that has to be attached to the top of the silk stockings he has purchased.

Sunday 16 July 1944
My Dear Gena,
Days seem but moments, a week just an hour. Time rolls by and mail is received, but alas! mail remains totally unanswered.
I did manage to run off a few most dull and uninteresting sentences, trying to regain the loss. I can only hope you and others will forgive me.
With a little luck I hope to write about a dozen letters and as yours is the first one. I have some hours of writing ahead. I did find time to do a small spot of shopping remembering you I popped it in to a registered envelope and posted it. I originally intended an undie set. They looked ok but after making a closer inspection, they would 'out utility' anything one can buy at home. I think they would last about two washings, so instead I managed to get a pair of real silk stockings, all silk except the very top where it is normal for you to attach the elastic thing or whatever you call it. I'm 'out of touch' so to speak. Usually it takes six weeks to arrive, so should reach you about middle of August.
Thanks so very much for the really nice letters you write me. I love to be able to sit down and attempt to repay you. Once could when in Africa, waiting to

start work. Since then you have had to content yourself with an occasional page of hurried scribble. In this case you are not alone Gena, all (so few this) my private mail has been the same, so I must ask your forgiveness hoping you will understand. Work! Work! Work! Heat! Flies! Heat! And million more flies. Just like a wet rag when I pack up. I have 3 cold rub downs a day, but always seem to be still hotter afterwards.

Sorry to hear that all is not well around. I often think about you. It must be frightening. I have had some very hot times just about now last year. Seems to me that one comes through if they carry on with the poo.

I am going to cut you short as the mail is now due out, so I can at least get yours away today. Love to mum. Hope you are both ok.

Write soon and keep smiling
Yours very sincerely,
Reg.

The next port of enquiry to find out more information about Major Webb was to place a question on the Kent History Forum, to see if anybody knew anything about either Major Webb or Gena Dawes. Later the same day I received an e-mail with some helpful information from somebody who had seen my request. So now I knew that

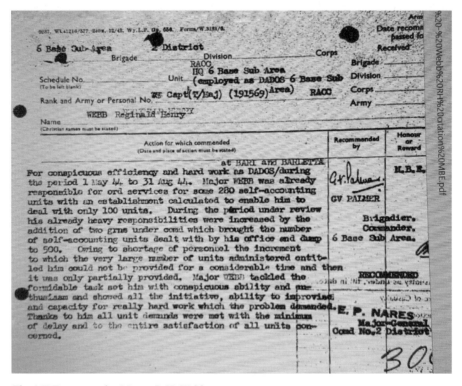

The MBE citation for Major R.H. Webb.

R.H. Webb was in fact Temporary Major (191569) Reginald Henry Webb, and that he had been awarded the MBE, the citation for which appeared in the *London Gazette* dated 19 April 1945. It read as follows:

For conspicuous efficiency and hard work as DADOS at Bari and Barletta during the period 1 May 1944 and 31 August 1944. Major Webb was already responsible for ordnance services for some 280 self-accounting units with an establishment calculated to enable him to deal with only 100 units. During the period under review his already heavy responsibilities were increased by the addition of two grns [garrisons] under comd [command], which brought the number of self-accounting units dealt with by his office and dump to 500. Owing to shortage of personnel the increment to which the very large number of units administered entitled him, could not be provided for a considerable time and then it was only partially provided. Major Webb tackled the formidable task set him with conspicuous ability and enthusiasm and showed all the initiative, ability to improvise and capacity for really hard work which the problem demanded. Thanks to him all unit demands were met with the minimum of delay and to the entire satisfaction of all units concerned.

He was recommended for the award by Brigadier G.V. Palmer, who was in charge of No.6 Base Sub Area. This in turn was endorsed by Major General E.P. Nares, the commander of No.2 District.

The cities of Bari and Barletta are both on the lower south-east coast of Italy. The area of Barletta includes part of the battlefield of Cannae, which wasn't as might be thought a battle of the Second World War, but from 216BC when the Roman Army took on the Carthaginians, under the command of the enigmatic leader Hannibal Barca, better known today as just, Hannibal.

My guess at where he had been stationed was incorrect, although with the Italian cities of Barletta and Bari being in the lower part of Italy, I wasn't too far off with North Africa.

CHAPTER 12

Kent's Victoria Cross and George Medal Winners

In this chapter we will look at the servicemen with Kent connections who were awarded either the Victoria Cross or the George Medal for their actions during the Second World War. This includes the award of the George Cross, an award that is available to either civilians or military personnel for acts of bravery, but not in the face of the enemy.

The following entries are in the date order in which they were awarded and the first two men survived the actions for which the award was made.

Thomas William **Gould** VC was born on 28 December 1914 in Dover. As a young man he enlisted in the Royal Navy and rose to the rank of petty officer (C/JX 147945). He survived the war and died on 6 December 2001, aged 86 years and is buried in the Peterborough Crematorium in Cambridgeshire.

The announcement for the award of his Victoria Cross was made by the Admiralty on 9 June 1942. It was made jointly alongside that of the same award to Lieutenant Peter Scawen Watkinson Roberts, for the same action.

Thomas William Gould VC.

HMS *Thrasher*, the submarine that they were on at the time, was in the eastern Mediterranean just off the coast of Crete, when it attacked and sank a German supply ship that was under heavy escort. The *Thrasher* managed to make good her escape, but only after she survived being depth charged by some of the German escort vessels and an aerial bombardment by the Luftwaffe.

The announcement appeared in the pages of the *London Gazette*:

The King has been graciously pleased to approve the award of the Victoria Cross for great valour while serving in HMS Thrasher *to Petty Officer Thomas William Gould C/JX147945.*

On February 16th, in daylight, HM Submarine Thrasher *attacked and sank a heavily escorted supply ship. She was at once attacked by depth charges and was bombed by aircraft.*

The presence of two unexploded bombs in the gun casing was discovered when after dark the submarine surfaced and began to roll.

Lieutenant Roberts and Petty Officer Gould volunteered to remove the bombs, which were of a type unknown to them. The danger in dealing with the second bomb was very great. To reach it they had to go through the casing which was so low that they had to lie at full length to move in it. Through this narrow space, in complete darkness, they pushed and dragged the bomb for a distance of some twenty feet until it could be lowered over the side. Every time the bomb was moved there was a loud twanging noise as of a broken spring, which added nothing to their peace of mind.

This deed was the more gallant as HMS Thrasher's presence was known to the enemy; she was close to the enemy coast, and in waters his patrols were known to be active day and night. There was a very great chance, and they knew it, that the submarine might have to crash dive while they were in the casing. Had this happened they must have been drowned.

The first of the two bombs was removed without too much fuss and was a relatively straightforward affair. It was the second one that caused them the problems, because it had penetrated further in their vessel than the first one. The casing mentioned in the citation was only two feet high in some places and the bomb in question was 150lbs in weight, easily the same as trying to move another man. Petty Officer Gould lay on his back and clasped the bomb close to his chest while Lieutenant Williams dragged him along the casement by his shoulders. It took the two men fifty minutes before they had managed to extricate the bomb and lower it gently over the side of their submarine before she could finally escape to safer waters. That fifty minutes must have felt like a lifetime to these two brave young men.

Awards of the Victoria Cross are not given lightly, but it strikes me that Gould's and Roberts' awards were even more deserving as they volunteered knowing full well that the outcome could quite possibly result not only in their own deaths, but that of their crew mates as well, if the bomb exploded before they managed to secure it and get it off the submarine. Most other awards of the Victoria Cross are quite often for spontaneous acts of supreme bravery by extremely brave young men, where they have little or no time to even think about what they are about to do. It is only afterwards when they have time to sit down and reflect about what they have done, when the enormity of it hits them. The criteria for the award of the Victoria Cross, 'for gallantry in the face of the enemy', is so high, that to win it often means that the recipient will be killed in the act of carrying it out.

Petty Officer Thomas Gould was awarded his Victoria Cross at Buckingham Palace in March 1943, by King George VI. His VC is on show at the Association of Jewish Ex-Servicemen and Women at the Jewish Museum in Hendon.

After the war Thomas Gould went on to become one of the founders of the English anti-fascist movement the '43 Group', a band of Jewish ex-servicemen who went on to

Henry Eric Harden, VC.

fight the fascists. Having returned to England after the war, Gould, and other ex Jewish servicemen encountered many fascist groups, including Oswald Mosley's Union Movement. A lot of the rhetoric which was coming out of these groups was of an anti-semitic nature. Their members carried out attacks on Jews as well as their property, and so Thomas Gould and his fellow Jewish comrades decided to fight back, which they did in numerous ways, including street fights. Like Thomas, many of the '43 Group's' members were decorated ex-servicemen. The group acquired its name from the number of people in the room at Maccabi House, on the night the group was founded. Henry Eric **Harden** VC who was born on 23 February 1912 in Northfleet, Kent, and served with the Royal Army Medical Corps during the Second World War. Harden was 32 years of age, held the rank of lance corporal and was attached to 45 Royal Marine Commando.

On 23 January 1945, during Operation Blackcock, the purpose of which was to clear German troops from what was known as the Roer Triangle, or the Dutch towns of Roermond and Sittard and the German town of Heinsberg, Harden was moving forward with 45 Commando, in the village of Brachterbeek, when three of the leading marines were seriously wounded by German machine-gun fire. Harden picked up one of his wounded comrades and carried him back to a temporary aid station which had been set up in a nearby house. In doing so, Harden was wounded in the side. He then organised a stretcher party to go back and collect the other two men, one of whom was a Lieutenant Corey. They picked up the other man first and began making their way back to the aid station, when they came under heavy German machine-gun fire which resulted in the wounded commando being killed. Harden and the stretcher party went back for Lieutenant Corey, the last of the three wounded marines, and whilst on their way back to the aid post, Henry Harden was shot through the head and killed instantly.

There are four members of the Royal Marines, 45 Commando, who are shown as having died on 23 January 1945. Corporal John Sidney Cocks, Marine James George Russell, Marine Frederick Edward Wale, all of whom were only 19 years of age, and Marine Charles Adam Lyon. One of these men, which one I cannot identify, is the second wounded Marine who was collected by Henry Harden and his stretcher party, only to then be killed whilst being taken back to the aid station. Lieutenant Corey survived. The first three of these men were, like Harden, buried in the Nederweert War Cemetery, which is situated in the Limburg region of Holland. The last man, Marine Lyon, is buried in the Mook War Cemetery, in Limburg.

The citation for the award of his Victoria Cross appeared in the *London Gazette* on 9 March 1945:

In North-West Europe on 23rd January, 1945 the leading section of a Royal Marine Commando Troop having come under intense machine-gun fire was ordered to make for some houses close by. Four of the section had been wounded and were left lying in the open. Under continuous fire Lance Corporal Harden at once went forward and with great coolness and bravery attended to the four casualties. He then carried one of them back to cover. He was ordered not to go forward again and an attempt was made to bring in the remaining casualties with the aid of tanks, but this proved unsuccessful owing to the heavy and accurate fire of anti-tank guns. A second attempt under a smoke-screen also proving unsuccessful, Lance Corporal Harden insisted in going forward with a volunteer stretcher party and succeeded in bringing back another badly wounded man. He went out a third time, and whilst returning with the stretcher party, he was killed.

Throughout this long period Lance Corporal Harden displayed superb devotion to duty and personal courage of the highest order. His action was directly responsible for saving the lives of the wounded brought in, while his complete contempt for all personal danger, and the magnificent example he set of cool courage and determination to continue with his work, whatever the odds, was an inspiration to his comrades and will never be forgotten by those who saw it.

Henry Eric Harden was a married man with two children. To commemorate his acts of supreme bravery, there is a plaque with his name on it on a bridge in the village of Brachterbeek (shown overleaf). The wording on it is as follows:

IN HONOURED MEMORY OF
HENRY ERIC HARDEN, VC.
LANCE CORPORAL BRITISH ROYAL ARMY
MEDICAL CORPS, WHO NEAR THIS
SPOT ON THE 23RD JANUARY 1945,
AFTER HEROICALLY SAVING THE LIVES
OF THREE COMRADES LYING WOUNDED
IN THE OPEN, WAS KILLED IN HIS
FOURTH ATTEMPT.
THE BRAVE SHALL LIVE IN ETERNAL
REMEMBRANCE.

Roderick Alastair Brook **Learoyd** VC was born on 5 February 1913 in Folkestone, Kent. As a young man he attended the Chelsea College of Aeronautical and Automatic Engineering Royal Air Force, but after completing his course he moved to Argentina where he worked as a farmer for two years.

He later returned to England and in March 1936 he was accepted for the Royal Air Force. Two months later on 18 May 1936 he was commissioned as an acting pilot officer and was posted to No.49 Squadron as part of Bomber Command. His status as a qualified pilot officer was confirmed on 23 March 1937 and a year later, No.49 Squadron moved to Scampton in Lincolnshire.

IN HONOURED MEMORY OF
HENRY ERIC HARDEN, V. C.
LANCE-CORPORAL BRITISH ROYAL ARMY
MEDICAL CORPS WHO NEAR THIS
SPOT ON THE 23 RD JANUARY 1945,
AFTER HEROICALLY SAVING THE LIVES
OF THREE COMRADES LYING WOUNDED
IN THE OPEN, WAS KILLED IN HIS
FOURTH ATTEMPT.
THE BRAVE SHALL LIVE IN ETERNAL
REMEMBRANCE

Remembrance Plaque to Henry Eric Harden VC.

Between 3 September 1939 and June 1940, Learoyd had already amassed twenty-three bombing missions over enemy targets throughout Europe. On 12 August 1940 Learoyd, by now an acting flight lieutenant, was part of an operation to bomb an aqueduct which crossed the River Ems, north of the German city of Münster. Eleven aircraft left Scampton to take part in the raid, including six from No.49 Squadron, one of which was flown by Learoyd. Two of the aircraft didn't make it back from the mission and another two were badly damaged. Learoyd's aircraft was also badly damaged due to the reception committee awaiting them from the ground in the proximity of their target – all of this before he had made his actual bombing run on to the target. Despite some serious damage to the undercarriage of his aircraft, Learoyd managed to get his crew safely home. But his troubles were not quite over. Realising that in the circumstances trying to land back at Scampton would not be the wisest thing to attempt in the dark, he decided to circle his base until it was light enough to land, so that he didn't cause any further damage to his aircraft or injure any of his crew. He just had to hope that he had sufficient fuel left to be able to stay in the air for as long as he needed to.

For his actions on 12 August 1940 in completing his mission and returning his aircraft and crew safely home, he was awarded the Victoria Cross. The announcement was made on 20 August 1940 by the Air Ministry and also appeared in the *London Gazette* the same day:

The King has been graciously pleased to confer the Victoria Cross on the undermentioned officer in recognition of most conspicuous bravery: Acting Flying Lieutenant Roderick Alastair Brook Learoyd 37860.

This officer, as first pilot of a Hampden aircraft, has repeatedly shown the highest conception of his duty and complete indifference to personal danger in making attacks at the lowest altitudes regardless of opposition. On the night of the 12th August 1940, he was detailed to attack a special objective on the Dortmund Ems Canal. He had attacked this objective on a previous occasion and was well aware of the risks entailed. To achieve success, it was necessary to approach from a direction well known to the enemy, through a lane of especially disposed anti-aircraft guns of all calibres. The reception of the preceding aircraft might well have deterred the stoutest heart, all being hit and two lost. Flight Lieutenant Learoyd nevertheless made his attack at 150 feet, his aircraft being repeatedly hit and large pieces of the main plane torn away. He was almost blinded by the glare of many searchlights at close range, but pressed home this attack with the greatest resolution and skill.

He subsequently brought his wrecked aircraft home and, as the landing flaps were inoperative and the undercarriage indicators out of action, waited for dawn in the vicinity of his aerodrome before landing, which he accomplished without causing injury to his crew or further damage to the aircraft. The high courage, skill and determination, which this officer has invariably displayed on many occasions in the face of the enemy sets an example which is unsurpased.

Learoyd served with No.44 Squadron for the rest of the war, which he survived, and he remained on the Royal Air Force Reserve until 1958, when he finally retired with the rank of wing commander. He had certainly done the people of Tunbridge Wells and the county of Kent proud.

George Albert **Cairns** was born in London on 12 December 1913, but by the late 1930s he was living in Sidcup, and working in the Belgian Bank in Bishopsgate, London, where he met his future wife, Ena. They were married in 1941 and set up home in the town. The following year George was commissioned as a lieutenant (198186) in the Somerset Light Infantry (Prince Albert's), but in early 1944, he was shown as being attached to the (Airborne) South Staffordshire Regiment which was a Chindit battalion.

He was killed in action on 19 March 1944 when he was 30 years of age. He is buried in the Taukkyan War Cemetery in Myamar (Burma).

The following details of why he was awarded the Victoria Cross, were printed in the *London Gazette* on 4 September 1945.

Lieutenant George Cairns VC.

At Henu and Mawlu, known as White City, near Broadway in Burma on 16 March 1944, the South Staffordshire Regiment, which formed a part of the 77th Independent Infantry Brigade, together with the 3rd/6th Gurkha Rifles, dug in and established a road and rail block across the Japanese lines of communication. Unbeknown to the South Staffords, they had in fact dug in their positions immediately adjacent to a small Japanese force, without either side knowing of the others presence.

At 11 am the following morning the Japanese reacted by carrying out an attack, throwing in large numbers of their men in to the affray. The men of the South Staffordshire Regiment were ordered to attack the hill-top which formed the basis of the Japanese assault. On reaching the hill top, the South Staffords discovered that their prize was no more than a plateau in size and in no time at all close quarter, hand to hand fighting ensued. It was brutal, bloody and merciless.

During this action a Japanese officer attacked Lieutenant Cairns, who had already been bayonetted through his side twice, and with one slash of his sword, cut off his left arm. Rather than falling under the ferocity of the attack, Lieutenant Cairns defended himself, and shot the officer, killing him outright with one shot. He then picked up the dead Japanese officer's sword, and with it killed or wounded several other Japanese soldiers, whilst still leading his men. A short while later he collapsed to the ground due to the amount of blood he had lost from the injury which he had sustained. He subsequently died from his wounds on 19 March.

His actions so inspired all of his comrades, that later the same day the Japanese were completely routed, which at the time was a very rare occurrence.

An interesting aside to these events was that it was some five years after his death that Lieutenant Cairns' Victoria Cross was awarded, and it was the last award of its type made from the Second World War. The reason for this delay was that the original recommendation for the award, accompanied by the required written evidence of three individuals who witnessed the events, had been submitted to General Orde Charles Wingate, who was then killed in an air crash in India on 24 March 1944. The original recommendation and the supporting statements of evidence were destroyed in the crash. Sadly, it was then simply forgotten about. By the time the recommendation was re-submitted, two of the three original witnesses had been killed during the war, which understandably caused a further delay.

Subsequently, Mrs Cairns heard a BBC radio broadcast in December 1948, which mentioned her husband's bravery and so she approached the Member of Parliament for Sidcup, Mr G.D. Wallace, who in turn made representations to the War Office on Mrs Cairns' behalf. To help matters, Major Calvert, who had been present when Lieutenant Cairns carried out his actions which led to the original recommendation, had the case re-opened.

The eventual award of Cairns' VC was mentioned in *The Times* on 21 May 1949, having appeared in the *London Gazette* the previous day. Cairns had finally received the acknowledgement that he so rightly deserved, five years after he was originally recommended for the prestigious award.

Lionel Ernest **Queripel** was a fourth generation military man. His father Colonel L.H. Queripel CMG DSO had served during the Boxer Rebellion in China in 1900, as well as during the First World War in Mesopotamia, Russia and France. Lionel clearly had a lot to live up to.

He was just 19 years of age when he was commissioned as a captain (108181) in the 2nd Battalion, Royal Sussex Regiment, just before the outbreak of the Second World War. In November 1942 during the Second Battle of El Alamein, despite its being an Allied victory, the Royal Sussex Regiment incurred heavy losses in the fighting. Out of those who survived, approximately 200 men from the 2nd Battalion, including Captain Queripel, successfully passed their parachute training and helped form the 10th Battalion, Parachute Regiment Army Air

Lionel Queripel VC.

Corps. Some of them were later landed at Arnhem as part of the 1st Airborne Division on 17 September 1944. A combination of bad weather, strong German resistance and problems with supplies and reinforcements, led to heavy British casualties. Lionel was one of those killed in action on 19 September 1944, during the subsequent fighting that took place after the airborne landings.

He is buried in the Oosterbeek War Cemetery at Arnhem, in the Gelderland region of Holland. As is the custom within the British Army, Lionel's grave stone is marked with the badge of the regiment he initially joined rather than the one he was attached to at the time of his death.

His parents, Leslie Herbert and Sybil Queripel, had moved the family to Tunbridge Wells, Kent, in 1926, Lionel was born at Winterborne Monkton, Dorset, on 13 July 1920.

The following details concerning the award of the Victoria Cross to Lionel Queripel appeared in the *London Gazette* on 1 January 1945.

In Holland on September 19th, 1944, Captain Queripel was acting as Company Commander. When advancing on Arnhem, heavy and continuous enemy fire caused his company to split up on both sides of the road and inflicted considerable losses. Repeatedly crossing and re-crossing the road under sustained and accurate fire, Captain Queripel not only immediately re-organized his force, but carried a wounded sergeant to the Regimental Aid Post and was himself wounded in the face. Nevertheless, he personally led an attack on the strongpoint blocking their progress, and killed the occupants, thereby enabling the advance to continue.

Later, Captain Queripel found himself cut off with a small party. Although by then additionally wounded in both arms, he continued to inspire his men to resist until increasing enemy pressure forced him to order their withdrawal. He insisted on remaining behind to cover their retreat with pistol fire and hand grenades and was not seen again. During nine hours of confused and bitter fighting Captain Queripel unceasingly displayed gallantry of the highest order. His courage, leadership and devotion to duty were magnificent and inspiring.

There are numerous memorials which commemorate Lionel's name, including the place of his birth, the college he attended, as well as the regiments he served with. In more recent times his name was added to the Tunbridge Wells war memorial. He has also had a poem written about him. When the award of his Victoria Cross was announced in February 1945, Tunbridge Wells Council had a poem commissioned about him by the Poet, Herbert Hope Campbell.

> *We who are burghers of your native town*
> *Hail you today with your illustrious name,*
> *Your knightly valour wins for you renown;*
> *We glory in your courage and your fame!*
> *May we be worthy of your daring deed*
> *Performed by you in England's hour of need.*

As a young man John Henry Cound **Brunt** VC MC had by all accounts been a bit of a dare devil as well as a keen sportsman, taking part in football, cricket, rugby, wrestling and water-polo. It appeared that there was nothing he was not afraid to do.

John Henry Brunt VC.

By the time he was 18, he was training the Paddock Wood Home Guard, ably assisted by his father. In 1941 he joined the Army, enlisting as a private in the Queen's Own Royal West Kent Regiment. The *London Gazette* records that he was commissioned as a second lieutenant with the Sherwood Foresters on 2 January 1943, although he never actually served with them. Instead he was posted to the 6th Battalion, Lincolnshire Regiment, a Territorial unit, and sent out to North Africa, as part of the 46th Infantry Division. By September 1943, Brunt had been promoted to the rank of substantive lieutenant and put in charge of No.9 Platoon, A Company, and it was his battalion that landed at Salerno during the Allied invasion of Italy, on 9 September 1943.

During December 1943 and January 1944, whilst still serving in Italy Brunt and his men were almost constantly in action, hardly a day went by without them being involved in some kind of contact with enemy forces.

The *London Gazette* dated 22 February 1944 included a citation for the award of the Military Cross to John Brunt, which provided the following information:

In the early hours of 15 December 1943 Lieutenant Brunt and his men received orders to go and destroy an enemy post that was situated in some houses approximately 200 yards north of the River Peccia. In his efforts to break the enemy line, Brunt crossed and re-crossed the river so many times, that his men took to calling it 'Brunt's Brook'.

After an intense five-minute British artillery bombardment, Lieutenant Brunt led a section of his men in to assault the intended target. The first two houses that they came across, contained only two enemy soldiers, whom they quickly dispatched, but it was the third house that provided the most resistance to them. Using grenades and Tommy guns, Brunt and his band of men managed to kill eight German soldiers outside the house. After some thirty minutes of intense, sometimes close quarter, fighting Brunt's section withdrew, having had one man killed and a further six more wounded. Brunt, his sergeant and a private remained behind to recover another soldier who had been wounded. For his actions that day Lieutenant Brunt was awarded the Military Cross.

In March 1944 Brunt and his comrades left Italy and headed for Syria and Egypt for some well deserved rest and recuperation, as well as to undertake further military training, before once again returning to Italy in July of the same year. It was around this time that he was promoted to temporary captain and became the second in command of D Company. As the year continued Brunt and his men had been involved in heavy fighting as part of what was referred to as the Gothic Line offensive. German Field Marshal Albert Kesselring had formed a last line of defence across the peaks of the Apennine mountains during the German army's retreat from Italy.

On the evening of 3 December 1944, the 6th Battalion, Lincolnshire Regiment commenced its planned attack on the town of Faenza, and after a few days of heavy fighting they finally achieved their objective and then set up defensive positions. It was for his actions during this time that he received his Victoria Cross. The citation for the award appeared in the *London Gazette* on 8 February 1945 and gives the following details:

War Office, 8th February, 1945.
The King has been graciously pleased to approve the posthumous award of the Victoria Cross to: Lieutenant (Temporary Captain) John Henry Could Brunt MC (258297) The Sherwood Foresters (Nottinghamshire and Derbyshire Regiment) (Paddock Wood, Kent).

In Italy on 9th December, 1944, the platoon commanded by Captain Brunt was holding a vital sector of the line in Italy. At dawn the German 90 Panzer

Grenadier Division counter-attacked the Battalion's forward positions in great strength with three Mark IV tanks and infantry. The house, around which the Platoon was dug in, was destroyed and the whole area was subjected to intense mortar fire. The situation then became critical, as the anti-tank defences had been destroyed and two Sherman tanks knocked out. Captain Brunt, however, rallied his remaining men and, moving to an alternative position, continued to hold the enemy infantry, although outnumbered by at least three to one. Personally firing a Bren gun, Captain Brunt killed about fourteen of the enemy. His wireless set was destroyed by shell fire, but on receiving a message by runner to withdraw to a Company locality some 200 yards to his left and rear, he remained behind to give covering fire. When his Bren ammunition was exhausted, he fired a PIAT and 2in. Mortar, left by casualties, before he himself dashed over the open ground to a new position. This aggressive defence caused the enemy to pause, so Captain Brunt took a party back to his previous position, and although fiercely engaged by small arms fire, carried away the wounded who had been left there.

Later in the day, a further counter-attack was put in by the enemy on two axes. Captain Brunt immediately seized a spare Bren gun and, going round his forward positions, rallied his men. Then, leaping on a Sherman tank supporting the company, he ordered the tank commander to drive from one fire position to another, while he sat or stood on the turret directing Besa fire at the advancing enemy, regardless of the hail of small arms fire. Then, seeing small parties of the enemy, armed with bazookas, trying to approach round the left flank he jumped off the tank and, taking a Bren gun, stalked these parties well in front of the Company positions, killing more and causing the enemy finally to withdraw in great haste leaving their dead behind them.

Wherever the fighting was heaviest, Captain Brunt was always to be found, moving from one post to another, encouraging the men and firing any weapon he found at any target he could see. The magnificent action fought by this Officer, his coolness, bravery, devotion to duty and complete disregard of his own personal safety under the most intense and concentrated fire was beyond praise. His personal example and individual action were responsible to a very great extent for the successful repulse of these fierce enemy counter attacks.

The following morning, 10 December 1944, whilst his men were waiting for their breakfast, their first proper meal in nearly 48 hours, Captain Brunt was standing in the doorway of the platoon headquarters, drinking tea and chatting with some of his fellow officers, when a German mortar round landed right in front of him, killing him instantly. He was just 22 years of age.

It is truly amazing when you read the above citation listing his heroic acts, knowing that he placed himself in so much danger and survived whilst saving the lives of others, only to be killed the following day in such a random way. He is buried in the Farenza War Cemetery in Italy.

Before the war he had lived with his parents, Thomas Henry and Nesta Mary Brunt, in Paddock Wood, Kent, where the family had moved in 1934, although his birthplace was in Priest Weston, near Chirbury in Shropshire.

John Brunt's Victoria Cross was presented to his parents at Buckingham Palace by King George VI on 18 December 1945.

There are numerous memorials and similar reminders that commemorate John Brunt's remarkable achievements, including the re-naming of a public house in Paddock Wood, where he was brought up. What was the Kent Arms was renamed 'John Brunt VC' on 3 September 1947, and despite a change of name in 1997, the name 'John Brunt VC' was restored to the public house in 2001, mainly because of local complaints. It retains the name to this day.

Robert Anthony Maurice **Palmer** VC DFC and Bar was born in Gillingham, Kent on 7 July 1920. He was educated at the prestigious Gravesend Grammar School for boys, where there is a portrait of him hanging in the school's main hall, along with the actual citation for the award of his Victoria Cross.

He enlisted in the Royal Air Force Volunteer Reserve in 1941 and flew his first operation in January 1941. In May 1942 he took part in the first of the 1,000 bomber raids on the city of Cologne in Germany and was also one of the first RAF pilots to drop one of the 4,000 lb 'Cookie' bombs, one of the largest conventional bombs used by the RAF during the Second World War.

On 23 December 1943, at just 24 years of age, and a squadron leader (115772) in No.109 Squadron, with a remarkable 110 bombing missions already under his belt, he took off on what would be his final journey.

Palmer was in command of twenty-seven Lancaster bombers as well as three Mosquitoes on a daytime bombing raid on the Gremberg railway marshalling yards in Cologne. His aircraft (PB371) was designated as the master bomber aircraft for the operation and was using the Oboe aerial blind bombing targeting system, based on radio transponder technology, equipment that was very advanced for its time. It had been in use with the RAF since December 1941.

Palmer's job was to mark the targets so that the other Lancaster aircraft knew exactly where to aim for. He did this by dropping flares. The air raid did not quite go according to plan. Two of the Lancasters collided with each other whilst passing over the coast of France, with the loss of both crews. As the rest of the aircraft reached Germany, the cloudy skies that they were expecting to find, and which were to provide them with much needed cover, had disappeared leaving them clearly visible

Painting of Robert Anthony Maurice Palmer VC DFC and Bar.

from the ground and easy targets for the German anti-aircraft batteries below. To counter this the decision was taken to allow the bombers to break formation and bomb their intended targets manually, rather than using their Oboe radio bombing equipment. Unfortunately Palmer and his crew did not receive the message and carried on their planned course which left them extremely vulnerable to ground attack. By the time his aircraft had reached its intended target, it had been hit numerous times and two of his engines were on fire. Rather than break off his attack Palmer continued on as planned, dropped his bombs and in doing so left a perfect target for his colleagues to attack. As his aircraft plummeted to the ground on fire, only one of the crew, the rear gunner, managed to extricate himself from the burning bomber, engaged his parachute and floated gently to the ground and survived, albeit to become a prisoner of war.

The following is taken from the *London Gazette* of 20 March 1945:

This officer had completed 110 bombing missions. Most of them involved deep penetration of heavily defended territory; many were low-level 'marking' operations against vital targets; all were executed with tenacity, high courage and great accuracy, so that he was invariably selected for particularly important missions. The finest example of his courage and determination was on December 23rd 1944, when he led a formation of Lancasters to attack the marshalling yards at Cologne in daylight. Before the target was reached heavy anti-aircraft fire was encountered and two of his plane's engines were set on fire. Squadron Leader Palmer ignored the double risk of fire and explosion in his aircraft and kept on. He made a perfect approach and his bombs hit the target. His aircraft was last seen spiralling to the earth in flames. Squadron Leader Palmer was an outstanding pilot. He displayed conspicuous bravery. His record of prolonged and heroic endeavour is beyond praise.

An act of true heroism by an extremely courageous young man. As if the action of 23 December 1944 wasn't enough, he was also a holder of the Distinguished Flying Cross and Bar. He is buried in the Rheinberg War Cemetery in the Nordrhein-Westfalen region of Germany.

His parents, Arthur Robert and Lillian Palmer, lived at Gravesend, Kent, along with his brother Douglas.

In addition to those men from the county of Kent who were awarded the Victoria Cross for their bravery during the Second World War, many more were awarded the George Medal, too many to mention in these pages, but who when called upon to do their bit and without any apparent consideration for their own safety, carried out acts of extreme bravery.

Below are some examples of the courage these individuals displayed. These are selected at random and no negative inference should be drawn in relation to others who were also awarded the George Medal, but who are not included in this chapter. It was simply not possible to provide accounts of every one of their acts of bravery.

On Monday, 30 September 1940, it was announced in the *London Gazette* that awards of the George Medal had been made to the following men of the Dover Fire Brigade, who also happened to be the first to have received the new medal.

Ernest Herbert **Harmer**, Executive Chief Officer; Cyril William Arthur **Brown**, Second Officer; Alexander Edmund **Campbell**, Section Officer.

The official account for the award of the medals stated that it was in recognition of their gallantry shown on the occasion of 29 July 1940, whilst dealing with a fire in Dover harbour that had been caused by attacking enemy aircraft.

His Majesty King George VI asked that the names of the following men also be included in the announcement, as having received commendations for their actions during the same incident: Ernest Alfred Foord, Fireman; Edward Jesse Gore, Fireman; Arthur Thomas Cunnington, Auxiliary Fireman; Lionel Rupert Hudsmith, Auxiliary Fireman; John McDermott, Auxiliary Fireman.

In the large-scale attack by enemy aircraft on Dover Harbour, fires were started both on ships and oil stores throughout the course of the day. During the air raid, members of the Dover Fire Brigade and the town's Auxiliary Fire Service, carried out excellent work in what were extremely difficult and dangerous circumstances, so much so that despite the carnage, all the fires were eventually extinguished.

Remarkably, the individuals named above volunteered to return to a blazing ship that contained a large amount of explosives, to extinguish fires that had broken out on the vessel – despite the fact that German aircraft were still in the skies above them – displaying courage and bravery of the highest order.

Temporary Lieutenant Frederick John **Hopgood**, of the Royal Naval Reserve, and the well-known master of a Dover harbour board tug, was awarded the George Medal, the news of which was made public on 24 January 1941. The date of the incident concerned was not divulged, but took place during an air raid on Dover. Three vessels lay abreast of each other alongside a jetty in the harbour but were in danger from the encroachment of burning oil. Mr Hopgood connected his tug to the middle of the three vessels, and then aided by his engineer and the tug's boy, he managed, after considerable difficulties and endeavour, to tow all three vessels clear of the burning oil, and in doing so, saved them from being engulfed in flames and lost.

Later he was also awarded the Distinguished Service Cross for his zeal, and dedication to duty.

During the same air raid Royal Navy Stoker 1st Class, George W. **Lowe** carried out a gallant rescue at the Sussex Arms public house in Dover, an action for which he too was awarded the George Medal.

Stoker Lowe displayed conspicuous courage and resourcefulness when he tunnelled under a pile of wreckage, some fifteen feet high and extricated the licensee, the sole survivor of the Sussex Arms. The entire time Stoker Lowe was carrying out his rescue, he was working in an incredibly small cavity in the debris. He was in danger of being crushed by the collapse of a large and heavy chimney breast, which leant precariously on the pile of debris under which he was crawling. After extricating the distressed licensee safely out of the ruins, Stoker Lowe once again volunteered to go back into the ruined public house, when it was discovered that there was a woman also trapped inside. He crawled back in under the debris, placing himself in extreme danger by doing so. He located the woman and removed her to a place of safety. She had been trapped under the debris of the ruined building for over three hours.

The announcement of the award of the George Medal to Calypso Clarence **Gammon**, a district officer with the Birmingham Fire Brigade, was made in the local newspapers, including the *Whitstable Times and Herne Bay Herald*, on Saturday, 29 March 1941.

He was in charge of the crews who were in attendance at the scene of a fire at premises that had been severely damaged during an air raid. An auxiliary fireman ventured too far along a passage way which ran along the side of the building. The heat of the flames was so intense, that one of the walls collapsed and the gallant fireman was struck by the falling bricks and other debris and knocked unconscious. When Mr Gammon located his fallen colleague, he was pinned underneath a concrete girder, and the rapidly spreading flames were almost upon him. With no apparent concern for his own wellbeing, Mr Gammon removed the extremely hot bricks which covered his colleague with his hands, and despite the fact that other sections of the same wall had started to collapse around him, he continued undeterred in his efforts, finally succeeding in extricating the man from under the fallen concrete girder, just in time to save the flames form engulfing them both.

Mr Gammon was the youngest son of the late William Gammon, the landlord of the Ship Inn at Whitstable.

Arthur Hugh **Grant** was an fireman with the London Auxiliary Fire Service, who carried out an act of supreme bravery on 12 November 1940, saving many lives in the process. His actions on that day were deemed to be worthy of the award of the George Medal. He was 29 years of age and a married man who lived at 107 Footscray Road, Eltham, Kent, with his wife Muriel Isabel Grant. His parents also lived in the same town.

The circumstances of the actions that were carried out by Arthur Hugh Grant, are recorded in the citation for the award of his George Medal, which was included in the *London Gazette* of 29 April 1941 but actually dated 2 May 1941.

On 12 November 1940, a high explosive bomb had dropped through the roof of a building which was in use as a temporary station by the fire service. Without any hesitation Auxiliary Fireman Grant removed it from the main hall to the area outside, quickly covered it with bags of sand. It subsequently exploded with only slight damage to the station. His heroic action undoubtedly saved many lives and much damage to property.

Two days after this incident he was killed as a result of enemy action at the Auxiliary Fire Station in Invicta Road, Eltham. He is buried in the Greenwich Metropolitan Borough Cemetery.

Arthur James **Foreman**, from Birchington, Kent, was a fire brigade officer with the London Fire Brigade, as his father and other family members had been before him. He was awarded the George Medal for the part he played in dealing with a fire in London.

The official announcement that told of the circumstances of how Arthur Foreman won his George Medal, stated that together with another fireman, he entered a magazine containing 60 tons of cordite outside which two trucks, loaded with explosives, were on fire. Both men were able to extinguish the fire in the truck, and then they returned to the magazine where they continued fight the fire until it was no longer a danger.

Mr Foreman was born in Birchington, Kent, where he was educated at the town's Church of England School. Between leaving school and up to 1936, he was employed at a local garage, which was also the year in which he enlisted in the fire brigade as a voluntary driver with the Birchington section of the Margate brigade. When the war broke out he became a full-time fireman with the Margate Fire Brigade, but in October 1940, he was sent to work in London, where soon after he made the move, he was promoted to the rank of brigade officer.

Mr Foreman's father, Arthur Foreman, was himself a fireman, who for many years was the driver of the horse-driven fire engine, which was the fire fighting appliance at Birchington. He gained a reputation throughout Kent of being a crack driver of horse drawn appliances and was single handedly responsible for the Birchington section of the local brigade winning several cups and shields in this particular discipline.

Edward Henry **Moore** was an auxiliary fireman who lived at Newington Road, Ramsgate. He was awarded his George Medal for an act of bravery at Ramsgate, Kent on 24 August 1940, during a German air raid on the town, and the Chief Fire Officer was mentioned in despatches for brave conduct in relation to civil defence. Both men had their deeds recounted in the *London Gazette*.

On the morning of the air raid Edward Moore was cycling in to his place of work along with fellow Auxiliary Fireman Herbert F. Wells, when an air raid began. Undeterred they continued on their way, with German bombs dropping from the skies above them, one of which landed in a nearby field as they cycled past and the explosion blew them off their bikes, across the road and into a hedge. Although Wells was knocked out by the blast, it appeared that Edward Moore came off worst as he was struck by a piece of shrapnel in his right arm, the wound bleeding profusely. Still Moore continued on, running to summon assistance at an aid post, which wasn't as easy as it might sound. The bombs had done their work, buildings had been hit and people injured, leaving Moore having to make his way through masonry, bricks, broken glass and fallen telephone wires, to get the help that was so urgently required.

While Moore was treated at the first-aid post, ambulance men followed his directions to where they could find his colleague Wells. They found him a short while later, unconscious and covered in blood. Both men were then removed to hospital, where Wells, whose home had been totally destroyed in a previous air raid, died.

In relation to the bravery shown by Chief Officer **Wain**, it was reported at the time that it was not possible to reveal the entire circumstances of what he did, on the grounds of national security.

At a meeting of the Ramsgate Town Council on 2 January 1941, the Mayor, Alderman A.B.C. Kempe, paid tribute to the two men, along with Chief Inspector **Butcher**, who it was announced, had been awarded the King's Police Medal for distinguished service. Each of the three men were subsequently sent letters of congratulation.

Henry Harrison Stephen **Kinlan** was awarded the George Medal, whilst serving with the London Auxiliary Fire Service. His award was announced on 1 February 1941. Mr Kinlan had served with the Fire Service since the outbreak of the war. Prior to this he had been a journalist working for local newspapers in Woolwich, Canterbury and Margate, and his parents lived at the Marina, Marine Gardens, Margate. He was a keen and popular local Thanet sportsman who took part in many sports but particularly cricket and football, the latter of which had seen him regularly represent the Old Centrals Football Club as well as Margate Reserves.

I could find no citation for the act of bravery Henry had carried out which warranted the award of the George Medal, but for some reason, not all such awards were announced in the *London Gazette*. However, I did find a newspaper article dated 14 February 1941 which described the incident.

Along with a Mr Storer, who worked for the London Auxiliary Fire Service, and also received the George Medal, they saved four buildings which contained high explosives. The two men remained at their post despite the obvious danger to their lives, and in the face of flying debris and exploding shells of various calibres, remained at their post, and by their actions set an example of courage to their comrades. They both insisted on remaining even when reminded of the imminent danger of an explosion.

Mr Kinlan was called up for full time service with the London Auxiliary Fire Service, originally being stationed at Abbey Wood, before becoming an acting section officer and being transferred to Plumstead Fire Station as a leading auxiliary. In early 1941, he was further promoted, this time to the rank of acting sub officer. During his time as an auxiliary fireman he attended many big fires, and on many occasions carried out his duties in conditions of extreme peril.

Arthur **Holme**, who was 40 years of age, married, and lived at 22 Hawkenbury Road, Tunbridge Wells, was a chief petty officer in the Royal Navy. Although he hailed from London, he had lived in the town since 1921. He was recalled for military service in March 1940 and was engaged on undisclosed work of a particularly dangerous nature, after having previously served in the Royal Navy for 21 years.

Mrs Holme, speaking to a local newspaper, explained how she had heard from her husband the previous weekend who had informed her of the award, but not what it had been awarded for. The fourth supplement of the *London Gazette* of 4 July 1941, records the following:

The King has been graciously pleased to approve the Award of the George Medal for Gallantry and undaunted devotion to duty to Chief Petty Officer Arthur Holme, C/J.4782.

The announcement did not include any specific information concerning the date, or what specific act of bravery Arthur Holme had carried out to be awarded his George Medal, possibly because of wartime security restrictions.

On 19 August 1941 it was announced in the local Kent newspapers that Edward William Robert **Morgan**, the son of Mr and Mrs W.E. Morgan of 73 Grange Road, Ramsgate, who was a district officer in the London Fire Brigade, had been awarded the George Medal. No date or exact location of the incident were provided, but his actions and those of his colleague, Sub-Officer G.W. Hill, who was stationed at Hendon, showed utter disregard for their own safety, or of any danger. Furthermore, they showed conspicuous courage and fortitude during a German bombing raid on London, when two persons were discovered trapped in the basement of a burning building, that was alight from the ground floor to the upper floor.

Morgan and Hill entered the burning building via a ground floor passageway. They located the two people and moved them to the front part of the basement, where they were lifted up into the street and safety. Sub-Officer Hill quickly followed, before Morgan, who was considerably affected by the smoke of the fire, and in a very exhausted condition, was pulled up with the help of a rope.

Whilst the two men were carrying out their act of bravery in the front section of the basement by rescuing the two members of the public, the rear part of the building collapsed, showing just how much danger Morgan, Hill and the two individuals whom they rescued, were in.

Two months earlier in June 1941, Edward Morgan, aged 34, was presented with the OBE by His Majesty King George VI at an investiture at Buckingham Palace for his courage and leadership when the officer in charge of the Watch was killed and other members of the team were severely injured when further bombs were dropped on their location while they were dealing with fires caused by an earlier direct hit on a large six floor warehouse. This incident took place on an undisclosed date the previous year.

Morgan was an extremely brave young man, because besides the two occasions of courage mentioned above, he had been recommended for his bravery on a third occasion during 1941, when he saved the lives of three women and a baby who were trapped by flames at the top of a tall building in which a fire broke out. On that occasion he received severe burns to his hands which incapacitated him for some time and saw him hospitalized for a few days while his injuries were treated. For this he was awarded the King's Fire Service Medal for Gallantry. As if this cache of medals wasn't enough, he was also awarded the London County Council Fire Brigade Silver Medal for gallantry.

John Lynton George **Warren**, a second lieutenant in The Buffs, was awarded the George Medal in September 1942 for an act of bravery which took place in Dover in March 1942. A house had been damaged during an air raid and a woman was trapped inside the ruined building under a mass of debris. John Warren tunnelled a way under the debris until he eventually reached the injured woman. With the aid of two small motor car jacks, he managed to slowly lift the weight of the debris off the woman's chest and prevented further movement of fallen wooden joists.

Lying in the small tunnel which he had made for himself, and with the constant threat and possibility that the debris above him might collapse at any moment, John Warren remained calm and stayed with the woman for five hours keeping her face and mouth clear of any dust and rubble, whilst talking with her and keeping her calm. On two occasions he gave the woman morphine injections for her pain, on the instruction of a doctor who was talking to him from outside the wrecked building.

When rescuers finally arrived to begin safely extricating the badly injured woman from under the debris, John Warren remained with her to offer them advice on the safest way to remove the fallen debris that was above him. It was undoubtedly due to John Warren's courage and perserverance, whilst at the same time placing himself in a position of great risk, that the woman's life was ultimately saved.

James Joseph Henry **Haywood** was 31 years of age, a married man, who before going off to war, lived at Petts Wood, Kent, with his wife, Ellen Elizabeth Haywood. He was an electrical lieutenant in the Royal Naval Volunteer Reserve when he was killed in action on 5 July 1942, whilst serving on board HMS *Niger*. The ship had left Murmansk in Russia on 27 June 1942, and was acting as an escort ship, when because of bad weather which in turn led to an error of navigation, the *Niger* strayed into an Allied minefield off Iceland, and at 2240 hours on 5 July 1942, she struck a mine and exploded, before quickly sinking. There were 149 crew members who were killed in the explosion, including the commanding officer, eight officers, one of whom was James Joseph Henry Haywood, along with 140 naval ratings.

I could not find the citation for the award of his George Medal, but then it was only first awarded after 24 September 1940, the date of its inception by King George VI, mainly to recognize the numerous acts of gallantry displayed during the Blitz, although at that time it could not be awarded posthumously. His body was never recovered for burial, but his name is commemorated on the Chatham Naval Memorial.

Mr A.E. **Twyman**, who had been the chief officer of Margate Fire Brigade until September 1941, left the service to take up the position as acting divisional officer for the north Kent district. He had been associated with Margate Fire Brigade for sixteen years, having joined in 1925 and went on to succeeded Mr H. Hammond as the town's chief officer. In August 1940 he was awarded the George Medal for his courage and leadership in connection to the bombing of an un-named RAF station in Kent.

Mr Gilbert **Mitchell**, 36 years of age and a farmer of Reach Court Farm, St Margaret's Bay, near Dover, was awarded the George Medal, whilst his wife Kathleen Mary Mitchell and her sister, Miss Grace Lillian Harrison, farm worker, now a tractor driver in the Women's Land Army, were both awarded the British Empire Medal.

The *London Gazette* in announcing the awards on 29 May 1942, said:

Mr and Mrs Mitchell and Mrs Harrison made an unexampled effort and have shown sustained bravery and devotion to duty in carrying on farming under the gunfire and air attacks of the enemy.

The farm in question was at the nearest point in England to mainland Europe and was scarred with filled-in shell holes. The farm buildings were probably the most vulnerable along the entire south coast of Great Britain yet work on the farm carried on throughout the entire period of the Battle of Britain and for the rest of the war.

During air raids the German pilots would regularly machine gun the farm, which resulted in work on the land having to stop until the raid was over. Despite the danger and continuous threat from these aerial attacks, the cows were still milked and tended on a daily basis.

When working in the fields cutting corn, for example, Mr Mitchell and Miss Harrison, would regularly have to take cover underneath their tractor, when German aircraft attacked them with machine guns. Attacking a farmer and one of his workers hardly constituted a legitimate military target. On one occasion, Mr Mitchell was sat astride his tractor whilst cultivating his fields, when a nearby balloon was shot down in flames, the burning fabric landed across his tractor, but he simply extinguished the fire and calmly carried on with his work.

Mr and Mrs Mitchell, along with Miss Harrison, remained working the farm throughout the war and gathered not only their crops, but those of nearby farms which had been abandoned because of the war.

It was announced on 18 December 1942 that both Police Constable Cyril **Ashley** and Mr George **Fenton**, from Folkestone, had been awarded the George Medal for their courage when they went to the rescue of a group of workmen who had inadvertently wandered into a minefield on the beach, which resulted in some of them being badly injured and three of them killed. The actions of PC Ashley and Mr Fenton, who in entering the minefield placed themselves in extreme danger and in the knowledge that they too could possibly be wounded or killed, were of the highest possible order.

Stephen **Jeeves** was 35 years of age and a married man, who lived with his wife, Kathleen Jeeves, in Slade Green, Erith, Kent. He was an able seaman P/JX 257401 in the Royal Navy, who was killed in action on 1 February 1943 whilst serving as part of the crew of HMS *Welshman*. He is buried in the El Alamein War Cemetery in Egypt. Once again, I could not find a citation in relation to the award of Stephen's George Medal, neither when or why it was awarded.

Anthony Reginald Joseph **Firminger** was 24 years of age and a lieutenant in Royal Navy Volunteer Reserve, who was killed in action on 23 August 1943, whilst serving on HMS *Cannee*. He had previously been awarded the George Medal and had also been mentioned in despatches. His name is commemorated on the Plymouth Naval Memorial and his parents, Lyle Douglas and Bessie Louise Firminger, lived at Bromley, Kent. Again, I could find no record of the citation for the award of his George Medal.

Alfred George **Spencer**, a flight lieutenant in the Royal Air Force, was the younger son of Mr and Mrs A.V. Spencer, who lived at 110 Northdown Road, Cliftonville.

An article in the local Thanet newspaper dated 29 December 1944, reported that Alfred Spencer was one of two RAF officers who courageously but sadly unsuccessfully, attempted to rescue the crew of a crashed British Wellington bomber aircraft that was carrying heavy bombs and incendiaries and had burst into flames. The entire wreckage was on fire, which resulted in the two officers having to break off their rescue attempts several times. It was not until the aircraft's bombs were red hot from the heat of the flames, and Alfred Spencer was certain that none of the crew could still be alive, that he and his colleague finally abandoned their rescue efforts. Both men were awarded the George Medal for their acts of bravery.

With the fighting finally over, acts of war-related bravery were still being undertaken. William Sangster **Borthwick**, aged 28 years, a lieutenant in the Royal Engineers, had, between January 1945 and January 1946, dealt with a staggering 1,600 mines. Once, after two mines had exploded and killed three prisoners of war and injured nine more, he managed to get the remaining prisoners out of the minefield, an operation made all the more dangerous by the fact that none of them spoke or understood any English. For his continuous acts of courage and bravery, he was awarded the George Medal. His mother, Mrs Borthwick, lived at 99 Buckland Avenue, Dover.

CHAPTER 13

Kent's Wartime Airfields

With the county of Kent being the part of the UK nearest to enemy-held territory, German-occupied France, it was imperative that there were sufficient airfields and aircraft to effectively deal with any aerial threat that Germany might pose. There were some twenty airfields across Kent during the Second World War, with thirteen of these being situated between the town of Maidstone and the Kent coast where it stretched from Folkestone to Lydd. Compare that with today's figures (2017) of seventy-eight airfields spattered across Kent.

Biggin Hill became one of the best known of Kent's war time airfields mainly due to the events of the Battle of Britain. It wasn't a new airfield, having first opened in February 1917 during the First World War, when it became home to units of the Royal Flying Corps. Although it was situated in Kent, it was also just twenty miles away from central London, which made it an ideal location from which to protect the capital from the joint threat of Zeppelins and German Gotha aircraft.

As German dominance continued to grow throughout Europe after the Nazi party gained power in 1933, so the peace that remained became more and more tenuous.

Biggin Hill.

To most political and military observers, it was more of a case of when the Second World War would start, rather than if, so with this in mind airfields such as Biggin Hill greatly increased in capacity and facilities in readiness for war. They became self-contained units where men could work and live and be in a position to react quickly to any threat posed by the German Luftwaffe.

During the Second World War more military personnel could be found in Kent than possibly any other county throughout the United Kingdom, except of course during the immediate build up to the D-Day landings. Part of this was down to the number of airfields, along with what were known as Advanced Landing Grounds, or short-term airfields, which in the main came into being because of the invasion of Europe in June 1944. A need had been identified, albeit an obvious one, that extra fighter aircraft along with light bombers would be needed to support the amphibious landings that took place on the Normandy beaches from 6 June 1944 onwards.

There were nine Royal Air Force bases across Kent. These were located at Biggin Hill, Detling, Eastchurch, Gravesend, Hawkinge, Lympne, Manston, Rochester, and West Malling.

Biggin Hill

The most well known of these was quite possibly Biggin Hill, which was a sector station as part of No.11 Group, Fighter Command, and is still in existence today. At the outbreak of the war the man in charge was Wing Commander R. Grice, who oversaw the resident squadrons, Nos. 32 and 79, which were quickly joined by No.601 (County of London) Squadron, an auxiliary unit which flew Blenheim 1Fs. By March 1940 they had changed over to flying Hurricanes, having already moved on to RAF Tangmere in December 1939. Tangmere was situated near Chichester in West Sussex.

As was the norm during the Second World War, RAF Squadrons were continually moved to different locations, sometimes only staying in the same place for a matter of weeks. No.79 Squadron left Biggin Hill in early May 1940, having been sent out to Merville in France to assist the British Expeditionary Force in their enforced retreat to the beaches of Dunkirk, but had returned to England by 21 May 1940.

The early months of 1940 saw squadrons coming and going at Biggin Hill, with No.610 Squadron, another auxiliary unit, arriving along with Nos. 213, 229, and 242 squadrons. These three were all part of the Royal Canadian Air Force, and more than played their part in the mass evacuations of British, French and Belgian troops from Dunkirk.

Such was the part played by the RAF and her Allied counterparts that Winston Churchill was moved to say in recognising the part that had been played by each and every pilot at Dunkirk:

Wars are not won by evacuations, but there was a victory inside this deliverance, which should be noted. It was gained by the Royal Air Force.

The RAF did not just protect the people and towns of Kent or the vastness of the English Channel, they were also sent on raids to parts of occupied Europe. In early May 1940 twelve Hurricane aircraft from No.32 Squadron took off from Biggin Hill to attack Ypenburg airfield in Holland which had been captured by the Luftwaffe. The raid was a success, with large numbers of German aircraft being destroyed on the ground, before they had a chance to take to the skies. This attack was carried out at the behest of the Dutch government.

On 10 May 1940, aircraft from No.600 (City of London) Squadron, raided Waalhaven airfield in Holland, after Dutch neutrality had been breached when German forces captured Dutch airfields at Ypenburg, Ocken, Waalhaven, Burg and Valkenburg.

No.600 Squadron, based at RAF Manston, sent six Blenheim aircraft from B-flight to carry out the raid.

L6616: Pilot: Squadron Leader 90081 James Michael Wells. Navigator: Sergeant John N. Davis. Air Gunner 800235: Basil A. Kidd.

L1335: Pilot: Flying Officer 90098 Charles Roger Moore. Air Gunner 800520: Corporal Laurence David Isaacs.

L1401: Pilot: Flying Officer Hugh C. Rowe. Air Gunner: Pilot Officer 77117 Robert Wyatt Hamilton Echlin.

L1514: Pilot: Pilot Officer Norman Hayes. Air Gunner: Corporal J Holmes.

L1515: Pilot: Pilot Officer 90497 Michael Herbert Anderson. Air Gunner: Leading Aircraftman Herbert C.W. Hawkins

L1517: Pilot: Pilot Officer Richard C. Haine. Air Gunner: Pilot Officer Marcus Kramer DFC.

Squadron Leader James Wells decided to take just one navigator on the mission, Sergeant John N. Davis, who was on board his aircraft. His reasoning for taking only one navigator was that they were a very precious commodity, and he knew that Sergeant Davis was more than capable of leading the other aircraft on to the intended target. The only potential problem with this was that if Squadron Leader Wells' aircraft had been damaged or shot down en route, the others would have had to abort the mission and return to base.

The six crews took off from RAF Manston at 10.30 am without an escort of either Spitfires or Hurricanes as promised. On reaching Waalhaven airfield, the Blenheims attacked and destroyed numerous German aircraft before they could even take off. There was only the opportunity to conduct one run over the target before they were attacked by twelve Messerschmidt BF110 fighters. The outcome for the six RAF aircraft from No.600 Squadron, was not a happy one.

L6616 – Crashed at village of Pernis. Squadron Leader James Wells and Air Gunner Basil A. Kidd were both killed, whilst the Navigator Sergeant John Davis managed to bale out. He landed safely and without injury and managed to safely reach the village of Herkingen.

L1335 – Crashed near the airfield at Waalhaven. Both Flying Officer Charles Moore and Corporal Laurence Isaacs were killed.

L1401 – Crashed at the village of Pershil. Pilot Officer Robert Echlin, a Canadian, who was the aircraft's air gunner was killed, whilst Hugh Rowe survived the crash but was in need of urgent hospital treatment. He eventually became a German prisoner of war.

L1514 – Was the only one of the six Blenheims that made it back to RAF Manston, with its crew intact, although the aircraft was so badly damaged that it never flew again.

L1515 – Crashed at Spijkenisse. Both Pilot Officer Michael Anderson and Leading Aircraftman Herbert Hawkins were killed. Anderson had previously been Mentioned in Despatches for bravery.

L1517 – Pilot Officer Richard Haine managed to carry out an emergency landing near to the village of Herkingen. Along with his colleague Pilot Officer Kramer and Sergeant John Davis, he made his way to the Hook of Holland, a journey which took the men three days, making sure that their true identities were not discovered. On arriving at the Hook and when their identities were confirmed, they were allowed on board HMS *Hereward* and taken back to England and freedom.

The seven airmen who were killed during the raid were buried by the Germans as 'unknown British airmen'. In the late 1980s their identities were discovered and their graves were marked accordingly. Kidd, Isaacs, Moore, and Wells are buried in the Grooswijk General Cemetery, which is situated in Rotterdam. Anderson and Hawkins are buried in the General Cemetery in Spijkenisse, and Echlin was buried in the Protestant Churchyard, in Piershil.

Flight Lieutenant 77345 Marcus Kramer, who had been awarded the Distinguished Flying Cross, was subsequently killed in action on 21 May 1941. He has no known grave, but his name is commemorated on the Runnymede Memorial in Surrey.

No.141 Squadron was stationed at RAF West Malling, flying Bolton Paul Defiant aircraft. On 19 July 1940 they were allocated to patrol in the skies over Folkestone, nine aircraft in total. Unbeknown to the RAF, the Luftwaffe had discovered a fatal weakness in the aircraft which the squadron flew. None of their four guns faced downwards, in fact they all pointed towards the rear of the aircraft, making them extremely vulnerable to a determined enemy. The nine aircraft from 141 Squadron had only been airborne for a matter of minutes when they came under attack from a group of Messerschmitt BF109s, swooping down out of the clouds. By the time the encounter was over, six of the Defiant aircraft had been shot down, and only one of the others managed to make it back to its base at RAF Manston. Such was the concern about the aircraft that No.141 Squadron was taken out of the affray and transferred to Prestwick in Scotland.

Those members of No.141 Squadron who were killed that day, were:

Sergeant 903401 Frederick Peter John **Atkins**, an air gunner in the Royal Air Force Volunteer Reserve, and a married man from Edmonton, north London. He is buried in the Eastern Cemetery in Boulogne. How he ended up in a French cemetery after his aircraft was engaged by the Luftwaffe over Kent, is not clear.

Sergeant 903506 Robert **Crombie**, of the Royal Air Force Volunteer Reserve, was 29 years of age and a married man from Lightwater in Surrey. He has no known grave, but his name is commemorated on the Runnymede Memorial in Surrey.

Hawkinge Cemetery.

Sergeant 747968 Albert George **Curley**, of the Royal Air Force Volunteer Reserve, was 33 years of age and from Bushey in Hertfordshire. He has no known grave, but his name is commemorated on the Runnymede Memorial in Surrey.

Flight Lieutenant 33306 Ian David Grahame **Donald**, of the Royal Air Force. He is buried in the All Saints Churchyard in Tilford, Surrey.

Pilot Officer 78543 Arthur Charles **Hamilton**, was an air gunner in the Royal Air Force. He was 28 years of age and a single man from Middlesex. He is buried in the Hawkinge Cemetery, in Kent.

Pilot Officer 41705 Richard Alexander **Howley** of the Royal Air Force was a native of Newfoundland, Canada. He has no known grave, but his name is commemorated on the Runnymede Memorial in Surrey.

Pilot Officer 41850 John Richard **Kemp** of the Royal Air Force was 25 years of age and a single man from Canterbury in New Zealand. He has no known grave, but his name is commemorated on the Runneymede Memorial in Surrey.

Pilot Officer 41297 Rudal **Kidson** of the Royal Air Force was 26 years old and a native of New Zealand. He too had no known grave and is commemorated on the Runnymede Memorial in Surrey.

Pilot Officer 44597 Dudley **Malins** was 26 years of age and serving with the Royal Air Force. He was a single man from Southsea, Hampshire and his name is commemorated on the Runnymede Memorial in Surrey.

Sergeant 746875 John Francis **Wise** served in the Royal Air Force Volunteer Reserve. His name is commemorated on the Runnymede Memorial in Surrey.

The first German Luftwaffe raids on British air bases throughout Kent took place on 12 August 1940. Spitfires from No.610 Squadron, who were at the time stationed at Biggin Hill, took to the skies and engaged a group of Messerschmitt Bf 109 fighters. As a result of the attack, the RAF station at Hawkinge was badly damaged and because of the large number of bombs that found their target, the runway was put out of action which resulted in No.32 Squadron having to redeploy to nearby Biggin Hill. This would become a regular occurrence throughout the Battle of Britain. Bases would be attacked, runways would be put out of action, resulting in resident squadrons needing to move to another airfield nearby and fast, so that they too weren't out of action.

Six days later on 18 August 1940 the Luftwaffe attacked Biggin Hill in a well-planned operation, with the intention of rendering the base inoperable and to cause as much damage as possible. Remarkably in just over ten minutes the attacking German aircraft managed to drop a total of 500 bombs on their intended target. Not surprisingly many of the buildings were damaged, some beyond repair, and the runway was put out of action, but despite the extensive damage caused and due to the dedicated hard work of the ground staff, it was back in operation later the same afternoon.

About 1030 hours on 30 August 1940 British coastal radar installations along the south coast, picked up a force of 100 incoming German aircraft heading straight towards Kent. The reaction to the threat was quick and within less than twenty-minutes Fighter Command had sent up sixteen of its squadrons to tackle the situation head on. Two of these squadrons were from Biggin Hill. They were No.79 Squadron, who were flying Hurricanes, and No.610 Squadron, who were flying Spitfires. This proved to be an extremely effective decision as this action prevented two waves of German bombers from reaching Biggin Hill. Not to be totally deterred in their attack, the Luftwaffe pilots dropped their payloads on radar stations that were dotted along the Kent coastline, and in doing so effectively knocked out Fighter Command's early warning defensive radar capability, which allowed the RAF's fighter aircraft to become airborne as quickly as possible whenever German aircraft approached the British coast.

The vulnerable situation Britain found itself in without an effective radar system was highlighted later the same evening about 1800 hours, when an undetected Luftwaffe raid on Biggin Hill, consisting of Messerschmitt 109s and Junkers JU88s, resulted in the deaths of thirty-nine members of the station's air crew, and one of the WAAFs, Lena Button, who was a nursing orderly from Tasmania in Australia, when the air raid shelter they had sought refuge in from the falling bombs, took a direct hit. Not all were killed outright but there were those who were injured in the attack who required amputations because of the severity of their wounds.

Another attack on Biggin Hill took place the next day, just before 1 pm, when twelve German bomber aircraft attacked the base. This resulted in a young boy, a member of the local Boys' Brigade who was helping out with signals duties, being wounded. He died in hospital a week later. Despite Spitfires from No.79 Squadron patrolling the skies over Biggin Hill, specifically to deal with the expected raid, the German aircraft, assisted greatly by thick cloud cover, managed to get to their intended target and drop their bombs. Numerous buildings were damaged, along with the gas, electricity and water supplies. The airstrip was so badly cratered that the station's own aircraft that had already taken off, had to land at nearby airfields, whilst those still on the ground at Biggin Hill, and who were able to, worked feverishly to fill in the large craters on the runway; but no sooner had the damage been repaired, than the Luftwaffe made further raids, damaging it once again.

This was also the same day that saw three members of the WAAF, Sergeant Emily Turner, Sergeant Elizabeth Mortimer and Corporal Elspeth Henderson, awarded the Military Medals for their bravery.

For the month of August 1940 Fighter Command of the RAF had lost eighty-five pilots killed, one was missing in action, whilst a further sixty-eight were wounded. During the same time scale, the Luftwaffe incurred considerably more in the way of casualties. Some 434 of their pilots were killed. A massive 804 were missing in action, whilst 201 of them were wounded.

Sunday, 1 September 1940 saw the funerals of those killed at Biggin Hill take place in the local cemetery, ironically against the backdrop of yet another air raid, targeted once again on Biggin Hill. But those present at the burial of their friends and loved ones were not deterred from paying their respects. The German authorities had obviously worked out the significance and the importance of the airfield at Biggin Hill to the RAF, and what its loss would mean to the British war effort, whilst at the same time how important it would be to their own chances of undertaking a successful invasion of the United Kingdom. The day was also notable for seeing the sixth attack by the Luftwaffe on Biggin Hill in just three days, which was unprecedented in its intensity. The problem for Fighter Command was fast becoming not one of a lack of aircraft, but of a lack of experienced pilots to fly them.

Sunday, 15 September 1940, was a notable day for the RAF and Fighter Command. Spitfires and Hurricanes from Nos. 72 and 92 Squadrons shot down a staggering fifty-six German aircraft in the skies over Kent and the English Channel, a morale booster indeed for the RAF, if ever it was needed. These were difficult times for the nation, possibly even make or break, but it was a monumental day for the RAF and is still commemorated as Battle of Britain Day.

Tuesday, 17 September 1940 was the day that Adolf Hitler postponed, indefinitely, his Operation Sea Lion (*Seelowe* in German) plans for the invasion of Great Britain. This was an operation that had come about as a result of Führer Directive number sixteen, issued on 16 July 1940, part of which included the following:

As England, in spite of her hopeless military situation, still shows no sign of willingness to come to terms, I have decided to prepare and if necessary to carry out a landing operation against her. The aim of this operation is to eliminate the English motherland as a base from which the war against Germany can be continued, and, if necessary, to occupy the country completely.

For the operation to take place, Hitler had decreed four conditions first needed to be in place:

(1). The Luftwaffe needed to defeat the RAF and control the skies over Britain.

(2). The English Channel needed to be clear of British mines at the intended crossing points for the invading German forces, and the Straits of Dover required to be blocked at both ends with German laid mines.

(3). The coastal zone between France and England needed to be dominated by German artillery.

(4). Royal Navy vessels already at sea needed to be engaged in other areas so as not to be able to prevent or interfere with the German crossing of the English Channel, and any vessels that had not taken to sea, first needed to be damaged or destroyed.

The intended invasion was to take place across a wide front, stretching across the Kent coastline from as far east as Ramsgate, and as far west as the Isle of Wight.

At the same time as deciding not to implement Operation Sea Lion, Hitler also changed his focus away from attacking the airfields of Kent, to targeting London, but Biggin Hill continued to play its part, as its squadrons were deployed to protect London. There is no doubt that Hitler's decision to stop the Luftwaffe from attacking the airfields of Kent helped to change the entire course of the war. By changing the focus of his aerial attacks away from Kent, he inadvertently allowed Britain's Fighter Command to recover, providing it with some vital breathing space. Its pilots were close to exhaustion, many having flown multiple sorties everyday for weeks without any kind of break. The stress levels they must have experienced can only be guessed at. How much longer they could have survived as an effective defensive deterrent is debatable.

Six Blenheim aircraft from No.601 Squadron took off from Biggin Hill on 29 November 1940 and made their way to Northolt on the outskirts of north-west London. There they joined up with six Blenheim aircraft from No.25 Squadron, and together the twelve aircraft carried out a raid on the German seaplane base at Borkum in the Frisian Islands. Its official title was the Naval Air Station Borkum-See, which was located at the far western tip of Germany. It had originally existed during the First World War but had then been dismantled as part of the conditions of the Treaty of Versailles in 1919. It was rebuilt during the course of 1935-36 under a Nazi-led resurgent German nation.

From December 1939 until March 1940, ice on the Wadden Sea, where the base was situated, had prevented the launch of any of the seaplanes which Germany had at her disposal. The RAF carried out further attacks on the base throughout 1941, but they had little or no effect on the final outcome of the war; they were never going to, which in turn raised the question as to what the purpose of these attacks actually was. On one particular raid which took place on 26 July 1941, British aircraft dropped forty-two incendiary bombs on the facility, and not one of them detonated on impact. All twelve British aircraft returned home safely from their mission.

Wednesday, 20 January 1943 would go down as one of the saddest days of the war connected to Biggin Hill. The call came through for the base's pilots to scramble to deal with the threat of fast approaching enemy aircraft. They managed to get airborne just as the German Focke-Wulf Fw 190 aircraft flew in low over the base.

The unexpected sight of fast moving Spitfires coming at them from below must have been a shock, and would have certainly caused panic amongst the German pilots, each of whom were still carrying their full complement of bombs on board. None of them would have wanted to risk getting involved in a 'dog fight' with bombs strapped to the underbelly of their aircraft.

Having already overshot the runway at Biggin Hill, and with the fear of being imminently attacked by Spitfires in mind, or for nothing more sinister than an instinctive reaction, they dropped their bombs on nearby Bromley, landing on a school and killing four teachers and forty-five young children. As they tried to make good their escape seven of the German aircraft were shot down in the skies over Beachy Head on the Kent coast.

As with such tragic events the numbers of those injured and killed is never an exact science. The figures quoted by individual newspapers sometimes added to the trauma of the occasion rather than assisting. One such newspaper article provides a good example of this. It was dated 22 January 1943, just two days after the tragedy.

IDENTITY OF SCHOOL DEAD DIFFICULT

Rescue workers were digging all night by the light of flares for the children still unaccounted for in the London school bombed in daylight on Wednesday, but it is not expected that any more bodies will be found.

The death roll, including six teachers, is now known to be forty-eight. Fifty children were injured and detained in hospital.

A mass funeral for the victims will take place on Wednesday next and the Mayor will attend.

Scores of parents who have children missing, gathered at the mortuary to try to identify the bodies. Now and again fathers and mothers, sobbing bitterly, were led out through the silent crowds to waiting cars which were arranged by the WVS to assist people to their homes.

Six of the children who were taken to hospital subsequently died of their injuries, but their deaths were included in the number of those who were reported as having been killed.

In keeping with the fact that there was a war going on, and security was paramount, especially in the reporting of such incidents in the press, exact details of the location of the attack or the name of the school were not mentioned, nor was there any mention in any of the newspapers that the German aircraft had been about to attack Biggin Hill airfield, overshot it and jettisoned their bombs before making good their escape. This in turn led to the belief in many people's eyes that the Luftwaffe aircraft had intentionally targeted the school. Some reports talked of the pilot of one aircraft waving and smiling after having dropped his 500lb bomb, whilst others mention him firing his machine guns at those he could see in the streets below. It would appear that the truth in this case is somewhere in between. The original target for one German aircraft undoubtedly appears to have been Biggin Hill airfield, but when unable to jettison his bomb, one of the German pilots, named in an article on Wikipedia as 28-year-old Hauptmann Heinz Schumann, was the man responsible for dropping the bomb that killed the members of staff and children at the school.

Even allowing for the numerous acts of brutality and the atrocities which occurred during the Second World War, it seems almost inconceivable that any man, regardless of the circumstances, would have intentionally targeted a school that had absolutely no military connection or worth whatsoever. It is worth pointing out at this juncture that Sandhurst Road School was a large building, which occupied many floors in height, so maybe it was mistaken by the German pilot as a factory, but if that were the case why the machine-gunning of those he could see below? As Heinz Schumann was killed in action on 8 November 1943, we will never know for sure why he dropped a bomb on Sandhurst Road School.

The six teachers who were killed in the tragedy were:

Mrs Constance May **Taylor** deterrant (58) who was buried in Hither Green Cemetery in a private ceremony on 27 January 1943.

Mrs Virginia May **Carr** (38) who lived with her husband, John Carr, at 38 Beckenham Hill Road, Catford. She is buried in Ballygen, Ireland.

Miss Mary Frances **Jukes** (38) who was buried in St Mary's Churchyard, Harrow.

Miss Harriet Irene **Langdon** (40) of 65 Manor Park, daughter of Charles and Eliza Langdon of Langley, Maidstone.

Mrs Ethel Jessie **Betts** (53) and Miss Gladys Maud **Knowelden** (51) years of age who lived at Hazledene, Furze Hill, Kingswood, Surrey.

One of the children who survived was 12-year-old Molly Kinnerman. Initially she had been trapped by fallen timbers which had resulted in both of her legs being fractured. One of those involved in the rescue was there for both professional as well as personal reasons. Police Constable Greenstreet worked throughout the night with others attempting to rescue staff and pupils who were still trapped amongst the rubble of the school. One of Police Constable Greenstreet's children had been discovered alive and well. He continued searching for his other child, only stopping when he discovered the lifeless body amongst the ruins.

Sandhurst Road School had only been re-opened a matter of months before the attack. It had closed as an educational establishment when the local children were evacuated to the safety of the countryside, and as far away as Wales, during the time of the London Blitz. Whilst the children were away it had been used by the Ministry of War.

Below is a list of the children who died in the attack at Sandhurst Road School, all of whom were buried in Hither Green Cemetery on 27 January 1943, unless otherwise stated.

Alexander, Malcolm Britton (11) survived the initial attack, but died later the same day at Lewisham hospital. He lived with his parents, William Walker Alexander, at 19 Verdant Court, Catford.

Allford, Brenda Jean (5) died in hospital with her sister Lorna Elizabeth (7) who lived with their parents, Charles Joseph and Mrs E.B. Allford, at 125 Torridon Road, Catford. Both girls were buried in Ladywell Cemetery.

Asbury, Olive Hilda (12) lived with her father, Walter Asbury, at 60 Scarlet Road, Catford.

Baker, Joan Elizabeth (12) lived with her parents, Stephen Rowland and Alice Baker at 59 Brookbank Road, Lewisham.

Barley, Betty (15) lived her mother, Mrs E. Barley, 9 Harvard Road, Lewisham. Her father was Lance Sergeant William James Barley of the Royal Field Artillery.

Barnard, Dennis Handford (10) and Ronald Edward (9) lived with their parents, Edward Handford and Dorothy Lilian Barnard, at 120 Further Green Road, Catford.

Biddle, Anne Rosemary and her twin sister Judith Maud (5) lived with their parents, Leslie George and Edith Biddle, at 22 Muirkirk Road, Catford. Leslie George Biddle, was a Corporal in the Royal Electrical & Mechanical Engineers.

Brazier, Kathleen Myrtle (13) lived with her parents, Henry William and Florence May Brazier, at 105 Waters Road, Catford. Although she survived the initial explosion, she died later the same day in Lewisham hospital.

Brewer, Donald Victor (10) lived with his parents, Mr and Mrs Robert Sidney Brewer, of 328 Verdant Road, Lewisham. He was buried on 26 January 1943 in a private ceremony.

Brocklebank, Joyce Agnes (11) lived with her parents, Mr and Mrs Robert Brocklebank, at 75 Longhurst Road, Lewisham.

Carpenter, Pauline Feo (5) lived with her parents, James and Florence Carpenter, at 121 Dowanhill Road, Catford.

Chivrall, Margaret Kathleen Grace (12) lived with her parents, Arthur James and Florence Eliza Chivrall, at Brockley Grove, Crofton Park, south-east London.

Cooper, Pamela Mary Joyce (15) was the daughter of Leonard Aubrey and Violet May Cooper, at 61 Woodyates Road, Lee, South East London. She was buried in Hither Green Cemetery on 27 January 1943, in a private ceremony.

Cornell, Winifred Mary (13) lived with her parents, Alfred and Elizabeth, Cornell, at 7 Launcelot Road, Bromley, Kent.

Davis, Eunice Joan (9) years of age, and her sister, Pauline Mary, (7) lived with their parents, Edwin John and Lillian Emily Davies, at 57 Killearn Road, Catford.

Day, Joan Margaret (12) lived with her parents, Francis Thomas and Dorothy May Day, at 109 Rushey Green, Catford. She was injured in the explosion and died later the same day in Lewisham hospital.

Deavin, Olive Annie Margaret (15) lived with her parents, Reuben and Grace Deavin, at 9 St Swithun's Road, Lewisham.

Drummond, Anthony (9 lived with his parents Leslie Albert and Mary Emily Elizabeth Drummond, at 224 Brownhill Road, Catford.

Dutnall, Janet Mary (5) lived with her parents, Mr and Mrs Archibald Dutnall, at 129 Torridon Road, Lewisham. She was injured in the explosion, but died later the same day at Lewisham hospital.

Fagan, Richard George (9) lived with his parents, Richard John and Georgina Caroline Fagan, of 35 Dallinger Road, Lee, south-east London.

Glennon, Cyril Arthur (6) lived his parents, Albert Ernest and Bessie May Glennon, at 102 Broadfield Road, Catford.

Greenstreet, Norman Frederick (8) lived with his father, Frederick Walter Greenstreet, a local Police Constable, at 73 South Park Crescent, Catford. Frederick's other son who was also at the school at the time of the explosion, survived.

Harrison, Norah Marie (9) lived with her parents, Thomas W. and Ellen E. Harrison, at 33B Southend Road, Beckenham.

Head, Sylvia May Ellen (12) lived with her parents, Stephen Edgar and Rosina May Head, of 80 Milborough Crescent, Lee, south-east London. She was buried in Hither Green Cemetery in a private ceremony on 27 January 1943.

Hobbs, Iris May (15) lived with her mother, Louisa Hobbs, at 13 Theodore Road, Hither Green. Her father, Albert William Hobbs, had already died by the time of her death.

Jarrett, Rodney Charles Ash (6) lived with his parents, Lewis Charles Ash and Sybil Lilian Beck Jarrett, at 4 Cobland Road, Grove Park.

Jones, John Edward (10) lived with his parents, Edward George and Mary Jones, at 46 Ardfillan Road, Catford.

Lay, Doreen Alice (6) lived with her parents, Archibald Baden and Violet Louisa Lay, at 68 South Park Crescent, Catford. She was injured in the initial blast, but died later the same day at Lewisham hospital.

O'Rourke, Mary Rosina (15) lived with her parents, Thomas and Mary Ann O'Rourke, at 148 Oakridge Road, Bromley, Kent.

Scholes, Evelyn Joyce (11) lived with her parents at 192 Firhill Road, Bellingham.

Silmon, Pamela Eileen (10) lived with her parents, William Melchior and Mrs D.M. Silmon, at 45 Ardgowan Road, Catford.

Tennant, Clive Derek (8) lived with his parents, Harold Archibald and Ena May Tennant, at 91 South Park Crescent, Croydon.

Thorne, Doreen (12) lived with her parents, Stanley Arthur and Florence Annie Thorne, at 9 Fernbrook Road, Lewisham.

Towers, Edna (12) lived with her parents, Mr and Mrs Richard Towers, of 27 Horn Park Lane, Lee, South London.

The deaths of such a large number of school children was a shock to the entire nation. It even resulted in questions being asked in the House of Commons. Mr Arthur Duckworth, the Conservative MP for Shrewsbury, asked the Secretary of State for Air if he had any statement to make concerning the raid and the reasons for the delay in sounding the air raid warning before the attack took place. Mr W.J. Thorne, the Labour MP for Plaistow, asked the same question, whilst Captain Charles Taylor, the Conservative MP for Eastbourne, asked him whether he was satisfied that everything possible was being done to combat the German raids along the south-east coast.

May 1943 saw the rise of both excitement and expectation as the pilots and squadrons at Biggin Hill fast approached the base's landmark of shooting down its 1,000[th] German aircraft since the beginning of the war. The news of this pending achievement had reached the ears of the Press, who had deemed it worthy enough to send down their journalists and correspondents to cover the auspicious occasion for both radio and newspapers. As the important moment approached, so the desire grew to be the man to score the 1,000[th] 'kill'.

The milestone was finally reached on 15 May 1943, but confusion initially reigned as to who had actually shot down the 1,000[th] enemy aircraft, and claimed the £300 'sweepstake' waiting for the man who was to collect the prize.

It was relatively late in the day before any of the base's aircraft were sent up. Just before 4.30 pm the order came through for Nos. 611 and 341 squadrons to take to the skies and make their way to Caen in Normandy. Whilst en route they were attacked by several Focke-Wulf Fw 190 fighter aircraft. Squadron Leader Edward 'Jack' Charles, the man in charge of No.611 Squadron, was definitely responsible for shooting down the 999th enemy aircraft, but determining who actually shot down the 1,000[th] wasn't as straightforward. Squadron Leader Charles shot down a second German aircraft, but Commandant Rene Mouchotte, the commanding officer of No.341 Squadron, also scored a hit. It could not be clearly determined who was actually responsible for the 1,000[th] kill, so the accolade was shared between the two men, as was the £300 sweepstake money.

Biggin Hill and RAF stations throughout Kent continued to play an important role in the war against Nazi Germany. As the war progressed its role changed from being defensive to an offensive one. On 13 June 1944, just a week after the D-Day landings of Allied troops in Normandy, Germany sent over the first of her infamous V1 flying bombs, aiming it towards London. It was at this time that Biggin Hill airfield became home to barrage balloon units whose job it was to provide a secure aerial ring around London, in an attempt at preventing German air raids being successful. By September 1944 the purpose of Biggin Hill had changed once again, returning back to its offensive fighter role with the job of escorting Lancaster and Halifax bombers on daytime raids deep into the heart of a slowly declining Germany.

In the immediate aftermath of the war it became more of a transport hub as part of No.46 Group Transport Command, as men, equipment and supplies were needed in various parts of a now liberated Europe that no longer had to cower under the threat and fear of occupying German forces.

Detling

Detling airfield had started during the First World War, but closed afterwards and wasn't re-opened until 14 September 1938, on a much larger scale and with a grass runway which stretched for 4,200 feet. Its first resident unit was No.500 (County of Kent) Squadron, which was part of No.6 (Auxiliary) Group of Bomber Command, and its main purpose was aerial reconnaissance. With war looming, No.500 Squadron became part of No.16 Group of Coastal Command in 1939, still with its reconnaissance role over the English Channel and the Dover Straits, but adding escort duties to its CV.

By the end of September 1939, No.500 Squadron had been joined at Detling by No.48 Squadron. As the end of the year drew to a close, the base suffered losses, not as a result of enemy attacks, but several fatal crashes, some of which were down to the worsening weather.

In Robin J. Brooks' book, *Kent Airfields in the Second World War*, he writes of an aircraft returning to Detling after having been involved in escort duties in the English Channel. As it approached Detling, it developed engine trouble and quickly began to lose height. Flying Officer D.G. Mabey (25) of Tonbridge, who was at the controls of the stricken aircraft, managed to keep her steady and even gain a little height. Leading Aircraftman Messent managed to bail out, but Mabey, Pilot Officer A.M. Paterson (29), and Corporal J.F. Drew, weren't so lucky. All three men perished in the crash on 7 October 1939.

Daphne Pearson.

In the build-up to the Dunkirk evacuations in May 1940, all of Kent's airfields were busy, not just with the coming and goings of their own aircraft but other squadrons that had claimed temporary squatters' rights, that's what it must have felt like to the resident squadrons, who suddenly found their airfields crammed with faces they didn't recognise and aircraft they had never seen before.

In the early hours of 31 May 1940 an incident took place at Detling which involved Joan Daphne Mary Pearson, known as Daphne, who had enlisted in the Women's Auxiliary Air Force soon after the outbreak of the war and who became the first woman to be awarded the George Cross.

Aircraft had set out from Detling earlier in the evening of 30 May 1940 to attack German barges near Boulogne. The codename of the operation was Dundee. One of the Anson aircraft of No.500 Squadron allocated to the raid was R3389. Its crew consisted of Pilot Officer Bond, Flying Officer Chambers, Corporal Petts and Leading Aircraftman Smith. As the aircraft approached its target and prepared to drop its pay load of bombs, Corporal Petts pressed the bomb release button, but nothing happened. He tried again, with the same result. The pilot, Bond, now had no option but to abort

Painting of Daphne Pearson.

his mission and get back to his base at Detling as soon as he could as he was fast running out of fuel. As he approached the Kent coastline, close to home, Bond's job became even more difficult with the combination of bad weather and a failing aircraft. As the wheels of the Anson touched the grass, it was already on fire and as it slithered sideways the undercarriage gave way.

Daphne made her way to the stricken aircraft over a fence and down a nettle-filled ditch, having heard it crash land from the nearby WAAF quarters. As she neared the aircraft, others appeared on the scene and started dragging the pilot clear. Running towards them, she yelled: 'Leave him to me – go and get the fence down for the ambulance.'

She began to drag the pilot further away from the blaze and stopped to give him first aid; finding that his neck was injured, she feared a broken back. The pilot then told her that there was a full load of bombs on board, so she pulled him further away, reaching the other side of a ridge just before the petrol tanks blew up. At once she threw herself on top of the pilot to protect him from blast and splinters, placing her helmet over his head. Then, as they lay there a 120lb bomb went off and she held his head to prevent any further dislocation.

Shortly after the pilot had been removed by ambulance, there was yet another, even fiercer explosion. Daphne was undaunted, however, and went back to the wreckage to look for the fourth member of the crew, the wireless operator, but found him dead. Afterwards, she returned to the base to help the doctor, and was on duty as usual at 8 am that day.

Two weeks later she was promoted to the rank of Assistant Section Officer, spending the rest of the war working mainly in recruitment.

She was originally awarded the Empire Gallantry Medal, at Buckingham Palace in August 1940, and returned to the Palace to be invested with the George Cross by King George VI on 31 January 1941, making her the first female recipient of the award. The citation for her award reads:

The King has been graciously pleased to approve the following Awards: The Medal of the Military Division of the Most Excellent Order of the British Empire, for Gallantry:

880538 Corporal (now Assistant Section Officer) Joan Daphne Mary Pearson, Women's Auxiliary Air Force

On 31 May 1940, an hour after midnight, an aircraft crashed near the Women's Auxiliary Air Force quarters at Detling in Kent, the pilot being seriously injured, another officer killed outright and two airmen slightly injured. Upon hearing the crash Corporal Pearson rushed out and, although she knew there were bombs on board, she stood on the wreckage, roused the pilot who was stunned, released his parachute harness and helped him to get clear. When she got him about 30 yards from the wreckage, a 120 lb bomb went off and Corporal Pearson threw herself on top of the pilot to protect him from the blast and splinters. She remained with him until a stretcher party arrived and then returned to the burning aircraft to look for the fourth member of the crew. She found him – the wireless operator – dead in the bomber. Her prompt and courageous action undoubtedly helped to save the pilot's life.

July 1941 saw the arrival of Wing Commander C.H. Turner, who was the new man in charge of No.500 Squadron. They added bombing missions, particularly on enemy held harbours to their schedule and were joined by No.53 Squadron, as summer arrived. Things really started to heat up on 13 August when Detling experienced its first air raid when it was attacked by Junkers and Stuka dive bombers. By the time the raid was over, many of the station's buildings had been damaged, more than twenty aircraft were destroyed on the ground and the runway was put out of action. A total of ninety-three service personnel were injured and sixty-seven were killed, with many of the bodies being reduced to unidentifiable remains, such was the ferocity of the attack. The casualties were initially taken to Preston Hall Hospital, in Aylesford, where some were treated whilst others were sent to other nearby hospitals.

The Commonwealth War Graves Commission website records that a total of eighty-seven RAF/Luftwaffe personnel were either killed or died throughout the United Kingdom on 13 August 1940. This includes fourteen German airmen, and fourteen RAF personnel who have no known grave and whose names are commemorated on the Runnymede Memorial in Surrey. It also includes nineteen British airmen who were buried in Maidstone Cemetery.

The same website also records that thirty-four soldiers serving with different regiments of the Army, seven of whom are buried in the Maidstone Cemetery. This accounts for twenty-six of the sixty-seven who were killed at Detling airfield on 13 August 1940.

Included amongst the dead was the man in command at Detling, Group Captain Edward Davis, although on the Commonwealth War Graves Commission website he is shown as being commemorated on the Runnymede Memorial, indicating that his body was never recovered and that he has no known grave. An entry on the *forum.12oclockhigh.net* and dated 4 August 2008, states that *The Times* dated 19 August 1940 announced that his burial service took place at St Simon's Church, Milner Street, Chelsea at 2 pm 20 August 1940.

Below are just some of those who were killed on that fateful August day:

Corporal (563962) William Frank **Bateman** of No.53 Squadron, Royal Air Force.

Sapper (1989620) Leslie George **Bishop** (30) of the 703rd General Construction Company, Royal Engineers.

Aircraftman 2nd Class (1168029) Albert Frederick **Brooker** Royal Air Force.

Aircraftman 1st Class (573086) Leonard Edward **Brookes** Royal Air Force.

Leading Aircraftman (526331) William **Collerton** Royal Air Force.

Leading Aircraftman (567998) Arthur Frank **Dancaster** (20) of No.53 Squadron, Royal Air Force.

Group Captain Edward Peverell Meggs **Davis**, AFC, Royal Air Force.

Sapper (2113035) Reginald Walter Sidney **Golds** (20) of the 703rd General Construction Company, Royal Engineers. He is buried in the New Churchyard at St Mary's Church, Washington, Sussex.

Gunner (1550631) Reginald Horace George **Heath** of 265th Battery, 67th (2nd/15th Battalion, The East Surrey Regiment) Anti-Tank Regiment, Royal Artillery.

Sapper (1989608) Winston **Holton** (23) of the 703rd General Construction Company, Royal Engineers. He is buried in the churchyard at St Nicholas Church, in Little Horwood, Buckinghamshire.

Sergeant (903368) Harvey Cecil **Rowan** of No.500 Squadron, Royal Air Force Volunteer Reserve. He was buried in Wimbledon Gap Cemetery in Surrey.

Gunner (1550619) Francis **Joseph** (22) of the 265th Battery, 67th (2nd/5th Battalion, The East Surrey Regiment) Anti-Tank Regiment, Royal Artillery.

Gunner (1461706) Charles **Kemble** (21) of 268th Battery, 67th (2nd/5th Battalion, The East Surrey Regiment) Anti-Tank Regiment, Royal Artillery.

Gunner (1550635) Ernest Victor **Kennewell** (23) of 268th Battery, 67th (2nd/5th Battalion, The East Surrey Regiment) Anti-Tank Regiment, Royal Artillery.

Sapper (1989454) Henry Arthur **Knowles** (25) of the 703rd General Construction Company, Royal Engineers.

Squadron Leader (33119) James Henry **Lowe** Royal Air Force.

Sergeant (812073) Frederick **Messent** (27) of No.500 Squadron, Royal Air Force (Auxiliary Air Force), a native of Kent, from Maidstone.

Aircraftman 2nd Class (812304) William **Neale** (26) of No.500 Squadron, Royal Air Force (Auxiliary Air Force). He was a native of Kent, born in Maidstone.

Squadron Leader (34109) Dennis Clare **Oliver** of No.53 Squadron, Royal Air Force.

Lance Bombardier (6142986) James William **Pendergrest** (25) of 268th Battery, 67th (2nd/5th Battalion, The East Surrey Regiment) Anti-Tank Regiment, Royal Artillery. James Pendergrest is buried in St Mary's Churchyard, Merton in Surrey.

Corporal (510925) John Idris **Price** (29) years of age, a married man who served with No.53 Squadron, Royal Air Force.

Sergeant (343318) William Harry Lindsey **Richards** Royal Air Force, a married man.

Aircraftman 1st Class (812240) Leslie Austen **Watchous** (24) of No.500 Squadron, Royal Air Force (Auxiliary Air Force). He was a Kent man who hailed from Paddock Wood.

Driver (1989695) William Frank **Wear** (27) of the 703rd General Construction Company, Royal Engineers. He is buried in the Sutton-in-Ashfield Cemetery, Nottinghamshire.

Gunner Clement Allen **Wood** of the 268th Battery, 67th (2nd/5th Battalion, The East Surrey Regiment) Anti-Tank Regiment, Royal Artillery.

Two members of the WAAF who were stationed at Detling were awarded the Military Cross for their actions during and immediately after the raid. One of these was Sergeant Youle, who was on duty in the telephone exchange when it took a direct hit from one of the German bombs. Despite the death and destruction this caused, she remained at her post and continued her work, with a professional calmness which ensured that communications with the outside world were maintained at a time when they were most needed.

The other was Corporal Josie Robins, who received her award for courage whilst in a position of extreme danger. The operations shelter that she was working in was caught in the blast of an exploding bomb that, although not a direct hit, landed sufficiently close enough to cause death and injuries to those she was directly working with. Both women were presented with their awards on 20 December 1940.

Detling was attacked twice more before the end of the month. The first came on Friday 30 August, when due to a major electricity failure, many of the coastal radar stations throughout Kent were inoperative, making the county's defensive system from aerial attacks reliant on the dedicated individuals of the Observer Corps. Thankfully they were able to provide early warning of a large enemy force of aircraft heading straight towards Detling, allowing for the sirens to be sounded, so that evasive action could be taken by those on the ground. The runway was demolished and the airfield was closed down for some fifteen hours once the attack was over and the German aircraft had made good their escape.

On Saturday, 31 August 1940 more than a hundred enemy bombers flew in over the Kent coastline, thankfully for those personnel at the Detling base they were not the main target for the German attack, although they didn't get off completely scot free. Having finished their attack, some of the Luftwaffe pilots strafed the airfield with machine-gun fire, which resulted in some minor damage but thankfully no one was killed as a result of the attack.

The next day the base was subjected to two attacks, Detling having seemingly become the favourite location for German pilots. The raids once again resulted in the base becoming non-operational whilst efforts were made to repair the damage and make the runway useable again as quickly as possible. This was the last direct attack on Detling airfield during the course of the war.

Thursday, 5 September 1940 saw possibly one of the most unusual incidents of the Second World War, when a Messerschmitt Me 109 fighter aircraft, flown by Luftwaffe pilot Oberleutnant Carl-Heinze Metz, landed at Detling. The aircraft approached the base, lowered its wheels and then circled once before landing. Metz pulled back the cockpit's canopy, stood up and held his hands in the air, indicating his surrender. He had become detached from his colleagues and realised that, desperately low on fuel, he was extremely unlikely to make it home, which would mean having to crash land in the middle of the English Channel. His other option was to locate a nearby airfield on the English side of the Channel and land his aircraft, whilst running the risk of being fired at by anti-aircraft batteries. If he landed safely, he knew that he would be taken prisoner and spend the rest of the war incarcerated in a British PoW camp. Having given the matter due consideration, Metz took the latter of the two options. His aircraft was flown to Farnborough for evaluation and to see if there was anything that would provide the RAF with either valuable information concerning any deficiencies that it might possess, or advantages that might be useful the makers of British aircraft.

On the website *www.aircrewremembered.com* there is a Hauptmann Karl-Heinz Metz. The entry for him states that on 5 September 1940, he collided with a Focke-Wulf-190 D-13 (Gotz) aircraft and was then fired upon by Flying Officer Johnson of No.46 Squadron RAF, before he managed to land at Detling airfield.

Metz purportedly shot down three British aircraft in his short wartime career: a Blenheim at Le Havre on 10 August 1940, a Spitfire at Portland on 11 August 1940 and a Hurricane, also at Portland on 25 August 1940.

After airfield security was handed over in its entirety to the RAF Regiment, Detling airfield saw the formation in March 1942 of No.2368 Squadron of the RAF Regiment. Just four weeks later, the squadron had the honour of carrying out guard duty at Buckingham Palace, the first squadron of the RAF Regiment ever to do so.

Detling played its part in the D-Day landings on the beaches of Normandy. By now the resident units at the station were Nos. 80, 229 and 274 squadrons. With the expectation that the landings were going to be successful and that the Allied troops would quickly begin to make their way inland, their job was to clear the way ahead. To achieve this, they had been tasked with attacking trains, lorries and any other form of vehicle that was found moving around in German-held territory. What a sight it must have been for them as they flew across the English Channel en route to carry out their mission. The English Channel below would have been awash with all kinds of vessels making their way slowly, to the beaches of Normandy, to begin the liberation of Europe from Nazi occupation.

As June 1944 came to an end the new threat to the British mainland was the V1 and V2 rockets that had begun raining on down on Kent, Essex and London. Aircraft from Detling did their bit to prevent the final death throws of Nazism from having any real impact in stemming the tide of Allied power that was gradually forcing enemy forces all the way back to Germany and certain defeat. Squadrons of RAF aircraft from airfields all across Kent, including Detling, along with a safety net of barrage balloons, strategically placed around London, and hundreds of anti-aircraft batteries deployed across Kent, collectively provided an impressive deterrent to Adolf Hitler's last real throw of the dice.

Detling's last major involvement in the Second World War was when her squadrons escorted the thousands of British airborne troops across the English Channel to Arnhem in Holland, as part of Operation Market Garden. For nine days from 17 September 1944, they escorted some 500 gliders and nearly 4,000 aircraft packed with soldiers who were taking part in the operation.

Eastchurch

Eastchurch, on the Isle of Sheppey, earned a place in aviation history as the first place to see a flight by British pilot John Moore-Brabazon in 1909. It was used as an airfield by members of the Royal Aero Club.

It was a much smaller airfield than some of its nearby and more illustrious neighbours and at the outbreak of war its basic function was one of aircraft maintenance. But by December 1939, it had taken on a whole new purpose. It had become a training centre for Polish pilots, but for some unknown reason, the German authorities believed that the base was part of Fighter Command which it wasn't. This would explain why the Luftwaffe attacked it throughout the first couple of months of the war. This belief by the Luftwaffe might have come about because in the early weeks of August 1940, Eastchurch was home to Nos. 12, 19, 142 and 266 squadrons, albeit only for a couple of days for one of the units.

Because of its geographical position on the east coast of Kent, it seems a strange choice of location for a training base for pilots as it was an obvious target for raiding

Eastchurch Camp.

Polish Pilots WW2.

German aircraft. With this in mind, how could it make any sense at all to fill an air base with a large number of trainee pilots and the extra aircraft needed for their training. By March 1940 there were 1,300 Polish airmen billeted at Eastchurch.

The first time that Eastchurch was attacked was just after 6.30 am on 13 August 1940 and it came as a surprise. The Commanding Officer of RAF Eastchurch, Group Captain Frank Hobbs, had just been informed in a phone call from Coastal Command that his base was in imminent danger from attack, when the first of the bombs were dropped. Many of the British aircraft were still on the ground, with their pilots not having enough time to get airborne and therefore sitting ducks for the attacking German planes as they jettisoned their cargo of high explosive bombs. By the time the raid was over, wrecked aircraft were on fire along with damaged buildings. Eleven aircraft had been lost included an entire wing from No.266 Squadron, and the overall casualties were twelve killed and twenty-six wounded. Nearly all of the wounded personnel from the base were initially taken to the nearby Sheppey Military Hospital.

One of those killed was Aircraftman 2nd Class (986486) James Burrows **Brawley** (20) from Glasgow in Scotland. He was in the Royal Air Force Volunteer Reserve and is buried in the Riddrie Park Cemetery in Glasgow.

The airfield was out of action for just ten hours before it was up and running again, such was the hard work put in by so many willing hands. The raids continued throughout August, but lessons had been learned from that first attack, with all non essential staff having been moved off the base to a nearby requisitioned house. Despite this, the Luftwaffe obviously still believed that Eastchurch was being used as a fighter base and continued their attacks.

Mid afternoon on 2 September 1940 a large force of incoming German aircraft were picked up on radar and just before 4 pm the first of the bombs landed. Many of the base's buildings were damaged including a direct hit on its ammunition bunker. By the time that the raid was over four members of the RAF had been killed with a further twelve wounded.

As the war continued and the Luftwaffe finally appear to have realised that Eastchurch was not the significant air base they had once believed it to be, nothing further of any real importance occurred there, and its use by the RAF was reduced to maintenance and training.

Gravesend

There had been an airfield in Gravesend from well before the Second World War, where aircraft were also designed and manufactured for the more affluent members of society. With a war in Europe becoming more and more likely, the Air Ministry rented the site from its owners with a view to turning it into a training establishment for newly enlisted RAF pilots as well as those from the Fleet Air Arm. On 25 September 1937 No.20 Elementary and Reserve Flying Training School came into being.

With the outbreak of war, everything changed. The Air Ministry requisitioned the site, the training school closed and Gravesend became part of No.11 Group, Fighter Command. For the first few months of the war nothing of any real significance took place, mainly because much needed construction work on the site was still underway. The first aircraft to arrive at Gravesend were the Hurricanes of No.32 Squadron in the early days of January 1940, but just two months later they had already moved on.

May 1940 saw the arrival of both No.56 (Punjab) Squadron and No.610 (County of Chester) Squadron, which was an auxiliary unit. With the evacuation from Dunkirk underway by the end of the month, both squadrons found themselves in action.

RAF Gravesend.

Squadrons did not tend to stay in one place for long periods of time and Gravesend was no different. Throughout the course of the war the base was home to thirty-three different squadrons, some returning on more than one occasion. They included men from the United Kingdom, America, India, New Zealand, Australia, Belgium, Poland, Trinidad, America, Rhodesia, Czechoslovakia and Mauritius. Here they are listed in the order in which they were stationed at Gravesend.

No.32 Squadron
No.56 (Punjab) Squadron
No.604 (County of Middlesex) Auxiliary Squadron
No.72 (Basutoland) Squadron
No.501 (County of Gloucester) Auxiliary Squadron
No.610 (County of Chester) Auxiliary Squadron
No.66 Squadron
No.421 Squadron
No.141 Squadron
No.85 Squadron
No.264 (Madras Residency) Squadron
No.74 (Trinidad) Squadron
No.609 (West Riding) Squadron
No.92 (East India) Squadron.
No.401 Squadron. (Canadians)
No. 121 (Baroda) Squadron
No.350 Squadron (Belgians)
No.71 Squadron
No.131 Squadron
No.277 Squadron
No.181 Squadron
No.245 (Northern Rhodesia) Squadron
No.174 (Mauritius) Squadron
No.244 (China British) Squadron
No.19 Squadron
No.131 (City of Bombay) Squadron
No.301 (Torun) Squadron
No.257 (Burma) Squadron
No.64 Squadron
No.266 (Rhodesia) Squadron
No.65 (East India) Squadron
No.122 (Bombay) Squadron
No.464 (Australian) Squadron
No.21 Squadron
No.487 (New Zealand) Squadron

Although many men were killed whilst serving with these squadrons at Gravesend during the Second World War, I have only recorded those who died whilst stationed at Gravesend and who served with either No.66 or No.501 Squadrons during the time of the Battle of Britain.

The first pilot to be lost was Duncan Alexander **Hewitt** (20) who served with No.501 Squadron, Royal Air Force Volunteer Force. He was killed in action on 12 July 1940, has no known grave, but is commemorated on the Runnymede Memorial in Surrey. He was a native of Canada.

The next loss came on 20 July 1940 with the death of Edmund John Hilary **Sylvester** who was a Pilot Officer (90556) with No.501 Squadron, and a member of the Royal Air Force (Auxiliary Air Force). He was a holder of the Distinguished Flying Cross, but sadly has no known grave. His name is commemorated on the Runnymede Memorial, which is situated in Surrey.

Philip Anthony Neville **Cox** (25) was a Flying Officer (33184) in the Royal Air Force, serving with No.501 Squadron, when he was killed in action on 27 July 1940. His name is commemorated on the Runnymede Memorial.

Two pilots from No. 501 Squadron were killed on 18 August 1940. Pilot Officer 90895 John Wellburn **Bland** (30) years of age of No.501 Squadron, Royal Air Force, was killed in action on 18 August 1940, whilst flying Hurricane P3208. He is buried in Gravesend Cemetery.

Flight Lieutenant 28119 George Edward Bowes **Stoney** (29), a married man from Liverpool, who served with No.501 Squadron, Royal Air Force, was killed in action on 18 August 1940, whilst flying Hurricane P2549. He is buried in St Helen's Churchyard in Sefton.

A further seven airmen from No.501 Squadron were killed throughout September.

Flying Officer (39762) Arthur Thomas **Rose-Price** (21) was killed in action on 2 September 1940. He has no known grave, but his name is commemorated on the Runnymede Memorial in Surrey. At the time of Arthur's death, his parents were living in Chile, South America.

Pilot Sergeant (742740) Geoffrey Wilberforce **Pearson** was one of three men from No.501 Squadron to be killed in action on 6 September 1940. He was 21 years of age from Oxfordshire and serving with the Royal Air Force Volunteer Reserve. He is buried in St Stephen's Churchyard at Lympne, Kent.

The other two men were:

Pilot Officer (85645) Hugh Charles **Adams** (22) was serving with the Royal Air Force Volunteer Reserve, when he was killed in action on 6 September 1940. He is buried in St Peter's Churchyard at Tandridge, Surrey.

Pilot Sergeant (745437) Oliver Vincent **Houghton** (19) from Coventry was serving with the Royal Air Force Volunteer Reserve, when he was killed in action on 6 September 1940. He is buried in the All Saints Churchyard Extension, at Allesley, Warwickshire.

Sergeant (742787) Edward James **Egan** (19) was serving with the Royal Air Force Volunteer Reserve, when he was killed in action on 17 September 1940. He is buried in the Brookwood Military Cemetery in Surrey. His family were based at Dulwich in London.

Pilot Officer (83988) Edward Maurice **Gunter** (20) was serving with the Royal Air Force Volunteer Reserve, when he was killed in action on 27 September 1940. He is buried in the Churchyard of St Mary's Church at Aldeby, Norfolk.

Pilot Officer (42707) Frederick Cecil **Harrold** (23) was serving with the Royal Air Force, when he was killed in action on 28 September 1940. He is buried in the Churchyard of St Andrew's Church, at Cherry Hinton, Cambridgeshire.

Flying Officer (72514) Nathaniel John Merriman **Barry** (22) of No.501 Squadron, Royal Air Force Volunteer Reserve, was killed in action on 7 October 1940. He was buried in the Churchyard of St Andrew's Church, at Finghall in Yorkshire. He was South African by birth.

Sergeant Pilot (745100) Stanley Allen **Fenemore** (20) was serving with No.501 Squadron, as a member of the Royal Air Force Volunteer Reserve, when he died on 15 October 1940. He is buried in the Allerton Cemetery in Liverpool. His family were from Whitewell in County Antrim, Northern Island.

Czechoslovakian Pilot Officer (81945) Vilem **Goth** (25) was serving with the Royal Air Force Volunteer Reserve when he was killed in action on 27 October 1940. He is buried in the Sittingbourne Cemetery, Kent.

There were nine men from No.66 Squadron who were also killed during the fighting of the Battle of Britain. The first six in the list below were all members of the Royal Air Force, whilst the remaining three were members of the Royal Air Force Volunteer Reserve.

Pilot Officer (41491) John Alnod Peter **Studd** (22) was killed in action on 19 August 1940. He is buried in the Holy Trinity Churchyard at Touchen End in Berkshire

Pilot Sergeant (41298) Peter James Christopher **King** (19) years of age was killed in action on 5 September 1940. He is buried in the St Botolph's Churchyard, Farnborough in Warwickshire.

Pilot Sergeant (5801530) Arthur Dumbell **Smith**, was killed in action on 6 September 1940, and is buried in the St Luke's Churchyard at Whyteleafe in Surrey.

Flight Lieutenant (37799) Kenneth McLeod **Gillies** (27) was killed in action on 4 October 1940, and is buried in the Thornton Garden of Rest, in Lancashire.

Sergeant (740913) Rufus Arthur **Ward** was killed in action on 8 October 1940 and is buried in the Mitcham Road Cemetery in Croydon.

Pilot Officer (81366) George Henry **Corbett** (21) was killed in action on 8 October 1940. He is buried in St Mary's Churchyard at Upchurch, Kent. He was a native of Canada.

Sergeant Pilot (561445) Charles Albert Henry **Ayling**, was killed in action on 11 October 1940 and is buried in the Monkton St Nichola Cemetery in Pembrokeshire. His brother, Albert Edgar Ayling, was also killed during the war.

Pilot Officer (43043) Hugh William **Riley** (22) was killed in action on 17 October 1940. He is buried in Gravesend Cemetery.

Pilot Officer (78976) John Romney **Mather** (25) was killed in action on 27 October 1940. He is buried in St Margaret's Churchyard, in Ifield, Crawley.

Hawkinge

There had been an airfield at Hawkinge going back to the time of the First World War, and after the fighting was over it remained an airfield as part of the newly formed Royal Air Force. With the beginning of the Second World War No.2 Squadron was the station's resident squadron, but it was quickly despatched to France, and Hawkinge became the newly formed No.3 Recruit Training Pool.

In early 1940 Hawkinge ceased being a training centre and became part of Fighter Command No.11 Group and became a Forward Operating Base, which meant that besides any resident squadrons that were stationed there, other squadrons flew in and out of it most days; how many, depended on the potential threat from the Luftwaffe. If large numbers of German aircraft had been picked up on radar, making their away across the English Channel, heading for Kent, then squadrons that were stationed at other bases around the county would fly to Hawkinge and hold there for deployment. As it was the nearest Kent airfield to the coast, it played an extremely important role in the defence of the nation. Strategically, it was of great importance and the Germans knew this, which is possibly why they attacked the base so many times, especially during the early months of the war. To deal with the potential threat of German paratroopers being deployed to take control of the airfield, soldiers from the 6th Battalion, The Buffs (Royal East Kent) Regiment were stationed at Hawkinge on airfield defence duties.

On 1 March 1940 the No.1 Pilotless Aircraft Unit moved into Hawkinge. In essence the unit brought with them radio-controlled model aircraft, which were used mainly for

RAF Hawkinge/Aircraft.

live target gunnery practice for anti-aircraft units. These were radio-controlled pilotless models made out of wood and plywood, and were known as 'Queen Bees'. In total nearly 400 of these were built for use by the RAF. The unit left Hawkinge on 22 June 1940.

In late May and early June 1940, Hawkinge played an important role in Operation Dynamo, the evacuation of Dunkirk. It was used by returning aircraft and crews to refuel and replenish, before once again flying back across the Channel to provide defensive cover for the escaping troops and vessels that were used to get them off the Dunkirk beaches and back to the safety of the British mainland.

As Operation Overlord got underway on 6 June 1944, Hawkinge had aircraft from the Fleet Air Arm as well as Nos. 854 and 855 squadrons stationed there. They patrolled the English Channel, their aim being to keep enemy vessels from leaving their bases and potentially interfering with the invading Allied vessels making their way across to the beaches of Normandy.

Lympne

As the military rumblings and uncertainty across Europe increased, Lympne became a military airfield on 3 November 1936 with the resident units being Nos. 21 and 34 squadrons, who were flying Hawker Hind bombers. They became part of No.1 Bomber Group. There were no nice warm, clean barrack blocks or individual private rooms for the pilots and other aircrew at Lympne, just the simplest of tented accommodation.

Pilots relaxing at Lympne.

The war was still over a year away but the authorities were preparing for its inevitibility. With this in mind, on 11 July 1938 the two squadrons moved to their new and larger home at Upper Heyford. Lympne was left as a maintenance and care base, but in the early months of 1939, it was handed over to the Admiralty, commissioned as HMS *Buzzard* and used by naval aircraft, and as a school for Royal Air Force Mechanics; but after about a year the naval aircraft left.

By May 1940 there were two resident units based at Lympne, Nos.16 and 26 squadrons, at a time where German forces were running amok across Europe, having pushed through the Low Countries of Belgium and Holland, and were in the process of pushing British, French and Belgium troops into a bottleneck at Dunkirk. The two squadrons were engaged mainly in tactical reconnaissance as part of the subsequent Dunkirk evacuations.

On 8 June 1940 the two squadrons left Lympne as it was redesignated as a forward operating base for the Biggin Hill sector, as part of No.11 Group, Fighter Command.

The Luftwaffe attacked most, if not all, of the airfields across Kent, and Lympne was no exception. Throughout July and August 1940, it did so on five occasions, two of which were on the same day, 3 July 1940. The first attack took place in the morning, whilst some personnel were still having their breakfast. The first of the bombs was dropped at just after 9 am as the German aircraft came in low over the airfield. By the time the raid was over, a further 140 bombs had followed. The damage to the airfield's buildings and landing strip was as would be expected for such a large deposit of high explosive ordnance landing on it from a great height, but thankfully there were no recorded deaths.

With efforts at making the base operative again, still underway, the Luftwaffe returned for a second attempt at putting Lympne out of action once and for all. This time nearly 250 bombs were dropped, causing even more severe damage. But despite having expended this level of devastation on one location the Luftwaffe didn't let up on their attacks of Lympne, following up with further attacks on 13, 15 and 18 August 1940.

During the latter months of 1941 into the early part of 1942, much reconstruction work was carried out at Lympne, but a Flight from No.91 (Nigerian) Squadron still managed to operate out of the base, and as time went on more followed, although they were not all in place at the same time. As one squadron left and moved elsewhere, another would arrive to replace it.

No.133 (Eagle) Squadron. Arrived 30 June 1942.

No.401 (RAM) Squadron. Arrived 14 August 1942.

No.65 (East India) Squadron. Arrived 2 October 1942.

No.91 (Nigerian) Squadron. Arrived on 23 November 1942 and joined up with their colleagues who were already at Lympne.

No.1 Squadron. Arrived 15 March 1943.

No.245 (Northern Rhodesia) Squadron. Arrived on 30 March 1943.

No. 609 (West Riding) Squadron, who were a Royal Auxiliary Air Force unit. Arrived 18 August 1943.

No.137 Squadron. Arrived 14 December 1943.

No.186 Squadron. Arrived 1 March 1944.

As the invasion of Europe drew closer, squadrons from Lympne became busier, although because of the extreme secrecy in place, the pilots would not have known the real reasons behind their missions or why they had suddenly been tasked with carrying out raids into parts of German-occupied France.

Still the squadrons kept coming:

No.73 Squadron. Arrived 15 – 17 May 1943.
No.74 Squadron. Arrived 15 – 17 May 1943.
No.127 Squadron. Arrived 15 – 17 May 1943.
No.310 Squadron. Arrived 3 July 1944.
No.312 Squadron. Arrived 3 July 1944.
No.313 Squadron. Arrived 3 July 1944.

The last three squadrons in the list above were made up nearly exclusively by pilots from Czechoslovakia.

No.130 (Punjab) Squadron. Arrived August 1944.
No.610 (County of Chester) Squadron. Arrived August 1944.
No.350 (Belgian) Squadron. Arrived September 1944.

With the invasion of Europe a success and the Allies pushing German forces back to the fatherland, certain air bases were no longer needed as the remaining Luftwaffe units had much more important things to think about, than attacking relatively small airfields on the south coast of England which by now, was way behind the front lines of the leading Allied forces.

As the war was coming to a close, two Australian units – Nos. 451 and 453 squadrons – arrived at Lympne in April 1945, but only stayed for about a month. The base saw out the war as an aircraft maintenance and care facility, after which time it then reverted to civilian use.

During the war years many different squadrons had flown from Lympne to carry out numerous missions, for all kinds of different reasons, in all different types of aircraft. A number of them never returned, nor the men who flew in them. Some of them, to this day, still have no known grave, the price that they paid in the service of their country.

Manston

During the First World War, Manston, which is situated on the top of the chalk cliffs on the Isle of Thanet, saw its first use as a military airfield in April 1916, when it opened as a Royal Naval Air Station, although prior to this it had already been used as a site for emergency landings.

Between the wars, and especially throughout the 1930s, Manston continued to have RAF squadrons based there, for training and reconnaissance purposes, but immediately before the start of the Second World War, Manston had been a School

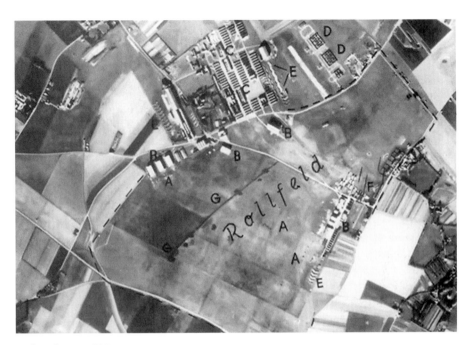

Luftwaffe pic of Manston.

of Air Navigation. As soon as hostilities began this was closed down and moved out. In its place came the Hawker Hurricanes flown by No.3 Squadron that were part of Fighter Command's No.11 Group, although they left on 13 November 1939.

Unfortunately for RAF Manston, as it was in such an open location, it was always going to be a prime candidate for attacks by the Luftwaffe, as its lofty position made it stick out like a beacon in the dark. It wasn't just air raids that the base had to consider, it was the real possibility that the Germans might deploy airborne troops against them. Accordingly, trenches were dug, machine-gun positions were in place and ground troops had been deployed to deal with any such eventuality.

The unit that arrived at Manston to replace No.3 Squadron was No.79 (Madras) Squadron. After them came No.600 Squadron, an auxiliary unit, which arrived on 27 December 1939. The winter that year was one of the worst on record, with the big freeze lasting all the way through until February 1940.

Manston was involved in Operation Dynamo, the evacuation of the British Expeditionary Force from the beaches of Dunkirk. During this time, No.264 Squadron was deployed to Manston to assist with the aerial needs of the operation.

On 12 May 1940 Manston was the subject of an attack by the Luftwaffe on the day that No.54 Squadron had arrived at the base. Although most managed to get off the ground before the German attack began, not all of the aircraft did. The damage was extensive, with buildings and aircraft destroyed and on fire by the time the Luftwaffe pilots had left, along with the landing strip having been extensively cratered by bomb blasts, although miraculously it didn't stop aircraft from either landing or taking off.

Throughout August 1940 it was Manston's turn to face the wrath of the Luftwaffe, with attacks on the base taking place on the 12th, 20th, 22th, and 24th of the month, but it was the last of these that was by far the worst. Not only had the airfield been badly damaged, No.264 Squadron, which had been flying out of the base on the day had lost numerous aircraft and seven people had been killed. Nine German pilots also lost their lives. Because of the loss of accommodation blocks in the raid, the contingent of Women's Auxiliary Air Force personnel had to be billeted at the nearby Ursuline Convent at Westgate-on-Sea.

In the aftermath of the devastation caused as a result of the raid on 24 August, Winston Churchill paid a visit to RAF Manston to see at first hand just how much damage had been caused. He was reportedly quite shocked at what he had seen, with a number of unexploded German bombs clearly visible. The damage was so extensive that it took nearly thirty-six hours before the station was up and running again, but even so more than a year later very little in the way of repairs had been carried out at Manston, something which was noted by Wing Commander R.P. Gleave when he took command of the base in late 1941. The main reason he had been put in charge was to bring it up to its previous standard as a fully operational airfield.

RAF Manston was in part involved in what must undoubtedly go down as one of the bravest acts of the war, which makes the story surrounding it one that is worth telling in the pages of this book. The story relates to the German Operation Cerberus, or what the British referred to as the 'Channel Dash'. It was an operation devised by the Germans to try and get their battlecruisers *Scharnhorst* and *Gneisenau* and the heavy cruiser *Prinz Eugen,* out of the harbour at Brest in France to make their way back to their home base at Wilhelmshaven in Germany. From a British perspective, if the German ships did manage to break out from Brest and make their way into the English Channel, then Operation Fuller was to be activated. This involved a fleet of six motor torpedo boats, six destroyers, and a number of torpedo-carrying Fairey Swordfish aircraft as well as Beaufort torpedo bombers, attacking the German Fleet. For the British operation to work, early warning of any movement by the German ships, was imperative.

The planning of an operation and its subsequent implementation can often be miles apart, which was definitely the case with Operation Fuller. The German vessels set sail from Brest Harbour on the evening of 11 February 1942, not by chance, but by a well thought out and executed plan. The escaping vessels were to be supported by a large number of fighter aircraft as well as a number of ships, which included both destroyers and E-boats. It would be twelve hours before the British authorities would believe that the German fleet was actually on the move, despite some of their own pilots telling them that this was the case. If the truth be known, what the Germans were doing was so audacious that the British authorities never really believed that they would attempt it.

This is where RAF Manston became involved. Although not based there, No.825 Squadron of the Fleet Air Arm, had six of its Swordfish aircraft, each armed with a torpedo, waiting at Manston for the order to play their part in a co-ordinated attack on the escaping German fleet. The man in charge of them was Lieutenant Commander Eugene

Esmonde, who had, earlier in the war been awarded the Distinguished Service Order, for his part in an attack on the German battleship *Bismarck* on the evening of 24 May 1941.

The British torpedo boats had already tried and failed in their efforts to stop the escaping German battleships. It was now the turn of Esmonde and his men in their Swordfish aircraft to try to intercept and destroy them. Esmonde knew that the aircraft that he and his men would be flying would be absolutely no match for their German counterparts, the formidable, Messerschmitt Bf 109, which was a much faster, sturdier, and more heavily armed aircraft. He also knew that what he and his men were going to do was as near suicidal as it was possible to be. But despite knowing this, all of his men climbed on board their aircraft and, in ever worsening weather, took off. It was a latter day version of the Charge of the Light Brigade – brave men venturing into the valley of death, knowing that their chances of surviving the day were slim. As they smiled at each other and shook hands, very few words would have been spoken, there was no need, as most of them had a strong inkling that it would be for the very last time.

The six Fleet Air Arm Fairey Swordfish aircraft and their crews on that fateful day were as follows:

W5907 – Kingsmill, Samples, Bunce
W5978 – Bligh, Beynon, Granville-Smith
W5983 – Rose, Lee, Johnson
W5984 – Esmonde, Williams, Clinton
W5985 – Wood, Fuller-Wright, Wheeler
V4523 – Thompson, Parkinson, Tapping

Esmonde had been promised a fighter escort to assist him and his men to be able to deliver their deadly payload of munitions to the escaping German vessels. The ten Spitfires he eventually left with were only a small fraction of what he had been promised, the others had been delayed by the snow flurries that Mother Nature had determined would be part of the day's weather.

It was not long before Esmonde and his men found what they were looking for, but in less time than it had taken them to get there, it was all over. Every one of the six Swordfish aircraft had been destroyed, with not one of them making it back to RAF Manston. The losses were dreadful with thirteen of the eighteen crew killed, including Esmonde. A ferocious barrage of fire power from the ships below and the Messerschmitts above, ensured that the fight did not last long.

The bravery and supreme sacrifice made by Esmonde and his men was recognised by both sides, including three German officers who were serving on board the *Scharnhorst* at the time of the attack.

For his actions that day, Esmonde was awarded the Victoria Cross. The announcement of the award appeared in the *London Gazette* on 3 March 1942. It read as follows:

The King has been graciously pleased to approve the grant of the VICTORIA CROSS, for valour and resolution in action against the Enemy, to: The late Lieutenant-Commander (A) Eugene Esmonde, DSO, Royal Navy.

On the morning of Thursday 12 February 1942, Lieutenant-Commander Esmonde, in command of a Squadron of the Fleet Air Arm, was told that the German Battle Cruisers SCHARNHORST and GNEISENAU and the Cruiser PRINZ EUGEN, strongly escorted by some thirty surface craft, were entering the Straits of Dover, and that his Squadron must attack before they reached the sand banks North-East of Calais.

Lieutenant-Commander Esmonde knew well that his enterprise was desperate. Soon after noon he and his squadron of six Swordfish set course for the enemy, and after ten minutes flight, were attacked by a strong force of enemy fighters. Touch was lost with his fighter escort, and in the action which followed, all his aircraft were damaged. He flew on, cool and resolute, serenely challenging hopeless odds, to encounter the deadly fire of the Battle-Cruisers and their Escort, which shattered the port wing of his aircraft. Undismayed, he led his Squadron on, straight through this inferno of fire, in steady flight towards their target. Almost at once he was shot down; but his Squadron went on to launch a gallant attack, in which at least one torpedo is believed to have struck the German Battle-Cruisers, and from which not one of the six aircraft returned.

His high courage and splendid resolution will live in the traditions of the Royal Navy, and remain for many generations a fine and stirring memory.

Eugene Esmonde and some of his colleagues.

Poignantly, the body of Eugene Esmonde was given up by the sea some weeks after the day of the attack, when it was washed up in the Thames Estuary close to the River Medway, still wearing his life jacket. He was buried on 30 April 1942, with full military honours, at Gillingham Cemetery.

Of the other men who were killed on the same operation, the first three in the list below were members of the Royal Naval Volunteer Reserve, the remaining seven served with the Royal Navy. None of them have any known graves, but all of them are remembered on the Lee-on-Solent Memorial, in Hampshire.

Sub-Lieutenant (A) David Robert **Beynon** MiD (27), a married man from Monmouthshire.

Acting Sub-Lieutenant (A) Peter **Bligh** was (20), a single man from Palmers Green, London.

Sub-Lieutenant (A) Eric Herbert **Fuller-Wright** MiD (22) a single man from Tunbridge Wells, Kent.

Leading Airman (FAA/FX 189404) Henry Thomas Albert **Wheeler** (30), a single man from Southend-on-Sea, Essex.

Sub-Lieutenant Cecil Ralph **Wood** MiD, a married man.

Sub-Lieutenant Robert Laurens **Parkinson** MiD (21), the son of Sir John and Lady Parkinson of Marylebone, London.

Petty Officer Airman (FAA/FX 82042) Ambrose Lawrence **Johnson** DSM (22) years of age, a single man from Yorkshire. His DSM was awarded for his part in the attack on the *Bismarck* on 24 May 1941.

Leading Airman (FAA/FX 76365) Ernest **Tapping** MID (26), a single man from Sydenham, Kent.

Lieutenant (A) John Chute **Thompson** MiD (27), a married man from Southampton.

Leading Airman (FX 79499) William **Granville-Smith** MiD (22), a single man from Poplar, London, serving in the Royal Navy. He is buried in the Woodlands Cemetery, Gillingham, Kent.

Petty Officer Airman (JX143258) William Johnson **Clinton** (22) of the Royal Navy. He is buried in the Churchyard Extension of St Martin's Church, in Ruislip.

Lieutenant (A) William Henry **Williams** was serving with the Royal Navy at the time of his death. He is buried in the Aylesham Cemetery.

Esmonde's great-uncle, Thomas Esmonde, had also been awarded one of the first Victoria Crosses, for his actions on 18 June 1855 at Sebastopol during the Crimean War. He was a captain in the 18th Regiment of Foot.

Five men, although all wounded during the operation, survived. They were Sub-Lieutenant Lee, Sub-Lieutenant Kingsmill, Sub-Lieutenant Samples, Petty Officer Donald Arthur Bunce, CGM, and Sub-Lieutenant Rose. I believe that all of the officers were awarded the DSO, which was the officer's equivalent of the CGM.

A few final facts about this group of men: Johnson, Esmonde, Thompson, Parkinson, Wheeler, Clinton, and Bunce also took part in the attack on the *Bismarck* on 24 May 1941. Parkinson and Thompson flew together during the attack on the

Bismarck as well as the one on *Scharnhorst, Gneisenau,* and *Prinz Eugen.* Bunce was the only man to take part in, and survive, both attacks.

Over the next few years squadrons arrived at and left Manston, many of whom had also been stationed at other Kent airfields as well as neighbouring areas such as Essex. Their duties were varied and understandably priorities changed as the war developed.

Between 17 and 25 September 1944 Manston was used as one of the departure points during Operation Market Garden, the mass use of airborne Allied troops parachuting into Holland, which up until that moment in time involved the largest airborne operation there had ever been.

Rochester

No. 23 Elementary and Reserve Flying Training School was formed at Rochester in April 1938, a facility for the training of Royal Air Force Volunteer Reserve pilots.

The then Rochester City Council bought the land that became Rochester Airport from the previous owner, by way of a compulsory purchase order, with the intention of building a municipal airport. Short Brothers had taken over the site as early as 1934, when the council let them lease the land for test flying their aircraft. It was where they also designed and manufactured their aircraft including the Short S29 Stirling, which was designed and manufactured at Rochester and went on to become the first four-engine bomber to go in to service with the RAF.

The first Stirling bomber aircraft came off the production line at Rochester on 14 May 1939. On returning to the base after its initial flight, one of the aircraft's brakes

Rochester Airfield.

seized, which in turn caused the undercarriage to collapse. Fortunately, nobody was injured as a result of the crash landing.

Due to the damage caused to Shorts factory and the runway at Rochester as a result of an air raid by the Luftwaffe on 15 August 1940, with 100lb bombs, production of the Stirling bomber was greatly affected. The attack was so severe, that it is estimated that production of the aircraft was put back by many months.

Although overall the Stirling bomber was seen in a positive light performance-wise by those who flew them, it was an aircraft which certainly had its shortcomings. The maximum height it could operate at was 20,000ft which brought with it a certain vulnerability from ground-based anti-aircraft batteries. It also required a crew complement of seven, meaning each aircraft lost was a drain on personnel levels. Between 1941 and 1945 a total of 582 Stirling bombers were lost in action, with a further 119 being lost by other means such as crash landings or mechanical failures. The last of the 2,383 Stirling aircraft built, came off of the production line at Rochester in the early part of 1945.

Developments in aircraft design saw the Stirling's demise as part of Bomber Command, last being used in a bombing capacity in September 1944. After this time it was given less confrontational operations, such as transport duties.

Many of the airfields scattered across the south of the country had some kind of infantry element attached to their defensive capability and Rochester was no different. Whereas most airfields were protected by Territorial Army units, and after 1 February 1942 by the RAF Regiment, Rochester airfield was protected by members of the 33rd Battalion of the Home Guard who were attached to the Short Brothers' factory that was situated there. Its commanding officer was Lieutenant Colonel J.M. Prower DSO. The men of the 33rd Battalion came from those who worked at the factory, who would usually have had to carry out two night patrols each week. Rochester as a town had its own Home Guard unit which was the 13th Battalion; its commanding officer was Captain H.S. Pickering.

West Malling

West Malling was originally used as a landing area during the First World War in the early days of flying. In 1930 the area became the Maidstone School of Aviation, before becoming Maidstone Airport in 1932, where numerous air shows and displays were put on, attracting large crowds, by such aviators as Amy Johnson.

With the war fast approaching it was one of the many local airfields that suddenly took the interest of the military authorities and became RAF West Malling in 1940. One of the first changes was the runway being upgraded from grass to concrete, so that bigger and more powerful aircraft could be more readily accommodated.

It became a forward operating base as part of Fighter Command and, in keeping with its new status, its ground defences were updated to include anti-aircraft guns and searchlight batteries. The station's initial squadrons arrived on 8 June 1940. First to arrive were No.26 (Army Co-operation) Battalion, their job being to photograph different locations of military interest in German-occupied Europe. The other unit sent to West Malling was No.51 Wing, which was made up of three or four squadrons of aircraft. Less than a month later on 12 July 1940, No.141 Squadron arrived in their Boulton Paul Defiant aircraft, which was a two-seater fighter. One of its 'unique' features was it did not have any forward firing guns, which was an unusual if not somewhat strange concept, leaving the aircraft extremely vulnerable. Although this was not too much of a problem when up against bombers, the type of aircraft it was designed to fight, when it came in contact with the Luftwaffe's more manoeuvrable Messerschmitt Bf 109 fighters, it was in big trouble, especially if the meeting of the two aircraft was during the daytime.

On 19 July 1940, a week after arriving at West Malling, No.141 Squadron was on patrol over the English Channel, when they came into contact with a large number of Messerschmitt Bf 109 fighters. It wasn't long before six of the nine Boulton Paul Defiants had been shot down, the remaining three aircraft only surviving due to the intervention of a number of Hurricanes from No.111 Squadron.

According to the Commonwealth War Graves Commission website, nine airmen from No.141 Squadron were killed that day. The first seven names on the list have no known graves, but are commemorated on the Runnymede Memorial. The remaining two men were buried in the cemeteries named against their entry.

Sergeant (903506) Robert **Crombie** (29) Royal Air Force Volunteer Reserve.

Sergeant (747968) Albert George **Curley** (33) Royal Air Force Volunteer Reserve.

Pilot officer (41705) Richard Alexander **Howley** Royal Air Force.

Pilot Officer (41850) John Richard **Kemp** (25) Royal Air Force.

Boulton Paul Defiant aircraft.

Hawkinge Cemetery.

Pilot Officer (41297) Rudal **Kitson** (26) Royal Air Force.
Pilot Officer (44597) Dudley Malins **Slatter** (26) Royal Air Force.
Sergeant (746875) John Francis **Wise** Royal Air Force Volunteer Reserve.
Pilot Officer (Air Gunner) (78543) Arthur Charles **Hamilton** (28) Royal Air Force. Buried in Hawkinge Cemetery, in Kent.
Flight Lieutenant (33306) Ian David Grahame **Donald** Royal Air Force. Buried in All Saints Churchyard at Tilford, Surrey.

Despite RAF West Malling having played no real part in the Battle of Britain, and the base being in a state of disrepair with building work being quite apparent, the Luftwaffe still saw fit to bomb the airfield numerous times. During August 1940 it sustained at least four attacks which resulted in lots of damage, and the death of a workman. The first was on 10 August when fourteen bombs were dropped causing damage to newly constructed buildings, and a group of seventy civilian workmen were badly injured, one of whom later died. Further attacks followed on 15th, 18th and 20th August, with different degrees of damage caused each time.

The worst attack happened on 10 September 1940, but this time just a single German Dornier aircraft was involved. The pilot flew in low over the base, dropped six anti-personnel bombs and quickly made good his escape. One of the bombs scored a direct hit on one of the camp's machine-gun positions, killing six members of the Queen's Royal Regiment (West Surrey), and wounded three more. All of the men were deployed on airfield defence duties and were hopefully a sufficient deterrent to prevent German paratroopers from attacking the airfield. Five were killed outright at the time, whilst the sixth died of his wounds the following day.

The first two men were buried in Maidstone Cemetery, the next two were buried in St Michael's Churchyard in Yorktown, Surrey, whilst the fifth was buried in St Mary's Roman Catholic Cemetery, Kensal Green.

Private (6089720) George Henry **Josland**, 2nd/7th Battalion.

Private (6088211) Edward Albert **Seymour** (19), 2nd/6th Battalion.

Company Sergeant Major (2690051) William George **Briercliffe** (38), a married man, 2nd/6th Battalion.

Lance Sergeant (6087030) James Leslie **Sergison** (25), 2nd/5th Battalion.

Private (6090598) Frederick **Collins**(19) 2nd/7th Battalion.

Private (6089905) John **Linstrom** 2nd/7th Battalion, died of his wounds on 11 September 1940, and is buried in Maidstone Cemetery.

Another interesting incident unfolded at West Malling on Sunday, 15 September 1940, when a Heinkel He 111, which was obviously in some kind of distress, with smoke billowing out of its engine, landed at West Malling airfield in mid-afternoon. The three German airmen were all uninjured and realising that resistance was futile in the circumstances which they found themselves in, they surrendered without a fight.

On 27 April 1941 No.29 Squadron arrived at West Malling in their Bristol Beaufighters. One of the pilots was Guy Gibson, who two years later would be awarded the Victoria Cross for his actions during the Dambuster raids in Germany, and go on to be the country's most decorated serviceman in the Second World War, all by the age of 26.

On the evening of 17 April 1943, possibly one of the strangest incidents of the war happened in West Malling. Earlier in the evening a number of German aircraft had carried out an air raid on Essex towns and, having completed their mission were on their way home, when they became confused by the heavy mist which had rolled into the darkness.

Having become disorientated as to their position, the pilots wrongly assumed that they were landing in their home base in occupied France. But they weren't; instead they had inadvertently landed at RAF West Malling. Although aircraft had been

FW 190A at West Malling Airfield.

heard in the skies above the airfield, there was no thought that this could conceivably be an enemy aircraft, even though it had been reported that some were known to be in the vicinity. The aircraft concerned circled the airfield twice, which simply added to the confusion of those on the ground below. It eventually landed and taxied to a halt next to the control tower. A soldier, still none the wiser as to the identity of the aircraft, and having not picked up on the Luftwaffe signage on the sides of the plane, ran towards it.

Gunner Lionel Barry of the 4th (Ulster) Light Anti-Aircraft Regiment spoke to the pilot informing him that he had landed at West Malling airfield. When the man replied it became abundantly clear that he was not English, and the assumption that he might be Polish or Czechoslovakian didn't appear to have crossed Gunner Barry's mind. As far as he was concerned, rightly as it turned out, the man was German. Realising the situation he now found himself in, and having approached the aircraft without his rifle, Barry did a quick about turn and ran off to retrieve it from the station's watch office. By the time he had returned to the aircraft, a Focke-Wulf Fw 190 (Yellow H of 7./ SKG10), this time properly equipped, the pilot of the aircraft, Fieldwebel (Sergeant) Otto Bechtold, having already assessed the dire, if not somewhat embarrassing situation that he now found himself in, was waiting for him with his hands held in the air, clearly indicating that he was surrendering.

Gunner Barry had acquired himself a prisoner in circumstances the likes of which he could never have dreamt possible. Bechtold was taken into custody, for him the war was over and a prisoner of war camp awaiting him.

No sooner had they deposited the prisoner in the guardroom than the noise of another aircraft could once again be heard circling overhead. Before those on the ground had any time to think, a second Focke-Wulf aircraft had landed, but the quick-witted German pilot, Leutnant Fritz Sezter, quickly realised his mistake and manoeuvred his aircraft to take off again. Leading Aircraftman Sharback who was in the airfield's armoured vehicle opened fire on the aircraft with his vehicle's twin Vickers machine guns. This had the desired effect. The Folke-Wulf veered off the landing strip, but Sezter tried to manoeuvre it back on course to try and take off again. Sharback opened up on the aircraft once again. This time the aircraft caught fire and rolled over, the pilot either managed to jump clear or was thrown clear by the momentum of the crashing aircraft. He had been wounded in the leg and shoulder from the machine-gun burst fired by Leading Aircraftman Sharback.

Two gunners from the 4th (Ulster) Light Anti-Aircraft Regiment rushed forward to try and grab hold of Sezter, but despite his injuries he managed to escape their grasp. His freedom was short lived, however, as he ran straight into the arms of the station's Commanding Officer, Group Captain Peter Townsend. A combination of Townsend and one of the gunners, managed to extinguish the flames that had started to engulf the German pilot's flying suit and pulled him clear, moments before the damaged aircraft exploded. Debris was scattered over a large radius injuring several of the station's firemen.

Within a matter of minutes, a third Focke-Wulf aircraft attempted to land at the airfield but crashed at Springetts Farm before reaching the runway. The pilot, Oberfeldwebel Otto Schultz, escaped with just a few cuts and bruises.

The pilot of a fourth aircraft totally misjudged his approach to the airfield and crashed into a nearby apple orchard at nearby Staplehurst and the German plane burst into flames. The pilot, Oberleutnant Kurt Khaln, bailed out but he was too low for his parachute to properly engage and he fell to his death.

The only one of the four aircraft to still be serviceable was that of Otto Bechtold. It was flown to Farnborough later the same day for evaluation and examination, and eventually became part of the RAF's 1426 (Enemy Aircraft) Flight.

No.322 (Dutch) Squadron, which had only been active since 12 June 1943, flying Mk 14 Spitfires, arrived at West Malling airfield on 20 June 1944. Their job was to try and intercept a new threat from the skies, the German V1 rockets that had been targeting London. The shooting down of the V1 rockets was given the apt name of Operation Crossbow. During their time at RAF West Malling, No.322 Squadron were responsible for bringing down 110 V1s.

A manoeuvre to try and make the V1s crash had first been successfully attempted in early July 1944 by tipping the rocket with the wing tip of his aircraft, by Flying Officer F.J.H. van Eijk of No.322 Squadron. The Germans became aware of this tactic and began fitting tampering buttons on the V1s so that any such interference would cause it to explode. On 12 July 1944, whilst trying to carry out this same manoeuvre, Warrant Officer (1549995) Justin Albert Maier of No.322 Squadron was killed when the V1 rocket exploded. Maier's body was cremated at the Kent County Crematorium in Charing, Kent.

The squadron had previously been stationed at RAF Hawkinge twice. The first time was between 31 December 1943 and 25 February 1944, and the second was for just eight days between 1 and 9 March 1944. They were also stationed at Biggin Hill between 1 November 1944 and 3 January 1945.

No. 322 (Dutch) Squadron.

CHAPTER 14

Isle of Grain Camp

The Grain Tower can still be found in the Medway channel on a tidal mudflat, its home since the mid 1800s when it was erected as a defensive structure because of growing fears of a French invasion. By 1940 the fear of an invasion had once again raised its ugly head, but this time the enemy was Germany, and the Grain Tower once again had a role to play in the defence of the nation. It was re-armed with a twin 6-pounder quick-firing gun to deal with the threat posed by a German naval assault. Just in case any such attack might be occasioned during the hours of darkness, a searchlight emplacement was added.

There was a military fort on the Isle of Grain, which had been completed in 1868 and was part of the River Medway's coastal defence system. It was an active location during the First World War because of its unique geographical location at the mouths of both the River Thames and the River Medway, immediately opposite Sheerness. Its level of importance hadn't reduced by the time of the Second World War where it provided a first line of defence in helping to protect the important naval dockyards at both Sheerness and Chatham.

Aerial shot of Isle of Grain Camp.

It utilised close defence guns, in the form of two 6.2-inch pieces, as part of its function as a defensive coastal gun battery, positioned seawards to deal with the threat of enemy shipping or an attempted invasion.

The men stationed there were from the 34th Battery, 12th Light anti-aircraft Regiment, Royal Artillery, which was a Territorial Army unit, and their job was to protect the oil refinery owned by the Medway Oil Company and the railway lines which connected the Isle of Grain to the rest of Kent and beyond. There was a camp which catered for up to 250 men in at least fourteen accommodation barrack blocks, along with other buildings such as the mess hall and air raid shelters.

In case of a German amphibious invasion, concrete anti-tank obstacles were installed as part of the area's coastal defences, which are still in place today as a constant reminder of a bygone defence facility that thankfully never had to be used.

The photographs on the following pages were those of Bombardier Steward, one of those who served with the 34th Battalion, 12th Light anti-aircraft Battery, Royal Artillery.

Army Camp on the Isle of Grain.

Soldiers guarding railway line Isle of Grain.

Above left: Soldier guarding railway line Isle of Grain.

Above right: Soldier guarding railway line Isle of Grain.

Below: Bombardier Stewart and his wife.

Soldiers of 34th Battalion, 12th Light anti-aircraft Battery, Royal Artillery. Winter 1940.

Believed to be Bombardier Stewart with Military Truck, winter 1940.

Bombardier Stewart with Military
Motor Cycle (1940).

Group of Soldiers of 34th Battalion, 12th Light anti-aircraft Battery, Royal Artillery.

Isle of Grain Military Stables 1940.

Group of Soldiers of 34th Battalion, 12th Light anti-aircraft Battery, Royal Artillery.

Police vehicle and officers of Kent County Constabulary 21 February 1940.

CHAPTER 15

Prisoner of War Camps in Kent

The following list of prisoner of war camps throughout Kent during the Second World War, is taken from the Twentieth Century Military Recording Project, which lists the PoW Camps which existed throughout Britain between 1939 – 1948.

Defining exactly what constitutes a Prisoner of War camp is difficult because of the immense variety of types, sizes, and classes of buildings used. The number and types of camps varied throughout the war. In addition to the base camps, a large number of semi-autonomous hostels were established out in the country, and a large number of PoWs were billeted at farms. For the purposes of this report a Prisoner of War camp will be any site or building that has been used to house military prisoners captured by the Allies and which appeared in the numerical listing system used by the British authorities.

Prisoner of war camps throughout the United Kingdom were allocated a number, which ranged from 1, Grizedale Hall, Ambleside, through to 1026, Raynes Park, Wimbledon. The camps are not in alphabetical order, and it would appear the allocation of a number to a particular camp came about for no other reason than when it was opened, it was allocated the next available number. Numbers were allocated also for security reasons so a camp could be referred to without giving away its actual location. During the Second World War, the British authorities would not reveal the actual location of its PoW camps to the Germans, because of fears that in the case of invasion they would be targeted, the PoWs released, armed and equipped, to quickly bolster the size of the invading army. The Germans for their part, claimed that the only reason they required the information was to ensure that they did not accidentally bomb the areas that the camps were in by mistake. This was highly unlikely as many of the camps were in the middle of the countryside, some with no residential properties anywhere near them.

Initially there was no standard design to the camps, but this was because there were different types of camps, which by the very nature of their specific purpose, meant that they would have different requirements. Command cages were usually in buildings and premises that already existed and that before the war had been used for totally different purposes. In some cases they were nothing more elaborate than a fenced off, tented compound with very basic amenities. Internment camps were built for German or Japanese civilians or from other nominated enemy nations, who had been detained in the United Kingdom. There were also interrogation centres where German military personnel were questioned to establish the depth of their political allegiance to Nazi Germany. Once identified, the more die-hard, card-carrying, fully paid up members of the Nazi Party, were usually sent to far off places such as Canada, to prevent their release by German paratroopers, and because of the distance from Europe, to try and deter them from trying to escape. Transit camps were initially used to keep PoWs while it was determined in what category they would be placed.

Until 1943 the numbers of German PoWs detained throughout the United Kingdom were comparatively low, and in the main were either airmen or from submarine crews, although a number of these men had Nazi sympathies. The number of PoW camps, along with the number of PoWs, increased greatly after the defeat and surrender of the German Afrika Corps in North Africa on 13 May 1943. This also coincided with the standardisation of how camps were built, with most comprising 18 ft 6 inch x 12 ft timber framed huts of varying lengths, although some were Nissen-type huts with concrete or brick built front and backs, a curved roof that stretched down to ground level and made of corrugated iron. These housed 48 men on average.

There were fifteen locations throughout Kent that were categorised as being Prisoner of War Camps, they were:

Camp No. 33. St Martin's Plain, Shorncliffe Camp, Folkestone.
Camp No. 40. Somerhill Camp, Somerhill, Tonbridge.
Camp No. 86. Stanhope Camp, Stanhope.
Camp No. 86a. Woodchurch, Ashford. See Camp No. 282.
Camp No. 117. Walderslade Camp, King George Street, Chatham.
Camp No. 154. Ministry of Works Camp, Swanscombe Street, Swanscombe.
Camp No. 233. Summer House, Ravensbourne, Bromley.
Camp No. 237. Co-Ed-Bel Camp, Lubbock Road, Chislehurst.
Camp No. 267. Mereworth Castle, Mereworth, Waterinbury.
Camp No. 282. Brissenden Green Camp, Brissenden. Ashchurch.
Camp No. 282. Honghorst House, Woodchurch, Ashford.
Camp No. 629. Mabledon Park, Tonbridge.
Camp No. 654a. R. E. Bridging Camp, Wouldham, Rochester.
Camp No. 670. St Radigrund's Camp, Dover.
Camp No. 670b. St Martin's Plain, Shorncliff Camp, Folkestone. See Camp No. 33.

German and other enemy PoWs were well fed during their stay in camps throughout the British mainland. The weekly rations each man received were the same as a British soldier, which meant that they received more than the civilian population. A German PoW who undertook his allocated work details received the following weekly food allowance: 42 ounces of meat, 8 ounces of bacon, 5 ½ pounds of bread, 10 ½ ounces of margarine. On top of this they also received vegetables, cheese, cake, jam and tea.

The three meals per day German PoWs received would have consisted of the following:

Breakfast: Bread, margarine and tea. Lunch: Pork and potatoes. Dinner: Milk, soup and bread.

Many of the Second World War Prisoner of War Camps throughout Kent no longer exist. Many of them have been totally demolished, without any sign of what once stood there and why. There are some that have partial remains which are now being used for totally different purposes. For the German prisoners of war who were detained in them, far away from their homes, families and loved ones, they were a home from home for the period of their detention. How long they would be held, or whether they would ever return home again, they did not know for sure.

CHAPTER 16

War Dead and Memorials

According to the Kent Roll of Honour website, there are sixty-four war memorials dotted around the county of Kent that commemorate the names of the county's men and women who lost their lives during the Second World War. Eleven of these are in Ashford alone. Add to that the number of rolls of honour that adorn the walls and windows of churches, schools, businesses and other similar locations, associations and clubs, a number of commemorative plaques, and we are talking about an awful lot of names. Some of the names will appear on more than one of the memorials, where the one in the main town has also included the names that are also included on the memorials surrounding villages and parishes. Take a look on the Roll of Honour website to see the names of those from your community who gave their lives in both world wars.

Most if not all big towns and villages would have already had a war memorial which commemorated the names of those who had fallen during the First World War, with most of these having been unveiled in the early 1920s. Just over twenty-years later, yet more names were being added to the memorials. In some cases the names would be the same, with fathers from the First World War being followed by their sons from the Second World War. Having said that, there are in fact fourteen communities throughout England and Wales that do not have a war memorial, as although men from their communities served in both wars, all of them returned home alive. None of them are from Kent, although Knowlton, near Canterbury did not lose any men during the First World War.

Maidstone War Memorial.

In Closing

I hope you have found this relative snippet of information about the seven years of wartime Kent both useful and informative. I do not suggest for one moment that it is a fully comprehensive record of the troubled times which the county faced, by any stretch of the imagination.

In this book I have attempted to balance what was happening to the county of Kent and the people who lived and worked in its towns and villages, against the events of the war in a global sense, and how they in turn impacted on Kent.

One thing is for certain, Kent and its people played a big part in the final victory of the war, from the work of the Dover Patrol, to the evacuations at Dunkirk, through the entire period of the Battle of Britain, Operation Pluto and the oil pipeline across the English Channel, and the success of the D-Day Normandy landings. Add to this the approximate 8,000 military personnel and civilians from Kent who lost their lives, and that adds up to one hell of a commitment.

It has been my absolute pleasure and privilege to have written this book, and even though I know that there was so much more that could have been in it, I hope that what I have included has proved to be useful, informative, and worthwhile.

Sources

www.a-e-g.org.uk
www.aircrewremembered.com
www.aircrewremembrancesociety.com
www.ancestry.co.uk
www.bigginhill.co.uk
www.britishnewspaperarchive.co.uk
www.cofepow.org.uk
www.cwgc.com
www.epibreren.com
www.exploring-castles.com
www.flightglobal.com
forum.12oclockhigh.net
www.historicengland.org.uk
www.historyguy.com
www.homefrontcollection.com
www.home-guard.org.uk
www.kenthistoryforum.co.uk
nelsonlambert.blogspot.co.uk
www.newsshopper.co.uk
www.nhs.uk
www.pastscape.org.uk
www.raf.mod.uk
www.rochester-airport.co.uk
www.uboat.net
www.unithistories.com
www.victoriacross.org.uk
www.victoriacrossonline.co.uk
www.2db.com
Wikipedia
www.worldnavalships.com
Kent Airfields in the Second World War – Robin J. Brooks
The Kent College Saga – 1886 – 1996 – Margaret James

Index

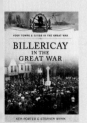

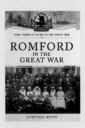
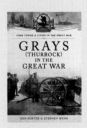
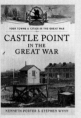

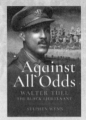